The Real 'Dad's Army'

The Real 'Dad's Army'

THE WAR DIARIES OF
LT.COL. RODNEY FOSTER

Rodney Foster Archive

Edited by Ronnie Scott

VIKING
an imprint of
PENGUIN BOOKS

VIKING

Published by the Penguin Group
Penguin Books Ltd, 80 Strand, London WC2R ORL, England
Penguin Group (USA) Inc., 375 Hudson Street, New York, New York 10014, USA
Penguin Group (Canada), 90 Eglinton Avenue East, Suite 700, Toronto, Ontario, Canada M4P 2Y3
(a division of Pearson Penguin Canada Inc.)
Penguin Ireland, 25 St Stephen's Green, Dublin 2, Ireland (a division of Penguin Books Ltd)
Penguin Group (Australia), 250 Camberwell Road, Camberwell, Victoria 3124, Australia
(a division of Pearson Australia Group Pty Ltd)
Penguin Books India Pvt Ltd, 11 Community Centre, Panchsheel Park, New Delhi – 110 017, India
Penguin Group (NZ), 67 Apollo Drive, Rosedale, Auckland 0632, New Zealand
(a division of Pearson New Zealand Ltd)
Penguin Books (South Africa) (Pty) Ltd, 24 Sturdee Avenue, Rosebank, Johannesburg 2196, South Africa

Penguin Books Ltd, Registered Offices: 80 Strand, London WC2R ORL, England

www.penguin.com

First published 2011

5

Diary extracts abridged and selected from the diaries of Rodney Foster copyright ©
The Estate of Rodney Foster, 2011, under licence to Shaun Sewell
Introduction and historical notes copyright © Ronnie Scott, 2011
The moral right of the copyright holders has been asserted

Licence for the Reproduction Rights for the 36 images from the Rodney Foster Archive
for the purpose of this book is by kind permission

Set in Bembo Book MT Std 10.75/12 pt
Typeset by Palimpsest Book Production Limited, Falkirk, Stirlingshire
Printed in Great Britain by Clays Ltd, St Ives plc

A CIP catalogue record for this book is available from the British Library

ISBN: 978-0-670-91982-6

www.greenpenguin.co.uk

MIX
Paper from
responsible sources
FSC™ C018179
www.fsc.org

Penguin Books is committed to a sustainable
future for our business, our readers and our
planet. This book is made from paper certified
by the Forest Stewardship Council.

To all those who served in the Home Guard during the defence of Great Britain in World War II

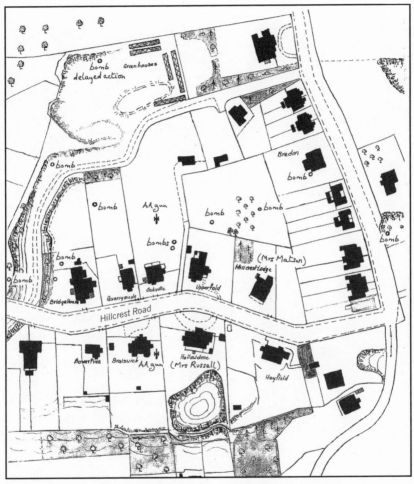

Rodney Foster's drawing of where the bombs fell on Hillcrest Road

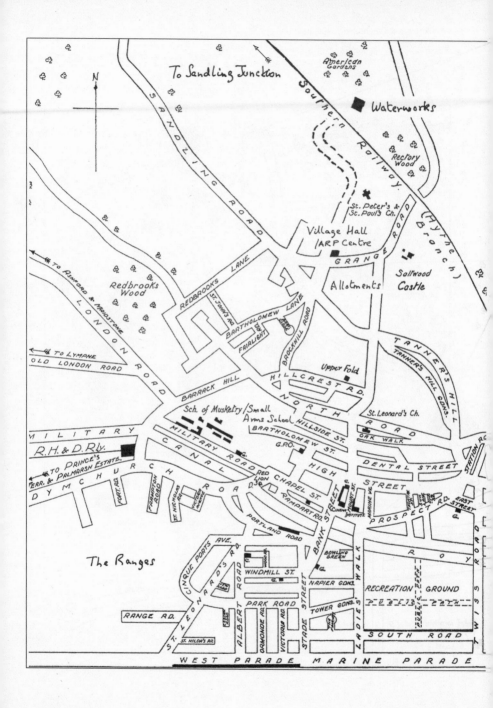

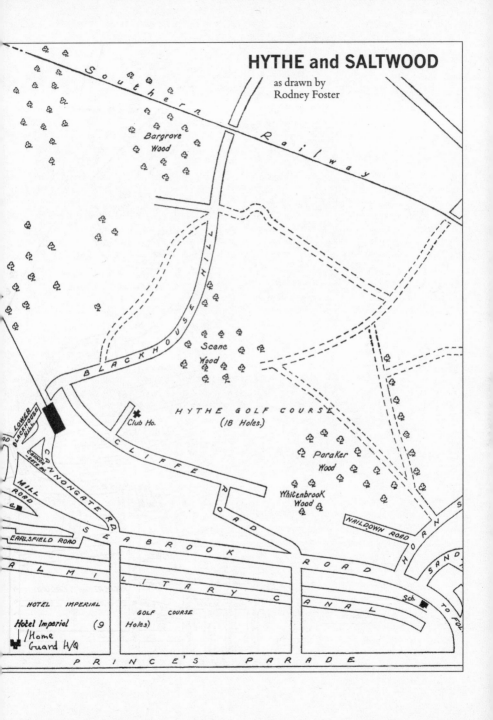

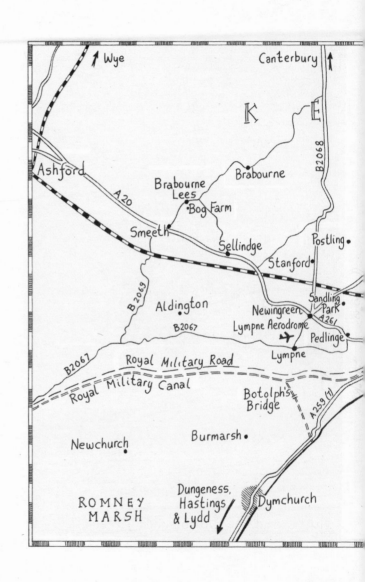

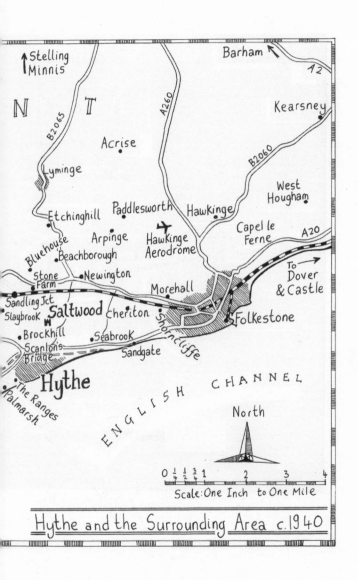

Hythe and the Surrounding Area c. 1940

Introduction *by Ronnie Scott*

R odney Foster, soldier, surveyor, Home Guard officer, ARP warden, family man and obsessive diary keeper, lived through stirring times, but as an individual he barely ruffled the pages of history. Now, fifty years after his death, his diaries firmly establish him as an important witness to life on the Home Front during the Second World War, with fresh insights into the development, training and activities of the Home Guard and the Air Raid Precautions service.

These diaries are an important testament to the humble heroes of the Home Front, the men and women who selflessly volunteered to defend their country against the horrors of fascism. They show, in meticulous detail, the everyday sacrifices of life on the south coast of England, under almost constant bombing and shellfire, and in imminent danger of invasion.

Rodney is a compulsive chronicler of the everyday, the routines and small events that make up our lives. His diaries throw a spotlight on the lives of his family, friends and Home Guard colleagues as they fight their own battles, and win their own wars, on the Home Front. To read these diaries is to step back into Hellfire Corner at the height of the Battle of Britain, and to stand shoulder to shoulder with the brave civilians who risked their lives defending civilization.

Rodney Foster was born in Saugor, in central India, on 27 May 1882, into a British Army family. His forebears had helped suppress the Indian Mutiny in 1857–8. Rodney was educated in England, and entered the Royal Military College at Sandhurst as a cadet in August 1900. As a young subaltern, he formed part of the guard at the funeral of Queen Victoria in February 1901.

Rodney was commissioned in the British Army later that year, spending the next five years in India, including on the North-West Frontier. But, feeling his career was unlikely to be advanced within the regimental structure of the Indian Army, he moved to the civil service and in December 1906 joined the Survey of India, the equivalent of the Ordnance Survey, where he worked as a surveyor and cartographer. During his early years in the Survey he returned to England in June 1910 to marry Phyllis Blaxland, a friend of one of his sisters, whom he had first met when he was at Sandhurst. Their daughter Daphne was born on 1 September 1913.

During the First World War, Rodney rejoined the Indian Army and rose to the rank of Lieutenant-Colonel. In April 1919 he returned to civilian life in the Survey of India, but remained on the Indian Regular Reserve of Officers. In these years, his pastimes included travel, sketching, tennis, cricket and big-game hunting.

Rodney retired from the Survey of India, with the rank of Superintendent, on 11 September 1932. Brigadier H. J. Couchman, the Surveyor-General of India, was generous in his praise of Rodney. He wrote: 'Lieutenant-Colonel Foster was a steady, painstaking officer of imperturbable temperament, whose whole service was spent in topographic and revenue surveys. He takes into retirement the good wishes of friends in all ranks of the department.'

Rodney outside his home, Upper Fold in Hythe, in 1939

Rodney's diaries present a family at home in England, living as routine a life as possible in wartime. They shopped, gardened, went to the cinema and visited friends. But they also battled daily with the dangers and privations of the Home Front. In the diaries' pages, Phyllis seems almost colourless, spending her time between working in Folkestone Library (where we occasionally glimpse Rodney consulting *The Times* and writing up his autobiography) and her involvement with the First Church of Christ, Scientist in that town.

Daphne, who had also worked as a librarian, spent most of the war working with the Girl Guides, as Assistant District Commissioner for South Kent.

Most of Rodney's relatives, friends and neighbours were evacuated from the south coast of England by a nervous government, who wanted to militarize the area not only to prevent an enemy invasion but also to assemble an Allied force for the invasion of Europe, away from the prying eyes of gossips and spies.

His mother, his sister Milly and his father-in-law Herbert Blaxland were evacuated to Guildford, and his brother Maurice's family were moved to Canterbury. This dislocation of families, who of course were already split by conscription, added to the pressure of life in the southern and eastern Home Counties.

The Indian-influenced hallway at Upper Fold, as drawn by Rodney Foster

Rodney, unusually, kept his car on the road, first by using petrol coupons connected to his work with the Home Guard, and later the Volunteer Car Pool. Most private motorists put their cars up on blocks for the duration.

★

In 1932, the Fosters bought Dane Cottage at 4 Hillcrest Road, Hythe, extended the upper floor and renamed the house Upper Fold. Rodney's sketches show the cluttered interiors, with their framed drawings and paintings competing for wall space with mirrors, shelves of bric-a-brac and military souvenirs. The hallway was dominated by animal trophies, including a much-prized tiger-skin rug and a stuffed and mounted tiger's head which he had acquired as a hunter in India. Much of the ornamentation recalled the family's life in India.

The house sat in extensive gardens. Rodney, as an experienced surveyor and cartographer, faithfully recorded the details of the garden in a map (see page xix).

To the west of the house was Oakville, the home of Albert Edward Palmar, and to the east Hillcrest Lodge, the house of Mary Matson. Opposite was Hollowdene, the home of Revd George and Mrs Muriel Waters. Hillcrest Road itself stood on high ground overlooking Hythe, with the village of Saltwood, a suburb of the town, to the north.

Rodney's diaries provide a detailed account of the formation of his local Home Guard, from its early beginnings on 14 May 1940 as the Local Defence Volunteers (LDV, quickly nicknamed Look, Duck and Vanish), then its reorganization as the Home Guard in July 1940 to its being stood down in September 1944. Rodney, who volunteered immediately, was first in charge of the Saltwood Platoon, then 'B' Company of the Cinque Ports Battalion.

A wartime issue of the *Folkestone, Hythe and District Herald* described the first meetings of the men who would make up the LDV: 'They were motley crowds; retired majors rubbed shoulders with workmen in their Sunday best, professional men sat with builders' labourers. But all were there with one purpose, to keep England inviolate.'

For the modern reader, mention of the Home Guard brings to mind the television comedy series *Dad's Army*. The popular BBC programme was devised by Jimmy Perry, based on his experiences as a seventeen-year-old member of the 10th Hertfordshire Battalion of the Home Guard.

Written by Perry and David Croft, the series followed the fortunes of a fictional Home Guard platoon in the south coast town of Walmington-on-Sea. Although the series was filmed in Thetford, Norfolk, Captain Mainwaring and his ill-assorted troupe were firmly located in west Kent, as were the real-life Rodney and his charges.

Readers familiar with the pompous captain, the surly recruits, incompetent commanders and the insolent ARP warden will find their antecedents in

Rodney's unvarnished account of daily life in the Home Guard. These diaries may only now have come to light, but they could easily have been the inspiration for the television series.

During Rodney's time in the LDV and Home Guard, he recorded the day-to-day duties of an officer, the initial shortages of uniforms and weapons, the sometimes chaotic approaches to training, the often problematic relationships with the regular army, his recruits' reluctance to submit to army-style discipline, and the stifling bureaucracy within which they did their best to operate.

The Home Guard

Rodney's Dad's Army, the elite fighting force of Saltwood Home Guard
(Rodney Foster Archive)

While he was clearly, as a former professional soldier, frustrated and often angered by the amateurish and inconsistent behaviour of those around him, he was a dedicated officer with an obvious attachment to those of his volunteers and, later, conscripts who committed themselves to the defence of their country. He had no time for slackers, desk jockeys or gossips.

He valued integrity and honesty, and had no respect for those of his superiors who lacked these qualities. Rodney was a professional and conscientious member of the Home Guard, and worked extremely hard for a country in which he was not born and in which he spent only ten of his first fifty years. He laboured far more than the maximum forty-eight hours a month on duty, spending each morning in the office or delivering uniforms, weapons and ammunition, dedicating countless hours to putting his men through their paces on the parade ground or the rifle range, and putting himself on patrol most nights.

He was also realistic and sometimes cynical about military and government announcements, and had a clear dislike of Prime Minister Winston Churchill and Field Marshal Bernard Montgomery. None of this, however, dulled his sense of duty or his obvious patriotism.

Despite Rodney's promotion to Major in September 1942, with 560 men under his command, and the obvious need for people of his character and conviction, his energy and enthusiasm had been eroded by the officious and small-minded behaviour of fellow officers, and the injured pride of the old soldier drove him out of the Home Guard.

His resignation in January 1943 was clearly delivered with regret, and he followed the fortunes of his former charges through regular meetings with old colleagues, but the palpable sense of relief in the diaries showed that he had made the correct decision for his own health and happiness.

He slept better, had some time to himself, and was able to indulge in long walks through the countryside. His renewed sense of purpose showed in his dedication to his new duties as an ARP (Air Raid Precautions) warden, for which he spent each Monday night on fire watch, and as a driver for the Volunteer Car Pool.

Both of these occupations served the diarist very well. In the former he was awake all night watching bombers coming and going, recording explosions and aware of activity along the coast. In the latter, he drove through the Kent countryside, documenting the impact of the war and the bravery of the locals. As 1944 progressed, Rodney noted the build-up of troops and the other preparations for D-Day, the Allied invasion of occupied France, then the coming of the V-1 and V-2 rockets, which rained as much destruction on the coastal towns as they did on London, often to less public notice.

During the war, the area around Dover, which was so much the focus of German shelling and bombing, was known as Hellfire Corner, and those residents who – like the Fosters – resisted evacuation and spent the war at home were often exposed to as much enemy fire as some on active service. The large houses in Hillcrest Road, abandoned by their owners who had been evacuated inland, were requisitioned by the military and used for billeting troops on the move from training camps to active service.

The Fosters were the only family left in Hillcrest Road, and faced the bombing without an air raid shelter. They may have baulked at paying for an Anderson Shelter, which were free only to householders with an income of less than £250 a year, or they may not have realized the destructive power of aerial warfare.

Rodney and his family, of course, spent the First World War in India, so had no experience of war from the air. They never built an air raid shelter, nor did they use one. When their neighbour Mrs Russell offered them the use of her elaborate shelter they refused, claiming they 'had a form of claustrophobia where dugouts were concerned and preferred to be above ground when bombs fell'. The family had been warned about enemy bombs and shells. Stanley

Baldwin told the House of Commons in November 1932: 'The bomber will always get through. I think it is well for the man in the street to realize that there is no power on earth that can protect him from being bombed.'

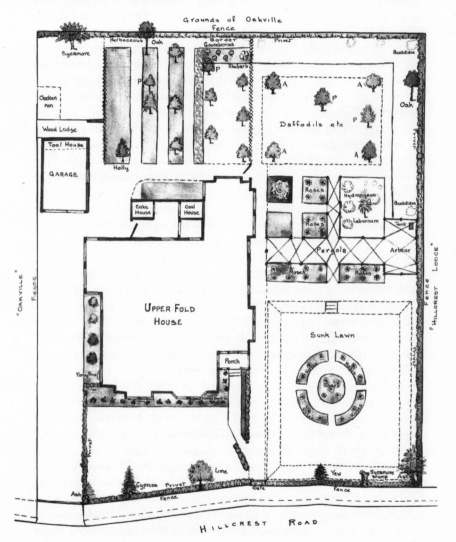

Rodney's drawing of his garden

And on the day war was declared, 3 September 1939, George VI broadcast to his subjects: 'There may be dark days ahead and war can no longer be confined to the battlefield.'

The family did temporarily decamp from the military zone, first to Bog Farm, in the Kent hinterland, and then to South Road, in Hythe. Rodney continued to live in Upper Fold, because it was nearer to his duties and, presumably, to keep their beloved house out of military hands.

Rodney and his family often despaired over the small acts of destruction waged on his orchard, garden gate and coal house by the billeted troops in Hillcrest Road, as well as the more criminal acts against some of the occupied houses. While these acts may have seemed insignificant compared with the daily horrors experienced by combat troops in the various theatres of war, Rodney viewed the social niceties as the building blocks of civil society: if we can't keep simple rules for respecting people and their property, how can we call ourselves civilized and claim the moral high ground when fighting a just war against a tyrant?

As well as physical damage from the effects of the war, the Foster family and other inhabitants of Hythe and other towns on the south coast suffered from years of extreme noise, from the almost constant bombardment by the big guns of the Germans on the French coast, the bombing by enemy aircraft, the anti-aircraft fire, the mines and depth charges, and various military exercises and training events.

The area surrounding Hythe was a strategic target for enemy fire. Nearby were Hawkinge and Lympne airfields, in the town itself were the Small Arms School and the artillery ranges, and the whole coast was being systematically shelled to make it both easier for a German invasion force to land and harder for an Allied invasion force to assemble and embark.

This almost-constant aural assault, with accompanying air raid sirens, shell warnings and other alerts, regularly shredded the nerves of the inhabitants and, as Rodney's diaries clearly show, made a full night's sleep almost impossible. Some of the insensitive behaviour shown towards Rodney by his colleagues and superiors, and his knee-jerk reaction to it, can perhaps be excused on the grounds that everyone was living on short rations and short sleep, and with the perennial fear of invasion, defeat or death.

Rodney recorded various military technologies in his diaries, but he does not mention radar, because the British public did not know about that breakthrough until after the war. The secret technology, originally known as radio direction and ranging, was pioneered in Britain by the scientist Robert Watson Watt, and patented by him in 1935. Other countries were working along the same lines, but Britain, concerned about the superiority of the German air force, led the way in using radar to detect enemy aircraft. Radar operators were among the unsung heroes of the Battle of Britain.

Rodney heard one hint, though. In February 1941, he wrote: 'George [. . .] says we are countering the night bombers with the aid of a wireless mast, which records the position of the raider, and this information is passed on to our own night fighters.'

Perhaps surprisingly, Rodney had a soft spot for animals. He had a dog (Jerry) and cats (Doris and Socks) of his own, and was a supporter of the Royal Society for the Prevention of Cruelty to Animals (RSPCA). His diaries provide a glimpse of the workings of the local branches of the charity. While the local committees were severely disrupted by the evacuation of civilians from the south coast, the demands placed on the charity's clinic in Folkestone, run by Mr Neville, continued.

One unknown aspect of the work of animal charities on the Home Front became apparent after the retreat from Dunkirk, when cats and dogs fleeing the noise and confusion of battle were transported from the French coast to Dover, Folkestone and other Channel ports. Rodney helped with this and also supported an appeal from the only cats' meat supplier in Kent, who was resisting conscription on the grounds that dogs and cats would suffer and die if her supply of meat was not continued. The short supply of pet meat was a consequence of the law insisting that all horse flesh should be supplied for human consumption.

Rodney's diaries offer an invaluable insight into the Home Front during the Second World War. Not only do they detail life on Hellfire Corner, they clearly depict the inception and development of the Home Guard from the point of view of a serving officer – something that, until now, has never come to light.

Home Guard personnel, especially those serving in the areas most vulnerable to invasion, were forbidden from keeping diaries, in case the information in them could be of use or value to the invader. So it is all the more remarkable that such an establishment figure as Rodney should break the regulations in this way.

Rodney was not a professional writer, although he produced more words in his lifetime than most authors, and his diaries are the unvarnished observations and thoughts of a down-to-earth, common-sense person. His accounts of bombing raids on Hythe, when he was in the thick of the action, are alive with human detail, compassion and fellow-feeling. He may have been a professional soldier, dealing death and destruction by his own hand, but when he is on the receiving end of mechanized slaughter, his cartographer's aptitude for minute observation and accurate recording bring the scenes to horrible life.

These diaries offer us a perspective far from the Western Front, or any other theatre of war, but they are indispensable documents in the overall history of one of the most traumatic periods of the twentieth century. That they are also humane, tender and touching is a credit to the observational and recording skills of Rodney Foster.

The Leas, Folkstone, before the war

1939

Friday 1 September
Daphne's birthday. Phyllis out to a board meeting in the afternoon and I had my usual afternoon with my father-in-law. In the evening we sat in our blacked-out house. Very stuffy, inconvenient and depressing.

The Fosters' living room

Saturday 2 September

War now imminent. Chamberlain being pushed on by Opposition and others.

Sunday 3 September

War declared by England and France on Germany at 11 a.m. I drove
Phyllis to church for 11.30 service. At 11.15 Chamberlain broadcast and as
soon as he had finished the local air raid warning started. There was a panic
among people in the street. I told the congregation, who came out and
wanted to disperse, that it was only sounded to say war was declared. We
learnt in the evening that Folkestone, having seen a single aeroplane out
at sea, thought it was a raider. Heaven help us if our nerves are to be
shattered by such false alarms. Hythe's siren followed suit but Daphne,
who was by herself, kept her nerve. Later we listened to the King's
broadcast, a very moving speech. More discomfort in the evening, with
Kenyon-Slaney the [ARP] warden coming around and complaining of
cracks of light.

Monday 4 September

A false alarm on the east coast early this morning. The Germans have sunk
a passenger ship with 100 Americans on board [SS *Athenia*]. All saved
except those killed in the explosion. First blood as far as we know. The
advance parties of the British Expeditionary Force have landed in France.
Mrs Matheson, her companion and Bessie Surtees to tea.

Tuesday 5 September

An air raid warning about 3 a.m. We slept through it. Phyllis went into
Folkestone in afternoon. About 6 o'clock, 70 reservists were billeted in
'Oakville', Mr Palmar's empty house next to us. They did not take long to
strip the orchards. I had an interesting talk with a man who was caught in
Vienna when Hitler came in. He says the Germans are starving. Our
Warden didn't warn us about a light showing.

Wednesday 6 September

We were woken up at 7 a.m. by the sirens. All different and very confusing.
Lympne and Hawkinge planes went up flying north-east. A warden told
me something was happening further north. 'All clear' at 9 a.m. As far as
one knows, it was an attempted raid towards the Thames.

Thursday 7 September

In the morning we heard the dropping of depth charges out at sea and what sounded like guns in the afternoon. It appears yesterday's raid was a false alarm. On the return of our machines they were fired on by our own Anti-Aircraft guns.

Friday 8 September

Mother's birthday. Daphne and I drove into Folkestone. She is to take a lesson in driving a car with ordinary gears. I had my usual afternoon game of bagatelle with Mr Blaxland [father-in-law]. It was a very hot day. We have had 10 days of real summer.

Phyllis with Socks the cat, Daphne and a rented car

Sunday 17 September

Our troops are in France. A French announcement gave the show away. The Government are not giving us news as they promised. The Poles have been gradually driven back, but Warsaw still holds out. Russia has been mobilised and has made a pact with Japan. About 21 ships have been sunk so far. The news that petrol was to be rationed from yesterday leaked out, and there was an orgy of hoarding during the week. News of the torpedoing of the aircraft carrier HMS *Courageous*, with the loss of 580 lives.

Monday 18 September

Russians advance and overrun eastern Poland. Finis Poland. Firing out at sea off Dover.

Tuesday 19 September

Janka Neumann, a Czech refugee, came as our servant. Her husband, a Jewish mill-owner, had been murdered after the German invasion.

3

Wednesday 20 September
Sent in my application to the Officers Emergency Reserve. General de Crespigny very kindly signed for me. He said he had sponsored all the old dug-outs and all the youngsters in the road. News of a serious revolt in Czechoslovakia. Hundreds killed, thousands arrested. That blackguard, Chamberlain; how different it might have been if he had not bolted in terror last September (and Baldwin is chiefly to blame for not rearming three years ago).

Thursday 21 September
A fellow called Francis rang up and asked Janka out. He is an electrical engineer who is off to Penang. He has known Janka for some time and they seem to be engaged. The papers say there was a U-boat hunt off Folkestone watched by crowds from the Leas. It may have been on Monday. The 54th Royal Army Service Corps column is billeted all round us, with their lorries in the fields.

Friday 22 September
Saw Mr Blaxland at Kingsnorth Gardens. He and I played dominoes; bagatelle makes him tired. I held my own. After supper we went to the cinema, taking Janka with us. *The Mikado* in colour, quite good. Had a bad time driving back without lights; soldiers all over the road.

Saturday 23 September
The 54th RASC packed up their kit and drove away in their lorries. In the afternoon the Channel had a line of ships from one horizon to the other. It was too misty to tell if they were men-of-war or merchant ships. About same time, four planes dashed across going southwards. Petrol rationing starts today.

Sunday 24 September
Third week of the war. France has a hold on the high ground above Saarbrücken but we appear to be going no further. We seem to have scotched the submarine menace. Roosevelt states the USA definitely stays out, and all other countries crying out their neutrality – which means they won't help us. No further news of the Czech revolt or troubles in Germany-Austria.

Monday 25 September

Captain Durham, regional organiser [of the RSPCA], turned up this morning. He has come about the meeting tomorrow to elect new officers for the branch. He wants me to be branch secretary.

Tuesday 26 September

Went to the Queens [Hotel], where Durham took the chair at the meeting. He asked if anyone was willing to take on the position of secretary, and turned to me. I said: Yes, if the committee wanted me. When I was proposed I watched to see if all hands were raised without hesitation; if they had not been I would have refused to stand. Had lunch with Durham, a well-cooked mixed grill. We seem to have common tastes. A U-boat captain wirelessed to the Admiralty saying he had sunk one of our ships at a certain latitude and longitude and would we please send a ship to pick up the crew. He has since been captured by us.

Wednesday 27 September

[John] Simon brought out his Budget: cruel and vindictive. He will squeeze us dry, and we will starve before the Germans. Warsaw has surrendered. Germany and Russia have divided up Poland and threaten us and the French with dire trouble if we do not stop the war.

Sunday 1 October

End of the first month of war. We are better off than we were after a month of the last war. Many U-boats sunk and the French army on German territory with the Saar coalfields out of action. Our airmen threw leaflets into Berlin. Coal rationing started.

Tuesday 3 October

A vindictive Budget. Income tax 7/6; ARP a scandal. Thousands of casual workers doing nothing on £3 a week. Two mines got adrift from the North Sea and washed past our coast in a strong easterly gale. One came ashore at Seabrook and the other close by. Cars were stopped on the Folkestone–Hythe road until the first mine was exploded.

Friday 6 October
In the afternoon to Kingsnorth Gardens, to see Mr Blaxland. A large convoy passed through. About 6 o'clock, heard guns or depth charges. Hitler's speech to Reichstag futile. Russia is absorbing the Baltic States.

MINE EXPLODES ON SOUTH COAST

Monday 9 October
German bombers attacked a British cruiser squadron for five hours and made not a single hit. We brought down four of their craft for certain. It rained the whole day.

Tuesday 10 October
My first RSPCA branch meeting at Captain Glennie's house: 18 present and everything went off well. Mrs Swinhoe-Phelan sent me a postcard to say she had no wish to continue as a member. I was not able to stop our new chairman [Harold] Burdekin from getting noisy over the clinic, but the meeting only lasted an hour. Had tea with the Glennies and others. Interesting talk with Glennie; he says the Navy is thrilled at the air attacks on ships. The first in history. Heavy showers most of the day.

Saturday 14 October
A lot more rain. Found someone had broken the French window of Hollowdene opposite and an attic window. Probably the men next door, who are a rougher lot than the first.

Monday 16 October
A bright autumn day – perfect. About 6 a.m. an aeroplane came over very low. In the afternoon I drove Phyllis to her [Christian Science] reading room and went to an RSPCA committee meeting at Kitty Haviland's. Everyone very noisy and some droned on futilely. Had tea with Tasker-Evans and went through finances and collections. A German air raid on the Firth of Forth; no damage done. All bombs dropping in the water. We brought down four planes. First raid on Britain. We made another flight over Germany.

Tuesday 17 October

A fine day with a clear sky. As we were finishing lunch, the sirens went, starting with Dover. I went out into the allotments but saw nothing. Getting quite impatient, I went down town and talked to Savage, the picture framer. His son is captain of an AA battery near Sevenoaks, and he saw much of interest when he paid him a visit. The 'all clear' went about 3 p.m. and I went up the High Street collecting for the RSPCA; very successful! In evening we learnt that a number of German planes were sighted coming over and the alarm was given from York to Dover!! This was done because when the Firth of Forth was raided, no alarms were sounded. We also learnt the *Royal Oak* was torpedoed at anchor in Scapa Flow!!! Lastly, one evacuee child gets an allowance of 10/-, whilst three soldiers' children get 10/-!!

Wednesday 18 October

North wind and much colder. Another batch of Royal Engineers (RE) came to Palmar's and Rowlett's houses. In the former, they pitched a large marquee on the lawn. More attempts by air on Scapa Flow.

Thursday 19 October

It poured with rain all day. Phyllis and Daphne went into Folkestone in the afternoon. Another party of soldiers have come into Hollowdene opposite. Two planes were shot down on 17th. The crew of one was captured and two officers from the other rowed ashore and were taken after two days.

> **FIGHTERS AND A.A. GUNS ACTIVE**
>
> ───
>
> **PEOPLE REMAIN IN CINEMAS**

Saturday 21 October

Left Sandling Junction at 11.30 a.m. Train packed. A talkative woman sat next to me. Arrived at Waterloo 1.45 p.m. and had a scratch lunch and got down to Guildford at 3.30 p.m. No porters, so had to hump my bag up from station. My sister Milly alone with two Jewish servants (Germans this time). Waterloo was crowded with Navy, Army and Air Force officers and men. Wireless says we have sunk the South American raider. Milly anxious about her John, who is on his way to Argentina.

Monday 23 October

Went up and saw Mother. She recognised me at once. Afternoon, took the dogs out.

Tuesday 24 October

Left Guildford 11.30 a.m. Had a curry at Veeraswamy [Regent Street, London]. Charing Cross Station at 3.15 p.m. A batch of the new conscripts came down in the train to a camp at Lympne. Every type imaginable.

Sunday 29 October

The rain at last held up after nearly 10 days. Floods everywhere. Orchard estate up to ground floor roofs. Canal overflowing, Sandgate flooded, Dover cut off and no one went to church.

Monday 30 October

An air raid warning about 9.15 a.m., 'all clear' soon after. We went on with our breakfast. Officials say no enemy aircraft about, but destroyers drove off bombers south of Dogger Bank. Locals say they saw planes and heard firing, and Dover say they beat off attack. Some of our neighbouring soldiers have gone, and a batch of old men of 50-plus have come. Hear that a number of places in Guildhall Street, Folkestone, have subsided, a bus falling into a big hole near the Town Hall.

Wednesday 1 November

Third month of war and no achievements to show. We and the French are obviously doing nothing, waiting for Germany to break up. Mrs Faucus, who is half German, says they won't last a year. She says they are worse off for food than they were in 1918. A large batch of the older reservists left today and about 80 new men came in. These are the Pioneer Corps of men up to 50. Nearly all have medals, some from the Boer War. I had an interesting talk with a sergeant of the Queen's Royal West Surrey Regiment. He says many of the men were 60, one having medals for five campaigns.

Friday 3 November

[RSPCA] Inspector came at 12.30 p.m. He says the news of the two German bombers being shot down by British and French AA batteries yesterday refers to an attempted raid on Boulogne. Drove into Folkestone in afternoon with Daphne, who was taking stock in the library with Mrs Johnstone.

Mounted cavalry in Kent, possibly Shorncliffe (War and Peace Collection 0007)

Tasker-Evans says that 30,000 troops are being billeted in Folkestone. Also a reserve cavalry regiment is being raised at Shorncliffe. Went to tea and 'matador' [dominoes] with Mr B.

Saturday 4 November
Several bodies of German U-boat sailors washed up on Hythe and neighbouring beaches.

U-BOAT MEN WASHED UP

FIVE BODIES FOUND ON SOUTH COAST

Wednesday 8 November
I drove Phyllis to her testimony meeting and went to look at Aunt Olive's house [in Folkestone]. It and the other Grimston Gardens empty houses and Kent College are full of these old ex-servicemen all camouflaged as REs – thousands of them. What use are they? Not a word about the war in the evening news.

Thursday 9 November
Discovered that the men in Hollowdene opposite have stolen our ton of coke. Wrote to OC General Labour Battalion and in the evening a dapper Major Collins (Sherwood Foresters) turned up very contrite and hopes to

replace it. Phyllis and I went to tea with Grove-White. The Lancashires there. Yesterday Leopold of Belgium and Wilhelmina of Holland offered to bring about peace. Today we hear that Germany is massing troops on the Dutch border. Do they really mean to go through? Hitler made a speech in his Munich Beer Garden yesterday. After he and his Nazi leaders left, a bomb exploded in the roof killing eight and wounding 60. Searchlights at night.

Friday 10 November
Major Collins phoned up; he had a ton of coke to give me. It was dumped in our side drive. Drove to Folkestone and gave Tasker-Evans £4. His son has 24 hours leave to prepare for being sent to France. On to Mr B, who took 6/- off me at 'matador'.

Saturday 11 November
Armistice Day. I forgot the 11 a.m. silence as there was no alarm to warn me. I humped half the ton of coke into the coalhouse and Harding the gardener came up and carried the rest. An aeroplane is said to have attacked Deal yesterday, and the story is that it was hit and crashed near Canterbury. This morning, planes flew over France and attacked the Le Havre to Dover cross-Channel boat; Dover AA guns blasted at it.

Tuesday 14 November
The Shetlands were bombed yesterday but the papers claim only a rabbit was killed. We sank a U-boat and the French sank another one. A letter from Daisy says South Africa was very near rebellion.

Friday 17 November
Heard from Milly. John, on his way to Buenos Aires, sighted a submarine. We had the Cantrells to tea. In the news, we were told a German plane has flown across England to the Irish Sea. Not much defence!! Air raid alarms in Marseilles. Definite unrest in Austria and Czech.

Sunday 19 November
A fine day, cold north wind. German submarines are dropping magnetic mines in the North Sea trade waters. Yesterday, a Dutch passenger steamer, the *Simon Bolivar*, was sunk with the loss of 140 men, women and children. German planes are also flying daily over Holland.

Trouble in Czech since Independence Day, 25 October: hundreds shot and thousands arrested.

Monday 20 November
We heard gunfire from Dover in the morning. Heard later that some German planes flew towards London. Some people in Folkestone saw the shell bursts. Took Phyllis to her library and I spent the afternoon at the free library. At 7.45 p.m. the sirens went and we dashed out to the allotments. No guns and no searchlights and the 'all clear' went at 8 o'clock.

Tuesday 21 November
Heard that a German bomber was attacked by three of our planes and shot down at sea off Deal this morning. The old Labour Corps men have been issued with rifles and none knows how to handle them.

RAID ALARMS IN COAST TOWNS

A 'plane with raked wings, believed to be a Heinkel bomber, was seen by people on the pier of a coast town in East Kent.

Thursday 23 November
Germans are laying mines in the trade routes. They have sunk a Dutch and Japanese ship (former with heavy loss of life) and a British destroyer. Their aeroplanes are also said to be dropping mines. The chief activity seems to be in the mouth of the Thames. Daphne met Giles (Church House caretaker) who, along with our gardener George Vale, is in the Hythe AA Battery at Dover. He says that German planes come up nearly every day. His battery has shot down one. Troubles in Czech; 1,000 are said to have been shot. 'Bone' Foster came over after tea and went through papers with a view to taking over RSPCA secretaryship of Hythe. Phyllis and Daphne went to Thanksgiving Service and I stayed late shopping.

Sunday 26 November
A raging storm last night with heavy rain. Mild today. Morning gave a rumour that the *Deutschland* had been sunk by us. Our news makes no

mention of it, but says the P&O armed liner *Rawalpindi* was sunk with all but 17. I expect the *Deutschland* did it.

Monday 27 November

Bad news on the whole: 14 British, two French and eight neutral ships sunk this week by magnetic bombs dropped by German aeroplanes. Another Dutch ship sunk in the Thames estuary. A British ship torpedoed on west coast. Sweden has protested over the mines and the Finns are sticking up to the Bolshies. Working on the Blaxland pedigree.

Wednesday 29 November

A perfect day yesterday, but rain again today. Yesterday we heard the *Rawalpindi* had been sunk by the *Deutschland*, as I thought. Russia is again abusing Finland but, not being Germany, I do not think they will fight if the Finns hold out. Rationing of butter and bacon to commence 8 January. Our Air Force attacked Borkum, going down to 10 feet off the ground to machine gun seaplanes, a patrol boat and machine gun posts.

Saturday 2 December

The Russians are well into Finland, but the Finns say they are holding them up. I consider the Scandinavian countries very foolish not to help out. The batch of Labour Corps around us went off this morning. I went into Folkestone about the fence of Aunt Annie's house, which the RE have knocked over. In the afternoon Colonel Wood the vet came up to see me about the National Air Raid Precautions Animals Committee [Home Office scheme to issue identity collars for pets]. Phyllis and Daphne drove Eva [Rodney's sister-in-law] and Joan [Eva's daughter] from Canterbury to Deal to see the ships collected there. They counted 60. They also saw a wreck. Got a wire from my sister Milly in evening saying Mother had fallen out of bed and broken her leg. She is 86.

Sunday 3 December

A good day for us. Our airmen attacked German ships off Heligoland, registering at least two hits with heavy bombs. An aeroplane definitely sank a large U-boat, and we have captured the whole crew of the U-boat which sank the *Courageous*.

Monday 4 December

I left by the 8.50 a.m. train and spent the day at the India Office Library [in London] and got to Guildford about 4.30 p.m.

Tuesday 5 December

Looked up Mother in the morning. She lies in bed, a tiny little woman living in the distant past and can only repeat one word several times. I thought in the end she recognised me or mistook me for Father or someone else. I doubt if she did even that. In the evening Milly and I saw *The Lion Has Wings*, quite a good film showing the men who raided the Kiel Canal.

Wednesday 6 December

Went in morning with Milly to see Mother. She has a nurse all day to be with her. Some Hun planes came up the Thames estuary last night, and one crashed into the sea without being fired upon. We have also captured another German liner.

Friday 8 December

Rained all day. Left Guildford at 10.30 a.m. and spent the day at the India Office Library without lunch or tea. Left 4.30 p.m. and arrived at Hythe at 6 p.m. Milly telephoned that darling Mother passed away.

Sunday 10 December

A fair, warm day. The King came back after six days in France. A number of German aeroplanes over, and we have two shot down. Four ships sunk. Finns appealed to the world for help.

Tuesday 12 December

Phyllis and I got off in good time at 11 a.m. and had a straight run. We had lunch at Westerham at the George and Dragon, an old coaching inn in a picturesque village. We reached the Malabar Hotel, Guildford, at 3 p.m. I found Milly had already gone to the Guildhall for Mother's inquest. I went to Pimms' mortuary chapel and left our wreaths and had a last look at Mother. When I got inside I knew I had seen it all before, even the attendant and the one wreath at the foot of the bier.

Wednesday 13 December
Drove up to the cemetery at 11 a.m. It is at the top of the Mount, up an almost perpendicular narrow road. Besides us four were Mai Ross and young George. Canon Buchanan led the service well and we gave him a lift back afterwards. In evening, supper with Milly and Eddie [her husband]. Battle of River Plate.

Thursday 14 December
Got back at 3 p.m. Aeroplanes over Ashford and big guns at Hythe. A gallant fight by three British light-armed cruisers against the *Graf Spee*. The *Ajax*'s Captain Harwood must be a fine man. Marvellous manoeuvring enabled them to dash in and hit like terriers with a badger. As usual, the first news made it into a defeat for us.

Monday 18 December
The *Graf Spee* sailed from Montevideo yesterday evening and was scuttled by her crew five miles out. It is said Captain Langsdorff sank with her. His action has saved life, but is ignominious. First British casualty list from France – a patrol. News of two of our submarines: one blew up a U-boat, sighted the SS *Bremen* and challenged her to stop, but was driven down by planes and later sank a cruiser. The other attacked eight cruisers and hit and possibly sank two. We also hear that the Canadians landed yesterday.

Wednesday 20 December
'Bone' Foster came round with the money collected from the RSPCA boxes. £3 of copper, mostly halfpennies and farthings. We had a job counting them.

Thursday 21 December
Explosions in the Channel and a number of aeroplanes about. Got in the last of my local collections (RSPCA). One collector is a daily maid who does it in her spare time. I sent her a special letter of thanks.

Friday 22 December
Inspector came with the last of our collections. After lunch I handed over £27 to Tasker-Evans. Went to play 'matador' with Mr B.

Monday 25 December

Christmas Day – no Mother to spend the day with. Janka left yesterday afternoon to be away for two nights. Phyllis got up at leisure whilst I did the before breakfast duties and we ate the meal in the kitchen. Weather much milder. Went over to 18 Kingsnorth Gardens for Christmas lunch. News that all leave boats from France are held up and Channel Isles steamer is a day late. Is the German fleet out?

Sunday 31 December

Thawed all day and froze again at night. None of us went to church. The men around us are increasing, but are a strange lot. One platoon is all NCOs, nucleus of the new Pioneer Corps. Some are our old soldier friends. A terrible earthquake in Turkey.

The Fosters' kitchen and the table they used as a bomb shelter

1940

Monday 1 January
New Year. We treated it as an ordinary day. Trawler *Young Harry* blown up with all hands off Folkestone: a local fisherman, his son and two deckhands had gone fishing in the prohibited zone.

Wednesday 3 January
The War Office have accepted my offer of service, and I am on the Emergency Reserve list. I do not know if they mean to call me up. More heavy explosions in the Channel. It is said to be mines.

Sunday 7 January
Daphne and I went to church in the morning. Great excitement over the re-shuffle of the cabinet. Chamberlain deposed Hore-Belisha from being War Minister and offered him the Dominions, which he refused. Mine sunk by gunfire off Copt Point.

Tuesday 9 January
Brigadier de Crespigny told me that the Army kicked out Hore-Belisha. He seems to have 'democratised' the Army too far. Liner *Dunbar Castle* mined off Ramsgate whilst with a convoy, her captain killed.

Wednesday 10 January
A very severe explosion in the morning, which shook the house, and others of less extent throughout the morning. It is said they are German mines which have drifted down from the North Sea and which we fire at to explode, being the quickest way to get rid of them.

Monday 15 January

A hard frost in morning and a cold day. I drove Phyllis into Folkestone to a meeting and I saw about Mr B's rebate. Meat rationing is to come in soon. The Germans have massed troops on the Dutch frontier, and the Belgians have mobilised.

Tuesday 16 January

Aeroplanes very busy in the morning. Germans about, I expect. It started snowing in the morning, ending up with a mild blizzard. The Germans have sunk three of our submarines in the Heligoland Bight, capturing about 35 of their crews.

Thursday 18 January

Snow lying deep everywhere, and still no buses up the hill. Explosion at Waltham Abbey [Gun]powder Factory; about six killed and 30 injured, said to be sabotage. Finns claim another victory. Explosion due to frost at officers' mess at Shorncliffe; several injured.

Friday 19 January

I believe I have solved the mystery of the Sylt raids. Both the Admiralty and Air Force say they are not British planes – they are Polish airmen. Nearly another foot of snow fell in the night; no buses running until midday. Had a very interesting talk with three officers of the Pioneers. They say Hore-Belisha was messing up the army, leaving it Bolshy. Our Czech maid, Janka Neumann, walked out at midday. She had worked herself into a nervous state due to not getting any letters from Hungary.

> ## NEW SYLT RAID MYSTERY
> ---
> ### 'PLANES SEEN AND GUNS HEARD

Monday 22 January

Slight thaw midday, but hard frost again in evening. Daphne went into Folkestone after lunch. The capture of a dossier by the Belgians from a German officer who had made a forced landing in Belgium details plans for invasion. They say it must be genuine and not a plant. Germany seems to be now turning against the Balkans. USA attitude disgusting.

Tuesday 23 January
A slight thaw midday when the sun was out. The Inspector rang
up that he was stuck in Horn Street and could not come. After lunch
I walked out up Sandy Lane to the main road. Beyond the [railway]
tunnel the snow was level with the banks. Came back through the
woods and across field into Saltwood. I went up to my knees crossing the
field.

Friday 26 January
Early after lunch into Folkestone. To Aunt Annie's house, met the new
CO of the Company – a stockbroker-looking Major with the MC and no
right arm. In two rooms the men had burnt out the fireplaces. On to
Kingsnorth Gardens and did some work for Mr B. At teatime it rained, at 6
o'clock it was snowing. Met two Canadian sergeants. On way up Church
Hill I crashed and broke a rib. Had a very painful night.

Saturday 27 January
Colonel Murray [a doctor] turned up about 9.30 a.m., thought I had dry
pleurisy because of the old scar, I expect. A nasty cold day for everyone,
but [I'm] warm in bed. More snow at night.

Sunday 28 January
Murray came again and completely bandaged me up. Weather worse than
ever. Had a better night.

Monday 29 January
Our dustbins cleared this morning. They had not been done since the 18th.
Gunfire in morning and heard later German planes had come over from the
Shetlands to the Kent coast. At 2 a.m. a mine drifted against East Cliff,
Folkestone, and blew up, damaging the promenade and several houses and
smashing hundreds of windows. Another is said to be ashore by West
Parade, Hythe. Bitter cold wind and snow in evening.

Tuesday 30 January
As much snow as ever this morning, with an east wind and no signs of a
change. Loud explosions during the day; probably mines blowing up. My
pain better in day but coughing gave us both a bad night.

Wednesday 31 January
A decided thaw; all the gutters dripping and slush everywhere. I got up at
noon and sat in a chair. A small noisy crowd of men have come in next door.
Papers say German planes attacked shipping all along the coast yesterday.

Thursday 1 February
Thaw continues. Houses around us again filling up with troops. Rather a
quarrelsome crowd. I was up from noon to 9 o'clock.

Friday 2 February
Still thawing but no impression on deep snow, and a frost and some snow
last night. Murray turned up early and said I had dry pleurisy not a broken
rib. Daphne went into Folkestone for lunch and had tea with her Grandpa.
Some explosions during day.

Saturday 3 February
At least 40 German planes are said to have attacked along the coast, three
being brought down. Our wireless went wrong. I came down and spent
the day in the drawing room.

Monday 12 February
Snow came down again this morning; about half a foot fell. Last night
the old tomcat died from an abscess, in the kitchen. Phyllis had a bad time
with it.

Friday 16 February
Phyllis went to Kingsnorth. She says Mr B looks fit and lively, but is very
wasted in the legs. My third week laid up. *Altmark* prisoners released by
HMS *Cossack*.

> *On 16 February, the SS* Altmark, *a German tanker and supply vessel that had
> rescued survivors of the* Graf Spee *sinking, was attacked and captured by HM
> Destroyer* Cossack *in neutral Norwegian waters. Around 300 British seamen
> captured by the* Graf Spee *were liberated.*

Saturday 17 February
Wind at night with more snow driven into drifts, yet the town buses
did not stop this time. Great excitement over the *Altmark* affair. We

were absolutely right and the Norwegian attitude was grossly un-neutral; through fear of Germany, we hope, not through partiality.

Wednesday 21 February
Very mild spring day. Primrose blooms just showing, snowdrops and crocuses are late. I went for a stroll after lunch. I have been indoors four weeks.

Primrose-picking time in Saltwood woods (Folkestone Library HS/PAR/2)

Thursday 22 February
Two loud explosions in morning with gunfire later and aeroplanes about all day. One seemed to zoom down three times round about Lympne making a noise like a siren. To me, it all sounded like chasing a submarine. I had an hour's stroll in morning and was out again in afternoon. A coastguard waded out and secured a drifting mine.

Friday 23 February
Daphne was in Folkestone all day taking car for overhaul and other doings. She and Phyllis went after supper to a concert given by our local refugees in aid of British and French Red Cross. It was amusing where it was not meant to be!

Friday 1 March

Very cold wind in morning. Inspector had a case against a farmer for cruelty to sheep at Seabrook Court and he was fined by Quested. After the case, he learnt that the sheep belonged to Quested!!

Saturday 2 March

Gunfire (big guns) and planes. It probably was German planes attacking a convoy, which we heard about on the wireless. Mine in Folkestone inner harbour lassoed by a [Royal Naval Volunteer] Supplementary Reserve man.

Monday 4 March

Our new maid Martha Graf arrived in evening. She is a German-Swiss who has been in service in Folkestone. Our scullery maid is Mary, so they are well named. We heard that yesterday's explosions were attacks on ships between Deal and Margate.

Wednesday 6 March

Aeroplanes very active in morning. A cold wind all day. Flakes of snow in afternoon. George Vale our late gardener is on leave and looked us up. He has been sick most of the time, but had one day's shooting at Dover and his [AA] battery has fired several times and claims one hit.

Saturday 9 March

Heard an aeroplane above the clouds in afternoon. A man on the allotments said by the sound of the engine it was German. Skeleton of a man, head on water bottle, found in [Folkestone] Warren.

Sunday 10 March

Drove Phyllis to church in the morning and round Sandling Park in afternoon to gather leaf mould. I saw my first lambs and a first bee. Our snowdrops and crocuses are pretty in front but we have practically no primroses this year. A lot of aeroplanes up in the evening, but we have no news of raids.

Monday 11 March

The papers full of Finnish peace talks. Sweden shows up badly over the affair. A warm day. A young lad of 19 named Hunter crashed and was killed on Folkestone Golf Course. His first solo flight. The men in the road very noisy in evening, singing and shouting.

Wednesday 13 March
Sweden is now frightened. The USA abuses us and the French. This afternoon at a meeting at Caxton Hall, a Sikh fired six shots, killing Sir Michael O'Dwyer [former Governor of the Punjab] and wounding Lord Zetland [Secretary of State for India] and two others.

Thursday 14 March
Blizzard started in the morning and the snow was blown in drifts finally lying about six inches deep. Almost impossible to drive against the wind.

Saturday 16 March
All the snow gone. Wind dropped, warm sun. Finland signed peace. An air raid on Scapa Flow, which – although Churchill said it was not – is still being used by our fleet. A large number of German machines came over, 20 bombs dropped round fleet, one of our ships damaged. Double that number of bombs dropped on land, one civilian killed and seven wounded.

Sunday 17 March
Daphne developed what is probably a mild attack of German (!!) measles.

Tuesday 19 March
Watched three Bristol biplanes firing on targets on the range. The third appeared to be a beginner and failed to open fire more than once.

Wednesday 20 March
Our local Air Force were out all night, landing finally in fields near Paddlesworth. This was probably in connection with the attack on the convoy. Everyone very gratified over the Sylt raid, including the neutrals.

Friday 22 March
Good Friday. A mine exploded near a cross-Channel steamer. Went to Kingsnorth Gardens in afternoon and played 'matador' with Mr B. A British trawler ran over a U-boat but doesn't know what happened to it. Another beat off and damaged a German plane, but not enough of the latter are

being destroyed. The USA are doing all they can to revive their trade with Germany through neutrals, and Germany must soon be better off than us.

Saturday 23 March
Mr Blaxland's birthday. Phyllis and I had tea with him. Daphne thought it best to stay away. About 10 p.m. a very violent explosion shook the house. It is said a mine was exploded six miles out at sea, but a ship must have gone up with it.

Monday 25 March
Easter Monday Bank Holiday. Two loud explosions in morning followed by what sounded like

> Beginning on Easter Monday, the butter ration will be doubled—eight ounces per head instead of four ounces.

gunfire. Other explosions during the day. Butter ration doubled, but the poorer people cannot afford the smaller ration.

Wednesday 27 March
Sunny, but a very cold wind. Drove Phyllis into Folkestone. Saw first ice-cream man on Sandgate Parade. I saw a smart corporal with a girl on his arm approaching an officer. He dropped the girl's arm as he saluted, and the officer acknowledged the salute. The officer had a girl clinging around his waist!!!

Friday 29 March
Went and saw Tasker-Evans. His son is an instructor at Sandhurst. He has put his car up on bricks, because he has to pay him as well as his daughter an allowance. Went on to Mr B.

Saturday 30 March
Our daffodils out. They are always later than other gardens. Saw a flight of five aeroplanes in formation. Churchill made a forceful speech to neutrals. It was relayed to USA, but the Yankees had their tongues in their cheeks. Germany cannot harm them.

Tuesday 2 April
Our R Es have cleared out, bag and baggage, from Oakville next door. We hear all the drains were clogged, and the town sewer pump has been

working all day. Trying to deal with the mess of 200 men with the drainage of a private house was impossible.

Thursday 4 April
I went to a RSPCA branch committee meeting held at Lady Macdonagh's house, not many there. Annual report and accounts: they praised my report. No one keen on lending a hand to find ways for making money. Meeting lasted from 3 p.m. to 4.30 p.m., but Lady M did not offer us tea!

Tuesday 9 April
The events [German invasion of Norway and Denmark] came over the air in rapid succession. Norwegian coastal forts put up a fine show and sank the *Karlsruhe* and *Blücher*.

Wednesday 10 April
The recapture of Bergen and Trondheim. Phyllis and Daphne, going into Folkestone, just missed seeing the Queen returning from her inspection at Broome Park.

Queen Elizabeth inspects the London Scottish at Broome Park
(Folkestone Library K/WW2/3)

Friday 12 April
Forty of the crew of the *Hardy*, the destroyer which ran aground at Narvik, landed fully armed and have marched inland.

Sunday 14 April

Took Phyllis to Folkestone, and went about Mr B's income tax return and RSPCA matters with Tasker-Evans.

Tuesday 16 April

They should give us full news. The Germans know it already through their spies and friends. Went to lunch and tea with Eddie at the Bristol Hotel [Folkestone] – a poor lunch. Coming away, we saw two destroyers rushing at full speed towards us from near France. They stopped opposite the harbour and an aeroplane skimmed the water quartering the sea as far as the Grand Redoubt. Then the convoy from Deal came up. Disappointed nothing dramatic happened. Italian press very anti-Allies. Is Italy joining the Germans? I say 'Yes.'

Wednesday 17 April

British troops have made contact with the Norwegians. A British submarine lost. The whole of Europe with the jitters. Japan wanting to take over Dutch East Indies. World war imminent.

Saturday 20 April

All the REs round here went away on a week's embarkation leave last night. A warm summer's day. Heard a cuckoo. Heavy gunfire after lunch. A convoy passing and sheltering north of Dungeness and aeroplanes flying high inland, but I saw nothing to connect the three. The air raid was on Deal. I hear the ships were sunk by aeroplanes not by mines.

**NAZI AIR ATTACK
OFF S.E. COAST**
GUNFIRE SHAKES
HOUSES

Sunday 21 April

A perfect 'mid-summer' day, and at night a full moon. Drove Phyllis, Daphne to church, then picked up Mr B and drove through Hawkinge, Acrise and Lyminge. The country coming out green. He had said he was

sure he could not get in and out of the car, but he managed it and enjoyed
the drive. Rumour that Allies have captured Hamar, 50 miles from Oslo.

Wednesday 24 April

A wet day. Some distant gunfire and a few explosions in morning. We have
undoubtedly had a set-back in Norway, and German air activity is very
strong despite our bombing of Boche aerodromes.

Friday 26 April

All our REs have returned from leave. Fine day. I am experiencing great
difficulty in getting extra petrol; have had none all April. To Kingsnorth in
afternoon; was not offered a peg.

Tuesday 30 April

Two COs of regiments captured in Norway. We are not holding our own.
Socks had kittens! A very heavy rainstorm with thunder.

Wednesday 1 May

News from Norway better. Phyllis said she heard an aeroplane flying low
overhead last night and felt sure it was a German. Local gossip says it was a
German and fell into the sea. Aeroplanes up all day.

Friday 3 May

Heavy distant gunfire morning and
afternoon and it broke out again at
10 p.m. and continued to midnight.
Northerly wind makes it probable it
came from Deal or the Thames
estuary. A warm day. Air battle off
French coast.

> **AERIAL FIGHT OFF
> ENGLISH COAST**
> ———
> **SHELLS SEEN FROM LAND**

Saturday 4 May

The Army needs a trumpeter like Churchill. Its work in Norway is hushed
up as something to be ashamed of. Yet it was most gallant, half-trained,
ill-equipped but rushed to the help of the Norwegians and saved a
complete invasion. The same story; not sufficient troops employed. Navy
and Army not co-operating, efforts half-hearted.

Sunday 5 May

Saw first bluebells and first wasps today. I fetched Mr B and Nancy [his daughter] over here after lunch to see the gardens and took them back. On my way home I met a mechanised unit of lorries and motorcycles, which stretched from Cheriton to Kick Hill. Couldn't tell to what branch of the service they belonged.

Tuesday 7 May

Sir Roger Keyes [Admiral of the Fleet] made a very fine speech; I am keeping a copy. Distant gunfire most of the day. A loud explosion at 8.30 p.m.

Wednesday 8 May

Chamberlain put up a poor show, talked only of his friends and enemies. Churchill made a poor speech full of lame excuses. In afternoon I drove into Folkestone with Daphne to pick up Phyllis, and gave two young cadets a lift in. I went in for a RSPCA meeting at 8 p.m. When I got to Miss Haviland's I found I was a week too early!!

Friday 10 May

I was awoken at 4 a.m. by explosions which shook the house: early morning raid on Boulogne. I am sorry for Chamberlain, but a man who has sacrificed the country's prestige and, one might almost say, its honour to preserve peace has not the mentality to prosecute a war. British troops enter Belgium and land in Iceland. Afternoon to Folkestone, about printing RSPCA branch annual report. Then 'matador' with Mr B.

Sunday 12 May

A fine day. Only two explosions. I drove the family to church, then drove Mr B to the golf course. Troops are out everywhere guarding bridges etc. and others standing to with their cars and lorries. Reservists have been taken out of our REs, armed and sent to guard Lympne Aerodrome. We saw hundreds of buses full of women and children parked by Folkestone Harbour. News from the Low Countries is not reassuring.

Tuesday 14 May

Rotterdam destroyed by bombardment. Our REs woke us up at 6.30 a.m. and I got up thinking it was 7.30. After lunch, went over and drove Mr B to Romney Marsh and all round and into his old Burmarsh farm. Very little land ploughed up, and that was the best arable land in Kent.

Wednesday 15 May

Again woken early by the men. A loud explosion at 7 a.m. In afternoon I went into Folkestone to tea with Ada Collins. She looked fit despite her illness. She is again worrying about her daughter who is said to be incurable, but she was full of energy. They are worrying about staying in Folkestone, whose authorities are now all for evacuation after having insisted on it being a reception area. After supper, I went to a RSPCA meeting at Kitty Haviland's flat. She resigned the secretaryship, as she says she is leaving. The usual pessimism and no one except Mrs Walton to do anything. I took over as clinic secretary, no one else offering. Finished at 9.30 p.m. and raced a thunderstorm up the hill. Thunder and lightning terrific. I have never experienced such a storm. The Germans have broken the Maginot Line at the first attempt. Holland capitulated at 11.00 a.m.

Thursday 16 May

Wind changed round to NE direction, strong and cold. I went to the police station and enrolled in the Local Defence Corps. Daphne also tried to do so but her friend the station sergeant would not have her. Men who sit in dug-outs and only come out when a raid is over get their £5 to £7 a week, but we who are to attack heavily armed parachutists have to do it for nothing! Rumbling of guns in the morning. Heard that Mrs Bush of North Road died during the thunderstorm last night. She had a weak heart.

Friday 17 May

Rumbling of guns early shook the house. A Dutch refugee ship, full of men, women and children, is said to have come into Folkestone Harbour, having been chased by Hun aeroplanes all the way. Lympne Aerodrome is now underground. A 30-mile breakthrough near Sedan and the Belgians retiring, possibly cracking. I said at the start the Maginot Line would prove useless.

Saturday 18 May

Received letters from Tasker-Evans and Jerry resigning the secretaryship of the branch and clinic. Tasker-Evans blocks everything, gives no help and resigns when there is any trouble. Saw Burdekin, and told him I would resign. They are a rotten crowd. Loud gunfire at night. I went to sleep still hearing it.

Sunday 19 May

Some distant firing in the morning, and planes flying overhead all day. Churchill made a stirring speech but it gave one the creeps. On top of that, at night guns and bombs went off from 11.30 p.m. until I went to sleep. The evacuees from London sent away from south-east coast.

Monday 20 May

I learnt from Driver, my tobacconist, that last night's affair was over Calais and Boulogne. He was on duty on the seafront. He mentioned a searchlight which went round in the sky like a Catherine wheel.

Tuesday 21 May

Five vessels outside Folkestone said to be refugee carriers; Fifth Columnists said to have been found amongst them. Squadrons of aeroplanes flying out to sea all day and I saw a mine explode in the sea. Continuous fire of heavy calibre guns started at 7 p.m. with one very loud crash. It died down about 9 p.m., and at 10.30 p.m. our siren went off. We went outside our gate, Daphne putting on my 'tin hat'. The fat Corporal from opposite told us that the British Expeditionary Force (BEF) was cut up and the Huns in Calais. At 11.45 p.m. planes were heard flying towards Lympne and searchlights were turned on but when we were expecting something to happen the 'all clear' sounded. They were our planes returning. We turned on the news at midnight but learnt nothing, except that the Duke of Gloucester had been wounded in the bombardment of Boulogne.

Wednesday 22 May

Wet morning, fine afternoon. Phyllis to Folkestone where she, Eva and Mrs Dix saw three barrage balloons high up, which they thought were parachutists. Some of our REs left at 5.30 p.m. At 7.30 p.m. I went down to the Town Hall to hear Major General RM Lucock explain the organisation of the Local Defence Volunteers. General AL Forster, Royal Marines, is to command the Kent Battalion, Major FW Butler the Hythe Platoon, Captain JS Fuller the Saltwood Section (which I joined) and

Colonel H Street the Hythe Section. There is a third (Lympne) Section. About 250 attended, Brigadier P Mortimer joined Saltwood Section and Major P Grove-White, Hythe. A peaceful night.

Thursday 23 May

British evacuated Boulogne. We hear that the Germans are in or almost in Boulogne and a U-boat is in the Channel. I drove Phyllis shopping in the morning; guns started at 11 o'clock and went on to 5 p.m. At 3 p.m. I had my RSPCA branch committee meeting at Burdekin's house; Mrs Walton, Miss Mullings, the Dales and Lancashire alone attended. We decided to close the clinic. An air raid warning at 6.30 p.m. I had a hurried supper and went to the SAS [Small Arms School] hut where our Section assembled and some of us were issued with P14 rifles. An instructor from the SAS gave us a short lecture. As James Kerr and I walked back with our rifles, two sentries, posted at the SAS gate below Barrack Hill, called out 'Any luck?' I replied: 'Not yet.'

Friday 24 May

Empire Day. Guns all day. Daphne drove me to Folkestone for an afternoon with Mr B. She applied for a job of driver to the police, but it was too strenuous, as she would have to live in Folkestone. We listened to the Empire broadcast, a fine speech by the King. A German air raid on Middlesbrough.

Saturday 25 May

A very hot, oppressive day. Heavy gunfire all day on French coast, and I saw what I imagine was Boulogne going up in smoke. People leaving Hythe and Folkestone like rats from a sinking ship. I don't blame them. At about 11.30 p.m. we heard the droning of many aeroplanes and stood at the windows watching the searchlights. Daphne saw them pick out aeroplanes, apparently our own.

Sunday 26 May

I hear we got the submarine which was in the Channel. Not a gun fired or bomb dropped all day. No news on wireless, except that children along eastern and south-eastern coasts as far as, but not including, Hythe are to be evacuated.

On 26 May, Churchill ordered the evacuation of Allied soldiers from the beaches and harbour of Dunkirk, after British, French and Belgian troops had been cut off during the Battle of Dunkirk. Between 26 May and 3 June, Operation Dynamo rescued 338,226 soldiers (198,229 British and 139,997 French) in a hastily assembled fleet of 850 boats, which ranged from merchant ships to pleasure yachts.

Monday 27 May

My birthday! (58) Another quiet day except for aeroplanes. At 6 o'clock I went out and looked for old Bush, and had a very heartening talk with him. He told me one of our own aeroplanes on Saturday dropped a bomb in Sandling Park. I feel sure the Germans are in Calais, though the French deny it.

Tuesday 28 May

Belgian army capitulated at 4 a.m. We heard of the Belgian king's surrender at about 8 a.m. Situation is hopeless. The Inspector told me he had seen a lot of French troops, many wounded, land and that they said they came from Calais. Distant gunfire in morning. At 1.45 p.m. the siren went and the 'all clear' 40 minutes later. Mr B, on the advice of his doctor, has decided to leave on Sunday.

Thursday 30 May

Commencement of Dunkirk evacuation. Woken up about 6 a.m. by hundreds of aeroplanes passing overhead. Spent day on RSPCA work.

Friday 31 May

Spent all day in Folkestone doing RSPCA work, ending up at Kingsnorth Gardens, no 'matador'. I had to write out his accounts and they were busy packing. Going in on the bus, I saw mines explode near the harbour; they were being trawled by a pair of small minesweepers very close to a destroyer. I heard no sound. I also saw a small party of French soldiers very clean and 'unused'. Trains dashing through every few minutes with troops.

Saturday 1 June

The Inspector has been busy killing scores of dogs, which have come over with the troops. All our Sappers left last night. They are building barricades etc. everywhere. Evacuation of Dunkirk completed.

Sunday 2 June
Order for all children to be evacuated. Most of them from Hythe went to Wales. Mr B and Nancy got away in Austen's car for Tunbridge Wells by 1.15 p.m.

Monday 3 June
Daphne saw a crashed British fighter carried through Hythe. Barricades up around the town, which are closed at 6 p.m. All small bridges over the Royal Military Canal dismantled and the others prepared for blowing up. Two naval guns by the Imperial Hotel. At 11 p.m. a German plane came over us and the searchlights were all on but they did not pick it up.

Tuesday 4 June
Our local Blackshirts arrested. A very hot day. Phyllis and Daphne to Folkestone for a church meeting. Churchill in his statement gave us the facts without any sugar to them. Also, news that all aliens must leave the area, so we lose our Swiss maid, Martha Graf. She was very upset about it, and exclaimed: 'I am not a spy, I am not a spy!', but we had our doubts. She had made friends with a boarding-house keeper near Folkestone Harbour, where there was considerable naval and military activity. Twice, on her afternoon out, she claimed to have missed the last bus and stayed the night there. We reported this to the police, but they made light of it.

Wednesday 5 June
End of evacuation. The Germans launched their attack on the French at the Somme and Aisne at 4 a.m. I walked along the seafront in the afternoon.

Thursday 6 June
I spent the morning doing RSPCA work in Folkestone. Had a personal letter saying I may yet be posted. News that the French are hanging on. We were woken up by sirens at 1.30 a.m. and the 'all clear' went at 4 a.m. We had heard German planes in evening but none during the alarm. I slept part of the time.

Friday 7 June
Martha left in morning. Our Sappers have increased: six lorry-loads turned up in morning. They have come back to feed next door. Met Fuller, who

said our planes deliberately unloaded three bombs in Sandling Park, thinking it was a clear area. He says the country around is swarming with troops who patrol all night with orders to shoot at sight and it is not safe for us Volunteers to go out. Sirens again about 1.30 p.m. and alarm lasted an hour. We saw only one searchlight and heard no planes.

Saturday 8 June
Aircraft carrier *Glorious* sunk off Norway. A cooler day. Saw the coast of France. Phyllis and I spent afternoon in Folkestone. Evening news did not sound very hopeful. About 11.30 p.m., as we had just got to bed, we heard a German plane and all the searchlights went on. Then we saw them catch the plane (Daphne saw two) in beams over Folkestone and showers of tracer bullets filled the air around it. Then two AA shells exploded above it and it disappeared and the searchlights switched off. At about 4 a.m., a number of loud explosions woke us up. Some sounded like naval guns.

Sunday 9 June
Norway capitulated. Hotter than ever. All three of us to church. At midnight I heard a German plane flying over, but was too sleepy to get up and see if searchlights were out. Single gunfire all night.

Monday 10 June
Cloudy, with a fog like an Indian dust storm coming up. I heard that Saturday's plane came down on to the water near Folkestone Harbour. An ex-regular NCO on the pier had a Bren gun aimed at it, but his Lieutenant, the town's music director, would not let him fire without orders. I also heard that it was later shot down off Dymchurch. The Police Inspector in charge of security called to ask us for Martha Graf's forwarding address, which we did not know, and what we knew of her movements. He refused to tell us the reason for his enquiries.

Wednesday 12 June
Ringing of church bells prohibited, reserved for warning that parachute troops were being dropped. A Hun plane brought down in Kent at 8 a.m. One would like to have a small gleam of good news. USA will be too late with their aid. They don't mean to give it.

Friday 14 June

Canadian Infantry Brigade lands at Brest. In morning, I went into Folkestone about RSPCA work and on Mr B's affairs. HQ is working with the Inspector, but keeps me in the dark. Some patrol let a gun off near us about 8.30 p.m.

Saturday 15 June

In morning, Captain Fuller brought my uniform and orders for tomorrow. He thinks the job we are being given is useless. Kept Phyllis awake all night with my coughing.

Sunday 16 June

Offer of Anglo-French union rejected. Wet all day. At 8.30 p.m. I went down to the Imperial Hotel and took charge of my group of volunteers. They were C Igglesden, proprietor of the Ashford newspaper; ET Kite, an ex-sergeant in the Buffs; WW Avery, labourer; W Burton; HS Gausby, gardener; Captain CF Newington, late of the Kent Yeomanry; BW Turner, chauffeur at Saltwood Castle; and WF Stone, shop assistant. I was the only one in uniform. Captain Fuller explained our duties and Kite gave some instruction in loading and handling weapons. At 9 o'clock we started our patrols from the hotel to Sandgate Old Lifeboat House along Princes Parade. I took the whole squad down to the end in daylight, making contact with the several posts. Our headquarters were two underground storerooms of the Imperial Hotel, accessible only through a small window, and we had mattresses to lie on. I stayed awake all night and personally saw to the relief of the patrols, which the others appreciated. Igglesden, a great talker, helped to pass the time. He had been over to France as a correspondent. Nothing happened. After pulling out the last patrol, I had a sleep at 3.30 a.m.

Monday 17 June

We came off duty at 5 a.m. As we left, a policeman told us to listen in at 7 a.m. and that France had given in. I did so, but only learnt of a change of government with Pétain as PM. However, at 1 o'clock we heard it was true. What a life!! As someone said, at least there is no one left now to let us down. Evacuation from Brest: transport *Lancastria* bombed and sunk, nearly 1,000 troops killed.

First Local Defence Volunteer guard at the Imperial Hotel, Hythe, 1940

Wednesday 19 June
Air raid by 100 machines along the Thames estuary and further north last night. I had Diggon, the RSPCA assistant secretary, to see me in the morning over my objection to them treating me as a nonentity. I got no satisfaction, however. Phyllis went into Folkestone in afternoon. Just after we got to bed at 11 p.m. we heard a Hun plane fly over and at 11.15 p.m. the sirens sounded. We watched the searchlights for a bit, then I went to sleep. I heard planes later on and the 'all clear' sounded at 4.30 a.m.

Friday 21 June
To Folkestone in afternoon. Posters were being put up all over the town, saying it would be evacuated if there was a possibility of an invasion. At midnight we heard aeroplanes but were not certain they were Huns, but at 12.30 a.m. the sirens were sounded. A few searchlights went up for a short time and some explosions, possibly anti-aircraft fire, were heard.

Saturday 22 June

The 'all clear' was sounded at 2 a.m. last night. A hundred planes are said to have come over, and we failed to bring down any of them. I had a RSPCA branch committee meeting at 3 p.m. at my house to elect Lancashire as treasurer – the Dales, Miss Mullings and Lancashire present. It did not take long. Lancashire stayed for a cup of tea but the sirens sounded and he had to go. We are beginning to hear some truths about the French and ourselves. Their socialist government, like ours, had frittered away the Army's equipment. Evacuation posters were put up this afternoon in Hythe, and visitors to the coast are banned.

Monday 24 June

We had an air raid alarm from 12.30 a.m. to 3.30 a.m.; I did not move from bed and heard no planes. I went into Folkestone in the afternoon to try and get news of the evacuation. I found Inspector Neville and his son hard at work destroying pet animals of every type: 60 dogs and cats up to that time in the one day.

Tuesday 25 June

Planes overhead in early morning. Vessels in Channel hunting mines or submarines. In the afternoon we three drove out to Smeeth (Brabourne Lees) to a cottage in a dell called Bog Farm where we met the owner Mrs Allen, and hired it for the duration for £1 a week furnished. It is a charming place, but has primitive sanitation etc., and is reputed 16th century and looks it!

Bog Farm, the Fosters' retreat, in more modern times

Wednesday 26 June

Signposts and place names removed. I was on duty again from 8.30 p.m. at the Imperial Hotel – Avery, Broom, Burton, French, Gausby, Prior, Stone and Turner were my squad. I had to put two sentries on the empty telephone exchange at the east end of the High Street and had to pass a manned barrier on Twiss Road. Each time they were good to us, but some days before had fired at Police Sergeant Jones. At dusk three of our planes with lights on flew along the coast from Dungeness to beyond Folkestone – a pretty sight. At 1 a.m. we heard a German, and searchlights came on from Dungeness side and my sentries said they lit up a plane for a short time. We were bucked at the news of our raid on the French coast.

Thursday 27 June
Germans reached Spanish frontier. Harman called in morning and drove Phyllis and me to Bog Farm to look into sanitary and other matters. In the evening I went round enrolling our volunteers. I slept soundly at night and heard nothing. Phyllis heard aeroplanes, machine gun fire and a very loud explosion. Folkestone pier breached.

Friday 28 June
Rumours that the affair last night was an attack on Lympne or the destruction of a submarine at sea. Actually, it was a Hun plane attacking searchlights in the Marsh and at Stone Farm. No one thought of reporting it to HQ Shorncliffe, who were peeved. In afternoon I went into Folkestone to the clinic and accompanied Neville round the empty houses in Folkestone, releasing canaries and budgerigars left behind by people who had gone away; it was the only thing to do as no one else would take them. We found many dead for want of food and water. Folkestone pier has had its centre blown up and a cargo steamer is moored by the harbour entrance. Naval gunfire from 6 p.m. to 8 p.m. General De Gaulle recognised as leader of the Free French.

Saturday 29 June
Went into [Major] Butler's office and joined orderly room, consisting of General Lucock, Colonel Street, [Colonel] Stansfield and [Captain] Fuller. I read intelligence reports, most interesting. Butler has gone sick and Street commands our platoon. We have apparently evacuated the Channel Islands and handed them over to the Huns without a shot. They speeded up the evacuation by killing about 40 civilians. The French overseas empire has given in and their fleet has surrendered.

Monday 1 July

I learnt in the morning that HM the King had motored with a following of Staff Officers, motorcycles, Military Police etc. down the Leas and Princes Parade inspecting our defences. I wonder what he thought of them; to me they are most inadequate. I was on duty again on the seafront at

Part of the coastal defence – a disguised pill-box along the Sandgate promenade (IWM H2177)

night. We had to use the hotel garages for headquarters as the hotel is closed. We were short of men, so Fuller came down and he and I each took a turn of duty. I took 1 a.m. to 3 a.m. We had to patrol Princes Parade, which now bristles with small pill-box posts, and we were challenged six times each way, 24 times in one tour of duty being made to 'halt, advance and be recognised'. At 10 p.m. several men in posts let off their rifles. At 11 p.m. two men from a post fully armed came to our garage and demanded food and we had difficulty in driving them away. A large sickle moon rising through clouds with the dawn was a beautiful sight at 3 a.m.

Tuesday 2 July

In the afternoon Phyllis and Daphne went to a meeting in Folkestone. I got my own supper and at 8.30 p.m. went to the Saltwood Waterworks. Fuller explained that we were to guard the pump-house building from tonight with two men and if possible three. It looked a peaceful spot in a small field surrounded by trees on three sides. I heard a Hun pass overhead just before going to sleep.

Wednesday 3 July

Rained at night and much cooler. We were packing up to lunchtime and were ready by 2.30 p.m. with all the kit outside, but Driver's lorry did not turn up, so Phyllis and Daphne left in the car with the animals about 3 o'clock. After phoning up Driver at Newingreen without result, I found the lorry man moving people into Castle Road. They had said they only had one load, and actually had four. About 4 p.m. I noticed three planes pass over which did not look British, but thought no more of them until the sirens sounded and I heard four explosions to the north. A little later, I saw a Hun plane flying fairly low and slowly from east to west followed at a long distance by bursting AA shells. It circled round Lympne and sauntered back the way it had come. After an interval it, or another, came back and did much the same thing. Three Hurricanes arrived but flew in the wrong direction. My lorry turned up at 5 p.m. and, despite sirens and gunfire, we loaded up and drove to Bog Farm. I had humped all the kit to the front gates, including five sacks of coke, and loaded and unloaded the lorry and was rather done in. The lorry man gave me a lift back to Newingreen; there the barriers were manned by Sappers who said bombs had been dropped at Lympne causing casualties. As no buses were running, I walked back via Pedlinge, the 'all clear' sounding as I got near Redbrooks. I was told that the cheeky Hun was brought down over the sea, also that bombs had been dropped near Hatch Park (in the morning) and at Ashford, Wye, Mersham etc. Thunder and rain at 8 p.m.

Thursday 4 July

The fight with the French Navy is a grim affair. I do not think our military policy is sound. The Hun which came over yesterday was definitely shot down. I got up early and made my own breakfast, and Mary came for an hour to wash up etc. At 10.15 a.m. the sirens sounded and I heard explosions Hawkinge way. 'All clear' at 10.30 a.m. I was in town all day, went to Stansfield's for sherry and had a cold lunch at the White Hart. Daphne turned up in the car in the afternoon to fetch cooking pots etc. They are having a difficult job with an old oil cooker, the water and drawbacks. There was a loud explosion at 8 p.m. I cooked myself a tasty supper.

Friday 5 July

Huns came over about 6 a.m. and woke me up. It is said we got two of them. Fuller came to talk over Section affairs. He told me the explosion I heard yesterday was caused by a Sapper Officer who demonstrated the firing of a new anti-tank bomb over the main gas-pipe in Sandling Park, and put out all the lights there and elsewhere. Inspector Neville told me he was at Stone Farm on Wednesday and the Hun machine gunned the cars parked on the road, but his bullets all went into the field beyond. All afternoon I was going round handing duty notices to the Saltwood Section. I cooked myself a lunch as well as all other meals. After supper I went to post the sentries at the Waterworks. Just about 9 o'clock, two machines, one whistling as if badly hit, roared over the church, over the trees surrounding the field I was in, their machine guns going hard out. I did not know it at the time but it was a Messerschmitt chasing one of ours, who managed to dodge the Hun when over me and get away to Hawkinge. The Hun then flew over me and out to sea. They say three of our planes chased it and brought it down into the sea. The British pilot died of his wounds.

Saturday 6 July

I was woken up again at 6 a.m. by AA and machine gun fire. It rained all day. I attended orderly rooms all the morning. Daphne turned up at 11.30 a.m. and took charge. Fuller came after lunch. He is fed up at our men having no uniforms and no arms, and wants me to help him make a strong protest on Monday. Explosions and single gunfire during the day. Bombs dropped on coast.

Sunday 7 July

A fine day after the rain. Daphne went to church. The siren sounded at 1.15 p.m., just as she returned, and the 'all clear' at 1.30 p.m. On my way to the Waterworks I met Seymour and, as we crossed the fields, we heard the Huns attacking a convoy and saw clouds of smoke east of Dungeness. As I got to Saltwood Green, our planes flew over and I with others watched a battle in the sky. Some said they saw two planes fall in flames, but I didn't. I went on to the Waterworks, where Prior had arrived. He is a nice man, has been a legal member of the Colonial Office in Sierra Leone and Kenya. He thinks everything out carefully and asks questions in a deliberate way. Fuller thinks he is trying to probe his ignorance, but it is not that. Planes hovered about for half an hour. We stayed up until 11 o'clock and I took the 11 p.m. to 1 a.m. and the 3 a.m. to 5 a.m. duties. It rained the whole night.

Monday 8 July

Rain all morning. Notices up saying all cars of owners who do not draw 'E' (Essential) coupons must be demobilised by tomorrow midnight. A great 'hoo-ha' in the town; the police tell me I must produce my 'E' coupons, which I have used up and won't take the note on my registration book. In the afternoon, I watched a convoy being bombed and a fight in the sky but could not distinguish friend and foe. I spent an hour at the SAS huts trying to get uniforms and shotguns out of Stansfield, who had been appointed Quartermaster. Supper at 8 p.m. then to the Waterworks to post my men and after that round the village enrolling other men etc.

No petrol, Kent, June 1940
(Kent Messenger PD1697397)

Tuesday 9 July

Town in the morning. Police had run out of car permit forms. Street made me Officer I/C of Saltwood Section, as Fuller has a job under the Ministry of Agriculture. Huns about all day and the siren went at 4.15 p.m. and was on for three-quarters of an hour.

> *The Battle of Britain, which lasted from 10 July to 31 October, was the first significant campaign fought entirely in the air. Germany's failure to destroy Britain's air defences was Hitler's first significant defeat, and forced him to postpone Operation Sea Lion, the plan for the invasion of Britain.*

Wednesday 10 July

The siren went at 11 o'clock and the alarm was on for an hour. A loud explosion at 12.45 p.m. The police said they do not give passes to LDV cars. Street, however, got passes from the military but the police say I must not bring my car back because it has been evacuated. About 1.15 p.m. a furious battle started out at sea; we went on with our lunch but it grew more furious. We went on to the balcony and saw the sea covered with smoke. AA puffs in the air, three Hun bombers pass (the second lot) east to west defended by their fighters and attacked by ours. The REs next door saw them go down and cheered each time. Daphne saw one airman come down in a parachute. We went into Mrs Russell's garden and saw the end of the convoy, a number of destroyers, a light cruiser, two motorboats and the Lydd fishing fleet apparently picking up survivors. Seymour, who had a grand view from the house at the end of the road, saw one of our fighters rush up from inland and down three Hun in as many minutes. The sirens went long after the start of the show.

Friday 12 July
After orderly room, I left by the 12 o'clock bus, and made a beeline for Bog Farm. On the way I picked up a wounded wood pigeon. After tea, Phyllis took me for a walk through a pretty wood and I went into the village to arrange for her supplies.

Saturday 13 July
Up early and brought Phyllis, the dog and cats into Hythe. At 6 p.m. the siren sounded when Phyllis and Daphne were in the town. Phyllis got back and we went to Mrs Russell's garden, but there was nothing to see; it was all over Dover way. The 'all clear' went at 6.20 p.m. and ten minutes later the siren again sounded. I was then on the allotments and saw three planes over the golf links, which might have been Huns. Later, some of our fighters were about and twice a gun went off. The raid was an attack on a convoy the other side of Dover.

Sunday 14 July
Phyllis and Daphne went to church. At 3 o'clock the sirens blew, planes flew over and anti-aircraft fire was visible. It was an attack on a convoy near Dover, which a BBC announcer broadcast from the cliffs. At 5.30 p.m. our aircraft passed over continuously for half an hour. I drove Phyllis back to Bog Farm after tea. At night we heard a Hun pass over as we went to bed. Later the siren sounded then the 'all clear' and shortly after the siren again sounded. I did not stir from my bed. This giving the 'all clear' too soon is becoming a habit. At 11.30 p.m. I felt my bedroom shake and thought it was big guns, but it was an earthquake.

Tuesday 16 July

A curfew has been imposed all along the coast. Drizzle and mist all day, and not a single plane up. Local Defence Volunteers are now the Home Guard, and organised on a county basis. Folkestone, Hythe and Dover LDVs have been made into a battalion under Kennedy-Craufurd-Stuart. Everyone here is very sick about the latter. Saltwood Section, under my command, is now No. 3 Platoon of 'A' (Hythe) Company, the 8th (Cinque Ports) Battalion.

Thursday 18 July

Phyllis and Mrs Dix were having tea in Ashford during yesterday's raid and heard a screaming bomb. Six bombs were dropped, one fell on the girder of a railway shed where 100 men were working and burst to right and left; one inch either way would have killed all. Some rain in morning. Alarm sounded at 10 a.m. and continued for half an hour. Going down town, I saw a line of destroyers firing at the French coast. Daphne cycled all over Shorncliffe Camp distributing copies of the *Christian Science Monitor* and was not questioned once. The sky full of planes in the afternoon.

Friday 19 July

I was woken up at 6 a.m. by planes roaring low over the house. Major General AL Forster, our CO [East Kent Home Guard Area], and Kennedy-Craufurd-Stuart both in full kit of rank turned up at orderly room at noon. Colonel Street, as usual, made no demands for uniforms or weapons; he considers the Home Guard is just a huge bluff and that the military authorities have no intention of arming them properly. The siren blew at 12.15 p.m. and 'all clear' at 1.30 p.m. Daphne at 3 p.m. went out to Bog Farm on her bicycle to leave it there. At 3.45 p.m., just as I had got into the town to buy sausages for my supper, the sirens sounded. I walked up slowly watching a scrap high in the sky over Dover and I heard one crash of bombs or perhaps a plane coming down as some people saw a parachute. 'All clear' at 4.30 p.m. At 5 o'clock I went with Lucock and Street to decide on defensive measures for my Waterworks post. I pointed out to them that only 11 of my men have arms. We went on to Lucock's house for sherry and to hear the news. Roosevelt made a straightforward anti-dictator speech. Now he is animated, perhaps he will do something for us.

Saturday 20 July

I went to orderly room, then drove to Bog Farm. We saw a French plane flying low, which I am sure was hostile. After tea we walked to the village and at 6 o'clock heard the Ashford siren and soon after saw rows of 'Archies' bursting in the sky in the direction of Dover and Hythe. Others said they were from land batteries, but I guessed rightly that it was a convoy being attacked. Then our planes came over flying very high. As there was a lull, Phyllis and I walked on and had just got to our drive when I heard our Hurricanes diving down and a crash and, shortly after, three of our fighters passed low down. I saw a parachute descending. The 'all clear' went at 6.45 p.m. I went up to the hill behind our cottage and watched our planes flying high up. I left at 8 o'clock. Daphne also had an alarm in Hythe at 1 o'clock and in the 6 o'clock raid she saw a parachute being blown out over Thanet and saw a plane crash on the hills behind Capel. I believe this was not the same as the one I saw.

> **PARACHUTE MYSTERY** 🌠
> Residents on the · south-east coast saw what appeared to. be a parachute being carried· swiftly inland. It was first seen at about 8,000 feet, descending very slowly. Nothing was heard of a fight overhead and no plane was observed.

Sunday 21 July

I drove Daphne and Mrs Welfare into church by the Newington Road and was stopped at the barrier by the Star Inn as usual by sentries of the Queen's Westminster's, who are usually sahibs. This time a constable also pulled us up and said we must have the yellow civilian's car permit as well as LDV by order of Beasley, Folkestone Chief Constable. As he said he would get into trouble if I insisted on going on, I turned back and dropped Daphne on the Sandgate Road and took Mrs Welfare back to her house. Daphne and I went to lunch with Colonel Street – salmon, pheasant and tart.

Monday 22 July

Kennedy-Craufurd-Stuart turned up at orderly room in mufti, not in full blaze of uniform and medals. He may be a nasty fellow but he gets things done. As Daphne and I were listening to Lord Haw-Haw's broadcast we heard a faint siren. Some Huns came over us; we stayed up until 11.20 p.m. when the 'all clear' sounded.

Tuesday 23 July
Kennedy-Craufurd-Stuart turned up with eight rifles, 40 uniforms and extra car passes. Daphne and I spent the afternoon at 18 Kingsnorth Gardens stacking the furniture. When we got back, we heard explosions.

Wednesday 24 July
It rained the whole day and half the night. I went to orderly room in the car and collected 40 uniforms and four rifles. We had an alarm at 11.30 a.m. which lasted half an hour. I had arranged for my platoon to parade at the Waterworks to show them our defensive posts, but it was so wet I stopped them by the old Vicarage and had a talk and distributed uniforms.

Thursday 25 July
Drove to Bog Farm. As I got to the village I heard an explosion and shortly after reaching the cottage another loud noise towards Lympne. Phyllis said they had heard a lot of gunfire towards the Thames estuary in the morning. Just as we were starting, the siren sounded but we decided to go on and I got through the Newingreen barriers by pointing at my LDV permit and saying I had to be on duty. Daphne told us when we got in that she had seen a scrap with lots of planes and Archie shells high over Folkestone or Dover, and we saw what we thought were Hun planes making smoke patterns in the sky, which made me very indignant. After a while our planes arrived but the others had gone. God help us if the Huns can do that sort of thing! At 3 o'clock as I was enrolling Chivers, a new man, the siren again sounded. There were a lot of planes high in the air and Archies bursting over Dover way. Then, after a lull, we heard the thump-thump of bombs and went over to Mrs Russell's and watched the end of an attack on a convoy of little coasting vessels which were being scattered. Our planes flew about until 6 o'clock. We heard heavy gunfire, so went over and saw four large destroyers steaming north close to the French coast and firing inland. One ship was evidently hit as it let out a cloud of black smoke, and we also saw bombs exploding in the sea but not near the ships. The 'all clear' sounded at 8.15 p.m.

Friday 26 July

I was issued three mackintoshes, four blankets, ammunition and field dressings today. Phyllis and Daphne went into Folkestone shopping and to the cinema. Whilst I was having my tea, aeroplanes flew over in increasing numbers, but I only realised there was a raid starting when the siren sounded at 4.40 p.m. The 'all clear' went at 5 p.m.

Sunday 28 July

Daphne went to Bog Farm after tea to sleep the night. I put myself on duty, young French having asked for weekend leave. I did not like to ask anyone to go on at short notice on Sunday. As I walked to the Waterworks at 8.15 p.m. the alarm sounded again. I found Street there, having a look at how I run my show, I expect. He was surprised at finding me on duty. I had Prior and Kerr with me. The 'all clear' sounded at 9.15 p.m. I was on 10 p.m. to 11.30 p.m. and 2 a.m. to 3 a.m. On my first watch, a plane which sounded German came over and I counted ten searchlights concentrated on it but failing to pick it out. During my second watch, a plane put on all its lights but was followed for a time by the searchlights. Kerr picked up a wild rabbit on his 4 a.m. to 5 a.m. watch.

Monday 29 July

Air raid warning at 7.30 a.m. and 'all clear' ten minutes later. Another at 9 a.m., and I had to walk down to the town. We all expressed annoyance at so many apparently unnecessary alarms, but we learnt in the evening that there had been a heavy attack on Dover Harbour of which we had heard nothing – 100 planes engaged and 15 shot down. I had a busy day over LDV affairs.

Wednesday 31 July

We heard AA fire or bombs in the morning. At noon, I drove over to Bog Farm and brought Phyllis and the animals back to lunch. A squadron of our fighters flew about for some time after lunch and soon after they left at 3.45 p.m. we had an alarm. Heard machine gunning Folkestone way, the machines too high up to see. Then squadrons of Hurricanes arrived and very soon after the 'all clear' went at 7 p.m. Ten minutes later the siren again sounded till 8.30 p.m. and again from 10 p.m. to 10.30 p.m.

Friday 2 August

A number of my platoon assembled at the Waterworks and turned the mound in front of the engine house into a fine rifle pit, whilst young Stone, up a 30-foot ladder, blacked out the windows of the pump house – a nice cheery crowd.

Saturday 3 August

A fine morning, but no planes about. We had an alarm between 7 p.m. and 7.15 p.m. On reaching the Waterworks I found only Seymour there, and at 9.50 p.m. I asked him and he said he had not warned the other two for duty. I went off to the village pub where I knew I would find Goodsell, who said he would go back for supper and tell Johncock's missus to let him know when he came back from Hythe. I hope they turned up all right as Seymour is very jumpy. An alarm between 11.30 p.m. and midnight.

Sunday 4 August

A lovely summer day with a low sea mist. Squadrons of our aeroplanes flew low over the houses in the morning, otherwise it was a quiet day. When I mounted the guard, a small black kitten came out of the engine house. I think Johncock, whose family have three, must have brought it last night. I do not see how he expects it to get sufficient food, as it is too small to catch mice.

Thursday 8 August

The siren sounded as I was going down town at 10.15 a.m. and lasted half an hour. It soon sounded again and the 'all clear' did not sound until 12.30 p.m., making me hang about because I had to cash a cheque. All the banks close during every alert, and the staff go down into their deep shelters. Daphne got away to Bog Farm between the warnings, as they do not now stop the buses running. At 2 o'clock I went down to pick up eight uniforms and saw a real cavalry regiment on horses pass through the town. From there I drove to the

Borough Offices, Stone Farm and Saltwood, distributing the uniforms. Another alarm 4 p.m. to 4.30 p.m. I was at the Waterworks soon after 7 o'clock supervising the camouflaging of our trenches, and did some digging myself. Daphne had returned when I got back. With all these alarms, I heard and saw nothing of the big fight. I cannot understand this Italian advance. I hope we are not finally giving up Somaliland.

Sunday 11 August

We had continuous air raid warnings from 7.30 a.m. At 10 a.m. I went to the allotments and saw the Dover barrage balloons and the sky thick with AA shells bursting and planes fighting overhead, whilst the sound of guns and machine gunning was continuous. I drove Phyllis to her church at Folkestone but did not go in myself. While sitting on the Leas I saw two Huns fly over us and dive at the Dover barrage and bring down one balloon. I met Kennedy-Craufurd-Stuart, who had been at Dover, who said three barrage balloons were brought down, and a gasometer was hit by machine gun bullets and the holes stopped with putty. He promised me more rifles and sandbags.

Monday 12 August

We had our first alarm at 8.15 a.m. and I went out and watched an air battle overhead, the sky full of planes. There was occasional AA shelling but it was nearly all scrapping in the air. I saw one plane give out smoke and fall like a leaf, but it may have been dodging. There were three more alarms in the morning. At 5 p.m. the siren sounded and the Huns came up and attacked Lympne and Hawkinge. The Lympne bombs made a terrific noise and the house rattled. Shortly after, three Dorniers flew low over the house followed by AA shells. They ploughed up Lympne Aerodrome killing one of the ground staff and wounding two, and caused a fire at Hawkinge, which one could see. They also dropped bombs all over Folkestone Golf Course, in Cornwallis Road, Millfield and elsewhere. In Millfield they wrecked the house of an old lady of 100 who had not long been evacuated. I had a digging parade at 7.30 p.m. but only four turned up. There was another short alarm at 11.30 p.m., but nothing happened.

Tuesday 13 August

I woke at 6.30 a.m., probably by the sirens as the 'all clear' went at 7.45 a.m. and I heard bombs or guns somewhere. Today, I received service rifles for my platoon. Being anxious to know how Phyllis had got on in yesterday's raid, I drove to Bog Farm after lunch, wearing uniform as I intended to go straight to guard mounting on my return. I

found Phyllis out, but let Jerry out and took him into the field at the back. The alarm sounded about 4 o'clock and a very large number of Hun planes came over and dropped bombs in the direction of Wye. To see better, I went up on to the higher part of the road then on to the top of Gun Hill. Fighting was going on in the clouds and now and then planes dropped lower. I saw one fly downwards with smoke coming from it and six Hun bombers flew fairly low over my head. When I came back to the road, I met the butcher's boy on a cycle. He said the whole village had been watching me, and he had offered to find out who I was. I found Phyllis back when I returned; she had bicycled to Ashford, was there when the alarm sounded and came back through the thick of it as they bombed Ashford behind her. Shortly after she had returned, a [ARP] Warden and an AA Scout turned up with the news

that they had seen a parachute from a German plane, discarded in the hollow. The Home Guard was turned out to search and one fellow said three Huns and one of ours had been picked up in the neighbourhood. Whilst we were at supper, the platoon commander came and seemed to think we had got the Hun in the cottage. Daphne on her way to Folkestone saw a Hun wandering low over Hythe and from a bus in Sandgate saw it crash into the sea. We had another warning at 11.30 p.m. but I stayed in bed.

Mr Willis and Mr Archer captured an enemy pilot near Smeeth (Kent Messenger PD1697264)

Thursday 15 August

We had an alarm from 10 a.m. to 11 a.m. and again at 11.45 a.m. when I was in the orderly room. We could see the Huns dive-bombing Lympne through our AA barrage. I saw one of them stop in its dive and fall like a leaf, definitely hit, whilst the other two went on. Others went for Hawkinge, causing fires, but one was brought down in flames and another went out to sea. One Hun crashed on the power station near Shorncliffe Station and cut off our electricity. The alarm sounded again at 3 p.m. The Hythe siren could only manage a faint cough and wardens had to go round blowing whistles. Huns came over high up and there was scrapping everywhere out of sight. In the middle of it, Phyllis arrived. At Newingreen she had seen the wreck of a machine flown by a Pole who had broken an arm when he crashed. At about 3.30 p.m. I was watching from the end of the road and saw a line of bombs dropped from the sea to Shorncliffe about where Horn Street runs. Phyllis left again by the 6 o'clock bus. At 6.30 p.m. there was another alarm and Huns passed over in shoals. There was one burst of firing along the seafront.

Remains of a crashed Messerschmitt in Shorncliffe Crescent, Folkestone
(Folkestone Library F/WW2/56)

Friday 16 August

There was an alarm at noon (the Huns seem to come later each day), whilst I was walking up from the town. There was flying overhead too far up but it was dead quiet half an hour before the 'all clear' sounded at 2 p.m. We had another alarm 4.15 p.m. to 6.15 p.m.; nothing happening near us. I had a digging parade at 7.30 p.m., five turning up. George Hovenden amused us with yarns of his poaching adventures.

Sunday 18 August

Just after 11 a.m., as I was about to drive Mrs Welfare and Daphne to church, the siren sounded. Mrs Welfare decided to stay with her sister, and I did not like leaving the car about so Daphne went by bus. The 'all clear' sounded at 12.30 p.m., nothing having happened near us, but at 12.45 p.m. the alarm again went off and a great number of planes flew over out of sight. After a time, the battle drifted back; there were fights in the air and one German plane flew low from the west towards the sea, evidently crippled. All the batteries fired at it, and so did the Sappers next door. I was in the road and bolted, more afraid of the Sappers than the Hun. Daphne was coming up North Road and met a Sapper with a rifle who, after asking her permission, opened fire. We had a late lunch and got away to Bog Farm at 3.45 p.m.; on the way we saw the crashed plane of the Polish pilot. The 'all clear' sounded as we reached the cottage. After tea, the siren sounded, German planes came over and a tremendous roar broke out in the direction of London (evidently the capital knows how to defend itself) and along the Thames. Daphne and I went to the higher part of the road. Three planes came over us fairly low, looking all the same to me. Suddenly, the middle one crumpled up and dived to earth and a high column of black smoke rose from beyond Smeeth Station. I hope it was two Huns chased by a Spitfire. I got out at Saltwood and Daphne drove the car home. I went to the Waterworks and watched the searchlights; there was a lot of activity mostly by our planes as they turned on their lights. I also saw a flight of our planes with all their lights on rise from Hawkinge: a pretty sight.

Monday 19 August

The evacuation of Somaliland is a disgrace and a great blow to our prestige in Africa and the East. We ought to smash Italy now. We can do it, and she will drop out of the war. We had a quiet day; evidently the Huns cannot attack two days running.

Tuesday 20 August

A quiet morning. The siren sounded at 2.30 p.m. and I saw a formation of 15 Hun bombers escorted by fighters fly overhead. There was a short scrap in the distance, and Dover put up an intensive AA barrage. Our fighters came up and cruised overhead for some time. The 'all clear' sounded at 4.20 p.m. Seymour came to ask to be put into another squad. He is definitely windy, giving false alarms which Goodsell and Johncock, two very old 'stiffs', resent and they make him stand guard all night. Daphne went to Bog Farm with Molly and Basil Harding, returning at 7 p.m. I went early to our post, hoping the Sandling men would bring the camouflage net, but they didn't. It soon started to drizzle and rained all night.

Thursday 22 August

Hun planes came over at 9.30 a.m. and at 10.30 a.m. No sirens were sounded. There was an alarm 12.50 p.m. to 2 p.m. with some fighting in the air. There was another alarm at 7.15 p.m. and from the allotments I watched fighting in the air and saw a plane crash in flames beyond Etchinghill. Whilst I was mounting guard a regular sound, as if a big gun firing, at Dover could be heard. On my way back I stopped and listened to it for some time by the allotments with Hovenden and some soldiers who said they could see the flashes of the guns on the French coast. Stansfield, who came back from London this morning, says the USA is definitely going to help us with arms and warships.

Friday 23 August

I heard that seven were killed and about seven injured by the shelling of Dover, a Royal Naval Commander and a blue jacket being blown to pieces. We had an alarm 11.40 a.m. to 12.10 p.m. Daphne went in the car to spend the night at Bog Farm. It was a nasty day with a fog so thick at 3.30 p.m. I had to put on the light to write, and the evening was wintry cold.

Saturday 24 August

We had an alarm between 8 a.m. and 9.45 a.m., Hun planes coming over being fired at by Archies, but I saw nothing and carried on cooking my breakfast. The next alarm was 10.15 a.m. to 11.15 a.m., with AA guns from Hawkinge firing at a few raiders. About 3 o'clock a terrific noise of bombing and gunfire broke out, and thick brown dust rose in clouds beyond the hills beyond Hawkinge, and planes were fighting high up all over the sky. At 4 o'clock there was a burst of AA firing, and I saw a plane crash behind the Bushes' house, and another I was not so certain of over beyond the golf links. The airman of the first plane bailed out and one of ours circled round him for some time. The 'all clear' sounded at 5.30 p.m. after a four-hour raid, one of the longest we have had. Fifteen minutes later a solitary Hun came over from the north-west and was fired upon but escaped. There was another alarm at 7 p.m. but I was in my bath. Daphne came home in the middle of it, with machine guns cracking overhead. The 'all clear' went at 8.15 p.m. This was the first raid on central London.

Sunday 25 August

Our first raid on Berlin. A peaceful day. 'A' (Hythe) Company Home Guard had a parade on the range at 10 a.m., firing a group of five rounds per man. Twelve of my Saltwood Platoon turned up. Prior shot better than Kerr. Smith, who has had very little practice, shot best of all; Gausby was disappointing; and Turner, who had never handled a rifle, was dangerous. Craufurd-Stuart and Gribbon looked on at the start. We finished at 12 o'clock. I spent most of the day driving around collecting the civil registration numbers from my platoon. At Stone Farm, Hobbs very pessimistic about the war. He told me of the terrible damage caused at Dymchurch yesterday – whole families killed. The Huns have found a gap in the AA defences there and go through unloading their unused bombs on the place when bolting back. We are closing the gap now! At 9 p.m., Johncock and Goodsell mounted guard, the former saying he never slept on guard and I would find them alert if I visited them any time in the night. I therefore decided that if providence took me I would turn out. I woke at 12.50 a.m. and took ten minutes to decide it was providence. I met no one going through Saltwood, got through the gate into the field and advanced to the power house with my torch alight. No one was outside and the door was shut. I at first thought they had packed up and gone home. I looked round the house, then knocked at the door and heard them scurry out of their blankets, open the door and stand ready with their rifles. So, calling out, I entered and found two sheepish-looking men.

Monday 26 August

The siren sounded at noon as the Huns came over in force, but our fighters were waiting for them and we saw two brought down in flames. The 'all clear' sounded at 1.20 p.m. I drove over to Bog Farm at 2.30 p.m. There was more than one alarm during the afternoon, but Phyllis and I took no notice of them. I got back to Hythe at 9 p.m. First all-night raid over London.

Tuesday 27 August

A quiet day. I spent most of the morning distributing uniforms etc. After lunch, we drove into Folkestone and mended Mr Blaxland's drawing room window. As far as we could see, besides that only a few tiles were dislodged. Two bombs were dropped in the playing field at the top of Kingsnorth Gardens close to the railway line. The top two houses were badly damaged. We then drove up Blackbull Road. The houses on both sides as well as those parallel to it are badly damaged, with tiles off and windows broken. We also looked at Salter's Laundry, which is a complete wreck. Two girls were killed there. Luckily it was a Monday, which is a holiday for the laundry girls. We had an alarm at midnight, the 100th since the war started.

Wednesday 28 August

The siren sounded at 8.30 a.m. and about 9 o'clock a large compact formation of Hun bombers escorted by fighters went over, our AA fire falling ineffectively far behind them. Some of our fighters attacked, and one encounter occurred overhead. The cartridge cases of our machine fell on the road and on our lime tree and hedge. We saw one pilot, a Pole fighting for us, bail out and make frantic efforts to come down on land. He fell into the sea just off the Grand Redoubt and was rescued. General Lucock, Welfare Officer for the London Division, was distributing vegetables to isolated posts and took me with him. We visited one on the ranges, on the Grand Redoubt and one at Botolph's Bridge. Coming up Lympne Hill we saw the craters of a row of bombs which fell on the Roughs and in Rushy Marsh field. We had drinks with a Sapper Colonel in Lympne Castle, a nice man but according to Lucock incapable of giving an order. We drove past Lympne Aerodrome. The landing ground has been repaired, but the hangers and huts are in complete ruins. We next visited a Royal Artillery Survey Unit in Sellindge, which ranges Dover's big guns on to the Hun guns across the Channel. As a young subaltern named Evans said, they are the only regular unit in the Army who are fighting. The siren sounded as we drove home. There was an alarm 2.30 p.m. to 5.30 p.m. Distant bombardment, and at 4.30 p.m. the Huns came back flying high up with our planes attacking them. I saw two parachutists descend, one behind the golf links and the other into the sea off Seabrook. The next alarm was 6.10 p.m. to 6.30 p.m., probably in error, and the next at 7.15 p.m. After a burst of machine gun fire, a Hun plane came low over the allotments, followed by one of ours, and crashed near Stone Farm.

Friday 30 August
Alarm 8 a.m. to 9 a.m. and 11 a.m. to 12.45 p.m. Daphne saw hundreds of enemy planes go over between 3 p.m. and 7 p.m. We went into the Choppings' garden and saw a squadron of Heinkels dive-bomb Lympne, where they killed five workmen. Planes came over in dozens, and we saw one squadron of ours high up but heard no fighting and there was not much anti-aircraft fire. After tea, we went out distributing fruit, took blankets to my post and drove out on to the Newington Road to Kick Hill where Daphne went across to see where the Hun had crashed on Wednesday. About 10.30 p.m. Huns came over and groups of searchlights came on. I have never seen so many. On the other hand, there now seems to be only one AA battery anywhere near us.

Saturday 31 August
Alarms 8.30 a.m. It started with a heavy attack on Dover, which brought down all the barrage balloons, but rumour says 13 Huns were brought down by the new Swedish pom-pom defences [Bofors guns]. The morning mist prevented one seeing anything. There was also one attack on Rochester between 12.30 p.m. and 2.15 p.m. Huns seemed to attack Lympne again. All quiet long before the 'all clear' sounded. Between 5.15 p.m. and 7.30 p.m., the Huns seemed to fly all over the sky being only occasionally fired at. Hythe sounded the 'all clear' at 7.15 p.m. just as a fight started not far up overhead, and the alarm sounded almost immediately after. A dockers' battalion, mostly from Tyneside, have moved in place of the old REs. They are a far more disciplined crowd, are quiet, march well and their NCOs give real orders. Palmar's is still a mess and Hollowdene is QM stores.

Sunday 1 September
Daphne's birthday. Alarm 10.45 a.m. to 12.15 p.m. A large number of

Huns, bombers escorted by fighters, passed overhead; the siren sounded after they were above us. There was some desultory scrapping later. I drove in and brought Daphne back from Folkestone; she was very late. The siren again sounded when the Huns were over, but our fighters were waiting and attacked them. Daphne and I drove out to Bog Farm, the 'all clear' sounding as we arrived. Alarm 4.0 p.m. to 5.15 p.m. As we were having tea in the garden, a squadron of Hun bombers flew over, dropped their bombs somewhere in the direction of Maidstone and returned as if the whole sky belonged to them. The sirens sounded after they had passed, one battery fired four useless shots at them as they went home, and there was not a sound or sight of one of our planes the whole time. When we got back, I changed into uniform and mounted the Sandling guard. Hun planes, searchlights and some firing at night. I felt very depressed at the thought of those Huns coming over unharmed.

Monday 2 September

Alarm 8 a.m. to 10 a.m. The siren again sounded too late; the Huns returned at 8.20 p.m. and Arpinge AA battery hit one. I was in the Webbs' [house], where it sounded as if it was coming down on top of me. It came down on the ranges almost intact, its young pilot hit in the head. Alarm 12 noon to 2.45 p.m. There was a lot of AA firing, some fighting overhead and columns of smoke beyond Hawkinge. We drove to Bluehouse distributing steel helmets and visited the place where the Hun came down on Hobbs' farm and picked up souvenirs to be sold for Guides funds. Alarm 4.15 p.m. to 6.30 p.m. Large numbers of bombers and fighters passed over, the AA fire seeming very useless. At 6 p.m. I was cutting my back hedge when a Messerschmitt skimmed over the trees with one of our fighters on its heels firing a burst as it came into view. The firing sounded terrific and I saw every detail of the Hun before I threw myself under the hedge, really frightened. The Hun got away, the Britisher breaking off the fight over the sea. Colonel Adams' nephew in the RAF turned up at their house asking them to drive him on to the Marsh as he had shot down a Hun there and wanted to inspect it. There were solitary raiders over at night. He was himself shot down and killed in a wood the next day.

Riddled with bullets, a crashed Me 109 on Romney Marsh
(Folkestone Library/*Folkestone Herald*)

Tuesday 3 September

Alarm 9.10 a.m. to 11.50 a.m. Siren sounded as two machines with British markings, the engine of one making noises like a Hun, flew over. There was some scrapping about 11 a.m. Our bombers gave the French coast a fearful hammering all morning. Alarm 1.20 p.m. to 4 p.m. During the last half, Huns were circling about high overhead with AA guns occasionally firing at them. Some of my men turned up at 7 p.m. to camouflage the rifle pit and place oil drums in the parapet. We now have two bathing huts in the engine house with spring mattress bunks in them. Alarm 9 p.m. to midnight. As I came home after mounting the guard, I went to bed but the 'all clear' woke me. It was a British night attack on the French coast.

Wednesday 4 September

A hot day. Alarm 9 a.m. to 10.30 a.m. The Huns came over a quarter of an hour before the siren sounded. There were four explosions, which shook the house; they were bombs jettisoned which fell on the ranges. Alarm 12.50 a.m. to 2.30 p.m. The Huns came over in large numbers and later drifted back, and there was some fighting in the air. At 2.30 p.m. when I was cutting the front hedge, a Hun Messerschmitt flew low over the house with a British fighter after it but neither was firing. Daphne went for the night to Bog Farm after lunch. I drove to Folkestone and looked at the smashed row of houses at the bottom of the Road of Remembrance. I then went on to Dover. As I drove into town, barrage balloons were being hauled down. I picked up two WATS [Auxiliary Territorial Services (ATS)] and a girl friend and I drove them to the station. There were a few minesweepers in the harbour, and one large cargo boat with its back broken up against the breakwater. I saw the damage by shellfire in Maison Dieu Road, many windows broken and tiles off, and St Barnabas' RC Church and a house at the corner of Penchester Road badly wrecked. I returned via the Alkham Valley. I also on the way back looked at the bomb craters on Folkestone Golf Course.

Thursday 5 September
Daphne returned about 9 p.m. She had seen two planes brought down in the morning. Sellindge had been bombed on Wednesday night, the church and cottage across the road being damaged. Phyllis on the bicycle had been run down by Orpens deliveryman's van, the bicycle badly bent and herself cut and bruised. 'Bone' Foster told me that three Huns and a Frenchman a few nights ago had come over in a rowing boat and had been caught by the Somerset Light Infantry in the Marsh. They had portable wireless sets and said that they had been instructed to conceal themselves with a view to guiding the invading troops through gaps in our defence.

Saturday 7 September
No early morning alarm, but one sounded at 11.30 a.m. as I drove off to Bog Farm. I brought Phyllis and the menagerie (increased by one kitten) and bushels of apples back by 1 o'clock. Alarm 3.50 p.m. to 7 p.m. Huns went over in masses, far more than there have ever been. At 5.30 p.m. the Huns were continuously passing for an hour and I saw several large formations. One lot flying home were attacked by Arpinge AA battery, and I saw a shell hit a bomber and heard its engine choke and saw smoke trailing behind it. It, however, kept on with the others. Daphne later saw a Hun fighter dive into the sea followed by its pilot and parachute and there was no boat nearby. At 11 p.m. the Huns came over again in masses for 15 minutes, the first time they have made a night attack in large numbers. It was most unpleasant. I hear there were Huns captured in a boat on Thursday. It made quite a stir – the whole garrison stood to arms thinking

it might be the commencement of invasion – among the Small Arms School class. This class dispersed the next day and at least one officer talked about it in a pub in Marlborough.

Sunday 8 September

Mother's birthday. Ninety-nine Hun planes brought down yesterday. Phyllis and Daphne went to church. Alarm 11.15 a.m. to 1.30 p.m. At 12.30 p.m. a wounded Hun bomber flying slowly at a low height was fired at by every kind of weapon but was badly missed and got away across the Channel. London was very badly knocked about yesterday. Alarm 8.15 p.m. to 10.30 p.m. I drove Phyllis back to Bog Farm, the siren sounding as I returned. After mounting my guard I was caught by the Saltwood Police with my sidelights undimmed. The village constable tried to be uppish, but a special was sympathetic and lent me a handkerchief to put round the lights.

Tuesday 10 September

Another overcast, rainy day so we had no Huns over. Hythe Company Home Guard have been issued with three Browning automatic rifles, of which Saltwood Platoon is to have one. I heard that in the bombardment of Dover yesterday, the Burlington Hotel and gasworks were hit. It is said that the Huns have made vast preparations in the harbours of Belgium and France for their invasion, but our Air Force bombs them to bits each night. It is also said that Goering spent three weeks in Hythe one summer and was so charmed with it he has ordered it to be spared as he intends living in Saltwood Castle after the war!!!

Sunday 15 September

Daphne went to church. I went to Cambridge Meadow where Hythe Company of the Home Guard were instructed in bomb throwing. Of my platoon, only seven turned up including Goodwin, a new recruit. In the course of instructing them I found I could throw more accurately than any of them. Alarm 11.40 a.m. to 1.30 p.m. The siren sounded when we were on the range and 50 or more bombers with their fighter escorts came over, showing clearly in the blue sky. Two AA batteries seemed to be shooting well but I saw no hit. Soon after they had passed, there was a lot of scrapping overhead. At 3.45 p.m. a wounded Messerschmitt flew low over us and was fired at by two batteries. It is announced that we have brought down 184 Huns!!

Monday 16 September

This was to have been the day for the [German] invasion. I was woken at 5 a.m. by the 'all clear'. They had kept the alarm on all night. At 8 o'clock four planes flew low across the allotments towards the sea, one at least firing. Hovenden said one was a Messerschmitt, which crashed into the sea. The high clouds were everywhere scored by the exhaust fumes of manoeuvring planes and had the appearance of ski tracks in the snow. Soon after this, more huge bombers (or troop carriers) flanked by light bombers and surrounded by fighters flew slowly over, showing black against the morning sun. Only one battery fired a few shots. They came back soon after and in fewer numbers, as if they had been badly beaten. I went over to Bog Farm and brought Phyllis back. Alarm 2 p.m. to 6.30 p.m. Nothing much happened at first. At 6 o'clock I drove Phyllis back to Bog Farm and took Jerry out in the field at the back of the cottage. There I heard the sound of engines and through the low scudding clouds I saw a huge four-engine Hun bomber so low I could almost see the bomb racks. It cruised around for some time without interference from our batteries or fighters, dropped two bombs near Ashford and came back and, when I could still hear its engines, Ashford gave the 'all clear'. It was a very depressing sight. I went to sleep wondering if I would be woken at 5 a.m. by the 'all clear' of the invader.

Tuesday 17 September

I believe the 'all clear' sounded about 11 p.m. I was woken by an alarm at 4 a.m. and again by the 'all clear' at 5.30 a.m., when there was a strong gale blowing with rain which lasted until 11 o'clock. Everyone is jumpy with thoughts of invasion. About midnight, a solitary Hun cruised over town, flew away, came back and dropped two bombs somewhere near. I suppose this is a form of terrorism, and a demonstration for us to think they have the mastery of the air. It certainly makes one think the latter, and have doubts about those reports of 180 hits and stories of the whole of Kent strewn with wrecks of Hun machines.

Wednesday 18 September

At 8.30 a.m. some Huns came over and were fired at by AA. Alarm 9 a.m. to 11 a.m. Huns came over in fair numbers at 9.30 a.m. and returned about 10 o'clock. There was some fighting overhead, but nothing to show for it. At noon, three Huns flew about the sky between Dover and Dungeness as if the whole world belonged to them, making patterns with their exhausts. As I drove up to Sandling to distribute pay, 12 Hun bombers with an extra large escort of fighters flew over. Hundreds of Hun fighters flew about all over the sky and later some of our fighters turned up. It was all quiet for nearly an hour before the 'all clear' finally sounded. Alarm 4 p.m. to 4.30 p.m. and again 4.45 p.m. to 6 p.m. Just after the first 'all clear' sounded, some Huns flew up and made a huge circle in the sky with their exhaust fumes and there was the sound of gunfire from Dover. At 5 o'clock, 18 large Hun bombers escorted by fighters flew overhead. They did not appear to go far and went back Dungeness way. Others, fighters, came back over us in scattered groups at 5.30 p.m. and were fired at by AA. One crashed into the sea.

Thursday 19 September
A cold and blowy morning with overcast sky, and a rainy afternoon and night. Phyllis came in by bus at 3 p.m. and was driven back about 6 p.m. by Daphne, who stayed the night at Bog Farm. At guard mounting, Turner told me that the Marsh round Newchurch was really strewn with Huns' wrecked planes; one large bomber lying by the roadside was undamaged except for bullet holes. The siren sounded as usual at 8.30 p.m. Some Huns came over, searchlights went up and AA fired at them. A violent storm in the night drove them away.

Friday 20 September
A wet, blowy morning, but it cleared up later. Alarm 10.50 a.m. to 12.15 p.m. It seemed as if only Hun fighters came over and flew about, defying the AA shells. One of ours was shot down, the plane falling near Paddlesworth and the young fellow bailed out and fell into some pine trees near Saltwood Castle. He was shot through the shoulder and ankle and the trees had scalped him and lacerated his thigh. He was not wearing flying kit, just uniform and light shoes. Coming back from orderly room, I felt very depressed. I only see our planes crash and the wounded Huns always seem to get away. The evening news said we brought down four Huns and seven of ours were shot down!!

Saturday 21 September
We did not have the usual alarm at 8.30 p.m. yesterday, but the man in charge woke about 1 a.m. and sounded the 'all clear'!! A Sapper who had laid a mine on the beach near the Imperial Hotel yesterday accidentally trod on it this morning and blew himself to bits. A large number of Huns

flew over as the siren sounded and returned apparently unmolested at
6.30 p.m. On my way back from guard mounting I watched for a while
the flashes and flares as our bombers thrashed the French coast with bombs.
The story keeps being repeated that the Germans, some time back,
attempted an invasion and were beaten back with the loss of 10,000 men.

Sunday 22 September

Hythe Company had a parade on the ranges. A Small Arms School NCO
gave us instruction in firing from behind cover. He had no medals, and it
was amusing to see all our old 'stiffs' standing around with expressionless
faces. We then fired our Browning automatics. Ross of Hythe, who had
been a musketry instructor, did some very accurate shooting, both
individually and burst. A thick drizzle fell most of the time. Phyllis came
in from Bog Farm at 3 p.m. and left at 6 o'clock. There was no alarm all
day until 8.15 p.m.

Monday 23 September

Alarm 9.30 a.m. to 11 a.m. The Huns came over too high for our AA fire
to reach them, but our fighters were lying in wait [and] were at them
almost at once. Alarm 5.30 p.m. to 6.30 p.m. There was some fighting high
up. Daphne went to a Guide meeting and on to Bog Farm for the night.
She took little Bingo, the kitten I found from our post, to a home in
Brabourne Lees. I wish he could have gone to a Saltwood Home Guard. I
was busy running round over platoon affairs and did not listen to the
King's speech. It is said some of our bombers went over after some
secretive objective – Berchtesgaden?

Tuesday 24 September

I was up early and cooked and ate breakfast by 8.30 a.m. Alarm 8.30 a.m. to
9.35 a.m. Seventeen large bombers came over showing up black against the
sky as the alarm sounded. Our batteries fired at them, but they sailed on
unharmed, a maddening sight. They returned in twos and fours from
9 o'clock onwards for half an hour, our AA fire again proving useless whilst
none of our fighters turned up. Alarm 11.30 a.m. to 12.50 p.m. A compact
force of 22 large bombers with their fighter escort flew over the town and
returned, I thought, with undiminished numbers at noon. As they passed
over Seabrook, there was an explosion of black and brown smoke in the air.
Immediately afterwards two columns of smoke and dust rose up. The Huns

had unloaded their bombs in a line from Beachborough to the sea. Stone Farm had one each side; another fell within a few yards of a searchlight near there. Ten or more fell on the golf links, two either side of Hythe Station, wrecking the ticket office and signal box. One fell on Red House on the Seabrook Road in which there were 40 Sappers; one was buried and suffered from shock and some others were cut by glass. Another completely demolished an empty bungalow opposite. Several fell between the canal and the sea. Phyllis and Daphne with the menagerie came back at 11.30 p.m. and a car full of apples and pears. Dover was again shelled and returned fire. Lympne was bombed by another flight of bombers as they went home.

Friday 27 September
Alarm 8.50 a.m. to 10.10 a.m. At 8.30 a.m. the AA guns fired at some advance scouts, and a convoy of small ships crept up from Dungeness close to the shore. The Huns flew up and down the coast as if they were unable to get through, and our fighters attacked them. They finally came in over Dymchurch and returned about 9.30 a.m. Alarm 11.30 a.m. to 1.10 p.m. Eighteen large bombers came over. One was left behind and was fired on, appeared to be hit and flew home. Another dropped as if about to crash, but straightened up and flew home. Between 12.30 p.m. and 1 p.m. there was very heavy fighting overhead. I saw two Huns break away and fly home, evidently hit. Alarm 1.40 p.m. to 4.30 p.m. Dover was shelled and replied. In the news we heard that 130 had been brought down.

Saturday 28 September
A cool sunny day. At 10.15 a.m. Huns, probably fighters, passed high overhead. About noon Dover AA guns had a regular battle and the Arpinge battery had shots at a stray Hun. About 2 o'clock there was a lot of fighting overhead. About 5.30 p.m. a solitary Hun flew over Folkestone, dropped bombs near Trinity Church and in Tontine Street and got away. Phyllis went to Bog Farm for the afternoon. I pushed a bicycle loaded up with greatcoats and tin hats up to our post and went on from there to Sandling Junction. I had to hump the bicycle over three stiles both ways and badly scraped the back of my hand. A ten-minute alarm at 7.30 p.m. Alarm 9.45 p.m. to 10.45 p.m. A tremendous shindy out Boulogne way.

Sunday 29 September
A gun barrage over Dover at 8 a.m. Alarm 8.30 a.m. to 9 a.m. A flight of 16

Huns flew over but appeared to be turned back by a cold rainstorm from the north. At 11.30 a.m. a Hun dropped bombs. Fuller having got 1,000 sandbags from the Sandling REs, we paraded at our defensive post and started work on building the parapets of our rifle pit and trench. Only the Sandling men and the youngsters turned up. When Phyllis and Daphne started off to church, the car conked out. With the help of an ASC [Army Service Corps] driver, Daphne discovered there was water in the carburettor. When I got back I also tried to start the car and failed, so had it towed to Swain's, who found nearly a gallon of water in the tank. It is a mystery how it got there. Alarm 4 p.m. to 5.30 p.m.

Monday 30 September

Alarm 9 a.m. to 12 noon. Scattered fighting and firing. I was too busy to see what was going on. After the 'all clear', a Hun cruised about and was fired at. I drove Phyllis to Folkestone in the afternoon. I found the road near the town hall and by the library roped off, as there were several unexploded bombs in Tontine Street and on the cliffs. A large area had its inhabitants temporarily evacuated. I met Beale and his wife, who had been away for the weekend and could not get to their home. On the beach near the swimming pool is a derelict Spitfire. Alarm 4 p.m. to 6 p.m. We drove up Bouverie Road and looked at Trinity Church. There is a huge crater up against the chancel, but this bomb broke only a few windows. As we arrived, a Hun bomber sailed over us and terrific AA fire was directed at it over our heads, so we bolted for cover. It is said we have had 200 air raid warnings since the start of the war.

IN A WEEK

Including the 49 'planes shot down in yesterday's air battles around England the Germans lost 259 machines in the past week.

In the same period the R.A.F. lost 79 'planes, the pilots of 39 being safe. The daily figures for the past week are:

	German	British
Tuesday Sept 24	8	4
	(3 R.A.F. safe)	
Wednesday 25	26	4
	(3 safe)	
Thursday 26	34	8
	(5 safe)	
Friday 27	133	34
	(16 safe)	
Saturday 28	6	7
Sunday 29	3	0
Yesterday 30	49	22
	(12 safe)	
Total	259	79
	(39 safe)	

64

Wednesday 2 October
A flight of Hun bombers flew down the Channel. At 11.15 a.m. a dozen Heinkels sailed through the ineffective AA shells and dive-bombed Lympne Aerodrome. Huns came over after the 'all clear'. Alarm 1.30 p.m. to 4.15 p.m. Near the end, a single Hun teased the Arpinge battery. At one time there was a lot of AA fire at a large bomber. I drove round Stone Farm, Bluehouse and Sandling on Home Guard business.

Friday 4 October
At 8.45 a.m. there was an explosion, and a column of smoke rose from Lydd. Alarm 9.45 a.m. to 10.15 a.m. Huns came over and were fired at. At 11.45 a.m. two Huns cruised about overhead. Taking Jerry into the fields at the back I watched one; the AA fire seemed to be absolutely futile. At noon the same or another cruised about in a similar way then turned for home, dived down and dropped two very heavy bombs. I was getting out of the car and Daphne was in the garden. The house shook and from the

The bomb damage in Hythe High Street after the attack on 4 October 1940

allotments one saw two pillars of dust and smoke rise up. I went out in the car, delivered a uniform in Tanners Hill Gardens and picked up greatcoats at the office. The east end of the High Street was impassable and debris was strewn as far as Tanners Hill. Two 500-pound bombs were dropped; one fell above the church car park making a hundred-foot crater and smashing the chancel windows. The other fell on to the middle of the Arcade, completely demolishing it and hurling its iron girders on to the shops on either side. The elder Mrs Carr, owner of the wool shop, and Mrs Stewart, owner of the Pixie tea rooms, are missing. Two girl assistants in the Bodsham Farm greengrocers were rescued badly injured and the owner of Beadle's shop was also badly crushed. They do not know if any shoppers or passers-by have been killed. The Congregational Church and the shops on either side are severely damaged. Young ES Dearman was blown out of the back of his bicycle shop. The alarm sounded at 1 o'clock!!

Saturday 5 October

I woke up to the drone of Hun planes and the exploding of AA shells, but there was no siren sounded. About 10 a.m. there were half a dozen Huns cruising about, the solitary Arpinge battery producing their usual inaccurate fire. A battalion of light tanks came down our road and there were numbers of soldiers in the town. At 11.30 a.m. 15 heavy bombers flew over and it seemed as if our fighters attacked them at once and I saw at least two dropping towards the sea, two of our fighters attacking one Hun. One of these fighters on its return gave the 'victory roll'. At noon, however, 20 Hun bombers came over; when about over Lympne they swerved seawards as if avoiding some area and went on towards Dungeness where they dive-bombed the empty camp of Jesson. The Huns were well over before the next siren sounded. A large number returned the same way and there was much scrapping overhead. At 5.45 p.m. when I went to mount the guard I saw numbers of Huns flying about, and there were firework displays on both sides of the Strait. Regardless of what was happening, the siren sounded at 8.30 p.m. and the 'all clear' at 5 a.m. A blockhouse on Folkestone Leas was hit by a bomb, and five men working on it, one a Home Guard, killed.

Sunday 6 October

An overcast day with low misty clouds. As we were having breakfast, Daphne and I heard the scream of a bomb followed by another, and dived under the table as the house was shaken as if by a violent earthquake. The explosion, however, went over our heads and was felt more by Phyllis upstairs. Poor little Doris was scared stiff, but Jerry and Socks did not mind it. When we had composed ourselves, I went out and learnt what had happened. A Hun had flown down the road dropping bombs as he went. One in Romney had made a fair crater and damaged the house a little, the next in Quarrymead had found soft earth, penetrated eight feet and made a small hole. One had hit the corrugated cookhouse next door without harming a man inside, and the next had fallen on to the tennis court. One struck the foundations of Bredon and cracked the whole of the south side of the house. Two fell in Fuller's garden, demolishing his hedge. Two more fell on the allotments but have not exploded. Our only damage is a piece out of a chimney pot. Bombs were also dropped on Folkestone, demolishing a pub near the Junction Station and killing a few people. I got to the Waterworks a quarter of an hour late. A good number turned up and we almost completed the sandbagging of the rifle pit. The siren sounded at 11 a.m.!! An hour after the damage had been done and when not a plane could be heard or seen. After lunch, a huge gun mounted on a truck came up our road and was driven on to Colonel Chopping's lawn. It had taken from early morning to drag it up Barrack Hill, and it must have been this gun, spotted by their reconnaissance planes, that the German bombers were aiming at. About 5.30 p.m. a strong south-westerly gale sprang up with torrents of rain. I had to go out to distribute pay and got soaked through, and again when I mounted the guard at 8.30 p.m. I got a second soaking. The gale continued all night.

Tuesday 8 October

At 4.30 a.m. I was woken up by six loud explosions which shook the house. The bombs sounded very near but were actually dropped on Lympne, falling in the wood. Alarm 7.30 a.m. to 12.15 p.m. A very large number of Huns came over, nearly all fighters. They appear to be making another attempt to overwhelm our Air Force. Having finished down town about 11.30 a.m., I had driven to Swain's and filled up with petrol. I saw two planes swoop down from the east on to the town and heard machine gun fire – a Messerschmitt chased by a Spitfire. Then there was a sharp crash; a column of smoke and dust rose up and the plane was blown right over by the blast. I lost sight of the planes as I was then looking at the explosion. I was told that a mobile Bren gun section blew the Hun to bits over Folkestone. The Messerschmitt's bomb dropped in the middle of Prospect Road, shattering the rows of old cottages on either side and killing two people. The house of Jones the tailor in Marine Walk Street was severely damaged, and the blast shattered windows in the High Street and Bank Street, including those of the Town Hall, and wrecked the back of the food office. Young Dearman, who had the front of his shop blown in by the Arcade bomb, had the back blown in by this one. He had the same customer in the shop each time. Alarm 12.30 p.m. to 1 p.m. As usual, all was over by then. We three and Jerry drove over to Bog Farm, had tea there, collected our fruit and saw a Hun bomber cruising around. Jerry was delighted to be back again in the fields. When I was mounting my guard, numbers of planes came over. I was told there are two lights down in the Marsh which burn all night. They can be seen from the end of our road but cannot be located down below. When a Hun drops bombs, the lights go out and go on again directly after the 'all clear'.

Wednesday 9 October
For several days now we have only brought down three or four Huns and lost as many or more ourselves. I think they have better and heavier armed planes. A gale of wind was blowing, and grew stronger during the morning. A lot of Huns came over and were fired at, but not one of ours came in sight. Prior, Kerr, Turner and Chappell came with me at 2.30 p.m. and we built up the inside traverse of our rifle pit. Two waves of Huns came over; one from the first batch was hit by Arpinge battery but managed to keep up high and follow its friends. One of the second batch came back flying low and losing height, and must have gone down in the sea. Daphne saw one hit by AA over Dover and two men bail out of it.

Friday 11 October
Alarm 7.15 a.m. to 9 a.m. The Huns were over us in large numbers unmolested in any way. The siren sounded and the guard-ships hooted after they had passed. What has happened to our Air Force? They only brought down four yesterday and lost four themselves. Alarm 10.30 a.m. to 1 p.m. The Huns were all over the place and there was promiscuous bombing. A thick haze of dust Canterbury way, I learnt later, was the bombing of the place, the cathedral being damaged. I drove Phyllis into Folkestone. As we reached Cheriton the AA broke out and sounded as if they were firing at the car! Several bombs had been dropped on the area

between the Dover and Black Bull roads causing extensive damage. We also saw more damage had been done near the hospital and in Shorncliffe Road. Just as we came out of Cave's Café after tea, a pair of planes flew about over the town diving down as if to bomb every now and then. A man with [field] glasses said they were ours, but a little later the AA fired at them. I did some RSPCA work. At 8.45 p.m. a battery of four guns at Gris Nez shelled Dover and were replied to by guns not far from us. I also saw the bombing of Gris Nez and Boulogne.

Saturday 12 October
A number of Huns came over. We heard the explosion of bombs Lympne way and there was the usual aimless manoeuvring overhead. I went with the wheelbarrow to the allotments and collected a sack of Moore's potatoes. As we were serving the meat at lunch, there was a loud explosion and as we dived under the table we heard the whistle of two bombs overhead and their explosion followed. The first bomb fell at the beginning of North Road, wrecking the front of the first house on the south and making a very large crater; the second fell into the high bank between 'Bone' Foster's house and the first house of Tanners Hill Gardens, filling the road with earth. The third fell in the grounds of Philbeach, the summer home for railwaymen's wives. Both it and the North Road house were empty, but next door to the latter were a Dr and Mrs Dodd, who had a shock. Dearman was blown off his bicycle. I was out distributing boots to my men at Bluehouse, Sandling and Saltwood. Numbers of planes passed over and there was a lot of scrapping in the air and AA fire. There was also firing out at sea, probably Dover again being shelled. Our escape last Sunday was clearly providential; eight 50-pound bombs fell in the gardens of the five houses, including ours, and eight more between Bredon and the allotments.

Sunday 13 October
Shooting on the range, Folkestone Company firing next to us. Eleven of my platoon turned up. The old soldiers were too full of beer, and young Gausby was again disappointing. The thin Broom made the best score: four bulls and an inner. I came next with two bulls and three inners. I believe I could have done better if I tried. It seemed as if the Hun was afraid to come over whilst the Cinque Ports Battalion were in strength on the range!!!

Friday 18 October

Canterbury was bombed yesterday afternoon and some damage was done to the [Cathedral] windows and Deanery. There was evidently some truth in the American stories of an attempted invasion. We are now told that [German] troops were embarked on the 16th [of] September, and some of the transports were sunk by the RAF when full of troops.

Tuesday 22 October

A misty morning and warm day. Alarm 10.15 a.m. to 10.45 a.m. Bombs were dropped on Deal disconnecting telephones and telegraph lines. Alarm 12 noon to 1 p.m. I had gone to our post to place blankets there and put up notices. As I moved away, I saw three Huns flying high, dive down and drop bombs on what I thought was Shorncliffe then turn and make off as the sirens sounded. After the 'all clear' solitary Huns came over, were fired at by AA, and some more bombs were dropped. Alarm 2 p.m. to 3.30 p.m. I went to the Waterworks with Prior, Kerr, Turner and young Hesketh and worked on our defences. Alarm 4 p.m. to 5.30 p.m. The Huns arrived as usual before the siren sounded. At 4.30 p.m. the sky was full of Huns, with some of our fighters amongst them, as the AA only occasionally fired. There was also some machine gun and cannon fire, but the noise was mostly the roar of their engines. When the bombs fell, Phyllis and I were in the garden and stood in the tool shed when they whistled over us. One fell on Saltwood cricket ground in front of the Brockhill Park. The next fell in Napier Gardens, shattering the roofs of five houses and blowing a coal lorry into Colonel Adams' front garden. The driver jumped to safety but his mate, an elderly man, was killed. Colonel Adams, Chief [ARP] Warden, was bicycling up the road. He threw himself off but was covered in debris, badly bruised and very badly shocked. Mrs Adams had just left her bedroom before a paving stone crashed through the roof on to her bed!

Thursday 24 October

Another foggy, cold morning. Alarm 2 p.m. to 2.50 p.m. At 1.45 p.m. I drove Phyllis down to the bottom of Barrack Hill to catch the Ashford bus. Soon after I had returned, I heard one or more planes dive down and drop at least two bombs on the town and I felt thankful Phyllis had got away. She had not. A car drove up trying to cross Scanlon's Bridge. Phyllis called out that the bridge was barricaded, and discovered that its occupants were her cousins Evelyn, Mace and Kitty Johnstone, who offered to take her into Ashford. Whilst she was talking she heard the whistle of the bomb and threw herself on the ground. It fell within 10 yards, pulverising a small hut used, but not then occupied, by ARP messengers. She and the car were covered by small rubble, but she was unhurt and suffered no shock. Young Fred Smith, one of my Home Guard, was blown from his bicycle and the road was cracked up to the car. The other bomb dropped on the canal bank opposite Twiss Avenue, shattering an elm tree and the water main and damaging several roofs. An oil drum fell in the Small Arms School camp; several bombs dropped on the Roughs and the Ranges.

Saturday 26 October
A very cold morning. The day was overcast and showery, and only odd planes flew over us at first. At 4.30 p.m., whilst we were having tea, a squadron of bombers came over about five of which turned back and bombed the town. We heard the whistle of two bombs as we dived below the table, Phyllis taking her cup of tea with her, without spilling it!! The bombs were mostly on the Roughs and the Ranges. One dropped in Front Road injuring one person but damaging the houses in the next parallel road. Another, a large one, fell on Gorsy Banks near Oak Wood. When are we to get these marvellous new planes and these efficient Canadian pilots?? About two days ago, a long canoe-shaped boat with mast and sail as well as oars was found on the beach behind the Ranges. It had no markings on it.

Sunday 27 October
I had just woken to a glorious sunrise of red, purple and gold when the alarm sounded. The Huns came over and were fired at by our AA batteries, one a new one which makes more noise and sounds nearer to us. Some of the Huns seemed to turn back almost at once and we heard two loud explosions. I got Phyllis downstairs but Daphne refused to move. A second wave followed shortly after the first, and by 9 o'clock they returned with our fighters attacking them. After that at intervals they came and went with an occasional fight overhead. At 4.50 p.m. several planes roared low overhead, the AA fired on them and we heard the whistle but not the explosion of a bomb. At 5 o'clock a squadron, said to have been Italians, circled over Hythe and Daphne saw them dive-bomb Hawkinge whilst AA and machine guns plastered the sky round them. For the next quarter of an hour, planes roared overhead. At the end I saw one crippled Hun fly out to sea pursued by AA fire.

Monday 28 October

I was about to start for Folkestone when some Huns flew north over the town and dropped bombs near Saltwood Castle. The noise of the bombs and our new battery sent me scurrying for cover. Other Huns dropped incendiary bombs near the Folkestone gasworks.

Tuesday 29 October

A cold but sunny day. Fighting overhead at 1.45 p.m. We went off and spent the afternoon packing at Bog Farm, as it had been sold and we had to vacate it. What looked like a squadron of ours flew overhead, others of ours flew about low and the squadron came back later. Just as they had gone, heavy firing broke out towards Folkestone and came nearer as each battery took it up and 12 Huns sailed over our heads; later on there was heavy machine gunning in the sky to the west, and one of our airmen bailed out coming down beyond Sellindge. We saw the planes flying low to protect him. The Huns returned about 5.30 p.m., passing over Aldington, and the 'all clear' sounded at 6 p.m. just as we got home. I learnt that Mrs Hesketh, sister of Broom, one of my Home Guards, was wounded in the back by the nose cap of an AA shell.

Wednesday 30 October

A cold clear day. I was in orderly room at 10.30 a.m. when there was a burst of machine gun fire above us, which did not sound British; a plane flew low over the town. Our ground defences burst into action and were followed by the crash of a couple of bombs. Bystanders told me it was over Saltwood, which made me guess it was Hillcrest Road, so I hurried up the hill. Phyllis and the two Mrs Drays were in the kitchen and Daphne in the garden and saw the two-engined bomber as it dropped its bombs. Two made huge craters in Bridge House, badly smashing the house and uprooting trees, whilst rocks flew over and made a hole in our roof and smashed the cookhouse next door, which had only just had the damage from the previous bomb repaired. An oil bomb, which did us no damage, was also thrown out and another bomb fell on the lip of the quarry where the nursery is and rolled to the bottom without exploding. Everyone agreed that the Germans were attempting to destroy the big gun on the lawn of Braiswick [Colonel Chopping's house]. The Sappers and Police arrived and told us we must leave the house. We had a fearful scramble, the two Mrs Drays carrying plates and dishes of food and we piling the car up chiefly with the numerous pets, and we all went to the Jenners' empty house for lunch and tea. There was heavy fighting overhead about 3 p.m. When it abated, I drove Phyllis to Sandling to see if the cottage-annexe of Captain Stuart-Lewis' house would suit us, but we decided it was not big enough for us. On the way back I drove up Seaton Avenue and had just stopped at Mr James Kerr's house when the delayed action bomb blew up. Phyllis was down on the ground at once, so were a lot of Sappers playing football in the field opposite. I could only sit in the car and gape at the columns of black smoke which rose straight up above the quarry. I felt no shock and nothing came our way. It completely wrecked the hut and greenhouses in the quarry, made another hole in our roof, smashed two windows and unhinged two doors. It also badly damaged two houses near us and did a lot of damage on both sides of Castle Road. After tea, Phyllis saw Miss Villiers about taking over her house in South Road. We then collected some of our kit and Jerry, leaving the cats and birds at the Jenners', and drove to Mrs Beatrice Dray's house in Martello Cottages, Dymchurch Road for the night. I had the son's room on the ground floor and she did us very well.

Thursday 31 October
A misty morning with rain. Phyllis and I drove to Bog Farm and completed packing and loading the car. Driver's lorry was an hour late, but we got away by 12.15 p.m. Deposited the kit at 40 South Road, which we had rented from Miss Villiers, picked up some sausages for lunch and a haddock for breakfast and returned to Mrs Dray's. In the afternoon I drove to our house, collecting uniform and kit. After mounting guard, I spoke with the bald-headed Sapper Captain and returned to our house for the night. I slept well.

Friday 1 November
Alarms sounded on and off most of the day. About noon there was a lot of scrapping overhead, and one of our men bailed out and landed at Hawkinge. At one time he looked as if he was rising. After lunch we settled into 40 South Road, collecting our kit from the other three houses.

Saturday 2 November
I had a very comfortable night in my new room. Alarm 8.30 a.m. to 11.15 a.m. In the first hour there was scrapping overhead and one Hun was

brought down on the Marsh. At noon a twin-engined Hun bomber flew very low over the length of the town, and our ground defences roared ineffectively at it. It, however, came down beyond Shorncliffe. The 'all clear' sounded before it had landed. A strong south-westerly gale and rain. We drove up to Upper Fold to collect more kit. A Hun tried to come in on the gale and dropped two bombs near the gasworks in the sea. I walked in the driving rain up to Saltwood and mounted guard and slept the night at Upper Fold. The news is good. We are mastering the solitary and night bombers. We are giving Berlin 'hell' and we are really going to help the Greeks. Later: Heard that the bomber which flew over the town was one of ours, a Hampden long-distance bomber. It landed unharmed at Hawkinge. Comment unnecessary!!

> R.A.F. bombers have this week-end inflicted on Germany the heaviest punishment it has ever experienced.

Tuesday 5 November

Frost in the morning and a fine sunny day. Huns came, passing over Folkestone, returning later with our fighters on them. At 10.30 a.m. after a burst of firing I saw one of ours drop from the sky like a falling leaf then recover itself and stagger off to Lympne. At 11.30 a.m. three Huns dived on the town from over Pedlinge and dropped bombs. Two fell on the Ranges, and one hit the quarters of the Quartermaster of the Small Arms School. The next hit and demolished the barricaded side of Nelson's Bridge over the canal, spattering the small houses nearby with black canal mud, and the last fell on Hospital Hill, Sandgate, killing a Sapper from the section in Hillcrest Road. Shortly after, the rain came down. On my way up to mount the guard I saw the strafing of the French coast in retaliation for the shelling of Dover. It came down in buckets as I left the post and I was wet through. Hillcrest Road was full of lorries, some backing into the Choppings', and there was great activity all night preparing to move the big gun. If the gun goes we ought to be able to return home. It is not pleasant having to go so far at night and sleep in a cold house.

Saturday 9 November

A strong south-westerly gale. In morning Captain Fuller drove me up to Saltwood and I walked all over the village distributing greatcoats. About

1 o'clock, two Huns flew over Hythe and dropped (some say ten) bombs on Cheriton. The London Division leaves today and a new Division comes in. The roads everywhere were full of troops and lorries and buses and there were pom-poms [AA guns] out on the ranges, in our allotments and in Sandling guarding against dive-bombers. Alarm 6 p.m. to 10.30 p.m. I again got soaked mounting the guard. Neville Chamberlain died today.

Sunday 10 November
A dark, raw morning with a storm threatening, but the wind had dropped. At about 8.45 a.m., 22 of our bombers flew overhead. Daphne took her 'Fortress' Patrol of Girl Guides to the Mayor's Sunday Service. Colonel Street had decided that it was not advisable for such a large body as our Home Guard Company to parade and march through the streets, with enemy aircraft continually flying over. Phyllis and I drove up to our house, and from there I went round Saltwood distributing overcoats. The AA batteries fired a few shots as the Huns came over.

Monday 11 November
Armistice Day. Daphne sold poppies in the High Street. A decided frost in the morning. There were bombs dropped out on the Marsh, and at 1.30 p.m. we heard the explosions as two Huns dived and dropped bombs on Julian Road, Radnor Park and the harbour area of Folkestone, one of which destroyed the old and interesting Fisherman's Bethel. Some children were killed; our fighters were up soon after the 'all clear'. A gale raged all the time. Learnt that during the day we shot down 12 Huns and 13 Italians, only losing two of ours. A good bag.

Wednesday 13 November
A few alarms during morning. Alarm 1.50 p.m. to 2.30 p.m. At 1.45 p.m. there was heavy firing to the west, then over the sea, and our ground defences burst into a roar. I saw two planes being fired at, one flew out to sea and the other along the shore to the west, then a number of our fighters flying round low. It seems the Huns nipped over and bombed Folkestone. Our fighters came along, were mistaken for the Huns, were fired at and one shot down. Phyllis and I drove up to Upper Fold, taking

some of our kit back. On our return we found barriers across Stade Street near the ARP Centre. It is said an unexploded cannon shell fell in the road. It rained and blew a gale at night, and we had one of the most violent storms on record, our South Road house rocking to the blows of the wind and the thumping of the breakers.

Thursday 14 November
A bright, clear morning. Broom, Foster and Mitchell turned up and enrolled themselves as volunteers; the former is to be in my platoon. We packed up the car and drove up to Upper Fold. I was told that Gausby had received his orders and that Broom had fallen off his motorbike, so I had to rush around Saltwood finding substitutes. We found our cypress tree bowed to the ground by the storm and nearly every house in the road had tiles off and some fences are blown down. A clear night with a full moon. Alarm 8.45 p.m. Huns were overhead before the siren sounded and the AA had fired at them.

Friday 15 November
I was woken at 6.15 a.m. by the 'all clear'. A bright morning with a very heavy frost. Alarm 9 a.m. to 10 a.m. There was hot fighting overhead for a time. Stansfield kept me helping him at orderly room to nearly 1 p.m. The news is bad: Coventry bombed to bits by 100 Huns, the cathedral a ruin and ten of our bombers shot down. The Russians more friendly to Germany, and the Spanish getting ready to join in.

Saturday 16 November
A raw, wet and blowy morning. I drove Stansfield to the ranges to try and get the 30-yard range, then on to the SAS to take over the TA Hut and finally to collect Foster's shotgun. Stansfield is very slow and we were all morning at it. At noon there was fighting overhead but I had not heard the siren. I took his gun up to Foster's house at 1 o'clock, and had a glass of sherry when the 'all clear' sounded. A storm came up and drove the Huns off.

Sunday 17 November
A coldish overcast morning, becoming finer. Twelve Hun bombers flew overhead. Two turned as if to bomb Dover, turned again when fired on by

AA and were chasing the first lot back. I had a digging parade from
10.30 a.m. to noon. 'Bone' Foster, Kerr and Prior, Turner, Johncock,
Stone, Dearman, Dray and Chappell turned up. We mended the fallen
parapets – very sticky work! About 1.30 p.m. the 'all clear' was sounded,
but was immediately followed by another 'alert'. Just before the second
'all clear' a Spitfire chased a Messerschmitt low over the house towards
Dibgate.

Monday 18 November

Sirens were sounded
every half-hour
throughout the night,
the last 'alert' being
between 7.30 a.m. and
8 a.m. The sounding of
them must have been
handed over to the
local authorities. There
were further alarms
throughout the
morning. At 4 a.m. this
morning two large
bombs (they call them
landmines) were
dropped on Beach
Street, Folkestone, near

*Bomb damage at Beach Street, Folkestone,
caused by parachute mines*

the Harbour and Junction stations, causing very bad damage and 70 killed
and wounded. They were digging them out throughout the day.

Wednesday 20 November

A blustery morning. The rain started and continued steadily all morning. I
went over to Folkestone on RSPCA work and was shown by Inspector
Neville over the two bombed areas. The area of damage was greatest near
Junction [Station] where houses for a great distance round were damaged.
It fell where there are eight pubs in a bunch and demolished five of them.
Neville seemed to think that the greatest tragedy!! About 30 people were
killed. The survivors excavating their possessions from the ruins were
wonderfully cheerful, and the owners of a café, half of which had been

demolished, were handing out cups of tea whilst a gramophone played cheerful records. The 'alert' was sounded continually throughout the afternoon. There were a lot of planes overhead during the night. They may have been our own bombers but, perhaps it was the effect of what I had seen, they got on my nerves.

Saturday 23 November

A clear frosty morning; alarm at 8 a.m. with a lot of fighting and AA fire overhead. Heard that last night's explosion was a bomb dropped between here and Folkestone, probably on the camp. Phyllis and Daphne, taking Mrs Welfare, drove into Ashford for a church committee, returning about 1 o'clock. Alarm 12.50 p.m. About 50 Huns came over from seawards, turned over Hawkinge when fired at by AA batteries, manoeuvred over Dover and made off home. Apparently, our fighters were waiting for them in a large cloud over the sea; as their lines of exhaust fumes approached they were cut off and altered to splashes and zigzags. Fighting continued overhead until about 1.30 p.m. I saw one of ours come down to land somewhere beyond Saltwood. I drove round Saltwood and Sandling and to Bluehouse and Stone Farm, handing in orders and collecting rifles, as we are to get our new rifles tomorrow. When I mounted the guard there was a severe bombardment going on Ashford way. There was nothing about it in the evening news.

Sunday 24 November

A frost in the morning, but the day turned out sunny and warm. I drove 'Bone' Foster down to the Small Arms School, picking up Prior on the way for the issue of our new rifles. We have received [Canadian] Ross rifles, clumsy weapons. I was able with Fuller's help to return all but three of mine. I next took charge of the shooting on the miniature range where Foster, Mitchell and some others passed their test. In the afternoon I went round Saltwood distributing the new rifles and when I was mounting guard there was again a bombardment, not so intense as last night but in the same direction. I think it must be the London barrage.

Wednesday 27 November

A morning of unnoticed alarms. Stansfield did not come to office, so Street got through the work quickly. After lunch and for most of the afternoon there was fighting overhead in which we brought down 11 Huns and lost two of our machines, the pilots being safe. One Hun came down near Horton Park – a sergeant wearing an Iron Cross. Street went to a conference with the new Divisional Commander, a Guardsman, in the afternoon. Street was very fed up at losing his golf – 'waste of an afternoon', he said.

Thursday 28 November
A clear, frosty morning. At 10.30 a.m. the Huns were over in considerable numbers before the sirens sounded, then the ships' hooters joined in. There was fighting all morning over the area. Street told us the Home Guard has come into favour with the military authorities. The idea is that there is still a probability of an invasion, or of raids on a larger scale. They have the men and the ships; the men are theirs, the ships belong to the beaten nations, and the Huns do not mind how many of either they lose in the attempt. The Navy are so shorthanded and busy elsewhere they cannot join in. Most of the afternoon there was scrapping overhead; our AA fired more than once and the Hun big guns shelled the Dover area. There was a big dogfight in the sky to the west when I went to Saltwood on Home Guard business. There was also much air activity at night. As I was leaving our post, I heard a Hun not very high overhead dodging the searchlights. Then I heard a 'clack-clack' which was repeated after a pause, the sound of bombs being released, and four flashes sprang up over the treetops in the direction of Newingreen followed by four explosions. The light from one stayed some time in the air.

Friday 29 November
Again much activity in the air round us. The military consider that as we can only mount guard between 7.30 p.m. and 5.30 a.m., owing to our volunteers' civilian duties, our guards in these long winter nights are of little use, so Street is abolishing the Hythe Guard from Sunday next. He said I could do as I liked, but I have to follow suit so I am stopping mine Saturday week. There was a lot of fighting in the air throughout the afternoon.

Saturday 30 November
A long day in orderly room and on to Stansfield's bungalow until 1 p.m. Alarms sounding on and off in quick succession. About 3 p.m. there was a lot of machine gun fire on the seafront, and a new gun beyond the golf

course fired a shot out to sea. I understand it was a Hun attempt on one of our convoys. The alarm was sounded later when two of our planes came over flying low. The Greeks still advancing, and we are doing nothing with our Army. It is better to wait and see and have a bloodless victory, but can we? My idea is to go and smash Italy out of the war.

Sunday 1 December

A severe frost at night, and clear frosty weather all day. The Hythe Home Guard fired grouping practice on the range; Street allowed all and sundry to fire with the Hythe platoons, so there was not enough ammunition for Saltwood. He also got his car stuck in the shingle, then found he had forgotten to bring the ammunition, so we were late starting and did not finish until 1 p.m. Whilst there, we saw a fight between two Spitfires and at least one Hun in and out of the mist over the sea. When one of ours came out of the mist doing the victory roll, half our men bolted for cover. There was heavy fighting overhead during and after lunch.

Monday 2 December

Bad news in the evening: the Greeks are being counter-attacked and we are giving them very little help. Our shipping losses are very serious, and the Huns bomb at night with impunity. Southampton has had two very severe raids.

Thursday 5 December

At noon a number of Huns came over and were fired on by AA batteries, which covered the whole sky with white puffs. I saw one plane hit and come away with smoke coming from it, but did not see it come down. After lunch I took greatcoats and rifles to my old men at Bluehouse. As I reached Sandling Station at 2.30 p.m., when no 'alert' was on, I saw half a dozen Messerschmitts dive-bomb Hawkinge. They were met by a heavy AA barrage and I heard later their bombs all went wide of the target. The AA was so intense I bolted to the station for shelter. Later, a formation of Huns came from the north flying out to sea where, it appeared, our planes caught them. Later, there was the sound of a heavy barrage to the north. As I left to mount the guard, a big gun on the seafront fired two shells, and one near the Hythe Station also fired. I saw two flashes, and to me it looked more like Hun shells exploding overhead.

Saturday 7 December
A very cold day. In the evening I mounted the last guard over our post at the Saltwood pumping station.

Sunday 8 December
Shooting on the range. A strong, bitterly cold west wind blew all the time. The men were late arriving, then Street found he had forgotten the ammunition. After lunch, Kerr, Foster and I cleared all our kit out of the Waterworks post. It was quite strange for me not to turn out to mount guard tonight. The Huns started to come over in numbers about 10.30 p.m., and about 11 o'clock one dived low over us and dropped two bombs not far off to the north, which shook our house. Later in the night at least twice planes came down low and on one occasion bombs were dropped.

Monday 9 December
Rain at night and a mild morning. I left Sandling by the 11.30 a.m. train and heard that the line beyond New Cross had been damaged. In my carriage to Tonbridge were three Petty Officers and one AB of the Royal Navy who played halfpenny nap all the time. From Tonbridge, where I changed to Redhill, I had a RAMC Corporal from Dover and, beyond there, a Wiltshire Corporal and a young gunner and his wife (?) who ragged each other. There were craters on the side of the line in the fields all the way, and some houses near the station at Dorking were damaged; otherwise I saw nothing. My train got into Guildford earlier than expected. I found Milly and Eddie both looking well but rather nervy. After tea I looked up Mr Blaxland and Nancy. I found him more feeble, and she worries a lot. Guildford is crowded, shops and pavements full and a solid stream of cars, very few with ARP or other labels on them. The troops are mostly Canadians. Eddie and I stayed up till midnight to hear the news. The advance in Egypt is most gratifying.

Friday 13 December
I had an amusing day in the office. Street had one of his 'don't want' moods and tried to clear out all the superfluous equipment in little Stansfield's 'mouse nest', and they nearly came to blows!! 'Dogsbody' [Kennedy-Craufurd-Stuart] blew in and Street went for him over a stupid return the Division had asked for, which Stuart had sent on for companies to comply with. Street ended by threatening to send it on to Grigg, the Under-secretary

for War. I was buzzing about the town up to 1 o'clock and round Saltwood all the afternoon ending up with tea with Fuller at the Home Farm, a fine old building.

Saturday 14 December

Another long morning in office. Street managed to make Stansfield give up quite a lot of stuff and cleared the office table and almirah [cupboard] of unnecessary papers. Stansfield dug in the wastepaper basket after he had left, and retrieved some. Vernal, the store-keeper to the Battalion, rang up to say more complaints had come in about the return, and would Street please not write to Grigg. There are many rumours about Italy. Internal fighting, threats of invasion by Hitler and Blackshirts surrounding the Palace [Palazzo Venezia].

Sunday 15 December

A mild foggy day. Fewer than usual of the Saltwood Platoon turned up. Firing at 200 yards with the Ross rifle, the first time I handled it. Mine was the highest score in the platoon!!

Monday 16 December

A wet foggy day, but very mild. The Australians have been brought up to finish off the war in Libya. I heard that Hitler made two attempts at invasion and is supposed to have lost 80,000 men! In the evening I had the first of Saltwood Platoon weekly meetings in the Territorial Hut on the canal bank. Twenty turned out – a very good attendance. I was tongue-tied, but Fuller gave them an opening lecture and young Kite instructed them in the firing position, fixing bayonets and shouldering arms.

Tuesday 17 December

Wind veered round to the east. About 9 a.m. a fearful din arose with ships' hooters joining in with the sirens; made me think the invasion was starting, but the 'all clear' sounded very soon. At 11 o'clock I saw what looked like a parachute over Etchinghill drifting eastward very slowly. Street said he saw it catch alight, and thought it was a balloon carrying leaflets. I was told afterwards that it was a loose balloon which one of our planes destroyed. I went to Saltwood village in the afternoon. There were no 'alerts' throughout the night. I wonder what the Hun is up to.

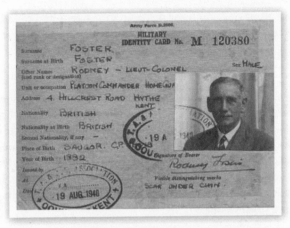

Rodney's Military Identity Card (Rodney Foster Archive)

Thursday 19 December

A dull morning with a few short 'alerts'. We had a punctual lunch and all three drove into Ashford for shopping. Whilst the others were still at it, I stood and sketched a corps sign on a lorry and was accosted by a Military Police Sergeant with an Oxford accent who wanted to confiscate my sketches, but let me off with a caution when I showed him my Officers Identity Card. Alarm 6.30 p.m. to 9.30 p.m. A number of Hun planes came over just as the wind rose to a gale. I went down at 7 p.m. to the miniature range, where Street organised pool [shooting] competitions. Kerr won the junior pool, six men made possibles. Our casualties in Egypt were only 72 killed and we have probably taken 50,000 prisoners. Warning by everyone that the invasion is imminent, this time by air.

Saturday 21 December

A cold morning, but some sun in the afternoon. Phyllis lost her green cock budgerigar. About 9 o'clock there was heavy gunfire at Dover from across the water, which went on for half an hour. During the firing our bombers flew over to retaliate.

Sunday 22 December

An icy cold wind all day. Shooting on the range in morning. I was so cold I could not think or supervise my men, and they shot very badly. Colonel Collins brought down a team of six of his stevedores (all regular NCOs) to shoot against six of ours. We beat them with 94 against 83, Broom of Saltwood Platoon making the top score of 18. I heard that Evie passed away suddenly last week; I am sorry for Carol.

Monday 23 December

A very cold day, never above freezing point. Street being away on holiday, Stansfield enlisted young Stanley Cosgrove, who lives near Stone Farm. Grove-White said it was not fair; he suggested we should toss for him. I refused! In the afternoon I went to The Field, Saltwood, where I met a London Rifle Brigade Officer who is training young NCOs of his regiment, who offers to demonstrate automatic guns and trench mortars to my platoon.

Wednesday 25 December

We were up only a little later than usual. No servants came and we ran our own show. A cold day, but not freezing, I took Jerry for a walk about midday. No carol singers this year. We missed the King's broadcast.

Thursday 26 December

Boxing Day. Not very cold, but with a thick fog. Alarm 12.15 p.m. to 1 p.m. This broke the 48-hour truce. No planes came over us. After lunch we three drove to Lympne. For some days, I had the feeling that Italy was about to cave in. The Pope's speech confirmed my idea and now on the news is the rumour that Italian peacemakers are on their way. Perhaps it is all wishful thinking. I had a bad night coughing, and kept Phyllis awake.

Saturday 28 December

A foggy and fairly mild day. There were no alerts all day. About 6 o'clock and again about 8 p.m. there was a tremendous din and commotion across the Channel, with lights of every colour and description appearing through the fog. The noise was greater than it has been during previous raids on Channel ports. It is said Hitler was present during the bombardment of Dover on Friday morning.

Sunday 29 December

A fairly mild, still day. I picked up Stansfield at 10 a.m. and drove to the ranges. Soon after we arrived there, two of our planes flew over and out to sea and there was the sound of continuous machine gunning for some time in the mist whilst men on the Martello Towers looked seawards. There was no raid warning on. Our men were late as usual. A young Wiltshire subaltern lectured and demonstrated the throwing of a Molotov Cocktail and a phosphorous bomb, and told us stories of a young friend of his who gained the MC using them against tanks. Stansfield took his men off to his hut for kit inspection afterwards. I sent mine home. There was an alert in the morning and several in the afternoon. After dusk the air was full of planes, probably a raid on London but some may have been our own.

Monday 30 December

The raid last night was on London, the whole City gutted by incendiaries, including the Guildhall and most of the churches. A very dark wet morning, but mild. I drove Stansfield round on Home Guard work. This took up the whole morning. We are told that Hitler is almost certain to attempt an invasion by air in the next week or so. No butchers had any meat today, and there was no fish either. Saltwood had their second meeting at the Boys Club hut; Captain Carter of the London Rifle Brigade sent two instructors to show us the Bren and Tommy guns. Very interesting. The elder NCO was good, the other was parrot taught and treated our men as if they were unintelligent NCOs. A very mild night.

A Heinkel He 111 bomber flying over Wapping,
London, during the Battle of Britain (IWM C5422)

1941

Thursday 2 January

I woke up to an 'all clear', and to a world covered in snow. There was another alarm at 9 a.m., then the snow came down again for a while. There were short 'alerts' all day. I went down to the SAS miniature range at 7 p.m. Barrack Hill was scored with the skid marks of Army lorries, and the road sign at the bottom was smashed. Stansfield, who had had a fall in the morning, felt rotten and went home.

Friday 3 January

A lot more snow fell at night. Short raid warnings all day. Stansfield did not grace the orderly room. Daphne returned about 9.30 p.m.; her train was not very late. Allen sent one taxi instead of two, and there were six stevedores and an officer crammed inside, whilst Daphne had to sit on the knee of a gentleman on the seat next to the driver. The stevedores were some of the original lot who had been through Dunkirk.

Saturday 4 January

Freezing all day, with occasional light falls of snow. There were the usual short alerts throughout the day and night. I stayed in all afternoon. We have at last made a move against Bardia. I was afraid we were going to sit down and starve them out. The trouble is the rationing. We are cut down to a minimum, and what we are told we can have cannot be bought. They are still afraid to tell us the truth that our ships have been sunk at sea and burnt out in our harbours. They allow Americans to learn our secrets and to publish them to the world and to our enemies.

Monday 6 January

Only a little snow fell, but it froze all day and the sky was again full of snow. Continuous alarms throughout the day, but none after dark. Twenty-three turned up for the evening parade of the Saltwood Platoon. Three NCOs demonstrated the working of the Army's new weapons: an anti-tank gun, a trench mortar and bomb throwing. Street turned up for a short time, and was very interested in the trench mortar and my efforts in securing these demonstrations. The prisoners from Bardia total 30,000, with our casualties at 500.

Tuesday 7 January

The frost still holds. There was a long alarm during lunch, when a plane had flown overhead and resulted in a burst of AA gunfire. There was prolonged machine gun fire towards Folkestone. Amy Johnson, acting as a ferry pilot, crashed into the Thames estuary and drowned. A naval commander who dived in to rescue her also lost his life. No alarms at night.

Friday 10 January

A clear sky, with a warm sun all day melting the snow. At noon I watched a squadron of our bombers come back from their successful

EXPLOSIONS FELT IN BRITAIN

daylight raid over France. Before that, there had been a continuous din which I thought had been the Hun's guns shelling Dover but was actually our bombs and their AA fire. In the afternoon I went to fill in a sketch of Saltwood village, which my platoon now defend instead of the Waterworks. At Bartholomew Close, a Sapper wanted to know 'what the 'ell' I was doing, and later on a counter-jumper with one pip rushed up in a car and wanted to arrest me, so I gave up.

Saturday 11 January

The thaw has started and most of the snow has disappeared. Phyllis and Daphne took the car out of cold storage and drove into Folkestone. During my tea, there was a long burst of machine gun fire with AA fire. Large number of planes flew overhead at 6 p.m. to raid London with more incendiaries, but this time the fires were successfully grappled with. We brought down six night bombers: a decent improvement. Our daylight raids over France continue. The bombing of Mannheim was to stop a big poison gas factory. The Huns are concentrating on bombing with incendiary bombs. They still get away with it.

Sunday 12 January

The slush froze at night but thawed by midday. Instruction in bayonet fighting by two Wiltshire sergeants at 10.30 a.m. at the Territorial Hut. Some of the older men showed up well; Prior did well but was slow at responding to commands. After dark, planes came over in considerable numbers for three hours and explosions shook the house. Probably stronger AA batteries, but some might have been bombs.

Monday 13 January

A thick mist in morning and evening, and most of the day it was freezing. Phyllis went by bus at Ashford to meet Mrs Dix, and Daphne had her Girl Guide meeting. Saltwood Platoon had their meeting, but only 20 turned up. Kite took the whole evening demonstrating the Browning automatic. He is not very good at it. The village constable informed me that he has orders to make two roadblocks on the Sandling Road and near the castle to stop motorists bolting from Hythe, and that a Home Guard is to be posted at each.

Thursday 16 January

Woke up to an 'all clear'. Dreamt that Saltwood Platoon and I were defending the village during an invasion, with Huns on the golf course and two Albanian prisoners being brought in. It froze harder than ever. The usual crowd turned up at the miniature range in the evening.

Saturday 18 January

Heavy snowfall with strong northerly winds. Swansea was bombed last night. Churchill made one of his foreboding speeches. Dive-bombing attacks on Malta commenced.

Sunday 19 January

The rain had washed all the snow away except in the drifts by morning. We had another bayonet fighting instruction parade on very slushy ground. Fuller and Kite have started their own show at Sandling. I do not like this idea, and must try and squash it. As I went to my bath the alarm sounded and planes came over in fair numbers. The explosions rattled our windows. At 10.45 p.m. a Hun hovered overhead and was occasionally shot at. I heard the change of note in the sound of his engine and said: 'He's going to bomb.' Very soon after we heard it explode fairly near the coast.

Monday 20 January

A pouring, raw day. I had to go into Folkestone to see my tailor and do some RSPCA work. The local vets have been whining that young Neville has been carrying out operations, which he denies. I returned via Saltwood, where 100 small incendiary bombs were dropped last night. Most fell in the fields and the churchyard, but some fell on the tops of the Rectory and Village Hall causing fires, which were put out by a Sapper extinguishing several on the ground with his helmet. I think it must have been an inexperienced Hun who spilt his cargo and went home. At Saltwood evening parade, 21 turned up.

Tuesday 21 January

A wet, almost mild day. Our guns were practising towards Lydd. On the news, it said our attack in Tobruk had started. I expect we have captured the place, but they must leave it to the morning papers to announce it.

Wednesday 22 January

Only Street and I attended the orderly room. Butler and his assistant were sick, and the fat typist had to attend Butler's house, so left the office in my charge. Our big guns were again firing all morning, and our planes were very active. The stevedores say that their leave has been stopped, and that an attempt at invasion is imminent.

Thursday 23 January

A very mild day, and the snowdrops are out. I went on a new way down to the miniature range, my torch petered out and I crashed into some iron railings, hurting my face and was half knocked out. Street stated that a rubber boat with German equipment and an identity disc marked Rudolph

Schmidt had been washed ashore near Sandling Castle. A suspicious person had approached a Wiltshire post near the Grand Redoubt and had been fired upon. In the afternoon we three motored with Phyllis Green and Molly Harding to Folkestone, and saw Charlie Chaplin's *Great Dictator*. The man who acted 'Musso' was the best. The film was good, but to me the pathos and comedy did not blend very well.

Sunday 26 January
The Shorncliffe Brigadier came to our bayonet fighting parade, for which 11 of my platoon turned up – a record number. After parade, the Wiltshire second in command asked Street, Stansfield and myself for drinks at the SAS mess. It was just 40 years ago that I was last in the mess! They said that the disturbances and unrest in Italy are really serious.

Tuesday 28 January
Some air activity and some speedboats dashing around in the fog. Six large explosions near Oathill Farm, but only a chicken house was burnt.

Wednesday 29 January
Only Street and I turned up for orderly room, so we took the opportunity to collar my fair share of warm uniforms, gas masks etc. for my platoon.

Thursday 30 January
I had a wire from my sister Milly telling me that Eddie was dangerously ill. After orderly room, I distributed seized uniforms and gas masks in Saltwood. Some air activity and big gun fire around noon. At the miniature range in the evening Kerr, Mitchell and young Thompson of the brewery tied for top score, the latter winning the shoot-off although he had a broken left thumb!

Friday 31 January
Not very cold, but foggy. Occasional Hun bombers flew over, one passing unmolested low over the town. 'All clear' given at 4 p.m. Colonel Knox of the USA says the next 90 days will be the crisis period, and that the Germans intend to use gas. All other high officials seem to think Hitler will attempt to invade soon as a last gamble. I hope he does not choose this area!

Saturday 1 February

Large flakes of snow during the morning. Street was out shooting and I drove Stansfield to the Wiltshire Quartermaster's stores to exchange coats and boots. Phyllis and Daphne drove into Ashford for shopping. It was given out on the wireless that Home Guard Company Commanders will be made Majors, and Platoon Commanders full Lieutenants. The present armlet will be changed for flashes on the collar.

Monday 3 February

Woke up to a country covered with thick snow, and more fell throughout the day. At evening parade I distributed a few gas masks. The sergeants returned theirs that had flimsy bags, and I handed these out to latecomers. Tiltman was late as usual and gave notice, but I checkmated him by accepting his resignation. Jesse Goodsell demonstrated the manipulation and care of gas masks very ably.

Tuesday 4 February

Cold morning with a later thaw. I could not use the car, so had to hump ten suits of Denham's [denim] from the Almshouse, but found a Wiltshire lorry to cart them down to orderly room. Clear sky with alarms all day. At 12.45 p.m. when I was out with Jerry at the end of our road, I heard and partially saw some Huns dive on Hawkinge Aerodrome and set an oil tank on fire. They were met by AA fire with much heavier calibre than I have heard previously. Our fighters came up too late to tackle the Hun. It was like old times!

Thursday 6 February

More snow fell during the night. Colonel Street was out shooting, so I commanded the company for half a day. We had a snap shooting competition at the miniature range; Prior shot well. The Divisional Commander is very annoyed that on more than one occasion German speedboats have come close up to shore (not in the Hythe section!) and had not been fired at by defence posts. Our Air Force went out in the evening and attacked the invasion ports – probably Dunkirk or Brest, as the noise was some way off.

Friday 7 February

Very foggy morning with slush everywhere. In the afternoon I recruited a civil engineer named Hickling. He had been in Palestine in the last war and had joined our local stevedores but has been invalided out through ill health. Our Air Force caused a heavy bombing raid on the invasion ports; the noise was loud and prolonged and lights of every colour filled the sky.

ANOTHER BIG RAID ON INVASION PORTS

Saturday 8 February
Great rejoicing everywhere over the capture of Benghazi. Wavell has certainly made his name. I cleaned the car after lunch, having not touched it for twelve months. At 3.15 p.m., without warning, a couple of Huns flew over Hythe and attacked Hawkinge. One was shot down in flames; the other fled back over Hythe, dropping its bombs on the ranges near the gasworks, and skimmed the waves on its way home.

Sunday 9 February
The Home Guard has no parade owing to the changing over of Brigades. A Battalion of the Queen's replaced the Wiltshires. The Prime Minister made a fighting speech, a little too long. The best news is that the aircraft carrier *Illustrious* has survived the heavy bombardment of Malta and been repaired and is out to sea again. It is also good that out of 150 German dive-bombers we have destroyed 90.

Monday 10 February
Warm day, with plenty of sunshine. Our planes made a daylight sweep across the water to raid Calais and Boulogne. Street told us that a Canadian officer said a device had been invented which enabled our night fighters to pick out and destroy enemy bombers [radar], but the authorities want to keep the Hun guessing, so we only announced that half of the actual bombers had been destroyed. Full attendance at Saltwood evening parade.

Tuesday 11 February
Thick fog all day. Street is on leave, as his daughter is to have an operation. I command the company until Friday. Alarms at 3 p.m., when the local stevedores were parading in the road. The American papers say we have raided into French territory, with troops on motorcycles getting as far as

Amiens. Street says we have done so once or twice with 19-year-old officers. Once they were put ashore on Sark by mistake, and had to swim back to their boats.

Wednesday 12 February

I went to orderly room as OC Company. Nothing exciting, except that the OC Queen's tried to make me take over a number of AW bombs, but I insisted on his waiting until Friday. I had hopes that Franco meeting Mussolini and Pétain meant peace, but it is said it's more likely to be an extension of the war.

Thursday 13 February

Phyllis and Daphne went into Folkestone. Street turned up at the miniature range, depriving me of my parade. The Queen's sentries were very jumpy, making me and several others hold up our hands. An officer arrested Hickling because he had no identity card and, after half an hour, sent him over to us on the range under a callow subaltern and a sergeant. Hickling slipped away from them in the dark and the subaltern's mild surprise was very comic! This battalion is a poor example of the smart Queen's. The news informed us via Italian sources that we had dropped parachute troops on the toe of Italy to destroy a big reservoir, but they were captured without causing any damage. Street says it is true.

Friday 14 February

I handed over to Street at orderly room. He is very pleased with my tidying up of our equipment and with the new equipment ledger. Terrific fight in the skies over Hythe. I thought I heard one come down. We only shot down one Hun and lost one of ours in the sea. At 11.30 p.m. there was a host of heavy explosions, and it sounded as if a heavy shell passed over the house. Alarms all day and night.

Saturday 15 February

Stansfield turned up at orderly room and behaved very well about my scrapping his books and tidying up his stores. A large formation of bombers with an escort of fighters looking very much like Huns made a spiral course from west to east. Daphne, who was in Folkestone, saw them go out to sea past Dover and thought they were ours. When I returned home I found Milly had rung up to say that Eddie had passed on yesterday. At 8.30 p.m. an intensive bombardment of the French coast commenced. Phyllis and Daphne said there were three rows of lights: our bombs, the Hun AA and the searchlights. Our house shook with the explosions as if the bombs were falling a few yards away. Daphne called us to the window to see a huge glow over Calais. It was red all round in the sky and behind the trees; in the foreground there was the light of flames. Soon these seemed to shift gradually to one side and upwards, and looked like a ship on fire. Then out of a cloud came a huge moon!

Sunday 16 February
The morning parade was a demonstration by a young Queen's officer (with a kiss curl!!) on fitting and drill for gas masks. Saltwood turned up 19 strong – a new record.

Monday 17 February
Almost a warm day. Two mines were washed ashore last night. One exploded off Sandgate, smashing half the windows in the place; the other is lying on Hythe beach near the lifeboat station. There was a record attendance of 25 at Saltwood Platoon meeting. Green lectured on arteries and first-aid treatment.

Tuesday 18 February
I left by the 11.30 a.m. train; both it and the Tonbridge trains were very empty. At Sandling Station a RE Sergeant said the Navy, Army and Air Force intend to finish off the Hun this time and will not allow politicians to stop them! On the Tonbridge train I had an interesting talk with a Middlesex farmer who, having had to sell out in the slump, had been taken on as farm hand to Sir William Wayland. He told me amusing stories, demonstrating the incompetence of Sir William, his Wye-educated agent and bailiff. In Guildford, I looked up Milly and had supper at the Angel [Hotel], where I was overcharged. In the evening there seemed to be an endless procession of girls having baths. The owners, servants and guests all appeared to be Irish.

Wednesday 19 February
A slight fall of snow made the rooftops white. The funeral was at noon. I joined Milly and George and we followed the hearse. The same Canon

who buried mother officiated. I had lunch in the town with Mr Blaxland, and tea with Milly and my nephew George. George, who works for a firm of electrical engineers, says we are countering the night bombers with the aid of a wireless mast [radar], which records the position of the raider, and this information is passed on to our own night fighters.

Thursday 20 February
A cold morning. I had difficulty in getting something for lunch in Guildford. There was a queue of hundreds at Sainsbury's cooked meat counter and a seething mass of women in Lyon's. I eventually got what I wanted in a narrow side street. My train was punctual, but I had a long wait at Redhill and Tonbridge.

Sunday 23 February
On the range we fired five rounds a minute. I made a four-inch group but, not knowing the rifle I fired with, the shots were all magpies. A Naval demolition squad arrived to remove a large mine, which had been washed ashore a few days earlier. Stansfield and I came across a mine trap just by the huts. The London Division started to return today.

Monday 24 February
Slight snowfall during the night. There was an explosion on the seafront at 9.30 a.m. A RE sergeant for some unknown reason took a section of the 7th Queen's through barbed wire on to a minefield – the one Stansfield and I had been near yesterday. Seven were killed and five injured, some very badly. The sergeant cannot be found and it is thought he was blown into the sea. There were wounded men lying about, no one knew the plan of the mines, and the troops were afraid to do anything. The foreman of one of the gangs on defence work rigged up planks which he let down and walked along and jumped into the crater and got the injured men out. At the Saltwood meeting, Green gave his second lecture on broken bones. He went on too long and bored his audience.

Tuesday 25 February
Craufurd-Stuart visited us at 11 a.m., 30 minutes of froth and inanities. We can be given all sorts of useless gadgets, but cannot have rifles and clothing, the only two things really necessary. We went to the Grove Cinema and saw the film *Irene* – a good show.

Grove Cinema, Hythe (Folkestone Library H/ENT/4)

Wednesday 26 February

Fine sunny day. Alarms all day. At 4.45 p.m. a large force of Huns came in from the west and were met by our fighters and AA fire. They jettisoned their bombs, some falling on Lympne damaging Berwick Manor, the Blaxlands' old home. Two dropped on 'E' Range and caught a party of South Staffords, killing two and wounding others. The evening sky was full of planes, and the gunfire shook the house. We saw flares and incendiary bombs over Canterbury. One bomb was dropped about 9.15 p.m. to the west of our house. A gale forced the planes away.

Thursday 6 March

Pouring wet day. Phyllis and I drove into Ashford to buy food. The shops were full of it. Later Phyllis and Daphne went for a bicycle ride to Lympne, Sandling and Postling. On passing Saltwood, they heard the scream of a descending bomb but there was no explosion. The AA was firing from behind Folkestone, so it may well be a dud bomb from our own batteries.

Friday 7 March

A large explosion shook the house during the night. I was told it was a sea mine off Dymchurch. Firing most of the morning. I went to tea with Lancashire, who is living alone. His butcher's wife cooks him buns and tarts and his gardener's wife cakes and scones!

Saturday 8 March

The big guns fired behind us, over the town into the sea. In the afternoon I took gas masks to Bluehouse and Stone Farm. I gave a lift to a soldier near the former and drove him into Folkestone and came back along the seafront, picking up Phyllis near Cannongate. The only bright spot in the week is our naval raid on the Lofoten Islands.

Sunday 9 March

'A' Company 8th Battalion Kent Home Guard paraded at their posts at 10.30 a.m. I placed the sections of my platoon near their positions around Saltwood, as we were not allowed into the houses we would occupy. Colonel Street inspected us, approved of my positions and tested the sections in the time they took to adjust their respirators on the command 'gas'. Plenty of AA gunfire during the evening, and I later learnt that a couple of Hun ships came inshore and were fired at by the coastal guns from Folkestone.

Monday 10 March

Fine sunny day. Continuous alarms all day. The sky was full of planes. In the morning Craufurd-Stuart told us that an invasion would certainly be attempted. The Germans have two divisions trained to be carried in gliders and dressed in British uniforms. Dive-bombers would attack at the same time. At 6.30 p.m., about seven Dorniers attempted to attack Hawkinge, but were forced back by the AA barrage and dropped their bombs in the sea

A Home Guard detachment patrolling the cliff paths of Folkestone or Dover (IWM H8111)

off Sandgate. Only 15 turned up at our evening parade. We had gas mask drill.

Thursday 13 March

I was woken by an explosion and burst of machine gun and cannon. Looking out, I saw our two watchdogs 'Gert' and 'Daisy' [AA guns] attacking some Huns flying low, and I saw tracer bullets all around one of them. The Huns were over the house where I could not see them. There was a very poor attendance at the miniature range.

Sunday 16 March

Shooting on the range in gas masks; much better than we had expected. Some good shots failed and some bad shots made big scores. 'Bone' Foster missed the target altogether and as usual blamed his tools!

Monday 17 March

Very busy morning, taking Stansfield back to his house, where we were followed by Craufurd-Stuart and his girl 'chauffeur'. My platoon paraded at their posts, and Major Scott brought his sapper group from Sandling and posted them. He ignored all the arrangements Street had made with him, arranging the barriers too far away for the platoon to defend.

Tuesday 18 March

A warm, sunny day. In the afternoon we saw Walt Disney's film *Pinocchio*. It was good, with no vulgarities. The kitten and the goldfish were two charming characters. Unadvertised, in the newsreel, we saw a thrilling episode of the Lofoten Islands raid. What a strange nation we are. Any other country would have made a full-length film of it and would have sent it all over the world, as well as to every cinema in the country.

Wednesday 19 March

I had a most disturbing night, waking to various alarms and 'all clears'. About 2 a.m. a plane dropped half a dozen bombs in Cheriton, breaking the railway line, demolishing two houses at Newington, and killing a woman and her two children and wounding half a dozen people. The alarms continued all day. At 6.30 p.m. when I was helpless in my bath, what sounded like a mine exploded.

Thursday 20 March

Cold, misty day. As I was going down Church Hill, two Huns flew low, circling around Lympne machine gunning, and were fired upon by ground defences. I saw them fly out to sea skimming the waves, passing low over a line of fishing boats and finally disappearing into the mist. They killed a soldier, and a fireman who had been up all night and was asleep in St Leonard's Road. Firing on the miniature range in the evening. Later on, the whole German air force seemed to be flying over us.

> A MURDEROUS attack by Nazi fighters was made on several small craft fishing in the Straits of Dover on Thursday morning.

Saturday 22 March

Misty day, with plenty of rain. A week of no good news. Yugoslavia is being gradually swallowed up by Germany. We are being too slow in Abyssinia, and are doing nothing elsewhere. Whilst the Huns with planes, submarines and even battleships are!

Monday 24 March

Very hard frost at night. We were awoken at 6.30 a.m. by a succession of explosions and the roar of low-flying planes. I dressed and was down early and learnt from Beatrice that the Greens' house had been hit, so I went up there with Daphne. Half a dozen Messerschmitts came in over Palmarsh, swung around Hawkinge and dive-bombed us. Two bombs were dropped on Tanners Hill, one in the road and the other on a house killing Samuel Wonfor, his wife and daughter. Two fell on St Anne's Cottage and the garden of the house Street is moving into. Three bombs fell unexploded in the fields behind Seaton Avenue and were soon extracted by the REs. Three or four bombs fell and exploded in Brockhill Road, but only damaging one house in which old Mr Smith living alone was unhurt. In Fairlight Road, one fell on a small house occupied by stevedores, completely demolishing the garage. About seven men were injured, none killed. The bomb had landed in the backyard of the Greens' house and demolished the whole house. Green was flung out of the bedroom window and partly buried. Mrs Green in bed had the floor collapse under her and the roof come down over her. They were both badly cut, but not

seriously hurt. Goodsell was first on the scene to rescue his brother Home
Guard. Phyllis Green was on night duty at the first-aid post. Her room was
blown to bits. She arrived soon after I did, having seen her parents off to
hospital. The demolition gang also came. We rescued some of their things,
then Daphne and I went back for breakfast and returned to collect more
until lunchtime. Afterwards, Phyllis and I carried on and Daphne went off
to Guides. I missed the Saltwood parade as I was done in from humping
and heaving boxes etc.

Thursday 27 March
After many days of bad news, good news has come in a lump. We have
finally taken Keren [Eritrea] and Harar [Italian East Africa] and young
Peter of Yugoslavia has brought off a coup and presumably reversed the
pact with Germany signed only yesterday.

Friday 28 March
Phyllis' birthday and a fair morning. It was a Hun bomber that destroyed a
fisherman's house in Folkestone. The woman living there had just left to
visit her married daughter, and the houses either side were occupied with
large families with children. Our daffodils in the orchard are in full bloom,
and so is the forsythia. Daphne picked handfuls of violets up the road. Our
primroses are also coming on.

Sunday 30 March
We were on the range judging distances and caused some consternation to
the Queen's by stumbling around in a large crowd. Some light snow fell as
we did a gas mask drill. Violent fighting overhead in the afternoon.

Tuesday 1 April
Another cold day, and another busy morning receiving and distributing
battledress. Craufurd-Stuart turned up and Colonel Tidmarsh joined
'A' Company and was posted to Grove-White's platoon.

Wednesday 2 April
Rain all day. Daphne was at the Greens' house all day, and I joined her
after distributing more battledress in Saltwood. We both got very dirty
sorting the stuff.

Thursday 3 April

Phyllis had a hen tea party. I went to the Greens' house during the afternoon and had my tea in the kitchen. We have been driven out of Benghazi by German mechanised forces who claim to have captured prisoners and material; we say we destroyed everything before we left.

Friday 4 April

A warm and sunny day, but everyone is depressed about Benghazi. They say that our troops have been transferred to Greece but, even so, it is incomprehensible. I worked on the panorama [painting] all afternoon and got well forward with it. Phyllis worked in the garden, and Daphne went to the Greens' and amongst other things rescued his rifle and ammunition. A large explosion at 9.30 p.m. rattled the windows on the north side of the house.

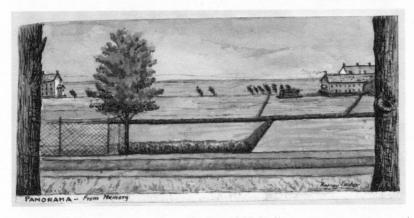

Rodney's panorama of the view from Colonel Stansfield's headquarters (Rodney Foster Archive)

Saturday 5 April

A fine day. I did the rounds in the car during the morning, and worked at the panorama all afternoon until 6 p.m. Daphne retrieved more of Green's kit. Poor old Jerry disgraced himself by cocking his leg in the drawing room.

Sunday 6 April

A bitter, strong north wind. The usual bad weather when Hitler invades a new country. Shooting on the range was very cold work, but it was good, snap shooting at head and shoulders. I wore my Buffs cap badge for the first time. Brigadier Gribbon and some of the Folkestone Home Guard were shooting on the same range. I worked all afternoon on my panorama but did not quite finish it. The Germans have attacked Yugoslavia and Greece. We have taken Addis Ababa – a useless gain.

Monday 7 April
Cold north wind all day. I finished the panorama in the afternoon. At our evening parade 19 turned up. We had a gas drill. Holmes, of all people, had suggested a church parade for Sunday week. I put it to the meeting and they all seemed in favour. I had a talk to Hickling afterwards. He is a queer mixture. He seems to have done nothing but live on his father who died six months ago.

Tuesday 8 April
Daphne drove me down to orderly room, clutching the panorama to the side of the car. Everyone, including 'Dogsbody' [Craufurd-Stuart], admired it. There was a lot of air activity from early morning till noon, and it started again in the afternoon. I drove to Saltwood and Bluehouse in the afternoon, and enrolled the new man Jenkins. He has just been discharged unfit from an AA battery station in Dover.

Wednesday 9 April
The news is grim, especially in Libya, where we have been caught asleep and Neave VC, O'Connor and Gambier-Parry [senior officers] captured. A disgraceful affair. To me, from the start, O'Connor appeared to be a newspaper-boosted general.

Thursday 10 April
Sunny morning. About 5 p.m. I watched three Messerschmitts race overhead from seawards; when the sirens sounded they were well over the hills to the north. It looked as if they were on their way to bomb Hawkinge, but our fighters saw them off. Going down to the miniature range I saw a squadron, presumably ours, making Prince of Wales feathers in the clear sky over the Marsh.

Friday 11 April
Good Friday, a sunny day and fairly mild. Spent the morning collecting denim suits and distributing kit. I was held up by a sentry as I passed

Shorncliffe Camp. Much air activity and a heavy bombardment to the north or north-west.

Saturday 12 April

A mild day. After duties in Saltwood and the orderly room, I collected young Stone's kit. I am sorry he is going, he is a charming young fellow and looks as strong as a horse. He applied for the Buffs but has been posted to the RASC in Scotland. Army methods are incomprehensible! I was very depressed and fearful, and must do something about it. Churchill's speech to bombed Bristol and Cardiff helped me.

Sunday 13 April

Easter Sunday. I got up early and went to Holy Communion at the Parish Church and sat next to Street. Norris is rather 'high' [Church]. I liked his reading, but it was rather on the fast side. The siren sounded in the middle, and he paused dramatically until it stopped. General Lucock drove Stansfield, Grove-White and me to Folkestone at 3 p.m. to catch a variety show. Tried to see a show especially for the troops, which was packed. Stansfield and I had tried to get out of it by saying we had no uniforms, but Lucock got permission for us and himself to go in mufti. It was a good show, though the vulgar bits were very crude. It was not the way I would have liked to employ Easter Sunday.

Tuesday 15 April

Phyllis went to Ashford in the morning to buy laying hens, but had no success. Daphne took her Girl Guides for a hike up Hythe Hill.

Wednesday 16 April

A perfect spring day. I had a look around our old post at the Waterworks. Our sandbags and revetments have stood up wonderfully well through the winter. Large numbers of planes overhead around 10.15 p.m., with a rumbling of bombs coming from the Thames estuary.

Thursday 17 April

A heavy raid on London last night. **HEAVY R.A.F. BOMBING** All night, planes were passing over and bursts of AA gunfire awoke us several times. The result of our bombardment on the French coast was evident by a pall of smoke hiding it from view in the morning. Prior left London just as the raid started, and saw incendiary bombs and fires on either side of the line most of the way down. Tidmarsh and his wife were in the Piccadilly Hotel for the night. A bomb fell across the Circus just as they returned to it from a public shelter, and later a landmine made a huge crater in the Circus.

Friday 18 April
An overcast day. News from Greece is very disheartening. I wonder how long this strain will last. Authorities say two more months. A sea fog in the evening, and there were no planes during the night.

Saturday 19 April
Street went on leave to his grandson's christening. In the afternoon I drove Stansfield and Baker, the Section Leader, out to No. 1 Section post, which is a pair of well-sited trenches near the sewage farm, close to the Romney railway line. As we left Hythe at 2.30 p.m., they started a practice 'surprise' gas attack in the town, and it was over when we returned an hour later. I believe it was not much of a success, as there was a strong wind blowing. Daphne bicycled through it and smelt no gas. There was another attack on London and Dover. At 9.45 p.m. a continuous stream of planes passed over us from the direction of Lydd flying on to Dover. There were huge flashes in places and parachute flares.

Sunday 20 April
A fine morning. Saltwood was strong for church parade, not good but more than I expected. Chivers, who says he goes to church when he is absent from Sunday parades, was not present! Revd Peters-Jones put us in the front seats. He preached a simple sermon on faith. Lucock read the lessons. There was fighting overhead with AA gunfire during the service. In the afternoon, the whole family worked in the garden of Quarrymead.

Monday 21 April
I was awoken at dawn by the cuckoo and an alarm. Planes were very active all day, and as I walked to evening parade there was AA fire over Lympne and Folkestone. We had a sergeant from the stevedore battalion to drill us in the field next to the church – an ideal setting for the modern village-trained man, with the huge yew tree in the old parsonage, not perhaps

quite old enough to have provided bows for Agincourt. Our instructor was good, but put his foot in it by saying that the way the Guards and some regiments swung their arms above their shoulders was 'damned balls!' We had two ex-Guardsmen on parade: Fuller was behind me but the face of Tiltman, who was my left-hand man, was a study.

Tuesday 22 April
The stevedore battalion is being disbanded and its personnel scattered. Most of the NCOs and men went away today. General Forster, our Home Guard Group Commander, inspected us and wished to see our posts. We went to Saltwood first and Street allowed me to show the General around and explain matters. I am to have five Tommy guns and perhaps some Browning automatics. Stansfield and Grove-White were left behind in the office and, without picking them up, Street went off from Saltwood to the Hythe and Seabrook posts. Poor little Stansfield was very hurt. I felt flattered that Street should consider I was not a hindrance.

Wednesday 23 April
St George's Day. It is extraordinary, how we English take no notice of it and what a fuss the Scots and Irish make of their days! In the afternoon we drove out to Brabourne Lees to buy eggs and a couple of hens. We looked in at Bog Farm, which has been bought by Collier, who has tidied it up and cut away a lot of trees and hedges all around, opening it up too much. His man, young George Brooks, who has just married, is living in it. We drove across the Ashford Road, meeting a whole fleet of lorries newly turned out from some factory and driven by ATS girls. Coming back, we went down to a small farm owned by a Mrs Hogben who lived in a perfect gem of a black and white cottage and owned half a dozen spotlessly clean yellow and white cows.

Thursday 24 April
About 8.30 a.m. a Hun flew in from the Marsh and dropped a blast bomb at the end of the Harveys' garden, halfway up the path between Brockhill and Fairlight roads. It was a blast bomb and shattered windows both sides of Brockhill Road and as far as North Road. I went around to enquire on little Mrs Smith, who had all her remaining windows shattered. Sergeant Perry, on leave from the Small Arms School, gave us a lecture and demonstration on the Tommy gun, of which we have received 15 for the Company.

Saturday 26 April

I was caught in the town by the police, having forgotten to renew my road licence at the end of last month, and I had not got my insurance certificate in the car. We drove to Brabourne to collect 'Gert' and 'Daisy', the two new hens, and bought more eggs. Whilst we were in Postling village, a Blenheim bomber which seemed to be in trouble flew low over us towards Lympne. Bombs were dropped in Cheriton. One cannot put down one's feelings on the war situation. One can almost believe [Charles] Lindbergh is true in saying our leaders know we have lost it already.

Sunday 27 April

A Hun bent on mischief flew overhead at 8 a.m., so we ran downstairs. There was the sound of large explosions in the direction of Shorncliffe, but I believe it was a Bofors gun firing. We had a scratch parade. Street started with a kit and rifle inspection. I had not warned my platoon beforehand, so most of them were deficient in kit, and John Goodsell had a dirty rifle. We then waited half an hour in the cold for a Queen's NCO who took us in elementary drill. Churchill's broadcast was not as pessimistic as I had expected, but Spain and Japan are on the brink of coming in against us.

Tuesday 29 April

Gunfire over Dover, and there were numerous alarms throughout the morning. At 3 p.m. there was a fierce fight in the clouds overhead. A Spitfire broke away to replenish its ammunition, a Blenheim bomber flew low towards Hawkinge and four Hurricanes rushed up. About 10 p.m., Hickling phoned up, asking if an invasion was on.

Sunday 4 May

All clocks are two hours ahead of time today, so we were up by 5.30 a.m. We were on the ranges in the morning firing at 300 yards; a good crowd turned up. There was much air activity, and at one time I thought two Huns were about to dive on us. AA fire drove them off.

Monday 5 May

War Weapons Week commenced today in Folkestone and Hythe. A poor prospect with both towns evacuated. During the afternoon, the Huns

HYTHE.

Air Raid.

Attack on Convoy.

1939 - 1945.

Home Guard.

Raid Warden.

1. The frontispiece page of Rodney's wartime accounts, which he donated to Hythe Council and currently resides in the East Kent Archive (East Kent Archive)

2. The frontispiece page of the World War II volume from the Rodney Foster Archive (Rodney Foster Archive)

3. Rodney illustrates how he dived for cover when a Messerschmitt skimmed overhead, pursued by a British fighter, on Monday 2 September 1940 (Rodney Foster Archive)

4. An aerial battle over Hawkinge and Hythe as British planes and AA fire disrupt a German bombing raid on Thursday 5 December 1940 (Rodney Foster Archive)

MESSAGE FORM

Army Form C2128. (Pads of 100).

| | | | | | Serial No. |

CALL AND INSTRUCTIONS — IN: Lieut. R. Foster — GR. — No. of Groups. Office Date Stamp

OUT:

ABOVE THIS LINE IS FOR SIGNALS USE ONLY.

TO: A Coy, B Coy, C Coy, D Coy

FROM: 8 K H G.

Originator's Number: 1 — Date: 7 — In Reply to Number:

Enemy force estimated one div landed
last night in CAMBERSAND DYMCHURCH area
Paratroops dropped in WESTWELL area
0200 HRS have been eliminated by details
1 Bttn. Main enemy force advancing on
ASHFORD by rd ROMNEY – IVYCHURCH – HAM STREET
has reached line of R.H. Canal at
1150 HRS Airborne troops landings estimated 50
far as ten planes reported in
area of ROTHER LEVELS still continuing
ALL INFORMED

THIS MESSAGE MAY BE SENT AS WRITTEN BY ANY MEANS. EXCEPT WIRELESS — IF LIABLE TO BE INTERCEPTED OR FALL INTO ENEMY HANDS, THIS MESSAGE MUST BE SENT IN CIPHER. — ORIGINATOR'S INSTRUCTION. DEGREE OF PRIORITY: IMPORTANT — TIME OF ORIGIN 12·15 HRS

Signed R. Foster Lieut — Signed R. Foster Lieut — T.H.I.

(BELOW THIS LINE IS FOR SIGNALS USE ONLY.)

SYSTEM IN — TIME IN — SENDER — SENDER — SYSTEM OUT — TIME OUT — READER — SENDER — SYSTEM OUT — TIME OUT — READER — SENDER — T.O.R.

5. Home Guard Message Form completed by Rodney as part of an invasion exercise; it was marked 'very good' (Rodney Foster Archive)

6. German bombing raid on Tanner's Hill, Hythe, which killed Samuel Wonfor and his wife and daughter, on Monday 24 March 1941 (Rodney Foster Archive)

7. Battle practice near Etchinghill, where a platoon of KOYLIs attacked a position under fire of live rounds, Wednesday 27 May 1942 (Rodney Foster Archive)

8. A crashed Dornier in the woods behind Beachborough. All the crew were killed, but it was rumoured that the pilot was alive and was polished off by someone, Thursday 5 November 1942 (Rodney Foster Archive).

9. A German bomber flies over Hythe on Sunday 10 May 1942, ready to drop a deadly cargo of bombs (Rodney Foster Archive)

10. A few minutes later, Trice's snack bar was destroyed in the the raid and his Home Guard platoon managed to dig out the survivors, but sadly his daughter and a fellow young Home Guard private lost their lives in the rubble (Rodney Foster Archive)

11. Coastal Artillery 6-inch guns manned by the Home Guard defending the south coast and English Channel (East Kent Archive)

12. Intensive AA gunfire from batteries in Romney Marsh during a German night raid, as depicted by Rodney from his vantage point above Hythe (Rodney Foster Archive)

13. Mobile Bren guns score a hit over Hythe as Prospect Road takes a battering (Rodney Foster Archive)

14. Spitfires blow up V-1 rockets as they approach the Hythe coastline (Rodney Foster Archive)

managed to come over unnoticed and attacked Lympne and Hawkinge aerodromes and two columns of smoke rose from the former place. There was a good attendance at our evening parade. The stevedore sergeant demonstrated the Bren gun. We were to have manned our posts with the Sappers, and the Brigadier was to have been present, but that fell through.

We sink ships in the Straits

Tuesday 6 May

Huns again flew over unnoticed and attacked Lympne, Hawkinge and the Dover balloon barrage, shooting down some of the latter. They looked and sounded so like our own that I did not realise they were Huns until the firing started.

Wednesday 7 May

A sunny day with a cold north wind. Only a short session in the orderly room. Stansfield

The railway mobile gun as captured in an artistic manner by Rodney (Rodney Foster Archive)

was absent and Street was late and stayed five minutes. Lengthy alarms all day. Our big gun on the railway, called the 'Boche Buster', fired at intervals all morning and the Hun retaliated by shelling Dover.

Thursday 8 May

I received my first commission 40 years ago, and it looks as if I will have my new commission about the same date. Intense air activity all day. At 3.15 p.m. there was heavy firing in a cloud overhead, followed by a burst from ground defences from the direction of the ranges. I heard that two Huns had been shot down, with every post in the neighbourhood claiming them as their victims. Parade at 7.30 p.m. at 'A' Company hut. Street seems to have failed to obtain an instructor, and told section leaders to demonstrate the Tommy gun to their men. There were 24 raiders brought down on Wednesday and 13 today – cheering news.

Saturday 10 May

Rudolph Hess landed in Scotland. At night, the Hun came over in large numbers on their way to bomb London.

The extensive Kent Home Guard exercise at Newland's sandpit (Rodney Foster Archive)

Sunday 11 May

The raid was on London last night. The House of Commons burnt out, and Westminster Abbey and many other places damaged. We brought down 33 of their bombers. Fifteen officers and NCOs of 'A' Company left in a lorry from the Queen's at 9.30 a.m. to Newland's sandpit where 4,000 Home Guards from East and West Kent watched demonstrations of all the weapons we may be issued with. Major Northover himself fired his projector into an iron contraption meant to be a tank. We were shown explosives and booby traps. One, like a large Molotov, which was fired by electricity, sent up a huge column of black smoke which curled over and singed the grass on the top of the pit, causing a stampede, and nearly all including myself fell or were knocked down. The only casualty was an anaemic fellow who had his glasses crushed on his nose. We looked like the soldiers in the battle in the woods in *Alice Through the Looking Glass*. We saw the very latest light tank demonstrations over rough ground attacked by Bren guns and dive-bombed by a Hudson aircraft. Finally, we were shown the right and wrong way for sentries at a post to hold up a lorry full of men. It was a fine sunny day, and the country looked beautiful. At 9.30 p.m., I watched six Hun bombers flying low over to Lympne, where they were met by our fighters, and the sky was soon full of tracer bullets like fireflies in the sky. I bolted indoors and saw one of our planes fly lower than the roof of the house next door. I believe we shot down two Huns.

Monday 12 May

At 1.45 a.m. I was woken by a barrage of fire towards the coast, and the windows on that side of the house rattled. I heard later that we brought down a night bomber near Willesborough (Ashford). Stansfield nagged Grove-White again, and the latter certainly was extra stupid. The first rain for nearly two months fell. I feel no inclination to listen to the news these days, and am impatient at the conduct of the war.

Tuesday 13 May

Everyone very excited at the Hess affair, and most people think it is the end of the war. I feel sure that it is a put-up job by Hitler, and they think we will fête him and he will manage to get away with valuable information. I trust we will treat him for the nasty brute he is. Daphne drove Phyllis into Folkestone to spring-clean 18 Kingsnorth Gardens. I went in the afternoon and brought them back to a marvellous tea of toast, butter and strawberry jam at the Frogmore. I found the clinic closed and young Neville gone with no word.

Friday 16 May

Phyllis went to Folkestone in the morning. At noon, the Hun got active and there was a huge scrap in the clouds. One Hun bomber attacked Hawkinge, was met and hit by ground defences and turned back flying low over Hythe with smoke streaming from it. It definitely came down in the sea. Daphne and I drove into Folkestone in the afternoon, picking up Phyllis after shopping and had tea in the Frogmore and saw the film *Kipps*. It was exceedingly well acted and was most amusing. We drove back about 7 p.m., and halfway down Grimstone Avenue a furious din started overhead and the sky was full of Bofors shells, so we abandoned the car and fled to the rather shallow porch of an empty house. About six Messerschmitts returning from Hawkinge sailed low over the town, machine gunning and being fired at by all manner of weapons. The air was alive with bullets, and I saw something crash through the trees in the square and found later it was a dud Bofors shell.

Saturday 17 May

A blazing hot summer day, and almost continuous air activity very high up. At 3 p.m. I met Major Scott and his subaltern, Williams. The new scheme is to make strong points at all the junctions where two roads meet, and turn the village into a keep. They are going to dump wire and other defensive material at each site for us to use. We have only 65 to 70 men, including the Sappers, to man these eight posts, and in my opinion Scott has made them too big in area. Williams is an interesting lad. He was in the Guernsey and Lofoten Islands commando raids. He said the former was a flop, as they got there too late; and in the latter our men were so cold they could not get out of their boats until the locals gave them hot coffee. After tea, I drove Phyllis around Brabourne collecting eggs; she gathered three dozen. At midnight, our bombers gave the Channel ports a severe pounding whilst the Hun bombers flew over us. Spain and France are openly helping the Germans, and there is talk of open war between us and France.

Sunday 18 May

I had a disturbed night, being awoken by bomb explosions around 5 a.m. I was picked up by Street in Castle Road at 7.45 a.m. and then we collected Stansfield and Grove-White at the Ritz Cinema. A very pleasant drive to

Maidstone, the country looking pretty. We drove around Leeds Castle grounds, passing a lot of houses in the woods where the Hun bombers, frustrated from reaching London last Sunday, had unloaded their bombs, killing a number of people. We parked the car at the gates of Mote Park and walked down to the Granada Cinema

General Montgomery inspecting the Kent Home Guard on one of their exercises (War and Peace Collection 2476)

where General Montgomery, the Corps Commander, lectured officers of the Home Guard from the whole of Kent. He is a non-smoker and teetotaller and after telling us we must not smoke, gave us 30 seconds to 'cough it up'. The result of such auto-suggestion was to cause far more coughing than there would have been. He insisted too much on the Home Guard being as fit as the regulars, and on us carrying out duties of patrols etc. At the end there was an amusing play of a Home Guard platoon rounding up a parachutist and other Huns from a troop carrier. We got back at 2 p.m. Daphne read in the papers of the escape from Greece of one of the last party of our officers and men, young Street being mentioned amongst them, so I rang up Street. He had heard nothing until he returned to find a phone message from his daughter. Stansfield had brought a paper with him, but Street had only looked up a race on which he had had a bet.

Friday 23 May
Cold, misty and wet. Craufurd-Stuart looked in for a short time and Dr Buttery, who has been made Battalion MO and a Major, also came to arrange first-aid posts, which Street suggested were not necessary. Phyllis

and Daphne drove to their dressmaker and after lunch to Brabourne collecting eggs.

Saturday 24 May
Empire Day. Rather cold and windy day. After lunch, we drove to Canterbury through the Elham Valley stopping at Elham to collect eggs. Canterbury full of troops and civilians. We found [Rodney's sister-in-law] Eva and [her daughter] Joan looking well and their flat was warm and airy. We took them to Lefevres for tea. The place was so crowded our party was seated between three tables at first. After tea, I took a stroll. The cathedral does not appear to be much damaged, and may have been repaired, but along the road every house and shop has been hit. A trip of 30 miles, the furthest I have driven for more than a year.

Sunday 25 May
I went to Communion at 8 a.m. Sounds like Dover was being bombed. It looks as if HMS *Hood* had the same faults in her magazine feed as our pre-Jutland ships. Very disgraceful, if true. The situation in Crete sounds hopeless. How can our troops fight without air support?

Monday 26 May
The military authorities are full of invasion scares, and say it is imminent. They now say we must not expect aid for the Air Force and Navy. We are told the *Bismarck* has been hit.

> THE Bismarck is being hotly pursued by our naval forces and aircraft of the Fleet Air Arm. This evening she was hit by one of our torpedoes from the air. "The hunt continues," says the Admiralty; and the whole world waits for news.

Tuesday 27 May
My birthday (59). A very happy one! We sank the *Bismarck*, HMS *Rodney* being chiefly responsible for silencing her. I heard the news at midday. Craufurd-Stuart turned up at orderly room full of lewd tales. We drove into Folkestone and had tea at the Frogmore. At 9.30 p.m. in a cloudy sky our planes rushed around skimming our chimney pots.

Wednesday 28 May

Planes flying around from early on. Machine gunning at Hawkinge and Lydd. Very sharp burst outside the house as I was taking a bath. At midnight, our 'Boche Buster' crashed out a salvo of six shots behind our house, which shook at the blasts.

MAYOR AND MAYORESS KILLED

Thursday 29 May

Two very large bombs were dropped on the residential part of Morehall [Folkestone] in which nine people were killed, including the Mayor and his wife. Swarms of troops poured in from the west. They were the whole Canadian Corps from around

Morehall Avenue, Folkestone, after the bombing
(Folkestone Library F/WW2/44)

Guildford on manoeuvres. They were supposed to be an enemy force that landed in the back areas of Kent trying to capture Folkestone. The umpires had declared they had been wiped out by the defenders around Ashford, but had been allowed to continue to the coast for exercise.

Sunday 1 June

Firing on the range. Little Chappell qualified at grouping, but completely missed the target at 200 yards. Jack Goodsell and Holmes shot well and scored 15. The Queen's had a ceremonial parade on Reach Field with band and colours to celebrate the Battle of Camperdown, in which engagement the regiment acted as marines. It was such an attraction that half our Home

Guard were late. The news came in the evening that we have been driven out of Crete and lost 10,000 prisoners and many dead. It was a most disgraceful show.

Monday 2 June
Cold overcast day, more like November than June. Not much of a bank holiday! We officers all turned up to orderly room, and afterwards I drove Stansfield to the police station and TA Hut counting ammunition and to Paddock House to collect rations. Twenty turned up to my evening parade – the last in the Boys Club. After this we must work out of doors. We had the Northover Projectors [anti-tank weapons] out and played with them. I picked up a recruit, a little fellow called Anthony Foord, only 5' 2" and looks 15 but is 16½.

Thursday 5 June
Shooting on the 30-yards range with the Tommy gun at 7.30 p.m. Several of my platoon shot well, others badly. Old Harding of No. 2 Platoon let off all his rounds in one burst, nearly knocking himself over and spraying the surrounding country with bullets.

Saturday 7 June
I woke myself and Phyllis by a violent fit of coughing. Soon after we heard the sound of Bofors, machine gunning, planes and AA fire. It sounded as if our night fighters were attacking bombers. Later I learnt that Hun bombers attacked a convoy of ours coming up the Strait and were met by AA fire from the ships and by our fighters. In the afternoon Phyllis and Daphne drove into Ashford shopping. There was much air activity, our fighters flying about the house tops whilst our bombers went over. Through Milly, I have heard that Maurice, who was doing Censor work and was last heard of in Crete but may have gone to Athens, had failed to arrive at the place of embarkation and is presumed missing. We should, now Germany is occupied in the east, launch our millions now in England across the Channel and win the war. But I suspect that our complements of tanks, planes and pilots are far below what they should be.

Sunday 8 June
We had a match on the range against the 2/7th Queen's, which was to have been 16-a-side at 200 and 300 yards range. No officer, markers or

ammunition turned up, and only eight of the team. Street gave them ammunition and allowed the men to shoot twice, which was some advantage to them, but our men shot very badly, especially at 200 yards when they led us by 40 points. At the 300 yards range, the scores were equal. Street and I were to have fired first, but he suggested we should stand down. Then, as Whiting did not turn up, he took his place. He is a very good shot, but he might have given the place to me. Some activity at night, but I was too sleepy to realise what was happening.

Monday 9 June
We and the Free French have crossed the Syrian border. Plenty of air activity, with planes quartering the sky and the constant AA and machine gun fire. Huns flew low over the house during the afternoon. Phyllis and Daphne went out with a small party in Bob Allen's taxi to a Christian Science lecture in Canterbury, returning home about 8.30 p.m.

Wednesday 11 June
I was awoken by 'alarms' and the sound of planes dashing about. Again in the afternoon there was considerable air activity, chiefly by our planes. Phyllis and Daphne drove out into the country collecting eggs, and brought back six dozen. Old Bush turned up after supper and stopped us hearing the news. He is here for two days from Bude, where he is being well looked after and looks remarkably well. He is 84 and still bathes every day, helps at harvesting and digs in others' allotments.

Thursday 12 June
I woke several times, and each time planes were zooming overhead. Our bombers attacked the cruiser which had accompanied the *Bismarck* and had run for Brest. At 4 a.m., the Huns dropped two landmines on Tower Hamlets, the most congested area of Dover, killing about 30 people. There was an explosion, and I saw a huge column of smoke shoot up above the houses and mushroom out. The Queen's blew up a mine beyond the ranges by mistake, but no one was hurt. I drove into Folkestone after lunch, visiting my tailor. In the evening we had the final shoot of the Tommy gun course. At the end, Street challenged me to 10 rounds individual. He had fired the gun previously but I had not done so. He got a possible 10. I had eight hits, but 'Bone' Foster hinted that he had put more than 10 rounds in my magazine!

Saturday 14 June

I cut the hedges in the afternoon. I have decided it is no use worrying about this war, and do not propose in the future to read the paper or listen to the news. The Libyan campaign, for example, is beyond my comprehension.

Sunday 15 June

I woke up dreaming that I was with my platoon at the back of Saltwood, glancing towards the seafront. I saw the sky full of descending parachutes. I called to my men to run home, put on uniform and man their posts, but they said there was nothing to fuss about and carried on with what they were doing! There was no morning parade, but the Intelligence Officer of the 168th Brigade came up to enquire if any of the Saltwood Platoon were still in his area. He was an absolute child, almost young enough to be my grandson, but addressed me correctly as 'Mr Foster' except when he forgot and called me 'Sir'. I met Street and Boxall, the new Brigadier of the 206th, to whom we now belong. The latter asked me to show him my scheme of defence.

Monday 16 June

We are deep into summer weather now. We were awoken early by our own planes tearing about very low. Distant boom of guns in the direction of the Thames estuary. I drove Stansfield into Folkestone, collecting kit from Battalion HQ. Coming back we saw Spitfires skim the cornfields near the top of Blackhouse Hill. The afternoon was a continuous rumble of guns and the sound of high-flying planes. In the evening, my platoon assembled in almost full strength in Sandling sandpit. Street, Stansfield, the village constable and two small boys being also present. We fired our Northover Projector, with Holmes getting a perfect bullseye, and the other three section leaders only just missed a sleeper stuck on its end at 75 yards. We threw some AW bombs by hand. A Spitfire circled the pit to find out what we were up to.

Tuesday 17 June

A piping hot day. Drove Phyllis into Folkestone. Large formation of our bombers flew overhead on their way to bomb the French

BIGGEST DAYLIGHT ATTACK

'invasion' ports. They were followed home by the enemy, who were attacked by our fighters and driven back across the Channel. I hear that the Air Force say the *Scharnhorst* and *Gneisenau* are so well camouflaged they do not yet know for certain if they have located them!!

Wednesday 18 June
Another hot day. Two stevedores broke through the fence and pulled up a bed of immature onions and did other damage. Daphne was very angry. I went over and saw a very canny Scotch Major about it. I left without being certain if he would do anything. However, soon after I went to see the damage Daphne caught him there and gave him a good dressing down! Phyllis and Daphne drove into the countryside for eggs but the supply is getting less. Our planes flew over throughout the day and evening and bombed the French coast.

Thursday 19 June
A hot night. We had firing on the range at 100 and 200 yards in the evening. My new recruit, young Foord, shot very well. A Lysander escorted by three Spitfires flew over our heads.

Friday 20 June
Daphne was in Folkestone having her hair waved. Everybody full of a possible attack on Russia by Germany. I am prepared to bet 100 to 1 it won't come off. Hitler must be mad or very desperate to do such a thing.

Saturday 21 June
A blazing hot day. Street and I met Appleby, the CO of the 14th Durhams, and two subalterns on Saltwood Green at 9.45 a.m. and rushed all over the place selecting posts for my platoon. I had originally to defend five posts, but now have only three, all new ones. That number, however, is at least one more than I can run properly. Modern warfare is a strange mix-up. All the posts, rifle pits, machine gun nests and .75 inch guns appeared to be sited to fire into each other's backs. In the afternoon, Stansfield and I collected ammunition, and warned his section commanders of manoeuvres which are to take place between the 24th and the 26th. After tea I drove to Stone Farm, Bluehouse, Sandling and Saltwood warning my people. The troops are to practise dropping from parachutes and landing by troop carriers, and we must impress on our people that there must be

no shooting. It seems strange to have it in sight of occupied France. I wonder if we are going over! Street suggested that it might be the real thing.

Sunday 22 June
Hitler, after his usual ranting speech, has launched Finns and Romanians against Russia. He must be mad, or desperate for supplies. I was prepared to bet 100 to 1 that he would not attack her, even though he is sure of a quick victory and will stop when he has the Ukraine. Another blazing hot day. A party of us drove out to Aldington to an old mill, once the weekend cottage of Jeanne de Casalis the actress, where we were joined by some other Home Guard and were lectured by two Sapper NCOs on the construction and laying of anti-tank mines. They had obviously only just read up on the subject, for they made mistakes and contradicted each other and themselves. They had a 10-minute break about 11.30 a.m. and at 12.30 p.m. broke off for 1½ hours for a visit to the pub and lunch. Afterwards, we went down to a field and exploded a mine. The whole show could have been done in two hours. The explosion was violent, but they said it would only damage a tank and not destroy it. The 14th Durhams came into the stevedore billets in our road today.

Tuesday 24 June
Intensive invasion scare is being started. The Corps Commander insists on all the towns on the coast as well as Canterbury being compulsorily evacuated.

Thursday 26 June
The manoeuvres ended in a pitched battle about 4 a.m. around Saltwood village. I slept through it, and no parachute troops came our way. Street told us that the new invasion scare entails the evacuation of banks, shops and the populace. They hope to keep 50% of the Home Guard by offering those in occupation £3.10 a week, an inadequate wage. We had shooting on the ranges in the evening. My platoon was represented almost entirely by my recruits, who shot very well at 300 yards, although most of them had never handled a rifle. I drove my three Grenadiers up the hill, and Hickling and I were caught by pretty Minnie Hesketh (now Turner) and invited to their Wedding Supper. There were only the Dearmans and two of the stevedore officers present. Minnie said most of the guests had gone,

but I believe the village boycotted the show. There were no signs of our planes in the evening.

Sunday 29 June

Captain Whitfield of 'B' Company of the 14th Durhams came round to see me at 11 a.m. and drove me to Saltwood village, where he showed me the only alteration in our last disposition: a couple of Northovers in Mrs Bryant's hedge. I had a lazy afternoon. After the 9 p.m. news, Quentin Reynolds, an American reporter, talked to Dr Goebbels – biting sarcasm in a Southerner's drawl and a very fine testimony to the British. The best speech I have ever heard. I would like a record of it!

Monday 30 June

Busy day collecting, exchanging and storing kit. At our evening parade, 26 turned up including all our recruits; a platoon of the Durhams demonstrated laying Dannert wire around the field opposite the old Rectory, and my people finished it off. The fat subaltern of the Durhams started our men off saying: 'Get a move on, you don't realise my men have already done a full day's work!' I explained to him that mine had done a full and in many cases a much harder day's work, and he apologised to them.

Friday 4 July

A silly fuss being made about celebrating American Independence Day in this country. What fools our rulers are! Fuller tells me the egg rationing is in a dreadful muddle. Poultry keepers, during the first week, had no quota returned to them for their own registered customers. Ashford centre is stacked with eggs, and they now tell the poultry keepers to 'use their own discretion' in bringing in their eggs. Hudson (Minister of Agriculture) is not on speaking terms with Woolton (Rationing). There was the usual air activity in the evening. We discovered that the Durhams had got over the fence and stolen a lot of onions and lettuces from the garden. Attack on our convoys in the Channel. Daphne and I went in our nightclothes to Mrs Russell's lookout, but it was by then almost over.

Saturday 5 July

I went over to see Captain Whitfield and complained about the theft of vegetables. He seemed genuinely upset about it. After tea, Phyllis and I drove to the Stansfields' and admired his roses and brought them back here to admire ours.

Sunday 6 July

The 7th Queen's left and have been replaced by the London Irish from up the Ashford Road. These latter have a comic-opera kit – black tam-o'-shanters, blue hackles, khaki tunics and tan kilts or 'plus fours'. My platoon had firing practice in Sandling rifle pit with Ross rifles, Browning automatics and Tommy guns. We shot off the last practice in the latter and passed three recruits with their eight-inch groups. It was very hot in the pit.

Monday 7 July

Hotter day than ever, about 80° in the shade. Violent explosion shook the house at about 6 a.m. The Durhams said it was a sea mine that our ships exploded. Only a few turned up at evening parade, so I had to send the Durham Sergeant away. Bean and Wright preferred to go to a dance! I took my men to view their several posts.

Tuesday 8 July

A Lieutenant Colonel Prawle turned up at the office with Craufurd-Stuart. He has just given up a Brigade on reaching 55 and has been made a sort of Staff Officer to the East Kent Home Guard. Street was in one of his 'don't want anything' moods. It was so hot I slept only with a sheet on.

Wednesday 9 July

Gunfire in the direction of Dover during the morning. About 4 p.m. a squadron of 12 light bombers flew out over the Marsh. They returned later, but I could not count 12. There are big troop movements behind us going north, and the German authorities are telling their people of a possible invasion of England. Phyllis slept in the porch on Daphne's camp bed.

Saturday 12 July

Cool breeze turned down the heat. I started my second round of hedge cutting. In the evening, there were sounds of big guns coming gradually nearer, so I went over to Mrs Russell's to see what was happening. The sky in the east was black. Coming back I realised it was thunder, and the storm soon came up and there was a heavy downpour of rain. By listening to Street and reading the 'Tory' papers I have come to the conclusion that our politicians believe the country won't stand the casualties of the last war. The Army chiefs know that if we attack we cannot avoid casualties, so they refuse to move. They are quite sure Russia will soon be beaten, but also expect a revolution to the Right there and an alliance of the Right with Germany to attack India with the Japanese joining in. But nothing is to be done to stop all this. We are to wait passively for Hitler to turn on us, and hope to defeat an invasion, but are not sure if they will. Street says the Germans cannot possibly invade us, but says it as if he was trying to destroy his own doubts.

ME109F CAPTURED WITH CRACK PILOT

A German crack pilot and his almost intact Me109F were captured on Thursday when a heavy British bomber forced the enemy pilot down in a field near St. Margaret's Bay, on the Kent coast. The German pilot is Hauptman Rolf Peter Pingel, who claims 22 victories and holds the Ritter Kreuz. *12. 7. 1941*

Monday 14 July
Margate was dive-bombed during the night. Sergeant Thomas of the police came to the office with instructions for the Home Guard to demobilise all petrol pumps; yet another job for us. We are expected also to close up all roadblocks and man posts all over the place. I watched 12 'E' boats come up from the east from Mrs Russell's garden. Great air activity again.

Tuesday 15 July
Street told us that Macnamara, Commander of the London Irish and an MP, told his officers that the Russians would be beaten in a month and an attempt at the invasion of England would be definitely made in the first week of December. The arrangement is for the whole of the coastal area to be devastated by us. The Navy cannot help us; the Air Force is not mentioned. When I protested, Street said it was all said to keep up the morale of the troops!!!

Thursday 17 July

The news today was all pro-Russian and of counter-attacks and German failures. The Durhams had arranged to demonstrate to us the methods of crossing barbed wire, but they failed at the last minute, so Street had individual shooting at falling plates. Prior, who is becoming a very good shot, knocked his three plates with his first three shots. Street challenged me, missed with every shot and was very annoyed with himself. I followed and did the same. A Spitfire and a Lysander returning from a patrol flew along the seafront below the level of the rooftops.

The village of Stelling Minnis (War and Peace Collection 0742)

Saturday 19 July

Daphne left at 9 a.m. for Bodsham Farm near Stelling Minnis, where she picked strawberries for jam making until 4.30 p.m. We talked about shooting in India at orderly room. I met the elder Dearman (employed on the railway) in the afternoon. He says they are very busy, and that a great deal of material, including heavy cranes, is going into Dover, and it was thought that the harbour would soon be re-opened. The news is that Goering said his air force was not fit for a war with Russia, and is in disgrace in a concentration camp, and that Hitler has had a fit. We are making a great song over chalking up 'V's in occupied countries. Unless we do something ourselves, in my opinion we will be hated when these poor devils are rounded up and shot.

Sunday 20 July

Today is the day the invaded countries have been asked to intensify the 'V' campaign, and 'V's have been chalked everywhere here. The Italians say we are going to do something. If we do nothing, the invaded countries will be told we have let them down again and all our sympathisers having given themselves away will be rounded up. At the sandpit in the morning, Saltwood Platoon had a record attendance of 30 out of 42. After 7.30 p.m., the Machkevitches turned up just as we were starting supper and stayed until 8.45 p.m. He is in a shipping firm and is a subaltern in the [AA] battery on the seafront. She struck me as being German or Swiss. He told us that at the 206th Brigade field day last week the London Irish destroyed a truck of the London Scottish, and the two units began throwing stones at each other! He also heard that guerrilla warfare had broken out in Norway.

Monday 21 July

The two Brigadiers are fighting over 'A' Company Home Guard. The 206th say many of its number live in their area, but only one section functions in it. At evening parade, 25 turned up. All the recruits turned up and were drilled by the Company Sergeant Major of 'B' Company Durham Light Infantry. He was too mild. Street came and passed four of my men for their proficiency badge. Kite took the rest in demonstrating the Browning, and Fuller lectured the NCOs on commanding their sections properly. Fuller gave me a lift home, as a squadron of Hurricanes circled over and headed out to sea.

Tuesday 22 July

Fighting overhead during the morning. We all went to see the film *No, No, Nanette*. It was quite amusing, but not much like the play. My friend Zasu Pitts was in it – very subdued and 'elderly'. In the evening our 'E' boats came up the Strait.

Wednesday 23 July

A very short orderly room. Daphne heard that the explosion yesterday morning was caused by three dogs running over a minefield; two of them were blown up. During the day, we lost five bombers and five fighters and only claimed five Huns down. Our casualties have been heavy for some time, and the results do not appear to justify them.

Thursday 24 July

Yesterday evening, 'B' Company Durham Light Infantry had a number of lorries outside their billets, and this morning a fleet of lorries came up the road and all day all kinds of stores were being loaded. I thought they were on the move, but they are still here. Our 'E' boats were on the scene early. Our bombers went over twice in the morning. A heavy tank passed through Saltwood. The battery at the Imperial Hotel had a practice shot at a towed target. In the morning, Vernal rang up to say the battalion wants a Quartermaster Sergeant with pay of 10/- a week. Stansfield suggested I should take it, and I felt like doing so as I want the pay, but I dislike the idea of being reduced to NCO. Street said it was just the job for me, as if he thought me no use as a Platoon Commander, but he may not have meant it that way.

Monday 28 July

At evening parade 25 turned up. I lectured them on being turned out smart; so many put their uniforms on anyhow. The NCOs drilled their sections, and we finished with a demonstration of constructing and dismantling a roadblock. Coveney's section, most of whom have been working on them, put a small one up in three minutes. Daphne went to an evening show given by the Air Cadets in Folkestone.

Tuesday 29 July

Daphne held a ceremony of enrolment of Brownies in the public gardens. Phyllis attended and presented certificates to some Guides. Our Intelligence Summary says our Air Force is now superior to that of the Germans, who had very heavy losses over here and in Greece and Crete, and they have now no hope of catching us up.

Thursday 31 July

At orderly room, I helped Stansfield make out a new return which was sprung upon us. The Russians seem to be holding the Germans so far. We, however, have to help them by bombing ports in north Norway, an expensive business. We lost 25 bombers and fighters, and only destroyed five Hun fighters.

Friday 1 August

Rain all night and in the morning. The Green Howards staged an invasion stunt, defending bridges in Sandling Park. They collected a number of civilians from Saltwood to represent a fleeing population.

Saturday 2 August
The sun came out in the afternoon, and so did our planes. There was not an alarm all day. The situation is beyond my understanding. The Russians are holding up the Germans and inflicting losses, not perhaps as great as they claim, but they may collapse suddenly or make peace. The Germans, according to our intelligence, have all their troops over there, only seven Divisions of troops being in the West; they have also got all their air force over there. Invasion in September and intensive bombing next winter is still the cry. Are we going over too soon? I hope so and sometimes I think we are.

Sunday 3 August
Mills grenade instruction in the morning. The four Saltwood men, although only one is an ex-soldier, were better at throwing than all the rest. Planes were busy in the afternoon, and in the evening there was a distant sound of bombing and a fight over Hawkinge way.

Monday 4 August
Bank Holiday. A misty morning, and a warm day. I walked up Seabrook Road to do some RSPCA business with Lancashire. Local manoeuvres began today, the 168th Brigade (London Scottish, London Irish and London Rifles) holding a position against the 187th and 206th Brigades, representing an invading force. The Durhams in our road left by the afternoon to take up their positions. At night there were isolated rifle shots, a motorcyclist roared up and down our road and a tank apparently lost itself. It repeatedly approached, turned and went off again.

Tuesday 5 August
The local war seems to consist of pairs of men hanging about every corner of the town. In the evening, a battalion of infantry, motorcyclists, Ironside tanks and lorries streamed along our road.

Thursday 7 August

When we awoke, the sky was full of planes, squadron after squadron flying on to France. A Durham Company cook told me they ('the Jerries') were slaughtered in Red Lion Square running into nests of hidden machine guns. Individual firing at 200 yards in the evening. The few of my platoon who turned up shot very badly.

Sunday 10 August

A fine day. Browning and Tommy guns assembled in the hut for inspection by an armourer tomorrow. Our grenade instructor did not turn up, so Street gave the men instruction in landscape targets. We had tea with Mrs Smith, widow of a Shropshire Officer I knew in India. The other guests were the Stebblings – why are most schoolmasters dirty? – and a girl called Gosling, who drives a YMCA Canteen van and is billeted with them.

August 11, 1940

Do you remember what happened a year ago today?

Four hundred German planes swarmed across the English Channel to bomb Portland, Dover, and British shipping. They made the biggest air attack ever launched against this country up to that day.

Sixty of them did not go back. The R.A.F., fighting on the defensive, shot them down at a cost of 26 British planes, with two pilots safe.

August 10, 1941

Do you know what happened yesterday?

Swarms of R.A.F. fighters, on the offensive, flew across the Channel several times and went hunting for German planes ove Occupied France.

They did not see one.

And not one German plane flew over Britain.

Monday 11 August

At 6 p.m. I drove down to the TA Hut and collected 12 rifles for my platoon. When I distributed them at evening parade, I found I was one short but refused to worry about it. Only 16 turned up owing to the bad weather. I gave them some marching practice to warm them up, then practice in the landscape target using the real landscape.

Tuesday 12 August
I went to the TA Hut and found my missing rifle with No. 9
Section's guns. No. 1 Section reported that their post camouflaged as a
haystack near Botolph's Bridge was missing! Street and Stansfield went
to look for it, and found it had been demolished. The London Rifles
knew nothing about it and it is not known who did it – some say the
Royal Engineers, some the Royal Artillery. The Home Guard
rationing is an extraordinary muddle. We have to provide our own
food for the first 24 hours of the invasion. The War Office give us an
emergency pack which we must not eat, the Ministry of Food
give us a two-day ration, we then have to buy our food from a retailer
who has remained behind after the evacuation, and finally the Army
feeds us.

Wednesday 13 August
As the Huns reach the Black Sea, we and Russia offer the Turks protection;
they will surely say: 'No thank you!' We lost 15 planes in daylight sweeps
today! A solitary AA gun fired at 10 p.m., and we went to Mrs Russell's
garden and watched pairs of sea-level searchlights at Folkestone, Hythe
and Dymchurch quartering the Strait with their beams.

Thursday 14 August
About 5 p.m. there was a fight overhead; neither the papers nor the
wireless ever tell us of these fights. We are given to understand that no
Huns come over England in daylight. We had team shooting at falling
plates on the range. Only 12 of my platoon turned up, so I made
them into two sections under James Kerr and John Goodsell. The latter
team shot well. We were officially told of the meeting of Churchill and
Roosevelt in the Atlantic today. Street says the rumour has been flying
about London that the Premier had left England for days, so those
in high places don't set a very good example [on spreading rumours].
It seems to me to be a very futile affair, leading nowhere, but I suppose
Roosevelt knows his own people. We bombed the invasion ports at
night.

Friday 15 August
We watched two destroyers in the Channel bombing France, and them
being bombed from there or the air. High columns of water shot up

around them. With the aid of glasses, we also saw one of our refuge rafts for RAF crews, which at first we thought was a submarine.

Saturday 16 August
I drove around distributing rifles at Sandling and Stone Farm, and arranging for the Waterworks men to shoot tomorrow. There has been a bust-up in our ARP. Stokes, the Controller, has booted out Holyoak and Captain Brown, the latter for his hasty temper and the former because he refused to do two jobs. Mrs Holyoak got up in the council meeting and said it was a lie. Carr is also resigning because he says there is no work to do. In the meantime, Stokes has put his own daughter in as a typist. In the evening, there was a scrap overhead passing from east to west. I could see the white lines of the exhaust flumes and puffs of white smoke, like AA shells bursting.

Monday 18 August
The town is again full of the old scares of invasion and compulsory evacuation. Our bombers in large numbers flew overhead towards France; I counted 36 but the Fuller girl counted 80. Apparently, a Hun followed them home. As soon as they passed, the alarm was sounded and planes zoomed overhead. Twenty turned up for evening parade, the last we can have out of doors, as the evenings are now too dark. Kite took them in bayonet fighting.

Saturday 23 August
A new moon, and the end of St Swithin's. It was raining when we woke up, rained all day with scarcely a stop and was raining when we went to bed!

Sunday 24 August
Another damp day. Parade in the morning at the SAS miniature range to pick platoon teams for the *Country Life* competition. Street planned it for 11 a.m., because he did not want our men to be mixed up with the London Irish church parade. The Hythe platoons turned up in force. I had told my poor shots not to come. Two good men were absent. Street did everything in a rush, and did not have the rifle sights adjusted. All my first men shot well, but the rifle threw high right, so their scores were low until at the end it was put right. I saw one of our planes get up from Hawkinge, and a

number of others come in from the south-east, but there was no sound of fighting.

Monday 25 August
Street attended our evening parade and passed four men for proficiency badges. John Goodsell passed with honours. His improvement is astonishing.

Tuesday 26 August
There were to have been manoeuvres around Ashford, Sellindge and the Marsh at the [coming] weekend and Street, Grove-White and I were to have umpired and to attend a conference on Thursday at Ashford, but today were told it was cancelled owing to the harvest being held up by rain. Daphne drove out to Burmarsh in a taxi with four other girls, to a cocktail party given by a company of the Royal Berkshires. She enjoyed herself and did not get back until after 2 a.m.

Saturday 30 August
Phyllis and Daphne drove to Brabourne after lunch and secured a dozen eggs and two pounds of blackberries. The Russians are still hanging on and the Japanese are not yet in. We do nothing except send our poor airmen over day and night on futile raids losing 10 to 20 planes a day.

Peaceful Saltwood village green before the outbreak of war

Sunday 31 August

Parade at 10.30 a.m. on Saltwood village green, at which 24 turned up. The second in command of 'B' Company, the Durhams, took us round our posts and those of the platoon guarding our area. He fully explained, very lucidly, the nature of and the reasons for the defensive positions. He made me feel very confident in the efficiency of the defensive scheme, the first time since the war started. There was much air activity from midday. This is nearly the end of the second year of the war. The prospect in many ways seems worse than ever, and the inertia of our Army if not inexplicable is at least indefensible.

Monday 1 September

Daphne's birthday. A disturbed night through both cats being out at bedtime and coming in at different times on to our beds. We went to the Savoy Cinema to see *The Letter* by Somerset Maugham, a well-acted tragedy but rather an unconvincing story. We left in the middle of the second (a wild west) film.

Wednesday 3 September

I was awoken at 3 a.m. by two bursts of gunfire from the direction of the Marsh. Great air and naval activity, although there was a thick sea mist over land and sea. Grove-White told us he heard that the Canadian Prime Minister, Mackenzie King, is very unpopular with his men. At an inspection of his Canadian troops at Aldershot the men hissed and booed his arrival.

Thursday 4 September

A perfect day. 'B' Company of the Durhams went off in lorries early, there was a 'stunt' on the canal banks, air activity at midday, our speedboats swept down the Strait at 3 p.m. and a large force of our bombers went over at 4 p.m. We fired off the competition in the evening; my platoon shot very badly and were last.

Friday 5 September

Last Saturday, the AA Gunners in the post near Botolph's Bridge set light somehow to some cordite stored in their office and five men, including Lieutenant Robins, a local man, were fatally burnt. Daphne drove me to Sandling to the 11.30 a.m. train. The Pullman carriage was called 'Daphne'. I saw the 'Boche Buster' out

Botolph's Bridge Inn, West Hythe (Folkestone Library H/HIP/1)

in the open being cleaned just short of Ashford. I reached Guildford at 2.30 p.m. I looked up Mr Blaxland, and he was looking well but pining to get home.

Sunday 7 September

Mr Blaxland sent for me in the morning, and went through his will, investments and request that we trustees should help Nancy. I have heard it all a dozen times.

Monday 8 September

Mother's birthday. In the afternoon I took Mr Blaxland down the London Road in a wicker chair. It was hard work pushing him, especially when Nancy, trying to help, pulled the wrong way!

Tuesday 9 September

Milly overslept in the morning. She only has a char in the morning, no other maid, and is generally up at 7.30 a.m. After lunch I again took Mr Blaxland out to Stoke Church and along the by-pass past Stoke Park to the river. It was a hot day, quite a long way and I had both Nancy and Mr Blaxland pushing against me. My left arm was numb when I got back.

Thursday 11 September

I went around in the morning to say goodbye to the Blaxlands and left after lunch. I had an hour's wait and tea at Tonbridge, and got back to Hythe at 6.30 p.m. In my absence, Dover had been shelled and Ramsgate bombed, with casualties at both places.

Saturday 13 September

I drove down early and helped Stansfield load up all our reserve rations, spare kit and equipment then drove round to Stone Farm, Bluehouse and Sandling. I heard the battalion of Durhams are shortly going, and the London Irish will take over Saltwood and that the whole London Division is to be replaced in November.

Tuesday 16 September

There was a 'stunt' on all day. The six-inch guns by the Imperial Hotel were supposed to be besieged by sea and land, and the Gunners had to eat their emergency rations. They fired at a target out at sea and bombers dived at them. Daphne and I went to the lookout in Mrs Russell's garden at night and saw a row of twinkling lights on the sea, some red star-shells and a searchlight on Gris Nez so powerful it lit up our shore.

Wednesday 17 September

Only Grove-White and myself attended orderly room. Spitfires and Hurricanes flew low from all directions criss-crossing the morning sky. Daphne met a Claims Officer at the Adams' house in Cannongate Road and found that all but a few poles and pegs of the Hythe Girl Guide camp kit sealed up in a basement had been stolen and the Adams' personal kit strewn over the floor. The house had been occupied by Queen's and then Sappers, who had deliberately broken in and destroyed all they did not steal. What an army! The officer suggested that the RE Quartermaster Sergeant had stolen the camp kit. He is an ex-antique dealer. Our bombers flew over in large numbers at 5.30 p.m. and returned at 6 p.m.

Thursday 18 September

The bombs we heard last night were dropped near the railway line behind Folkestone cemetery. They did no damage, but two boys stealing apples from the back gardens of the Shorncliffe houses were so frightened they were taken to hospital. Bombs were also dropped on Dover, some people were killed and the streets were machine gunned. Heard that a German agent with an unpronounceable name and a spotty face is loose in the country, having last been seen near Liverpool. Phyllis spent the day at 18 Kingsnorth Gardens spring-cleaning, and I drove in and fetched her back in the evening. Watched a biplane flying boat cruising about inland. Miniature range section competition in the evening. No. 10 (Sandling) Section with averages of 22 and 21 defeated No. 3 and No. 4 Sections. Old Kite, who cannot see, got 21 and 23.

Friday 19 September
A lorry-load of Durhams last night coming down Blackhouse Hill turned a somersault; every man was injured and at least one killed. The officer was driving, which was against regulations. They lay about a long time until an ambulance from the first-aid post picked them up. They were only 500 yards from their billets, but seem to have no medical arrangements of their own.

Monday 22 September
At orderly room Stansfield and I had an argument with Street, who insists that we cannot possibly invade the Continent. I had a record attendance at my evening parade: 29 present and only six absent. Captain Whitfield gave us a lecture on the defence against the invasion of Kent. It gave me personally a feeling of confidence. In the middle of his lecture there was a violent explosion.

Saturday 27 September
A Spitfire crashed in a wood near Sandling Park. The pilot, who was unhurt, said he had run out of petrol. Air activity continued for some time afterwards. Some papers are full of the imminent collapse of Italy.

Sunday 28 September
Our parade was firing Northover Projectors in Sandling sandpit. No. 2 Platoon had a succession of bursts close to the muzzle, due to faulty loading and inadequate cleaning, but they put it down to the fault of the gun. I had a shot and got a bullseye!

Tuesday 30 September
After tea we went to a musical film, chiefly at my suggestion because one

Susanna Foster, a pretty girl with a harsh American accent, acted in it. Thought Churchill's speech on the situation was stupid! The rest of the news was just padding. In the evening, trains were passing along the main line north of us, in a continuous stream. Tanks for Russia, I suppose.

Saturday 4 October

Rain in the morning but a fine afternoon. Some distant bombing in the morning. We went blackberrying in the quarry, with Jerry and Socks coming with us. The Huns have got far into Russia but have gained nothing yet. It is impossible to say if the Russians are beaten.

Sunday 5 October

Slight rain. Saltwood Platoon paraded on the village green at 10 a.m. No. 11 Section, with only Sergeant Coveney and the two Goodsells, and No. 13 with Newington attached went forward and defended our old Waterworks position, whilst the other two sections attacked it. I umpired for the

The rural setting of Saltwood Castle (Folkestone Library HS/STR/25)

defenders and Fuller the attackers. No. 10 had the easier task, attacking through wooded gardens. They came down the railway cutting and saw Jack Goodsell in the upper trench, but they missed the younger [Jesse] Goodsell up a tree by Garden House Bridge, who enfiladed them as they advanced. No. 12 Section went right around Saltwood Castle and had the harder task of advancing over open country, but the youngsters' leader Holmes worked well and got within 60 yards of the defence before being seen. They might have succeeded, but made an incorrect guess at the positions of the outpost and exposed their flank to Hickling. Everyone enjoyed himself.

Saturday 11 October

Our lecture on Sunday was put off, and I had to walk around Saltwood and Hythe and telephone to let my people know. The Intelligence Officer of the London Irish was to have talked on the German dispositions on the opposite coast, but discovered that the information could not be imparted to the rank and file. Street thought it would not be worth the man's while to turn out for four officers. I was sorry not to hear it, as it would have been very interesting. Everyone is talking of the inaction of our Army. I do not know if it is an attempt to make the Government act, or if the rumour has got about that they are about to and newspaper proprietors and other busybodies want to make out they forced the Government's hand.

Sunday 12 October

A fine day but definitely colder. No parade, so I drove Phyllis into church about midday. The troops tried out a new form of horn alarm for gas. It is supposed to be heard five miles off, but sounded feeble. The night was disturbed by bombers passing over. There were casualties in Dover.

Tuesday 14 October

General Sir Bernard Paget, Army Commander, wants to give a cup for the best Home Guard platoon in Kent. General Forster and Craufurd-Stuart came to the

BOMBER SAVED BY SHEILA'S "LOVE AND KISSES"

The story of a girl's message of good wishes that saved an R.A.F. bomber and its crew of four was told by Mr. ATTLEE, Lord Privy Seal, in a speech at Norwich last night.

The bomber, he said, had to fly through a lot of flak over Germany and one of its wings was damaged. On the homeward journey the fabric began to come away from the wing, but the tearing suddenly stopped.

The pilot made a safe landing and then found that the stoppage of the tear was caused by some extremely careful stitching of the fabric. Removal of this disclosed a message: "To the airman who will fly this plane. All good wishes, love and kisses from Sheila."

Sheila was discovered, added Mr. Attlee, and the pilot showed her the message. When she admitted that she was the writer, he told her she had saved his life and added: "Now I have come for my kisses."

orderly room to find out Street's views. Street, of course, turned it down. Certainly, it would be difficult to set a test which would be other than ornamental which could be carried out by town and country platoons whose roles are so different. Afterwards, I heard from Vernal that Gribbon had one platoon that has been trained for ceremonial duties only, and I imagine Stuart did not agree with Street but was afraid to say so. The town was full of London Scottish.

Wednesday 15 October

A Wellington bomber, badly shot up and trying to come home, with a pierced tank and on fire, flew overhead. The crew bailed out safely at Hawkinge. The plane circled around Hythe and crashed into a fir plantation at the top of Cannongate Hill and was burnt out. Part of the engine fell at the front door of the top house, and debris fell all around it and the next house, but neither was touched or their occupants injured.

Saturday 18 October

The Durhams are off shortly, and I hear that all this division including the London Scottish will leave next month. Eva heard through the Red Cross that Maurice is well and free in Crete. It appears he deliberately left the party going down to embark, and Eva thinks he was with a couple of Cretans who worked under him. I suppose being over military age and a non-combatant, the Germans leave him alone so as not to have to feed him. Lord Gort's dispatches published today. What a disgraceful affair, and all our Socialist wind-baggers can say is that it shows we cannot do anything on the other side [of the Channel] without adequate equipment. Who sent the force over in that state? The same crowd who are still at the head of affairs, and after three years' effort they say we still have no tanks and not enough planes. They admit that the workers have been slacking for two years. It is said that a day or two ago a young German pilot flew over and landed on a disused aerodrome near Dover, his aircraft, one of the latest type, being only slightly damaged. He is the son of a high-ranking official in the German Legation in London before the war who was born in England and says he joined the Hun Air Force on purpose to do this act. Twice lately Dutchmen have stolen a machine and flown them over to this country.

Sunday 19 October

Overcast day. Shooting on the range at 400 yards. Street put up second-class targets instead of first-class targets to make it more difficult, but agreed it was not fair on the older men with poor eyesight. I was pleased at getting a score of 13. Street challenged me to a shoot, but in the end did not take me on. All day the Durhams were cleaning up their billets and London Scottish were rushing around in lorries. The whole regiment are quartered around Saltwood whilst the Durhams have closed up towards the west.

Monday 20 October

For evening parade, 24 turned up. We spent the time distributing kit and filling in receipts for kits. We are now fully equipped with everything. Grove-White says that harbours in Northern Ireland are full of thousands of barges and motorboats. We, however, have missed the fine weather and our chance of going over this year.

Tuesday 21 October

A clear, cold day. All day, our fighters and bombers were going over and returning. At 4 p.m. one of our Spitfires crashed beyond the hills north of Bluehouses, the pilot bailing out. In the morning, convoys of lorries full of troops passed through the High Street going east, and Folkestone was full of Royal Fusiliers. We had an early supper and drove to Folkestone to see a film, *Moon over Burma*, a regular Hollywood construction; a travesty of Burma, but a good story. One of the heroes was Preston Foster, a good actor. Daphne drove back in the blackout very skilfully. The sky was full of planes all night.

Wednesday 22 October

Mary Blackman, our maid, told us that Dover was dive-bombed yesterday evening. There is supposed to be a new Hun bomb called 'the pencil', thin and pointed, which goes down deep, making the thud of a cricket ball and houses crumble to pieces.

Sunday 26 October

My platoon paraded on Saltwood village green and drove in a Durham LI lorry to the Odeon Cinema in Folkestone, where No. 7 (Canterbury) and No. 8 (Cinque Ports) Battalions, Kent Home Guard, were given a display of films on camouflage, manning a post, scouting and booby traps; all very good. There was also a film on how Germans get information out of prisoners, which was rather too much like a play, and a fifth column spy film which was pure Hollywood.

Monday 27 October

Phyllis went off to Guildford by the 11.30 a.m. train. A young fellow named Ross, during a stunt with ball ammunition by the London Scottish, was shot in the thigh and died of a haemorrhage whilst being taken to Folkestone in a lorry. It seems strange that none of these regiments have a doctor, ambulance or any form of medical aid attached to them. Only 21 turned up in the evening. I lectured them on slackness when they assembled on the green, and when they came out of the cinema yesterday they ran about like sheep and their NCOs did nothing. We then discussed the films, old Green holding forth on psychology. Coast searchlights were on as I returned home and there was a smell of burning rubber.

Thursday 30 October

Daphne and I drove into Dover. It has been very badly knocked about by bombs and shells. On the Folkestone Road beyond the Priory Station was an area of destruction railed off with men working in the ruins of at least six houses. Market Square has old scars, especially on Flashman's and the Westminster Bank. The Grand and the Burlington hotels and Clarence and Guildford lawns are ruins. Mother's old lodgings have been repaired and smashed a second time. All the damage up to the last has been on the east side of the town. On Capel Hill, the field next to the Valiant Sailor has been enclosed with a tall barbed-wire fence and soldiers are excavating it, building deep concrete foundations and throwing up the earth in mounds. There are some Nissen huts inside the enclosure. On our way home, we were held up by young George File and his sister with a flock of sheep.

Sunday 2 November

As I was finishing breakfast, a sergeant of the Durhams turned up and informed me he had a lorry-load of Northover charges and Molotov anti-tank bombs and did not know where to put them. Captain Whitfield had told us nothing about returning them. I sent the lorry to Saltwood. I put the charges in the almshouse then drove up and down Sandling Road to find an empty house for the bombs, but they were all occupied by London Scottish, so I took them to the garage of Street's old house, Castlemead.

Monday 3 November

At the evening parade we had 23, and we had a night march in gas masks to Stone Farm and back, about three miles. I led and was told I made the pace too hot. At Garden House corner I ordered a halt, having found it very difficult to breathe walking up the hill through the cutting. Here Kerr, Green, Hickling, Jack Goodsell and old Kite dropped out. I did not wear my mask the whole of the way to Stone Farm and not on the way back.

Tuesday 4 November

A snow-filled sky, and a very cold day. The London Scottish pipes and drums played up and down our road at 4.30 p.m. Phyllis and Daphne went into Folkestone for a board meeting.

Wednesday 5 November

A day full of shelling, and bombers flying over in large numbers. The town is full of York and Lancaster regiments, a party of whom had come into our road yesterday. A Durham Corporal came to orderly room to have his maps showing our posts brought up to date which, with the return of the Northovers, indicates they are off. I hear that the London Irish and London Scottish are also going. In the evening I saw Leslie Howard in 'Pimpernel' Smith, a very good film.

Thursday 6 November

As Daphne was going into Ashford by bus to see the Claims Officer about the theft of the Girl Guide kit, I decided to go with her. She enjoyed herself tackling the officer. I strolled around until teatime, and we both managed to catch the same bus home. A couple of explosions around 7 p.m. shook the house, and there was continuous bombing in the direction of the Thames estuary. In the miniature range rifle competition, my No. 12 Section beat No. 5 and No. 3. In the former, Sergeant Howard fired on his neighbour's target, dropping about 30 points, but No. 12 made a good score and would have beaten them.

Friday 7 November

One of our planes crashed near Botolph's Bridge; the Canadian Sergeant pilot was killed.

Saturday 8 November

Heavy air activity throughout the day. Dover was dive-bombed again. We learnt on the wireless that our bombers ran into exceptionally bad weather last night and 37 were lost! Also that we lost 14 fighters today – 51 in total! A pleasant nightcap to go to sleep on!!!

Sunday 9 November

Remembrance Sunday, and enemy planes over Dover. The Hythe platoons under Street went to the Parish Church. I took my platoons to Saltwood, but only 20 turned up. The Revd Peters-Jones preached a most excellent sermon on Christian attitudes towards war. Some thought it was rash, but it was the truth. The hymns were also most appropriate, but the choir was feeble. Planes were flying overhead all through the service. After listening to the pipers of the London Scottish on the village green, General Lucock took Hickling and me to his house for drinks.

Monday 10 November
Old General Metcalfe looked in at orderly room to congratulate Saltwood Platoon on their smartness. At evening parade, the younger men were put through bayonet fighting by Sergeant Kite. The others drilled with their Brownings and Tommy guns. Everyone was very optimistic that the war would soon end.

Tuesday 11 November
Armistice Day. Street came up to Saltwood early to collect a Northover Projector for the Seabrook Platoon.

Wednesday 12 November
Three braw Scotties came into Miss Goodyear's garden in Castle Road. The owner told them a previous unit had robbed her vegetables and hoped they would not do so. 'No ma'am,' said one, 'we were only hunting for a stick to get back our wee ba'.' The 'wee ba' was a football and it was 10 feet up a tree.

Thursday 13 November
The Durhams have gone, the KOYLI are replacing the London Irish in the Small Arms School and the York and Lancaster, the London Scottish in Saltwood. The latter were fine men and a very nice lot. Miniature shooting competition in the evening: No. 7 (Seabrook) won both their matches making an average of over 23 against No. 4 Section. When we went to put the miniature rifles back in our hall of arms, we found that the London Irish had stolen seven of our shotguns! None but they could have done it, as the room is inside the barracks close to a guard room.

Friday 14 November
Went to Stone Farm to collect his kit from Hobbs who, after failing to attend a single parade, resigned. Our planes were busy all afternoon. The

London Scottish were loading lorries until late at night. Daphne went into Folkestone to a meeting presided over by Miss Lewis to discuss the raising of a cadet unit of the ATS.

Sunday 16 November

Snap shooting on 'N' range. I obtained a couple of trucks from the York and Lancaster Regiment to take my platoon there. It was very cold on the range, but the shooting was good. Sergeant Dawkins brought the Seabrook Section in one of his coal lorries with a homemade corrugated iron hood on it. The wind blew the hood off, which turned a somersault, dented his radiator and passed my car causing only slight scratches. A marvellous escape! There was an interesting article in the paper which said Von Papen said Germany would *demand* an Armistice. No one who is winning would ever demand one.

Tuesday 18 November

Our planes were very active in the morning and Bren carriers and lorries were tearing about the roads. The new recruits manned their posts throughout the day. Craufurd-Stuart turned up at orderly room. He said he was fed up with Brigadier Gribbon, and Forster was coming down next week to see about getting rid of him. Higher authorities might be tired of Gribbon's volumes of paper, but old 'Dogsbody' I am sure would put up with anything. He told me to keep something under my hat, and made me think I would be offered 'B' Company. I would much rather stay with Saltwood Platoon and would not get on with the Folkestone crowd, but I also feel it would be foolish not to accept promotion.

Wednesday 19 November

The activity at dusk yesterday was caused by a Hun dropping two huge landmines on the village of Sturry, east of Canterbury. A pub was engulfed and about six people, including soldiers, killed. I went over to

Bluehouse and brought back a P14 rifle which William Fifield had picked up one night close to the main road.

Thursday 20 November

In the morning, we heard of our advance in Libya. The authorities are reluctant, but the papers blare out paeans of victory. In the miniature range competition, No. 10 Section were one short as Newington refuses to turn out at night and says he will resign if he is made to. He is 65 but he is a good little chap and one of our original members.

Friday 21 November

Drove Stansfield to Folkestone, where we got some kit out of Vernal at Battalion HQ, and then went to the TA Drill Hall, 'B' Company's HQ, and got more kit than we expected from Gribbon. It is a very big place, and 'B' Company do themselves well with two typists in trousers and a fully licensed bar. Although Russians say they are holding their own, it is a fact that they have lost the whole of the Crimea except Sebastopol and almost certain that they have lost Rostov-on-Don.

Sunday 23 November

The company was given a lecture on gas by Captain Coote of the old soldiers' battalion of the Buffs in the lecture hall at the top end of Turnpike Camp. Street marched us from the TA Hut as a company, giving the words of command himself. He gave us eyes right when my platoon, which was leading, reached the sentry at the lower gate and kept us at it until the last man had passed the quarter guard. Grove-White thought he had forgotten, and gave the order to his platoon to 'eyes front', which annoyed Street.

Monday 24 November

During evening parade, 22 turned up; young Wright was absent dancing with his girl. Old Kite found an undraped window in the village and spent the evening trying to make the people black out and the ARP and police take action. We played the game of 'O'Grady says', which cheered them up. John Goodsell reported to me through Fuller that some of the men when in the pubs allowed Tommies and civilians to handle their arms and take them to pieces, so I jumped on them for that. They guessed that it was Goodsell and went for him afterwards; young Dearman was so *insubordinate* I threatened to turn him out.

Wednesday 26 November

Street drove Stansfield and me into the Territorial Drill Hall, Folkestone, the two former to give evidence and I as a member on the Committee of Enquiry into the loss of our shotguns. The other members were Major Braine of 'G' Company (RASC Colonel) and a young fellow from the Gas Company platoon. Vernal, the head clerk, horrified Street by turning up with Miss Lumsden, the Battalion civilian typist. Street was so shocked that he gabbled his evidence so fast she couldn't take it down. Stansfield handed in a typed statement, which no one read. Braine seemed to know nothing about the procedure, and Street was very rude to Gribbon about his trousered typists.

Saturday 29 November

Russia seems to have gained a real victory at Rostov-on-Don. It is very unfortunate that a South African brigade has been cut up in Libya with 1,200 casualties. At the start of the war, they said they did not want to chance a disaster similar to what happened to them in France in the last war.

Monday 1 December

There were 25 on evening parade and we had another gas mask route march, a longer one, past Saltwood Castle, Garden House and Stone Farm, down Kick Hill and across country over the railway line back to the castle. I only lasted [wearing the mask] as far as the sandpit. Nearly all the rest seemed to stick it out. It was quite three miles up and down hill – a severe test. A fine moonlight night – very inspiring.

Wednesday 3 December

Stansfield took a holiday, so I was left in charge and took the opportunity to tidy up. Daphne went to inspect the Folkestone Guides in her new capacity of Assistant District Commissioner.

Saturday 6 December

Inspector Neville in the morning drove me into Lydd where the Mayor, Alderman Paine, presented RSPCA certificates to Frank Paine (who turned up in Home Guard uniform) and George Coleman for rescuing horses when Ness Farm cowsheds had incendiary bombs on them. The Mayor wanted to do all the talking, but the Town Clerk, Kinnard, insisted on me reading out the account of the rescue, which was written in Neville's rather bad English. We looked over the badly ruined Lydd church (the Cathedral of the Marsh) and the gutted barracks, and nearly half the houses have also been damaged. Passing through Dymchurch I saw for the first time the damaged bridge to the west of the town.

Japan mounted a surprise attack on Pearl Harbor, a United States navy base on Hawaii, on the morning of 7 December, which President Roosevelt labelled 'a date which will live in infamy'. Almost 2,500 men were killed in the attack, which finally brought America into the war.

Sunday 7 December

I left in the car at 9 a.m. and arrived at the Drill Hall, Ashford, at 9.20 a.m. There were eight of us Home Guard officers on the course. A Captain Mathews, Intelligence Officer 46th Division, a nice fellow, was our instructor. To explain the Signals point of view, he had brought the Divisional Signals Officer, a baby captain, who had been at school last year with the son of one of the Home Guard officers. He gave us a situation and told us to put it into a message as Battalion Intelligence Officers. To my amusement he marked mine 'very good'; none of the others received more than 'fair'. We adjourned for lunch, which I had at the Kent Arms [Inn] at the entrance to the station. Mathews showed us the working of an Intelligence office and explained the differences between a British and German Division, showing how the latter is organised for attack and ours for defence. He told us that from the top downwards the Army has not got a spark of aggressiveness in them. We heard on the news of the Japanese bombing Manila whilst their envoys were negotiating in Washington.

Monday 8 December

A hard white frost in the morning. I had 27 present at evening parade, only seven absent. Sergeant Kite took the youngsters and Prior and Hickling in arms drill. The Tiltmans had again been absent from the range yesterday, so in front of Sergeant Coveney I told the elder Tiltman he could resign or be discharged. He protested he could only be discharged for inefficiency and that he was more efficient than the rest, but he had delivered himself into my hands. I replied: 'A man who claims to have served in the Guards and comes on parade with a dirty rifle cannot call himself efficient.' Fuller had suggested a rifle inspection; I had asked him to help me and took care that he should inspect Tiltman's rifle and he found it dirty.

Tuesday 9 December

From what one can gather the American fleet were wiped out at their anchorage [Pearl Harbor]. America is now a united nation. Daphne went to her Guide meeting.

Thursday 11 December

The searchlights were very strong during the night. Poor Admiral Tom Phillips, who I think is a nephew of Uncle Tom, went down with the *Prince of Wales* off Malaya, and Cunningham has been kicked out of command in Libya. Churchill made a very optimistic speech, and everyone has declared war on everyone else.

THERE is bad news from the Far East. In furious air attack, the Prince of Wales, one of our newest battleships, and the Repulse, an old battle-cruiser, were sunk this morning off the Malayan coast. Details of this heavy loss are anxiously awaited.

The Japanese have made several

Sunday 14 December

A wet day, but it stopped raining sufficiently to enable 25 of us to meet on the Glebe Field in Saltwood to practise grenade throwing, with sand-filled canvas grenades. The young fellows thoroughly enjoyed themselves. I hope they will behave more soberly next Sunday when they throw live grenades. At 12 p.m. I went down to the Small Arms School to an 'at home' given by the 2nd/4th KOYLI Brigadier Campbell, a quaint-looking fellow from the Black Watch.

Thursday 18 December

Mary Blackman, our maid, rang up in the evening that she had obtained a special licence and was being married on Saturday, so would not turn up tomorrow. The new regulations governing the Home Guard are published. They say conscription will only be brought in when necessary. Our volunteers were afraid that under conscription they would be forced to leave their homes and be sent anywhere.

Saturday 20 December

The news is alarming and disgusting. Penang gone and almost certainly Hong Kong, and we have made the same mistakes we made at Dunkirk and Crete. How many more Dunkirks must we have before we learn our lesson?

Sunday 21 December

Phyllis got up very gallantly to cook me an early breakfast, and I got off just before 9 a.m. and reached Ashford in half an hour. Besides Captain Mathews, we had three other officers to talk on paratroops, prisoners of war and tanks. They were all interesting. At lunch I was placed at a table where a little woman was just finishing her meal. She said quietly: 'You have been having an exciting time here.' Not knowing what she meant, I said: 'Yes.' 'Was there any damage?' she replied. 'Oh no, there was no damage,' said I. I thought she was pumping me, but it seems some bombs were dropped last night near Ashford.

Monday 22 December

A company of the KOYLI went into Sandling Park and practised advancing under fire. They fired rifles, Tommy guns and Bren guns across the road, bullets hitting the roofs of the houses and narrowly missing several people in the park. Fuller managed to stop them. Only 21 turned up at evening parade. I talked to them on some of the subjects I had learnt at my course, and Fuller gave his views on the live grenade throwing. He told me he thought Street rushed things to a dangerous extent, considering most of them had never handled a grenade.

Tuesday 23 December

As Daphne and Phyllis were starting their journey to Folkestone, they saw two men bending over Socks near Minnie's gate. They brought her in and found that one hind leg was broken or dislocated. There was a series of alerts at teatime, and I went to the end of the road and saw flashes and heard rumbles in the direction of Hawkinge. A plane came over from the north, and as it came over the allotments there was a blinding flash and an explosion near Summerhouse Hill, the blast of which I felt.

Wednesday 24 December

Last night's explosions were a couple of landmines dropped near Lyminge. One man was hurt, but not a sheep was touched. In the morning, I drove round the town and to Sandling and Bluehouse on Home Guard work.

Thursday 25 December

My family prepared my meals, including a sumptuous breakfast, and we stayed together and fed on simple fare. We listened in to the King, a manly speech full of sympathy for those in sorrow and danger. I thought the broadcast of Churchill and Roosevelt guzzling and joking in Washington was disgraceful. I refuse to listen to it. I wonder what the poor fellows in Hong Kong, fighting for their lives, thought of it?

Friday 26 December

I drove into Folkestone to try to get the vet for Socks but failed to find him. She is, however, better. A very cold night.

Saturday 27 December

I went to the office after three days' holiday. Street was busy finding out for the Corps the number of men eligible for the Home Guard who have not joined up, and finds some 150 – this is very surprising. They must be men who have lately returned. I had an interesting talk with Dr Maudy, 'Timber' Wood, Hickling and Perrin on the military situation. I was, as usual in such circumstances, very 'Bolshy'. Our planes bombarded the Channel ports in the evening.

Sunday 28 December

A clear sunny day, just above freezing point the whole time. My platoon assembled at Sandling Park for a field day, 24 strong. The Tiltmans absent as usual. No. 10 (Sandling) Section acted as parachute troops who had captured the aerodrome, represented by the paddock. Nos. 11, 12 and 13 attacked them. No. 11 lost touch with their right and got mixed up with No. 12, but the two made a good final assault. No. 13 got lost. Old Tom Kite, a born poacher, hid in some reeds and I nearly trod on him without seeing him. George Piper felt cold so put his tin hat on (which only the attackers wore) and I mistook him for one of No. 13 Section. During our attack, Spitfires swooped down on us.

Tuesday 30 December

Daphne went down town for an interview in connection with her 'call-up'. She had a number of references showing she was a full-time worker for the Girl Guides and was totally exempted. The Fuller girl has been accepted in the WAAF.

The Cinque Ports Battalion cleaning weapons in the field (IWM HN8130)

1942

Saturday 3 January

Our Spitfires were roof hopping at midday. About 5 p.m. large planes were manoeuvring in the clouds Hawkinge way. A mild day, but a wind got up in the afternoon. The convoy action was a great success. I wonder if the Huns thought Churchill was in it!

Monday 5 January

By mistake, I woke everyone up an hour too early. I was nearly dressed before I discovered my mistake. Alerts throughout the morning in short bursts. Planes were active for the rest of the day, and a big gun fired several shots. Alert 6.15 p.m. to 8 p.m. There was an attack on Dover. Phyllis thought a Hun flew low over us but I thought it was one of our fighters as after the 'all clear' a similar plane flew back inland. We had a record attendance of 26(!) on evening parade and only five absent (one sick and Fuller held back by work). We played with hand grenades.

Mr Hills with his Auxiliary Fire Service vehicle stationed at Convent, Ravenlea Road, Folkestone
(Folkestone Library FWW2/76)

Tuesday 6 January

Frost at night, and a very cold north wind all

day. A short 'alert' at 9.30 a.m. Craufurd-Stuart visited us in the orderly room. Much stir over conscription for the Home Guard, and several forms sent to fill up. Over 250 men are employed in Hythe in ARP, Fire Service and Special Constabulary, and 120 in the Home Guard. Our planes went over and strafed the coast in the afternoon, and were busy overhead and to the east up to dusk. About 6.30 p.m., big guns fired for half an hour. We went to a cinema show in Turnpike Camp in the evening. I marched my platoon down from Saltwood. The films were on camouflage (which we had seen before) and German tanks and air force. The shore searchlights were on when I returned home.

Thursday 8 January
Somewhat milder. In afternoon, I drove Phyllis round servant hunting. It was a Saltwood platoon evening at the miniature range. No. 12 won both their matches with their usual luck. Shore searchlights were again out.

Friday 9 January
Bright sun in the morning, but very cold at night. Planes were manoeuvring in the sky during the afternoon. I wrote up my year's accounts. A hopeless outlook: my pension reduced by £700 and fuel and electricity prices have doubled.

Saturday 10 January
We were woken at 6 a.m. by an 'all clear'. A very cold day. Alerts at 9.50 a.m. to 10.15 a.m. Big guns fired Dover way at noon and again in the afternoon, and there was much air activity. The war situation seems desperate, yet our leaders are complacent. A few Indians trying to stem the millions of Japs, and now the Hun making a bid to capture Malta. I suppose we will send Air Force and troops from Libya and will be driven back again to the Egyptian frontier.

Sunday 11 January
We woke up to find the world deep in snow. My platoon assembled on Saltwood Green at 9.30 a.m. The York and Lancaster lorries were late, and one was an open one. Our young fellows rushed for the covered lorries but Kite, Corner, J Goodsell and Hickling said they did not mind, so I joined them in the open truck. It was not a pleasant ride. We were shown four films at the Odeon, two on day and night patrols, one on a tank trying to

force roadblocks and the fourth a confused unintelligible battle scene. At half time, Colonel Prawle, GOC Kent Zone HG, gave a talk. He emphasised very well how the country was always unprepared for a major war, and gave his reasons for considering the threat of invasion was still here. Street of course said it was all rot! It began snowing again when we were in the cinema. When we came back to our lorries, I gave the order for all under 24 to ride in the open truck, and the lads did so quite cheerfully. I got home at 1.30 p.m. Phyllis had a young private (Cheedle) of the South Staffordshires to tea, and Molly (Jenner) turned up afterwards. The private was settled in the drawing room by the fire with the papers, and stayed till 8 p.m.

Monday 12 January
It froze all day, but no more snow fell. Only 22 turned up for evening parade. I formed them into four squads, piled two lots of chairs up opposite each other to form sap-heads [trenches] and made them throw dummy grenades at each other. The old men of No. 13 Section did well, but were forced to give in from fatigue! Old Tom Kite of Sandling was one of the best throwers. It was thawing when I walked home.

Sunday 18 January
A heavy fall of snow at night and a very cold morning, but slight thaw in afternoon. Great rejoicing over Churchill's return [from America], but the Malay situation goes from bad to worse.

Thursday 22 January
A cold morning, but the east wind died down and the sun came out. The battalions in the area have been turned into Depot Battalions full of recruits, and most of them have been moved to St Martins Plain and Dibgate for training. All the York and Lancasters have gone from Hillcrest Road, and the South Staffordshires no longer defend Saltwood. My Home Guard platoon has it to themselves. The Huns shelled Dover in the middle of the day for four hours at least, one shell damaging Market Square.

Saturday 24 January
The rain washed all the snow away, and when the north wind subsided it turned into a mild day with some sun. Big guns were firing all day

from behind us and in the Lydd area, the latter sounding as if a convoy was being attacked. In the afternoon a bomber, escorted by two fighters, wandered aimlessly overhead. It rained all evening. The War Office are taking over a large area near Postling for a tank manoeuvre ground. Although there is plenty of hilly ground covered with coarse grass, they have picked some of the best arable land in the vicinity, and insist on having it.

Tuesday 27 January

A hard frost, and a very cold morning with snow on the ground. Our planes were active overhead early in the morning. We had a very busy morning in orderly room. Craufurd-Stuart came to deal with Sergeant Wood and Tiltman. The latter came first. Street said he was absent from parades, but Tiltman argued that he had attended more than some others had. Stuart said that was not the point, and asked Street what he wanted. Street replied: 'I do not want him in the Company.' 'All right,' said Stuart. 'Very good,' said Tiltman, and walked out. Of Sergeant Wood, Street said he was argumentative and insubordinate. Wood immediately became both. Stuart reduced him to Volunteer, but said he could stay on if he liked. 'I must think it over,' said Wood. There was a short alert at 1.30 p.m. At 4 p.m. we had a heavy fall of snow, which turned into sleet and by 7 p.m. into rain. Getting into bed, Phyllis caught her foot in the flex of the electric kettle and brought the tray down with a crash, which broke everything except one cup. Churchill's speech was very clever. Knowing he himself was safe, he took the whole responsibility on himself so that the critics could not demand the dismissal of this or that Minister.

Wednesday 28 January

Thaw in the morning with a blue sky. About 10 o'clock, a whole squadron of Spitfires flew overhead coming from a raid over France. I heard they are a new squadron just arrived at Hawkinge. Alert from 12.00 p.m. to 12.20 p.m. then heavy explosions in the direction of Boulogne or further south. More air activity in the afternoon, and salvos of gunfire in Dungeness direction. The debate in the Commons was a futile affair. It seems Churchill has made himself dictator.

Royal Marines during an invasion exercise in Kent (Kent Messenger PD1542066)

Saturday 31 January

I have a pouring cold. At 10 a.m. I met Street and Colonel Angier of the KOYLI on Saltwood Green in an incipient snowstorm. The South Staffordshires have been moved further east, the KOYLI have taken over the whole of Hythe, and Saltwood has been forgotten. Angier was very 'nervy' and did not want to sanction anything. He also was worried about the defence of the area all round the village, and wanted me to be responsible from Sandling Junction to Saltwood Castle. It snowed after lunch but did not freeze. We lost a number of ships in the Mediterranean at the end of November, including the *Ark Royal* and *Barham*, and lost command of the sea. The Huns have been severely bombing our bomber aerodromes in East Anglia.

Wednesday 4 February

Slush everywhere and a thin drizzle most of the day. Daphne had a difficult time driving back from her Cheriton Guide meeting about 8 p.m. The searchlights lit up the roads then went out suddenly, plunging everything into pitch darkness. She gave three soldiers a lift in Sandgate. A strong cold north-east wind all night.

Sunday 8 February

A hard frost at night. As there was no parade, I stayed in all day. A blue sky in the afternoon with renewed air activity, and our speedboats were in the Strait in the evening. Stafford Cripps' broadcast was good. His contact with Communism has made him almost a Tory. The news is so depressing from everywhere. I dread listening to it.

Monday 9 February

A clearer sky, and a definite thaw throughout the day. A short alert at 3 p.m. We had a record attendance at evening parade – 29 out of 31. The younger Kite gave an excellent lecture on the Battle School he attended on Saturday and Sunday. They had to do everything at the double under live-round fire from Bren guns and rifles. Only one of the Home Guard NCOs gave in, but he too eventually carried on. The Commando instructor was pleased with them, and gave them an extra tea.

Tuesday 10 February

A continuous thaw with thick slush. I took the car out; the roads were slippery in places. I drove Stansfield to Turnpike Camp in the morning, and Phyllis round the town in the afternoon. Hythe Corporation are imposing the demand for iron railings in a very Hunnish manner. They send round no notice nor do they concede any necessity for retaining them. They have employed a gang of soldiers in mufti. I am thankful I have none round my house.

Wednesday 11 February

Frost at night and a sunny day. Much snow still lying about. Grove-White picked up two RAF leaflets written in French in his garden. Our planes were about for a short time at midday. There was a burst of gunfire or bombs at 7 p.m.

*The German Navy scored a significant victory in February 1942, when a Kriegsmarine squadron (*Scharnhorst, Gneisenau, Prinz Eugen *and a number of smaller ships) defeated a British blockade and sailed from Brittany to their home bases in Germany. The manoeuvre was dubbed the 'Channel Dash'.*

Thursday 12 February

Frost with slight hail in the morning. None of us here realised what was happening across the water [the 'Channel Dash']. The first alert sounded at noon. At 12.20 p.m. there was heavy gunfire and bomb explosions in the distance as the 'all clear' sounded and the alert was again sounded. The second 'all clear' sounded at 12.35 p.m. followed by continuous gunfire and the sky was full of hundreds of our planes flying along the coast from west to east. At 2.30 p.m. two of our Spitfires came roof hopping over us.

Saturday 14 February

A sunny day. Several short alerts with spasmodic air activity; our windows occasionally rattled, and big guns firing to the north and west. All the troops except the KOYLI have been taken away from in and around Hythe and are to shut themselves up in Folkestone 'Fortress' (?). The two Hythe Home Guard platoons have positions facing out to sea and no protection from attack from the rear. My platoon is left to itself in Saltwood. We have a vague position, not agreed to by the Brigadier, given us but we can do nothing because the houses are occupied. It seems as if the defence of England is a bluff – like everything else.

Sunday 15 February

Almost a warm day. There was activity in the air early. Saltwood Platoon marched to the paddock in Sandling Park and fired our Northovers at their extreme range of 200 yards. The guns fired very accurately and we had only three prematures, but many bottles did not explode owing to the soft ground. Some of our Spitfires were flying about low most of the day. Churchill spoke in the evening. He told us of the surrender of Singapore and croaked of further disasters. He said only our follies would lose us the war – OURS!!

> **SUNDAY, February 15**
>
> SINGAPORE has fallen. Except an announcement broadcast by the Prime Minister to-night, there is no British report. A Japanese communiqué says the defending army surrendered unconditionally at 12.30 p.m. to-day. The siege had lasted

Monday 16 February

A cold wind all day. I recruited Major HFH Master for my platoon. He was in my Company at Sandhurst. There was a burst of air activity at noon, with guns booming in the distance. I had 27 present for evening parade. Kite lectured on the second part of his course. The shore searchlights were on when I returned.

Thursday 19 February
A five-minute alert at 10.30 a.m. Heavy gunfire to the north-east during the morning and afternoon. We were told that we are to have an additional 125 conscripts in 'A' Company. Street at once said we cannot have them, we cannot train them and he would resign his commission! In the shooting match No. 13 Section beat No. 10.

Saturday 21 February
I took sandbags up to Saltwood in the morning and drove Phyllis round town in the afternoon. Street as usual had thought it over and is not going to resign, but has worked out a way of absorbing our conscripts.

Monday 23 February
Light snow fell at 9.30 a.m. and continued to midday. Despite the bad weather, 24 of my platoon turned up. I showed them our new positions, then marched them to the Vicarage field where Kite taught them how to search a field for parachutists. Coveney and Kerr were both hopeless, Holmes improved. Kite then demonstrated throwing oneself over Dannert wire and climbing a wall. It was a rigorous parade, but all the old men saw it through.

Kent Home Guard during an exercise (Kent Messenger PD1542043)

Friday 27 February

We had a very busy morning at orderly room making up monthly returns and winding up the rifle competition. Craufurd-Stuart came in and Molyneux [Mayor of Hythe] turned up to try and get an Admiral for his Warships Week – four had failed him. We could only offer him a Post Captain. About 11.30 p.m. a large force of bombers flew over. Their engines had a very different sound to the usual noise of a bomber. I wonder if they are the planes carrying our parachute troops!!

Rodney's painting of road barriers on a country lane

Sunday 1 March

The sun came out and the day was much warmer. My platoon paraded on Saltwood Green and cleaned up and put in order the nine roadblocks we are responsible for, ending with a half an hour's drill on the school parade ground. Young Dearman has at last got his orders; he has been waiting nine months. At 8.15 p.m. violent bursts of big gunfire shook our windows. We went to the lookout in Mrs Russell's garden, and the sound seemed to come from the direction of Gris Nez. At 8.45 p.m. firing again broke out, the noise seeming to come from every description of gun and cannon fire as well as the engines of 'E' boats. There was a mist over the sea and we only saw (or thought we saw) one or two flares or rockets.

Monday 2 March
The show last night was given out as being cross-Channel shelling at first, but it was obviously not that. A fine sunny day, and pleasant temperatures at night. There were nine absentees on evening parade. There was a total eclipse of the moon starting just before midnight in a perfectly clear sky.

Tuesday 3 March
A pleasant day with a warm sun. At 9.30 a.m. there was a heavy strafing over towards Calais but sounding more inland. A continuous rumble of heavy explosions for a quarter of an hour, then a mist at sea and one could see nothing, but every now and then a flare lit up the sky above Dover. Our planes were up and at one time we saw one flying towards France silhouetted against the clouds. Later, our bombers flew over, there were occasional rumblings and once our windows shook.

Friday 6 March
A bitter cold day. In the morning, Street drove Colonel (Lieutenant) Mackay, Battalion Ammunition Officer, to inspect our caches of explosives. It was rather a farce. Alert 2.30 p.m. to 2.50 p.m.

Saturday 7 March
It froze all day and was bitter cold in the evening. I have not commented on the war for some time. I do not know what we and the Americans are playing at. The Russians are urging us to do something and are entertaining their new Japanese Ambassador. The Dutch, after a dignified reproach at our desertion, are fighting like heroes.

Sunday 8 March
Bright sun in morning, a perfect day. Shooting at 200 yards on 'A' range. My younger men shot very badly, and asked for a second shot for practice, so to show them how it should be done I got down and made 19/20! Speedboats were out and planes up whilst we were shooting. I had a talk with young Bryant afterwards, and booked him to give us a lecture on our parachute troops, of which he has experience. Alert 6 p.m. to 6.30 p.m. A

lot of air activity but nothing came of it. Later, searchlights were up and there were some planes about.

Monday 9 March
At 8.30 a.m. a wave of planes passed over, and there was a 20-minute alert. All afternoon there was intensive air activity, and at one time the sound of bombing or gunfire. Only 23 turned up for evening parade, chiefly due to the Sandling men being on farm work. Phyllis and Daphne watched the fireworks. In Saltwood, it sounded as if Folkestone was being attacked. The Boys Club hut shook with the explosions.

Tuesday 10 March
Phyllis was woken by explosions, which I was told later were bombs on Folkestone or gunfire in the Strait. Our big guns fired during the morning. We had a very busy morning in orderly room with the arrival of rifle-grenades and a lot of useless kit. We were told to contact our local Labour Exchange to begin enrolling the 125 conscripts 'A' Company is to have, but the former told us Canterbury was dealing with the matter and there was little hope of expecting the first conscripts for six months. In the evening, the Huns fired their guns at us and there were periodical sounds of distant bombing.

Wednesday 11 March
Rain fell all day. In the morning I drove Stansfield all round his area distributing kit. He gave it to Mitchell to do, because Street wanted to make Mitchell a platoon officer, but the man is incapable of doing the simplest thing and, acknowledging the fact, told Street he would not take a commission.

Saturday 14 March
We heard that eight bombs were dropped in the area, from top of Coolinge Lane [Folkestone] to Cheriton; no one was hurt. A spring day. Alerts at 11.20 a.m. and 11.40 a.m., the second just as the Mayor was opening Warships Week. Rear Admiral Round-Turner [Naval Officer Commanding, Folkestone] made a very good speech. Sir William Weyland, pandering to the tradesmen who now have a monopoly of the council, talked of 'people who ran away and hit the local tradesmen'. There was a procession in the afternoon: sailors, soldiers, Home Guard, all the town services, and Daphne leading her Guides brought up the rear. As

Stansfield was away, Street made Grove-White take No. 1 Platoon and I had Nos. 2 and 3 combined. Street then marched us back all the way to Scanlon's Bridge, where he had left his car.

Sunday 15 March

A warm, sunny day. Only 20 turned up for parade at Slaybrook [Hall]. We went up to Leney's woods and practised clearing a wood of parachute troops. The elder Kite and Jesse Goodsell acted as enemy, whilst Fuller and I acted as machine gunners and umpires. They made a mess of the action, Goodsell and Dray got up against each other and had a fire-fight and Dray and Wright talked the whole time. Sergeant John Coveney again failed to command his section. He came round later and resigned. I am sorry for him, but he is hopeless as a NCO. In the afternoon our planes were up in large numbers and bombers were over at night.

Wednesday 18 March

I drove to Bluehouse in the morning to give the post a box of grenades. At 6 p.m. I attended, in Street's place, a committee to interview 16 youths who had reached the age of 17. On the board were Alderman Molyneux, who took charge, Miss Butcher of the Youth Movement and Bedford the schoolmaster. It was very interesting. The young bank clerks were all talkative, and one definitely obstructive. One farm lad refused to join anything, but agreed to join the Home Guard when his friend said he would join. Molyneux wanted to put everyone into the Home Guard. I stood up for the Air and Sea Cadets, but later I thought he was right.

Friday 20 March

In the town I saw two men with new shoulder flashes, but did not get near enough to ask details. Later I saw a USA Officer in Lloyds bank. I wonder if it means anything.

Sunday 22 March

A heavy gale at night. Daphne got up to cook me an 8 a.m. breakfast. Officers and NCOs of 'A' Company, Kent Home Guard, left in two Army trucks from Red Lion Square at 9 a.m. I sat next to the driver of the leading lorry, and guided him to Eastwell Park, north of Ashford. There was fog on the high ground in the morning, and a biting north wind blew all day, freezing us all to the marrow. A large number of Home Guards from all over

Kent attended the demonstration. We were shown day and night patrolling, manning of roadblocks and ambushing tanks. We got back by 4.30 p.m.

Monday 23 March

We had 26 on parade in evening, and Street also turned up for a lecture on British parachute troops by young Captain Bryant of the Grenadier Guards. He was in charge of secret agents, Poles and Czechs, and said the Poles were marvellously brave, better than us. His talk was the most interesting I have heard up to now. At 8.45 p.m. there was an alert, and at 9 p.m. a very heavy raid on Dover started and went on for half an hour. The AA fire and flashes were intense, and many of the explosions were so heavy the bombs might have been dropped close by.

BOMBER REPORTED DOWN

Wednesday 25 March

A sunny day. At 11 o'clock there was a burst of cannon fire in the air over the town. Alerts throughout the morning, with the final 'all clear' at 12.30 p.m. Further activity during the afternoon. Our bombers returned from a raid on France at 5 p.m. and at 9 p.m. we heard them again over there. At 11.10 p.m. a plane flew over us, and from the noise of his engines we three all remarked that it was a Hun. A few minutes later there was the explosion of a bomb and the Hythe siren sounded the alert. Soon afterwards Dover was attacked; the bomb flashes and AA fire were very intense and the noise was terrific. The attack died down by 11.30 p.m.

Saturday 28 March

Phyllis' birthday. In the morning I had to drive all round my area altering details of Sunday's parade. My men balloted to attend services, and Street agreed. All through the afternoon, our bombers were flying over and pounding France. Although the bombing was far inland, the explosions shook our windows. Whilst it was going on, the sirens sounded at 5.45 p.m. and there was a scrap overhead. Our planes were flying round up to 10.30 p.m. The King was very fired up in making his speech in the evening.

Sunday 29 March

The sky was full of planes from early morning. A distant alert at 9.30 a.m., but Hythe siren was mute. My platoon, 25 strong, marched to Saltwood Church for the National Day of Prayer. The Rector, Peters-Jones, preached a good sermon on the lines that our life should be one long prayer and not ignored except on special occasions.

Thursday 2 April

We are receiving long-winded instructions on the matter of conscription for the Home Guard, and will have to take on a full office staff. Spitfires rushed towards Lympne low overhead. In the evening at the miniature range our 12 marksmen and recruits fired; the former shot badly. Two of my recruits only just failed to qualify. Searchlights were busy and planes were about. The troops were out on night operations, and a stream of Armoured Vehicles clattered down our road. At 12.30 a.m. Hun planes flew over us, the alert sounded and Dover was very heavily attacked, with a number of casualties.

Friday 3 April

Good Friday. In the morning I drove to Bluehouse. There was great air activity throughout the afternoon, and our speedboats were out in the Strait. A misty evening. Alert 8.30 p.m. to 9.40 p.m. Some planes about, but no searchlights up. It appears that on Thursday night a raid was expected; all the troops were turned out and stood at 'action stations' and the 'B' Folkestone and Bridge (Canterbury) Companies, Home Guard, were also called out. The latter said that some parachutists were dropped, but I think that was a yarn.

Tuesday 7 April

In the morning Street drove us four officers to the Odeon cinema in Folkestone to listen to an address by the Divisional Commander to all officers under him, both regular and Home Guard. He told us of the distribution of the troops in his area and talked of the training of the

Home Guard. He spoke as if he was bored or tired. At the interval, Street said the rest of the talk concerned only the regulars and took us home. I sat next to Craufurd-Stuart, who said orders had come that all over-65s must definitely go. It will be a great blow to Stansfield. It means I will be Captain and second in command of the Company, and must give up the Saltwood Platoon. I dislike the idea and the job, but am also sorry Stansfield goes. 'Bone' Foster also goes. We went back to orderly room, where Stansfield refused to do anything. From there I went to the Community Restaurant, where I met Phyllis and Daphne. It was a well-cooked, plain meal but a fuggy atmosphere. A strong gale got up at night.

Wednesday 8 April

A very large number of our planes flew over to France about 7 a.m. I went to orderly room and a morning of hard work. I felt rather bewildered, as it is difficult to adjust to my new duties with the presence of Stansfield, who is staying on as a sort of civilian officer clerk. At 7.30 p.m. I went to my first recruits' parade at the hut. Stansfield came and showed me the ropes. They are rather a weedy crowd, but may look better when they get their uniforms. Planes over at night.

Thursday 9 April

A cold overcast morning. Early in the morning, planes were about in large numbers. There was an alert 7.30 a.m. to 7.45 a.m. It rained the rest of the day. Trice turned up at orderly room, his first appearance as a platoon commander. He was not as 'matey' as I feared. Daphne left at midday to instruct in mapping at a Guiders course in Tonbridge. In the afternoon, I handed my platoon over to Captain Fuller. Just before he arrived, [Major] Master turned up and complained that the Home Guard was untrained. He has missed all the training by joining late, and had not realised that we must have done some training in two years! I went down to miniature range with the recruits at 7.30 p.m. A raging gale at night. The US troops have abandoned the Philippines, and we have had two cruisers sunk by the Japs.

Friday 10 April

Another busy morning at orderly room. In the afternoon I drove Phyllis into Folkestone. Coming back, three WAAF sergeants signalled me for a lift into Hythe. One, who sat in the front, had a bull terrier and a foreign accent. She said she had been in Folkestone on summer holidays. A very large force of our bombers flew over homeward bound about 5 p.m. We lost 13 bombers this day.

Sunday 12 April
Phyllis cooked me an 8 a.m. breakfast and I drove round picking up Street and Grove-White and drove them to Maidstone. Officers from the whole of Kent Home Guard were present at the Granada Cinema. General Montgomery, who spoke to us here just a year ago, gave us a résumé of the situation on the Russian and Far East fronts. He then told us what the Home Guard should do to keep fit and efficient. Amongst other things, we are to be subjected to live-round fire and dive-bombing. He told us some confidential information. I believe, however, it is faked news he wants us to spread about. Anyway, all he said could have equally been told us by our local Brigadiers, and it stuck me it was a great waste of petrol and time. He was late finishing, and it was after 1 o'clock before we got away. All afternoon, our bombers were flying in large numbers high overhead with occasionally a Spitfire flying low. At 10.30 p.m. we bombed Calais and again at 11 p.m. we strafed the French coast.

Monday 13 April
Alert between 11.30 a.m. to noon. At 3 o'clock, a large number of planes passed inland high up to the east and then minutes later the sirens sounded. Our bombers passed over in large numbers all afternoon. At one time, there appeared to be a fight and there was one loud explosion. I took recruits' parade in the evening, and gave them marching drill on the Reach Field. From there, I went up to Saltwood and looked up my old platoon. Holmes and all the Sandling men (except young Kite) seemed pleased to see me. Dear old Prior came up to me and expressed his sorrow at my going and old Kite waited for me outside and said the same.

Tuesday 14 April
Street went to London for the day but his dog, Tom, found his way down to orderly room and I had to take him home. Heard that a Brigadier and 15 officers and men were killed and 30 injured when a dive-bomber made a shot 300 yards short. Some were Home Guards. This is a good beginning

for teaching the Home Guard steadiness under fire. A very large number of planes flew back from France. A wind got up at night, and the frequent strong gusts brought sounds of very heavy bombing somewhere in France. There was nothing happening on the coast, so it must have been very heavy for us to hear it.

Wednesday 15 April

All six officers of 'A' Company attended orderly room. At 2.30 p.m. planes were dashing about in the air and MTBs on the sea, and there were sounds of heavy bombing across the Strait. The alert sounded at 2.45 p.m. The bombing continued until 3 p.m., when our planes began to return, and at 3.30 p.m. the 'all clear' sounded. I went to a recruits' parade on the Reach Field in the evening. About 7.30 p.m., there was a burst of machine gunning to the east, then about 10 planes flew out to sea over us. Our lads said they were Spitfires, but I was sure they were Huns. Next, to the north, there was a burst of cannon fire and we saw a plane zooming down with smoke coming from its tail. The 'all clear' sounded at 8 o'clock.

Searchlight piercing the night sky above Kent (War and Peace Collection 0256)

Friday 17 April

At 10 p.m. there was a 'blitz' across the water. At 11 p.m. our guns behind Hythe and on the seafront loosed off. Searchlights at the back were up, one every now and again semaphoring across the sky, and the shore searchlights were also on. During the evening I wrote out orders for 'Stand to' and 'Action Stations' for 'A' Company.

Saturday 18 April

A long day at orderly room with recruits, stores etc. At 12.45 p.m. the 30th Buffs rang up to say they wanted the Lewis gun lent to us, and would give us a Browning MG in its place. We went to the cinema at 5 p.m. to see *King Solomon's Mines*, entirely spoilt by bringing in a silly Irish girl and otherwise changing the story. News of the bombing of Augsburg, with the loss of seven out of 12 of our newest type of plane. I do not understand why they went so very low all the way.

Monday 27 April

Heard the first cuckoo this morning. Hythe garrison started a week of night ops. They have a 'supper' at 12 noon and go to bed, get up at 9 p.m. and have 'breakfast' and are out all night. There is a great wave of optimism that the war (at least as far as Europe is concerned) will be over this autumn. People like Benes [exiled President of Czechoslovakia] are saying so, and local people are taking bets on it. I took recruits' parade alone; Street did not come as he had Admiral Hall-Thompson staying with him. At night our bombers were overhead. The Bren carriers of the York and Lancasters woke us up.

Friday 1 May

I had a long morning helping Stansfield in the storeroom. We had lunch at the Community Restaurant. At 7.30 p.m. a big force of planes came from France double S-ing just like the Hun bombers used to with their fighter escorts. Our Spitfires rose from Hawkinge and Lympne, and Folkestone's sirens screamed. When the formation was over Hawkinge about nine swung eastward, then turned out to sea and were chased by planes from north and west, and white puffs as if from cannon fire appeared in their trail.

Tuesday 5 May

There was a lot of bombing and machine gunning about 3 a.m., but I heard none of it. Street left early for 10 days' holiday, fishing in Devonshire. I took command of the Company. Alerts all day. At

6.30 p.m. four Huns came in at rooftop level, dropping four bombs near the Cheriton Power Station and machine gunning the streets. One woman was killed, and four marines in a train wounded. I was starting a bath with the geyser tap running and heard nothing before the siren, which sounded after it was all over. Our bombers were over at night.

Thursday 7 May

I was out of bed just after 6 a.m., when a plane roared over our roof and there were two explosions to the west. Looking east, I saw a black snub-nosed Hun fly over my head. Another flew past to the north and the blast of an explosion caught my eye. Then I saw a third over Seabrook Road and saw a bomb leave its rack. This fell

Sandling Park House, Sandling Park, cut in two by a single bomb (Folkestone Library/*Folkestone Herald*).

on the Hythe cricket pitch. The first bomb cut Sandling Park House in half, the other two fell in trees. The siren sounded after it was all over! The Huns did no machine gunning. I was so interested, I forgot to tell my family to go to safety. In the afternoon I drove Stansfield to the funeral of Sergeant Baker's wife. We went in the procession from Palmarsh to Horn Street cemetery. Recruits at miniature range in the evening.

Sunday 10 May

Street being away, I told platoon commanders to run their own shows. Nos. 1 and 2 decided to man their posts in full kit. I went up to Saltwood and watched No. 3 start an attack through barbed wire, then drove down to Twiss Bridge and looked at the defence of No. 2 Platoon. From there, I drove along Prospect Road. As I passed the Ritz [Cinema], I saw two women dive into a shop and further on two policemen bolt into the police station. At the same time I heard two thumps and, realising something was up, I dashed from the car and dived into a narrow doorway. Low overhead, a black Hun flew spraying the roads with bullets and, with a loud explosion, a brown column rose up from Red Lion Square. One bullet made a hole in the canvas top of my car. I parked my car at the town bridge and followed Trice and his platoon. One bomb had exploded just behind Trice's snack bar, demolishing a large tin barn and flattening the bar premises. Trice and his platoon, joined by some soldiers, started at once on the wreckage; the ARP came much later. A few soldiers had got out of the ruins only slightly hurt. The first to be brought out was young John Nicholls, 19, a young Home Guard in Trice's old section. He had only just received his papers for joining the Army, and was not on parade. He died soon after. The next was young Dray, brother of a Home Guard, very badly hurt. Then Old Hardinge, ex-soldier and Home Guard over 65. He could walk supported, but was very badly scalded. The last to be got out was poor Frances Barbara, Trice's daughter, who was dead. Two bombs were dropped in the [Small Arms] School staff quarters, but fell between the rows of houses. Mrs Allen, our late cook, got a piece of shrapnel in her back and a small boy was hit. The sirens sounded 10 minutes after it was all over. The Huns said on their wireless that they had destroyed a factory!

Wednesday 13 May

A misty wet day; no air activity. In the evening I had the training squad and the recruits all by myself on the range; Grove-White was in the butts. I did not even have an NCO to help. The former behaved themselves. There was an alert at 7.30 p.m. as we were assembling. The Hun came in over Folkestone and hit something in Hawkinge. I saw the column of dust rise. Alert at 8.30 p.m. and again at 9.30 p.m. The whole 138th Brigade were out in their Bren carriers dressed up like commandos, with woolly caps on their heads.

Thursday 14 May

No alerts all day. Orderly room 10 a.m. to 12.45 p.m. After lunch, I picked up Stansfield and Grove-White at the Ritz [Cinema] and drove to Red Lion Square. We drove up to the cemetery and attended young Nicholls' funeral. Daphne attended the Trice girl's funeral, as she was a Ranger. Miniature range in the evening.

Friday 15 May

I drove Street round to the KOYLI orderly room to arrange with their new CO details of our training fortnight. Street was in one of his worst 'can't do anything' moods, and made me very ashamed of him. I went back and helped Stansfield sort ammunition until nearly 1 p.m. Air activity at midday. Gunfire at 9 p.m.

DIRECT HIT ON CHURCH

Sunday 17 May

A warm day with a thick mist lying low on the sea. This was the first day of 'A' Company's ten days' training with the KOYLI, and we started it by manning our defensive posts in full kit. About 10.15 a.m., four Huns flew in, dropped bombs on Folkestone and swung round and out to sea machine gunning. Street stood gaping in the road; I made a bolt for one of No. 2 Platoon's houses but found it locked. The sirens sounded quite 10 minutes later, and our planes turned up later still. One bomb damaged the Grand Hotel, one fell on an empty house in Godwin Gardens and two fell right on top of Christ Church, reducing all but the tower to rubble. Two women, one of them the verger's wife, were killed. Luckily, the service did not start until 11 o'clock. The Huns flew so low it must have been deliberate. There was spasmodic gunfire at sea, as if a convoy was being attacked, then at 11.30 a.m. a very heavy blitz started in the direction of Calais and moved down the coast. I walked up the canal and was in time to see the attack on No. 1 Platoon. I returned to Twiss Bridge then walked up to Smalls Cottage on North Road where the KOYLI had a signal-receiving centre. Here Colonel Wheeler with Street and two of his officers picked me up and drove me to Saltwood to see the attack on No. 3 Platoon. Fuller had disposed his men skilfully and the enemy found no gap. Two of the KOYLI had been dressed in German uniforms. Their advance was hampered by the church congregation coming out as they approached. They were captured by a well-concealed party under Chappell. There was a very heavy blitz across the Strait about midnight.

Christ Church, Folkestone, destroyed by a high explosive bomb

Tuesday 19 May

Street went on ahead and left me to march 'A' Company to the Range. Our men were allowed to fire with service rifles and the Bren gun and we were given a demonstration of firing the Bren at parachute flares with tracer bullets. Finally, Trappit fired '68' grenades from the grenade rifle, exploding most of them only halfway up to the target. This, in my opinion, is a nasty weapon. I did not get home until 10 p.m. as Street and I were taken by Colonel Wheeler to the staff quarters where there is a small mess. Bombers and speedboats were out at midnight.

Wednesday 20 May

At 11 a.m. two Huns sneaked over through the haze and swung round over the Roughs to drop their bombs, but our two Spitfires were up and they bolted back out to sea dropping their bombs and machine gunning local fishing boats manned by Harry and Jesse Wire. The bombs dropped wide. The Spitfires chased them and shot one down. There was an explosion at 2.30 p.m., which sounded like a landmine. In the evening we had a demonstration of street fighting in Miss Villiers' old school, at 40 South Road. Daphne was very shocked when she heard of it. We also worked sets of field wirelesses. The new Brigadier, about the 12th we have served under, watched us, and a Colonel Scaife. The latter has been appointed to

one of the latest Home Guard staff jobs – GSOI [General Staff Officer I].
Gribbon, phoning Street, said he understood Scaife had served in the
Burmese Navy in the last war! I had visions of an Irrawaddy steamer
captain. The story ought to follow him round.

Saturday 23 May

A fine day. About 12 noon, our planes flew over to France in large numbers.
There was an alert for ten minutes at 1 p.m. The sky over the Channel was
covered with white streamers. At 3 p.m. the Hun guns on Gris Nez fired at
Dover, one shell hitting the castle. Then an intense battle broke out in the
direction of Boulogne. The wave of optimism sometime back was a strange
phenomenon. Everyone seemed certain we would finish off the Germans in
a few months. Now it is all shouting for a 'second front', that arch villain
Beaverbrook leading. To me, the situation seems as backward as it has ever
been. The Russians, in all their boosted winter offensive, have gained no
ground. The Germans have not given up. The winter weather killed large
numbers of Germans. We are pouring tanks, planes etc. into Russia and
have lost our Far East empire. The poor Chinese, having been forced to
come to our rescue in Burma, are now completely cut off and attacked from
three sides, and we do not move a finger to help them. The much-boosted
American naval victory off the Coral Seas may have been a blow to the Jap
fleet, but the Americans seem also to have been put out of action. Now we
are cheering Mexico on to come to our help. We have surely learnt the
Bolshy lesson – scream for help when attacked but refuse help to one's best
friend. At home, it is nothing but strikes. Sixteen pits idle and we are
threatened with coal rationing.

Sunday 24 May

Whitsuntide. A strong west wind all day. We had platoon battle drill on
the Roughs in the morning. The officers did not themselves command
their platoons, which to my mind wasted the exercise. Street went off to
see No. 1 Section, leaving me in command for most of the time, and I tired
myself out walking the length of the Roughs four times as well as up and
down the hill. A thunderstorm at 2 p.m. Our planes busy in the afternoon.

Tuesday 26 May

Six of our conscripts turned up in the morning and enrolled. In the
evening, Stansfield and I enrolled another 20 between 6 p.m. and 8 p.m.

On the whole they were not a bad lot, though a few were full of excuses and reservations. The Company had gas drill.

Wednesday 27 May

My birthday! I have reached the age of 60. Daphne's present was three bright wren farthings for my collection. A wet morning, but the sun came out later. In the afternoon there were bursts of bombing to the west, and later the Huns shelled Dover. In the evening we were all driven in trucks to halfway up Etchinghill and marched to a funnel-shaped valley beyond the railway line. Here a platoon (less one section) of the KOYLIs attacked a position, under fire of live rounds from both flanks. Then our younger men, about 30 in number, in two sections under Sergeant Kite and another NCO, carried out a similar attack. Only young Denis Morgan flunked it. The others behaved well and shot straight. It was a well-run show, though Colonel Wheeler confessed he was in a panic lest an accident happened. The rain came down hard as I reached home.

Thursday 28 May

We had night manning of our posts, with evacuation of wounded to the ARP posts and an attack by the KOYLI. Street sent me to Battle Headquarters in Small's cottage in North Road, where I went after seeing the Saltwood Platoon assault. I had a KOYLI signaller to send messages, and talked about India to a York and Lancaster subaltern, whose company mess was in the cottage. Nos. 1 and 2 Platoons sent me no messages. I got indirect information about them through 'B' Company KOYLI, and Trice sent one short note after that. Fuller in Saltwood started well, but was later too busy. Wheeler and Street, keen to test the ARP, kept asking Captain Fuller for more casualties until he had sent half his platoon. Then the York and Lancaster Regiment had a show on, unknown to us, and scuppered one of his posts.

Friday 29 May

A very busy morning at orderly room, chiefly over our conscripts. Major Stokes, the Chief Warden [ARP], wrote and Stainer, the Town Clerk, came and grumbled about our enrolling all their fire-watchers. I explained that we have orders to take what the Labour Exchange sends us. About 5 p.m., motorcyclists, Bren carriers and the biggest tank I have ever seen, loaded with infantrymen, came down our road, and a major battle developed. The whole town below soon became full of all kinds of tanks, guns and carriers and the noise of blanks and crackers was deafening. A very noisy night.

The first Allied 1,000-bomber raid of the war took place on Cologne, on the night of 30–31 May, with the stated intention of weakening German morale and hastening the end of the war.

Saturday 30 May

A disturbed night owing to men and lorries moving about in our road. Probably returning from manoeuvres. Also planes overhead. I cut the hedgerows in the afternoon. Street has his son in Libya and Stansfield has a nephew there. Both are very anxious.

> THE R.A.F. made a world's record in air raids last night. Over 1,000 bombers attacked Cologne, at least twice as many as have on any one occasion been sent over this country by Germany. For more than an hour and a half high-power explosive bombs fell in quick succession on the city, and the number of incendiaries was, as one German report says, " colossal "

Sunday 31 May

Nos. 1 and 2 worked on honing their position under instruction of the KOYLI NCOs and No. 3 Platoon were taught judging distances by a KOYLI officer in the fields beyond Saltwood Church. I went to the latter at the start, then spent the rest of the time with No. 2 Platoon. Violent thunder and lightning and heavy rain all afternoon. I saw a number of planes coming in high overhead, shining in the sunlight. Our savage attack on Cologne horrifies me. We make no pretence now that we are out to kill women and children. Perhaps owing to that, I had a restless night. I heard no alert, but at 1.15 a.m. I woke to the sound of a distant plane and the throb of bursting bombs or gunfire, which every now and then rattled the windows.

Monday 1 June

The raid last night was on Canterbury. Our defence was most inadequate. The damage to the town was very great; all communications have broken down, and even the roads blocked. Worried about my sister-in-law Eva and niece Joan, I was not able to telephone and the police, as usual, could do nothing. I finally persuaded the Post Office to accept a telegram. Alert 12.30 p.m. to 1 p.m. In the afternoon, the sky was full of planes and during the evening parade I saw a large formation of planes returning from France. Alert 8 p.m. to 8.30 p.m.

Tuesday 2 June

I was woken up at 3.15 a.m. by all the sirens sounding. The attack was similar to last night, but not so intense. The 'all clear' at 4 a.m. I heard that the Huns again attacked Canterbury, but chiefly with incendiaries. In evening I went to orderly room and enrolled 16 recruits (conscripts). A few groused, but one recruit named LA Griffiths was a bad man – a shuffling gasbag of a Welshman. I then walked to the 30-yard open range, where Street was firing, all the men armed with a Tommy gun.

Wednesday 3 June

A hot summer day. Another disturbed night with planes, which sounded German, flying about. One roared over the rooftops from east to west. It was another attack on Canterbury and one on Ashford. Alert 2.10 p.m. to 2.20 p.m. In afternoon there were sounds of big guns beyond Dover, with the usual air activity, and there were two small ships out in the Strait. Evening parade – training squad with Mills grenades under Sergeant H Wire.

The Government announced that it would nationalise coal reserves in June 1942, and place them under the control of the Coal Commission. The mining industry remained in private hands until 1946.

Thursday 4 June

I woke at 6 a.m. with the 'all clear' sounding. Then our planes flew over and for 15 minutes there was heavy bombing on the opposite shore. This was the raid on Boulogne. Another hot day. Alert 1.40 p.m. to 2.20 p.m. First parade of conscript recruits; 23 received rifles and Trice gave them a little preliminary drill. There were only four absentees. Owen of Lloyds Bank was very peeved, as he was made to stay on. It is now known that there had been far more strikes in 1941 than there had been in any year since 1920. The first half of 1942 must be even worse. Miners all over the country are now on strike.

Friday 5 June

It is extraordinary how American naval victories take them each time further from the east and nearer their own shores. People are predicting the next victory will be off Alaska. A hot cloudless day, but no air activity. Our guns were practising in the afternoon. A short alert at 9.45 p.m. as our bombers came home.

Saturday 6 June

Another blazing hot day. Vernal had promised to send us the recruits' kit by lorry this morning but failed, so Trice and I accompanied Stansfield to fetch it in our cars. I had my first sight of Christ Church since it was bombed. Daphne spent the day with the Red Cross getting an empty shop ready for a display for the Girl Guides and the Red Cross, and she got me to draw a poster for her in the evening.

Wednesday 10 June

I hear that many of the unexploded bombs and incendiaries in Canterbury when examined were found to contain sand. Parade of training squad in the evening. A farce with Street, me and Sergeant Wire supervising 12 small boys. The fighting in Libya and Russia both depress one.

Sunday 14 June

Cold but fine day. Recruits' parade in morning; only one absent out of 37. I find it very difficult to carry on with Street, who gives out-of-date orders, rushes everything and tells the men they are good when they are making mistakes. Our bombers came over in large numbers at 11.30 a.m.

> **SUNDAY, June 14**
>
> FORCING his movement against Tobruk, Rommel is trying to break through the right wing of our Eighth Army and cutting its coast line of communications. The bulk of the German armoured divisions are said to be engaged in this desperate battle.

Tuesday 16 June

A cloudy day, some sun in afternoon and a few planes about. Wondered if one of them might be the Beaufighter which dropped a tricolour on the Arc de Triomphe.

Wednesday 17 June

An overcast day with showers. At 6.40 p.m. the ground twice shook, and the front door rattled as if it were earthquake shocks. I went to the lookout in Mrs Russell's garden and saw a line of ships passing up the Strait partly hidden by mist or rain, and a huge column of water rise up behind the last of them. I also thought I saw flashes from the ships as of guns, but I rather think it may have been minesweeping. Sergeant Wire said that when fishing they have been passed by frequent convoys lately. Parade of the training squad, to which Street did not come. After Sergeant Wire had finished his lesson in grenade throwing, I let him go and myself drilled the squad in arms drill. Our instructors give their words of command parrot-like; neither explains each movement nor corrects faults.

The aftermath of a bombing raid on Canterbury with St Augustine's Abbey in the background (IWM Q(HS) 299)

Saturday 20 June

A perfect summer day. I went by bus to Canterbury to look up Eva and Joan. Canterbury has been half destroyed, and they had marvellous protection. A big area of houses at each end of their small lane has been burnt and flattened, and the only incendiary in their lane failed to ignite. I did not go sightseeing, but one passed a lot of the damage. I saw one very big crater as big as a mine crater of the last war. The extraordinary thing is that only 60 were killed. The town is now surrounded by barrage balloons which, I am told, were available but had not been ordered up on the first (and worst) night raid. That nasty smell of high explosives and burning filled the air.

Sunday 21 June

A summer day. This Libya defeat is very bad. The obvious reason is we have somehow lost command of the sea. When Churchill makes a blunder, he is afraid to face us; he bolts to America as he did at the time of Singapore. Poor Ritchie [Commander of the Eighth Army in North Africa] will be sacrificed and perhaps Auchinleck [Commander in Chief Middle East] too, but the fault is with the Government who will now weaken some other theatre too late to help Egypt. There will be the usual debate: Churchill will take all the blame and they will be afraid to turn him out.

> A DISASTER has befallen British arms. Early this afternoon an Italian communiqué announced the fall of Tobruk. Half-an-hour later

Monday 22 June

In the early morning, whilst a battle was going on at sea, Phyllis had a nightmare, calling out 'there they are!' I was not able to wake her, although I shouted at her. Our morning woman left without giving notice for a £2 job at Boots. Everyone profoundly shocked at Libya. Shooting on the range by recruits in the evening. The recruits shot well.

Tuesday 23 June

In the evening, the training squad and six men from the platoon threw live grenades on 'N' range instructed by Trappit and one of his sergeants. They all threw very badly, probably due to nervousness. I had suggested to Street that the Cadets should not throw, but they enjoyed themselves hugely, watching from one of the bays. They were very pleased when debris hit the watch tower and made us all duck for cover.

Wednesday 24 June

Our wedding day! We were woken up by the alarm clock and sirens at 7 a.m. A short orderly room; very few planes about all day.

Saturday 27 June

Churchill is back. Evidently he thinks our indignation has cooled sufficiently, but it is worth noting that in every by-election lately an Independent has defeated his nominee, and they have made some very outspoken speeches.

Monday 29 June

A very hot day. Our new morning woman, a Mrs Johnson, started work. There were a lot of planes flying high all day, and the booming of distant guns or bombing. Recruits shooting in the evening. Feathers in the sky over Dungeness, then heavy AA or cannon fire all up the Strait.

Thursday 2 July

Our speedboats were out early. Alert at 7.45 a.m. In the evening the recruits shot from the 300-yard range with credit. Churchill, as expected, got a vote of confidence with a big majority. All parties are afraid he will resign and won't have anyone else in his place. He knows this and won't change his ministers, however incompetent. I hope this last reverse will be a lesson to him and make him give up trying to win the war by bombing German women and children, and helping Russia to the detriment of our security. Planes over in the evening. About midnight a battle raged round our neighbourhood and Saltwood.

Monday 6 July

Warm and windy. Mitchell came to see me after lunch. Owing to a breakdown, he cannot remember anything and even had to write down what he had come to talk about. When Stansfield had to resign, Street wished to make him Platoon Commander, but Stansfield asked me to back him up and say he was not fit for it. I imagine to prove his point, Stansfield abruptly told Mitchell he was appointed and ordered him to take over. It seems to have thoroughly upset Mitchell, who says that Stansfield bullies him and is telling him he has been appointed Company Gas Officer. Mitchell wants me to see that he is consulted before being given any job. I think I was able to put his mind at rest.

Tuesday 7 July

On arriving at orderly room, I found Stansfield sitting in the CO's chair with papers spread over the table and his arms round them like a spoilt boy grabbing all the toys. He hung on to the chair all morning. Later we enrolled about eight more conscripts. Their whining and excuses made me feel fed up.

Friday 10 July

Heavy rain all day. I drove Stansfield into Folkestone in the morning to collect kit for our recruits. I stored the kit and drove back to Sandgate, where I met Brigadier Gribbon and went over to the castle, where both companies are to store their superfluous explosives. Sandgate Platoon have the castle for a post, and have it well fitted out. I begin to think Gribbon is a better man than Street. His men really guard their homes and do something useful.

Wednesday 15 July

A busy morning, ending up with driving round the town delivering kit. Our Air Force were practising dive-bombing Lympne; some big bombers took part. Some Huns seemed to come in over the Marsh. St Swithin's Day, with no rain. Folkestone had a tear gas test, the public were not warned and there were a number of casualties.

The Battle of Stalingrad, which began on 17 July 1942, was one of the largest and most significant battles of the war. The bitter struggle, which ended on 2 February 1943, cost almost two million lives. Russia's eventual success made a German victory on the Eastern Front impossible, and the battle was a turning point in the war.

POST MAY BE CENSORED

Warning by P.M.G.

Beware of "careless talk" when you write letters; they may be censored.

Friday 17 July

A dawn patrol, a heavy shower then the alert at 7 a.m. woke me up. 'All clear' at 7.30 a.m. with more rain. I met 'young' Gausby, down here on leave from an AA battery which mans invasion barges and has had extensive manoeuvres in Scotland. I hear also that his (the 46th) Division are off on manoeuvres. Gausby agreed with me that it is all bluff.

Saturday 18 July

We woke to more rain. In the morning, I drove Stansfield into Folkestone and with Trice and his car brought back 28 Sten guns, a lot of ammunition, grenades and a Northover. After lunch, Eva and Joan came over from Canterbury. Phyllis regaled them with plates full of raspberries, of which we have a bumper crop this year. Lyttelton [Minister of State for War Production] tells us we are in a worse plight than we were after Dunkirk, yet the wireless and papers are full of the imminence of a 'second front'. Bluff and rotten propaganda is all they can do. Their idle boasting of the 1,000-plane bombing we were going to do, like everything else, has gone with the wind.

Tuesday 21 July

Our planes were active, flying roof-high in the morning and again in the afternoon. There were two loud explosions and some gunfire. I watched a tug towing a raft with a sort of crane on it manoeuvring off the end of Stade Street whilst another winked 'Morse'. I learnt afterwards they were mending or laying a cable. A section shooting competition at falling plates on the range in the evening. They did not shoot well. Afterwards, I distributed Sten guns. Whilst driving, two Huns flew in over Folkestone, were met by AA fire and flew home over Seabrook. I heard no bombs. One of our Spitfires went after them very soon.

A flight of Spitfires over England (IWM CH11479)

Thursday 23 July

Overcast, but no rain. Phyllis was woken up by a loud explosion and machine gun fire. A short alert at midday. The new recruits parade for the first time in evening. The nine old soldiers and one sailor showed they had not forgotten how to handle their arms. The other six were given squad drill. Street let me go when he dismissed the 'old stiffs'.

Saturday 25 July

A big bomber roared over the house sometime in the early morning so low I was sure it would hit something. I watched from Mrs Russell's a line of ships steaming down the Strait through the rain squalls. The local Brigade left today for manoeuvres, and our road is very peaceful. The Royal Welch Fusiliers are relieving the KOYLI, and the SWBs the Lincolns. Last Thursday I noticed the white noses on the planes which flew over us; now I find they are our new fighters, the Mustangs.

Sunday 26 July

We had a company route march up the Dymchurch Road, behind the Prince of Wales to Botolph's Bridge then up to the Grand Redoubt and home. No one fell out. Street set a very slow pace at the start. He gave a 'gas' and 'spray' alert marching out. I enjoyed myself, bringing up the rear. All the mothers and wives watched us pass by, and on our return called out to their men to fall out or there would be no dinner for them! At the start, Street allowed me to post markers and fall in the Company on them, a great difference to the scrimmage it has always been before. Whilst on the march, I saw four of our planes dive-bombing ahead of us, perhaps part of the manoeuvres.

Tuesday 28 July

A perfect day. Alerts 8.45 a.m. to 9.30 a.m. (longer than usual), 11.30 a.m. to noon, and 12.45 p.m. to 1 p.m. In the afternoon I took a walk up through Sandling Park then along the fields to the back of Hayne Barn and through Garden House woods to Saltwood. There is not one rabbit to be seen in the whole countryside. Distant booming of guns in the north all afternoon. Our motorboats were out in force in the night.

Tuesday 4 August

A cold, overcast day. No air activity. General Forster and Craufurd-Stuart visited us in the morning. The latter was in one of his exceptionally silly moods; his way of covering up his ignorance of his own Battalion's requirements. Phyllis and Daphne were both in Folkestone for the afternoon. Gandhi full of bounce, now. Let's hope we are just giving him rope to hang himself. Talk of the 'second front' has died down lately.

Wednesday 5 August

Alerts 11.45 a.m. to 12 noon and 12.15 p.m. to 1 p.m. Daphne had done most of the spadework getting up a Guides and Scouts sports meeting in Radnor Park. I offered to help, but did not realise

Lt-Col. Charles Kennedy-Craufurd-Stuart, CVO, CBE, DSO

what I had let myself in for. Daphne drove me in at 3.30 p.m. calling at several places for tug-of-war ropes etc. The sports started at 6 p.m. and I was on the gate from 5.30 p.m. to 8 p.m. I did not collect a large sum, as the other gates had not been locked and many got in through them. Daphne was wonderful, always in the right place and answering every question in her quiet, thorough way. Castle, the Folkestone Mayor, turned up and gave a speech. The Mayoress gave away prizes for the first half of the sports, and Daphne the rest. It finished at 9.30 p.m. and we got back to supper at 10 p.m. We ate it fast to race the blackout. All through the meeting, I wondered what would happen if a couple of intruder planes flew over; it was an ideal day for them, with an overcast sky.

Friday 7 August

Alert 9.40 a.m. to 10 a.m. In the afternoon I went to a garden party given by the KOYLI at the Commandant's house to meet their Colonel, General

Sir Wyndham Deedes. I met their late padre, now attached to the parachute troops, who sports the badge having done his seven 'jumps'.

Sunday 9 August
The day developed fine. Street staged a field day. Nos. 1 and 2 Platoons marched from Scanlon's Bridge to Slaybrook and attacked No. 3, who held a position in Sandling Park in front of the Home Farm. I was allowed to go with the latter, and enjoyed myself lying in the sun on the grass. Grove-White was slow coming up on the right to occupy the high ground and Trice, becoming impatient, attacked too soon and was engulfed by an advance section of Fuller's men. The York and Lancasters have again damaged Quarrymead. They put up a marquee for a Sergeants' dance and tied the tent ropes on the trees, smashed down part of the fence and stole some green apples. I showed the damage to two subalterns, who said it was the RSM who was responsible.

Wednesday 12 August
Alert 2.30 p.m. to 3 p.m. Planes high up in the clouds. Street had our machine gunners on the range. I collected Grove-White and his machine gun

Guildhall Street, Folkestone, after a dairy had been hit and the proprietor killed
(Folkestone Library/*Folkestone Herald*)

from Twiss Road, and took duty in the butts. The evening closed down very early and Grove-White, Owen and I had a job to put the machine gun back in the dug-out on the canal bank in the dark. The York and Lancasters kept up their dancing until midnight. As they dispersed, a heavy cannonade broke out from our guns and from the enemy across the Strait.

Saturday 15 August
Four heavy-engined Huns were over the golf links as the alert sounded. I heard them come in, then saw them lit up by the sun as they circled round and dived for Folkestone. More planes, I believe Huns, came in over the Marsh. I heard the bombs drop, mistaking the noise for AA fire. 'All clear' at 4 p.m., but for some time after planes were milling about the Marsh. We heard bombs had fallen in a dozen different places in Folkestone, from Ingles Meadow to the Skew Arches [railway bridge].

Sunday 16 August
Driving Phyllis into Folkestone, I drove along Guildhall Street and on to the Bayle, but saw no signs of damage. At 9.15 p.m. the house shook with explosions. At 11 p.m. I went to the lookout and saw across the Strait huge flashes light the sky and the flashes of salvos of guns. Also a strange red ball which seemed to float down along the coast above our seafront.

Tuesday 18 August
I was woken up by a gun at 12.30 a.m., which shook the house and nearly blew me out of bed. It is either a new gun or one placed in a new position. I was again woken at 6 a.m. by all the sirens hooting; Dover was hit. Craufurd-Stuart came in over some voluminous training instructions just issued by the Corps. We are expected to keep tabulated records on the training of every man in every conceivable subject. At 4.50 p.m. there was a sound of bombing in the Lydd direction, and I went out to the lookout. Two planes flew past me over the town, one seeming to me to be a Hun. On the 9 o'clock news we were told our old friend 'Binge' [Montgomery] was taking over the [8th] Army in Egypt. He will have to cancel the talk he was giving us next month. I wonder if he will try to teetotal the men in Egypt.

The Dieppe Raid, an Allied attack on the German-occupied port, began at 5 a.m. on 19 August 1942. Five hours later, the retreat was sounded, with around 60 per cent of those who went ashore killed, wounded, or captured.

Wednesday 19 August

I woke at 5 a.m. There was a continuous rumble of guns to the south, and the house shook repeatedly with loud explosions. Squadron after squadron of our planes, including many Mustangs, flew in the direction of the gunfire whilst others flew back. This continued up to 9.30 a.m., when there were bursts of gunfire at intervals (it was a heavy raid on Dieppe) and the planes went over less frequently until about noon when all was quiet.

Friday 21 August

I drove up to Saltwood about 12.40 p.m. Soon after, there were two loud explosions. Young Bryant's orderly said he could see two Huns and hear them machine gunning. A bystander called out: 'There's where the bombs dropped.' Looking down Brockhill Road, I saw a column of smoke rising above Hillcrest Road houses. I had a terrible shock, and exclaimed: 'My house is gone!' I dashed home and was relieved to find all well. Daphne and I went to the lookout, and saw the Grove Cinema and the Hythe Motor Works in ruins. In the afternoon, I went down into town. I found all the windows of our storeroom blown in, and [Major] Butler's office blasted in its upper storey. The fat Carr girl was singing as she cleared up the mess. Hall, the solicitor, who had been in his own office, was cut about the face. I met Igglesden at the Cinque Ports Club gate and went in with him. The whole club interior had been wrecked. He told me he had been sitting with Dr Maudy on the sofa whilst Craufurd-Stuart stood talking to [Major] Metcalfe. Something hit Stuart, smashing his head, and Metcalfe was untouched but badly shocked. A bullet entered Mandy's arm, severing an artery, and he may have to lose his arm. Old 'Timber' Wood was hit in the back of his head, but only bruised. The club butler was badly cut about the face by glass. I looked in at the Hythe Motor Works, where they were sweeping up the glass roof. They were machine gunned. Young Roger Hammond, son of one of our Sergeants, was killed and Dunkin (the manager) and Wiles (the mechanic) were badly wounded; the former, hit in the lung, is in danger. The bomb was the most destructive one we have had; roofs and windows in an extensive area were shattered, including half the length of the High Street.

Saturday 22 August

Trice turned up at orderly room with his face bandaged; he was in the Conservative Club, which was wrecked. Street was away visiting the new

Brigadier at Shorncliffe, the battery on the seafront and other places. The area from Folkestone to Dungeness is to be defended by only one Brigade, and we are to start patrolling the seafront next Wednesday, with headquarters at the battery.

Wednesday 26 August

Disturbed from 5 a.m. by the tramp of feet and rumble of AVs. Street was up in London for the day – marvellous how he gets out of funerals! I drove Stansfield and Grove-White into Craufurd-Stuart's funeral at the Parish Church, Folkestone, at noon. All the Mayor, Corporation and Police there, two Brigadiers and three Marine Officers. An elaborate ceremony, very inappropriate at times, and the parson in his oration forgot his words and made bad blunders. Most of us were excused going on to Hawkinge Cemetery. Stansfield, Tidmarsh, Wood and others gained a cheap advertisement, making out they represented clubs and associations. Stansfield claimed to represent Street!!

Thursday 27 August

A tropical day. Ships and speedboats in the Strait at 12.30 p.m. Various alerts throughout the afternoon and early evening. Alert 6.10 p.m.; looking up 10 minutes later, I saw two planes high up, lit up by the sun, wheel around and dive-bomb Folkestone and heard the explosion of at least two bombs. Sometime after, AA fire burst out over the sea. Young Wanstall, working in the garden, said he counted six. 'All clear' at 6.30 p.m. The bombs dropped either side of the railway. At 11 o'clock, there were two separate explosions; I felt the blast through the open window lying in bed.

Sunday 30 August

Shooting on the range at falling plates at 100 yards. The men shot very badly. After lunch, Gribbon rang up and asked me to take Command of 'B' (Folkestone) Company. I was afraid it might come. Street would not take over the Battalion if he had been asked, and he would not go to 'B' Company; it would mean too much work. Apparently, Gribbon turned up on the range to consult Street and suggested Tidmarsh, Grove-White and other impossible people. I went round to get Street's advice after supper. He was very kind and said nice things, such as not knowing how he could get on without me, but he said I ought to take it and that

I was wasted as second in command of a small 'A' Company. I hope he was sincere!

Monday 31 August

I drove out over to Folkestone in the morning, met Gribbon at the Territorial Drill Hall and was introduced to [Captain] Vinson of 'B' Company, my second in command, Miss 'Jackie' Green the typist and some of the officers. Gribbon has surrounded himself with officers and NCOs, nevertheless he works up to 8 p.m. in the office. He goes about with a suitcase full of secret files, which he said belonged to the Company but which he asked leave to keep as he had not digested them! I got away soon, but came back in the afternoon. The Adjutant of the RA Brigade turned up to arrange for 28 of our men to defend the guns on East Cliff (which they call West Folkestone!). At 'stand to', Gribbon sat in the chair and alternately gave me a file which he said he must explain and didn't, phoned up someone and gave Miss Green a letter to type. A very heavy thunderstorm commenced about 5.30 p.m. and looked as if it would go on forever so I borrowed an AG [anti-gas] cape to go home in.

Tuesday 1 September

Daphne's birthday. She had a very dull day. Alerts all day. I had another unsatisfactory day at the office, morning and afternoon. There was a tip-and-run raid on Lydd, the Huns flying very low. One bomb hit a gang of Hythe men, killing two and wounding several others. I heard Amos, who used to work at Bluehouse Waterworks and was in Saltwood Platoon, was one of them.

Thursday 3 September

Alert 6 a.m. No second in command or typist; the latter was in Maidstone passing her medical for the Wrens. National Day of Prayer. I didn't take much notice of the 11 o'clock broadcast. There was an alert in the middle of it. I drove Phyllis to her church service in the evening, and went on to the Drill Hall where about 80 of 'B' Company and Electricity Platoon paraded under Stokes and marched to the Parish Church, where I joined them. The service was too long, the parson giving an address of 40 minutes. I had agreed to say a few words to the men, having assumed command, but when we got back to the hall I found it filled by two platoons. I made a hash of my speech as usual. Poor Phyllis was waiting all this time at her church, and we did not get home until 9 o'clock. I was out of practice driving in the dark.

Friday 4 September

I was woken at 6 a.m. by a loud explosion, which shook the house. I got up and woke Phyllis, who was sound asleep. Going out of the door, she fell on the landing. I called to Daphne, then there was a splitting crash on the other side of the house. Daphne got under her bed and hurt her nose. She soon got into her siren suit and went out to Mrs Russell's lookout. The 'all clear' sounded at 6.15 a.m. One bomb had bounced off the road bridge near Sandling Junction and exploded in a wood. The second went through the roof of Philbeach and exploded in the air between two houses near the Roman Catholic Church. Alert 6.30 a.m. to 7 a.m. I was at orderly room morning and afternoon. Phyllis and Daphne went by bus at 1 o'clock to Brabourne to buy plums. In the evening on my way home, I met Owen, Manager of Lloyds Bank, who showed me over the ruins of his house. He and his family had a marvellous escape. He and his two boys were on the landing, Mrs Owen flung herself on the bed over her small daughter and they went down with the floor, the roof being held up by a door. There was heavy damage for a large area around, but no one was killed.

Sunday 6 September

I had a most interesting morning. I picked up Vinson at the Drill Hall and drove to East Cliff where Crump was posting his 28 men for guarding 213 Battery with Captain Kearton, the Commander. Kearton showed us his guns and magazines. He remarked that Girl Guides would be a welcome addition; I found Daphne's label was still on the windscreen of the car. I next drove to a brickfield at the back of Cheriton and saw [Captain] Archer and [Lieutenant] Axford firing the spigot-mortar. Then to Sandgate Castle, where No. 1 Platoon under [Lieutenant] McHutchison attacked a skeleton enemy along the lower Sandgate Road. On my way home, I dropped in at Gribbon's for sherry. Mrs G is a dark-haired Frenchified little woman, and their son, who's in the Navy, is exactly like his father in looks and voice. Heavy bombardment of Dover at night, with the sky lit up with flashes.

Thursday 10 September
Huns flew in and dropped bombs on Ham Street early in the morning. I heard they did no damage. Had a talk with Vinson, who claims to have joined the Tanks at their inception and carried out most of the experimental tests. Phyllis and Daphne saw the sky over the Strait full of drifting balloons. Some people said they were meteorological, but they would be useless to us if they fell in Europe. I drove into Folkestone in the evening and saw No. 4 Platoon parading. I was so hopeless in the dark I crawled home via Cheriton.

Friday 11 September
I was woken at 6.15 a.m. by the siren; soon after there were two explosions followed by the rattle of machine gun fire along the front. Then speedboats chugged out at sea. Alert 7.40 a.m. with distant gunfire. Our big guns carried out target practice at midday. I heard from a Lyminge Home Guard, who heard it from a staff officer, that yesterday's balloons each carried a cylinder full of incendiary bombs and had been let loose by us timed to explode over somewhere in Germany.

Tuesday 15 September
In the morning I met all 'A' Company in the town and learnt that Street is making Hickling second in command and Vincent, the dentist, second in command of Saltwood Platoon. Stansfield has cracked up lately and is having an operation, and Yearsly takes his place. I went by bus in evening to Folkestone and round to Shorncliffe and managed to find No. 6 Platoon. Gribbon and Vinson run the officers [Axford and Welsh] down, but they struck me as rather quiet but nice men and Welsh has a breastful of medals. I looked in at No. 1 (McHutchison's) Platoon at Ingles Hall and went on to the Drill Hall. I noticed much damage in parts of Shorncliffe – more than I had been aware of.

Friday 18 September
Alert 6.50 a.m. A couple of Huns were driven off from Folkestone, turned,

fired on a couple of fishing boats, damaging one, and flew along the shore machine gunning. When they came past Hythe they were met with heavy fire from Brens etc. Phyllis went for a short visit to Guildford. Daphne was out in the evening and I got my own supper.

Saturday 19 September

Daphne and I had high tea at 5.00 p.m. and I went by bus to Sandgate, from where the CO drove [Captain] Bagshawe and me to Dover. I noted some more damage in the town, and much of the old damage cleared. We went up to the castle where I was a member of the court martial with Major Bently, Cheshire Regiment, and a subaltern of the Queen's to try a Home Guard named Marshall for deserting his post. There is no power to confine a Home Guard pending trial, and when the 14th Queen's escort went to collect Marshall, he was not at home. They spent the whole afternoon hunting him, without success. The court martial was to have commenced at 7 p.m. When at 7.30 p.m. the escort were returning to report failure, they met Marshall walking up to the Castle in uniform. He explained he was coming up to say he would not attend the court! Both the prosecutor and the soldier's friend were barristers disguised as officers. I thought the defence by the latter was legal quibbling, but he had had no opportunity of seeing the man except for 10 minutes before we tried him. Dover Companies' Home Guard orders were non-existent and I felt reluctant to convict the man, but he was obviously guilty. We sentenced him to two years' imprisonment, which the Corps Commander reduced to one. We finished at 9.30 p.m. and I did not get home until 10.30 p.m. For a short time, bombers flew over the coast in large numbers. At 10.40 p.m. and again at 11.00 p.m. there were violent explosions behind us. They were, I believe, our heavies firing. The house was shaken to its foundations.

Sunday 20 September

There were two heavy showers in the morning, which broke up the fine weather. When I got out of the car I found a back tyre punctured and I had to use the very threadbare spare. I looked up No. 6 Platoon in Shorncliffe and went on to Quested's brickfields where some of No. 2 under Webb were firing the Northover. They were firing at the extreme range of 150 yards and were not bursting the bottles. I discovered that Webb had served in the Kent Cyclist Battalion [First World War]. I next drove to the polo ground, where Lieutenant Gill was putting 160 men through the gas chamber. Then I saw the black street musician we used to call 'the Abyssinian' whose name is Thomas and joined the Home Guard with the last batch of conscripts.

Monday 21 September

I drove Hickling into Folkestone. He was all togged up as a Lieutenant although he won't be gazetted for a long time. He was going to have his photo taken. He turned up at the Drill Hall in time for a drink and to be taken home. I had to go in again in the afternoon because Gribbon wanted me to meet the Brigadier, so I changed into uniform intending to have supper in Folkestone. Gribbon kept me to 5 p.m. I glanced through my papers at the Drill Hill and on coming out ran into Molly, Miss Dix's maid, who reminded me of the latter's standing invitation, so I went to the flat with her and was given tea, cheese and tomatoes. Colonel Wilson, commanding the 50th Buffs, inspected the Company of Cadets under [Captain] Cox, with Gribbon and Bagshawe present. The garage delivered the car at the Drill Hall, so I had to drive it home. There was, however, a moon and I got home without too much trouble.

Friday 25 September

We were woken by the siren at 7 a.m. Gribbon arranged that one Battalion or Company signaller should be in the Drill Hall guard each night. It was clearly laid down that the man had to do his turn of guard, but last night Sergeant Dunn, who is to be promoted to Battalion Signals Officer, refused to allow the man to take his turn. He had also got the Adjutant to transfer two men by name to Battalion without asking me. I went over to Gribbon, and got an assurance from him that he had given no orders. He promised to reprimand Dunn and cancelled the order about the signallers. I am determined to show them that I command the Company. Phyllis went to her [Christian Science] reading room at 3.30 p.m. and Daphne drove to her Cheriton Guides at 6.30 p.m. I made my own supper. 'B' Company had a dance at the Leas Cliff Hall in the evening. I was sure Phyllis would refuse to be hostess, so asked Mrs Gribbon to do so once more. The hall was packed. Admiral Round-Turner and the Chief Constable were our guests. I met most of the families of my officers. I notice all my officers are decidedly plain, nearly all their wives good-looking and their daughters without exception pretty. Daphne was caught by a policeman parking her car on the wrong side of the road, and couldn't find the insurance certificate or driving licence. When she got home she found her driving licence was out of date!

Saturday 26 September

Daphne came into Folkestone with me in the morning and went on to Cheriton on Guide business. Alert 11.15 a.m.; AA gunfire and planes charging about the sky. At 11.40 a.m. Huns flew in from the sea over Folkestone and Hythe and heavy AA fire was opened by every gun around Folkestone but hit nothing. I heard that they dropped their bombs in the sea. Alert 9.30 p.m. I heard that the ARP had orders to stand to, and at 10 p.m. some of the Hampshires marched off down the road. I thought there was to be a commando raid, but instead a torrent of rain fell with lightning and thunder which crashed and echoed down the coast. A big convoy got through to Russia this week. I wonder how many ships were sunk. We guarded it with 75 warships; no wonder we can do nothing elsewhere. The raid on Oslo by Mosquito aircraft on Friday was a bright spot.

Sunday 27 September

I picked up Axford in Sandgate and drove to Quested's brickfield where Nos. 1 and 2 were firing their Sten guns for the first time under Lieutenant Archer, who is a good instructor. General Forster arrived about 11 o'clock and talked to the men. At 12 o'clock I took him down to the harbour where Martin with No. 4 Platoon (Crump being sick) was looking out a scheme with young Captain White of the South Lancashires. On my way home I looked in at the Gribbons', where Daphne had preceded me, and met a Lieutenant Foster RN. The day turned out sunny and warm. The Queen ill with bronchitis.

Monday 28 September

Rain at night and all day. The 9th Buffs taking over from the 14th Durhams. The latter no loss; they are a poor crowd. An officer from each came to find out where the post stores are. I give them Gribbon's wonderful chart, which the Durhams man said he had not received. This wasn't true. He next said the HG were not keen to man certain posts, which annoyed me and I flared up. The trouble is that Gribbon has led us into doing more than we are capable of.

Thursday 1 October

Heavy rain at night and a wet morning, but fine after 11.30 a.m. I went into Folkestone in the evening but got fed up with office work and did not get round to other platoons. A small advance in Libya. Most papers decry Hitler's speech. I think it was a scathing indictment of our policy.

Friday 2 October

A hot summer day. About midday, guns round Folkestone fired for nearly an hour. Alert 1.45 p.m. A plane making a double drone flew in from seawards, circled overhead and slowly made off westwards. It was grey in colour and gave out a thick white trail. There were bursts of AA fire, a cluster of shell bursts over Folkestone and others wide of the place. All very mysterious! When walking down to the Drill Hall in the evening, I watched our planes with all their lights on homing back to Hawkinge – a very pretty sight. It was the end of raids by us and the Americans, which had lasted throughout the day. I listened to a lecture on wireless given by the 46th Divisional Signals Officer to 'B' Company Signallers. A nice young captain, but he was not lucid.

Sunday 4 October

I drove into Folkestone, picking up Bagshawe in Sandgate, and learnt from him that Gribbon was taking the Brigadier of 206 Brigade round my spigot-mortar sites; he had not asked my permission, or asked me to accompany him. I picked up Stokes at the Drill Hall and went round his positions overlooking the golf links and round the Central Station. We next drove to East Cliff and went round Crump's positions. I went back and watched a soccer match between Nos. 1 and 3 Platoons. A big troop-carrying plane flew over several times. Stalin was rather caustic about the 'second front' and 'aid to Russia'. We are not allowed to remind him of his pact with Germany and the thousands of Poles he interned. We staged a small commando raid on Sark to carry off a prize Jersey cow!!!

Monday 5 October

A warm, overcast day. Alert 2.30 p.m. and gunfire in the Strait. I went in again to orderly room in the afternoon and did some useful work. Alerts 4 p.m. and 6.15 p.m., with fighting overhead high up. The 'all clear' went at 6.50 p.m. followed immediately by another alert. About 8 p.m., big guns began to fire, some sounding like AA, others shaking the house, then our bombers came over in hundreds. I went out to the allotments. The French coast was covered in cloud and only now and then flashes burst out above them. Over the golf links towards Dover, there were vivid flashes and one huge semicircular orange glare. The big guns fired at intervals, even those on the seafront joining in, whilst all the time our bombers went over.

Thursday 8 October

The Sark raid was a daring one. There must be something true in German allegations that we tie up our prisoners. We still teach the acts of savages in our Battle Schools. (The Germans chained prisoners captured at Dieppe, but released them when we retaliated.) A dark damp morning. Alerts 7.15 a.m. and 7.45 a.m. Phyllis' budgerigar died. Alerts 3.20 p.m. and 6.15 p.m. In the evening I spent my whole time in my office, but I cleared off a lot of outstanding work. On my way home, Lydd guns were firing half a dozen rounds.

Friday 9 October

Alerts in early morning. Huns came in over Lympne and were fired on by AA guns. As I arrived in Folkestone about 10.15 a.m. all the sirens were sounding. People commenced to run and a woman went round in a circle in Alexander Gardens saying: 'What is happening? What shall I do?' I pushed her into a deep doorway but she bolted out again twice, so I let her go. The police were seizing people and throwing them down the shelters. Some rifles were fired, and a burst of six shells from the AA gun on the Leas made me look up; I saw the sky full of double-tailed machines diving on Hawkinge. They were American Lockheed fighter-bombers, very fast. Daphne heard that one plane was hit.

Saturday 10 October

I was busy with an assortment of affairs in the morning. Daphne went to Maidstone for the day to a Guides' conference on Lady Baden-Powell's visit and on the scheme for sending Guides into liberated countries.

Tuesday 13 October

I was kept in the office until nearly 1.30 p.m. by Vernal arguing about 'B' Company bills. Training films in evening; two out of the three were new. I came back in one of 'A' Company's lorries. Phyllis, phoning Mrs Dix, crossed a line on which two officers were talking of troop movements. She chipped in and suggested to the officers to remedy it, but they did nothing. Daphne wanted to start a conversation in German!

Wednesday 14 October

Alert 7.30 a.m. Two explosions rattled the windows at 1.45 p.m., followed a little later by an alert. Daphne drove me into Folkestone in the afternoon, and I worked out a training programme with Archer. At 7.30 p.m. I left and went to Cheriton, where Daphne picked me up and drove me home. She was fined 10/- for her parking offence.

Sunday 18 October

I went into Folkestone by bus, and met a young 9th Buffs Captain named Miller and, with Archer, showed him round the positions of Nos. 1, 2 and 3 Platoons, which his company has to man until we get there. Miller told me the 9th Buffs were raised after Dunkirk and composed of men from Northampton and London. The Chief Guide, Lady Baden-Powell, visited Folkestone in the afternoon. All the Guides and Brownies met her at Miss Lewis' flat. Daphne worked out the whole show and coloured a pretty programme (also her idea) to give her, signed by all the patrol leaders.

Wednesday 21 October

Trafalgar Day. I had more interference with my Company. Bagshawe sent for Archer, told him his training programme was wrong and ordered him to alter it. I lost my temper, went over and had it out with Bagshawe and Gribbon, but he is a slimy toad and a liar. Fine speech by old [Jan] Smuts [Prime Minister of South Africa], such an honest Christian outlook. Everyone up in arms (rightly, I think) over us copying the Hun and chaining prisoners.

Thursday 22 October

Heavy rain at night, and a dark morning. Alerts 8.15 a.m. and 8.45 a.m. Gribbon rang me up to say Brigadier Tremellan would like to meet me at the Drill Hall at 3 p.m. I came home a little earlier than usual, changed into uniform and was back there by 2.30 p.m. At 3 p.m. I was rung up and informed he could not come. I stayed on until 8.15 p.m., when I drove home by the light of the moon. Zone orders out: Fuller made captain and second in command of 'A' Company, but I have not been gazetted to 'B' Company.

Friday 23 October
A very mild, overcast day. I had a long talk with Gribbon, who is very chastened. I went in again for evening parade and stayed late, discussing the coming exercise. Smuts and Churchill were in Dover in the afternoon. Mrs Roosevelt is in England. Our bombers were again over us in large numbers in the evening. The 8th Army began their attack on El Alamein.

Sunday 25 October
Four loud explosions at 7.15 a.m. followed by cannon fire; Spitfires flew over at rooftop level. Dover balloons were out and the minesweepers were in the Strait. I heard bombs were dropped on New Romney and Littlestone, causing casualties. I picked up Gribbon and drove to East Cliff to show him round the battery positions. Scaife, the 12th Corps Training Officer for HG, was inspecting and I had arranged with Bagshawe to take him to Hythe ranges; but his fatal attraction for generals and staff officers made Gribbon ring them up and tell them to meet us. I took them all to the Warren tunnel, where a Company team was shooting against teams from the Navy and South Lancasters. Just as we arrived, the rain came down and washed out the match. The Home Guard were leading. I suggested to Gribbon he should go back with Scaife, and so got rid of him. I brought Phyllis home.

Tuesday 27 October
Rather cold, but fine. In evening, I went in for a training film. I was absorbed in accounts with [Captain] Vinson and [Private] O'Keefe, and was nearly late. Just as I was leaving, I was phoned up from the Town Hall by the Adjutant, who said the film had not turned up. The Brigade say the 12th Corps have repeatedly let them down like this. I asked him to dismiss my men, but collected my officers and had a conference on the coming military exercise, as I had received some further instructions. I got home at 10 p.m. On Monday afternoon, I had met Street who told me he considered it too stormy to patrol the seafront and when he went to mount

his patrol he would dismiss them. Brigadier Tremellan chose that night to visit the sea defences. He found my Sandgate Castle guard on the alert. 'A' Company patrol were absent.

Thursday 29 October
Alert 8 a.m. Later, a number of planes flew over the sea above the clouds. Alert 1 p.m. I saw two Mosquitoes. Alert 5 p.m. Saltwood Platoon got up a sing-song at the Village Hall and got some of the rest of 'A' Company to join in. They were due to start at 7.30 p.m., but by 8.15 p.m. the band had not turned up and nothing had developed. I had been persuaded to wear my tunic and felt a fish out of water amongst the battledresses! I was also not greeted with much enthusiasm, got a fit of depression and went home.

Saturday 31 October
I went into Folkestone morning and afternoon. Gribbon fussing about small details. Brigade Signallers filling my officers' room with phones, crossed their lines and put half out of order. The Brigade sent us .303 guns but no blank ammunition. There was a lot of gunfire everywhere, but I put it down to the sham fight. Actually, it was a heavy attack on Canterbury with casualties (10 killed in one bus) and much damage; we brought down nine of the raiders. I wondered about Eva and Joan. Dover was also a blaze of searchlights and AA. Two bombs were dropped near Park Farm, Folkestone. One Hun flew very low over Hythe. 'All clear' 9.15 p.m. and I went by bus into Folkestone [for the military exercise], reluctant to leave my family. Vinson gave me a camp bed and I slept with two blankets for pillows and two over me.

Sunday 1 November
All Saints. At 1.15 a.m. I was woken by heavy AA fire round me and planes flying low. I was too sleepy to stay awake. I woke again at 6.45 a.m. and got up. Message from the Brigade to 'stand to' arrived at 7.45 a.m. At 8.30 a.m. I was going to Vinson's restaurant when Gribbon turned up; I got rid of him by 8.45 a.m. and had a big meal. At 10 a.m. I went round Nos. 1, 2 and 3 Platoons' positions. After that I was held at the Drill Hall sending and receiving messages. My first news was that the forward troops had fallen back to Coolinge Lane and that Axford had unaccountably vacated Sandgate Castle, but his signaller got the telephone receiver away and reconnected himself with us from Observer Hill. Then Brigadier

Tremellan arrived and suggested I should report to 9th Buffs that my shortage of men were casualties from enemy air action. I received a Platoon from them. I sent them soon after to counter-attack up Bouverie Road, where it was reported the enemy were in force. Next, the Electricity Company arrived, having come through without seeing the enemy. I gave them a breather, preparatory to sending them up Sandgate Road, having heard that the Lyndhurst and Majestic [hotels] were taken. Just then, some enemy carriers, which I heard had got through, dashed up Shellons Street, headed by a police van full of soldiers. My men spotted the ruse and fired on them, but an umpire riding behind gave us out of action. However, I had got out the Electricity Platoon and they passed on. The former made their counter-attack, met the carriers and put them out of action. That finished the show. I was too busy to eat my rations, and some of the HQ scoffed the lot. Ceasefire was declared about 12.30 p.m. and I got home about 3.30 p.m. Eva rang up in the morning to say they had a very bad time but were unhurt.

Tuesday 3 November
Heavy rain in the morning. Orders received to hand in all Lewis guns immediately. These had been sent by the Admiralty to Shorncliffe for Naval defence, but had been intercepted by the Army and given to us. I went to Folkestone by 9.45 a.m. and, with Vernal doing the collecting, got them all in and handed over with only a few minor gadgets missing. Gribbon again 'badgering' me, as he himself calls it. I drove him home, when he told me his son was home for a day and gave me detailed information of his journey in a passenger steamer to take over a convoy, with its destination and cargo. I said: 'A man was shot in London last night for giving away convoy secrets.' It was on the 1 o'clock news.

The Second Battle of El Alamein, which ended on 5 November 1942, was a significant turning point in the Western Desert Campaign. The Allied victory ended German plans for occupying Egypt, controlling the Suez Canal and securing access to oil supplies.

Thursday 5 November
The Italians in Egypt are Guy Fawked!! Old 'Binge' has definitely broken the Axis lines, 9,000 prisoners, Huns bolting back and leaving the dagos [Italians] to do rearguard. Alert 12 noon. At 2.35 p.m., Daphne

came in declaring a German was overhead. It flew low from over Folkestone. There were a couple of shots from an AA gun and the alert sounded. It was a Dornier, which crashed into the woods behind Beachborough. Its bombs rolled down the hill without exploding. All the crew were killed, but there is a rumour that the pilot was alive and polished off by someone.

Friday 6 November
Rain and north wind in the morning, fine later. Alert 11.15 a.m. I went into Folkestone in the evening and had a Platoon Commanders' conference. Stokes came in halfway and in his bumptious manner said: 'Am I invited to this meeting, sir? I heard nothing about it until now.' Vinson said: 'You got a notice.' But he said 'no', and that he had looked in his box. I asked each Platoon Commander if he had a notice, and they all said 'yes'. Later, Stokes found his notice in his box and apologised to me. More rain in the evening. Fighting in Madagascar is over.

Sunday 8 November
A fine sunny day. First day of our training fortnight. I drove up Etchinghill, past the bomber which crashed near Beachborough, and to Grove Farm where Major Williams of the 9th Buffs was taking a class of officers in field tactics. From there I went through Cheriton to Shorncliffe, and saw three other classes. Intense air activity all morning. Alert 5 p.m. Bombers started going over in the evening. We hear that the bus service is to be drastically cut in south-east England. No buses after 9 p.m. and none on Sunday mornings. A huge army of Americans landed at Algiers, Oran, Casablanca etc. supported by the British Navy. Hints of a large convoy for some time. The Huns were completely deceived as to its destination.

Tuesday 10 November
I went to see the damage by shellfire in Folkestone. Behind the fish market, about four houses demolished, the bottom of Tontine Street badly knocked about, and behind the Dover Road schools about a dozen houses down. I hear only one man killed. I cannot understand what we gain by starting these bombardments. I went in by bus in the evening, first visiting Shorncliffe to see the officers and the Browning machine

gun classes. I had to dismiss the latter because No. 1 Platoon's gun had gone astray. I went from there to Ingles Hall to enquire about the gun, then to the Drill Hall where I met Gribbon. There, a young Buffs Corporal was showing at least two ex-sergeant majors how to put a pull-through into a rifle butt. This training is a farce. They have lost sight of its object, which is not to instruct but to pick out instructors. The Americans have taken Algiers, Oran and Casablanca, and are marching on Tunisia. At midnight, there was another gun duel across the Strait.

Wednesday 11 November

There was no damage in Folkestone last night. I went in uniform in the morning and with Captain Vinson placed 'B' Company's wreath on the war memorial at 11 a.m. Daphne placed the Girl Guides' wreath at the memorial at Hythe. At 10.30 p.m. the heavy guns again fired. One explosion was so sharp it appeared to be near Hythe. French forces in Algeria and Morocco surrender.

Friday 13 November

A very cold winter's day. I learnt that the 8th Army has entered Tobruk and Gaza. I went in the evening and visited the officers' and two other classes in Ross Barracks in Shorncliffe, then to the Drill Hall. At 9.30 p.m. four lorry-loads of ammunitions arrived; they had had a bad time hunting out the Headquarters, where they had to deliver their stuff. They were expected to return at 6.30 p.m. We arranged for them to doss down in the hall for the night.

Sunday 15 November

Church bells ordered to be rung by Churchill for 'Victory in Libya'. I disagree with the idea; it will cause slacking, and we have gained little so far. It was anyway a feeble show. Alert 10.30 a.m., and Huns flew over. I got held up in orderly room all morning and did not get out to see anyone. A fair number of our bombers flew over about 8.30 p.m. and returned at 1 a.m.

Sunday 22 November

A white frost. I picked up Archer and Bennett, the new Platoon Commanders, and met Colonel Ashe and Captain Kearton on East Cliff, where we discussed the new platoon and its duties. Crump again failed to send his men for instruction by the battery. Ashe showed Archer and me round the Copt Point battery. We saw a working model of the coast from Grand Redoubt with batteries and beachlights. Lieutenant Mont accosted me at the Drill Hall about his case. He is a gunner, and declares Gribbon promised him the platoon if it was formed. As Gribbon turned up late, I brought Mont up before him but Gribbon shuffled out of it. I did not get away until 1.30 p.m. In the evening our bombers were flying over us for an hour.

Monday 23 November
Gribbon left for a week's leave in Dorsetshire. A hard frost and very cold day. I went to office in afternoon. Alert 4 p.m. with much air activity and gunfire. We have taken Dakar and French West Africa, but that scoundrel [Admiral] Darlan is being boosted by the Yankees and De Gaulle snubbed.

Friday 27 November
The battle again raged all day round Beachborough. Two bombers set the grass on fire. At 3.15 p.m. two Hun bombers sneaked in through the mist, one came along the High Street firing its cannon. Daphne was up a tree. During the battle, two of our bombers had flown low over the house. She thought at first this was simulated, but realised that the firing was the real stuff and came down, taking the skin off her legs. Indoors, I heard the cannon fire then a loud explosion to the west, which brought me out. The sirens sounded quite 10 minutes after the Huns had gone, and one Spitfire came along later still; the Hun was brought down near Lydd. An hour later there was another explosion. When I went into Folkestone at 7 p.m., the battle was still raging: the sky was lit with red flashes, Verey lights and flares. The Huns marched into Toulon early this morning, and the French scuttled their fleet, many officers going down with their ships.

Monday 30 November
Alert 9.10 a.m. I drove Daphne in and we both stayed in Folkestone the whole day, having lunch at Central Town restaurant. I had the Quartermaster of the Ulster Rifles round to see me about taking over Post Store weapons. He tried to make me sign for what I did not have.

Wednesday 2 December

I stayed in Folkestone all day, getting back at 4.45 p.m. Gribbon, back from leave, rang me up three times and I saw him once. He gives me at once a feeling of dislike and opposition. I also met the Signals Officer of the new 8th Brigade and the CO of the local Women's Home Guard. Troops moving on all roads.

Thursday 3 December

Bombers seemed to be over us all night. Ours attacked Frankfurt etc. The Hampshires left at 4 a.m. Most of the morning I was engaged in handing over Brigade signal equipment, the new 8th Brigade Signals Officer complaining that Roberts of 206th Brigade was getting him to sign for non-existent articles. I went in to evening parade, but could only stay a short time as all the buses stop running by 9 p.m. now. I heard that Jenkins, the new Chief Constable, has already got into trouble over ARP rations.

Tuesday 8 December

A boy named Daniels working in Martin Walters Motor Works was brought to me by the manager for stealing £18 from the insurance fund. He is in [Lieutenant] Stokes' 'commandos' and says they gamble all night for 1/- stakes when on guard. The boy said they had forced him to join in, and he lost considerably. The manager and his father want him discharged from the Home Guard, which I was able to do, as he had wrongly given his age on enrolment. In the evening, I was able to inspect No. 2 Platoon at Cheriton and look in at No. 4 at the Drill Hall. Our bombers started flying over again from 6.30 p.m.

Wednesday 9 December

A sunny day. A Hun flew in at 9.10 a.m. Great air activity all day up to dusk, with an alert at 3.50 p.m., then at 6 p.m. our bombers came over continuously for an hour. They went to Turin last night and I guess they were paying a second visit. About 8 p.m., explosions shook the house. At 11 p.m. four rifle shots rang out on the front. At midnight our bombers returned.

Thursday 10 December

Last night Gribbon rang me up and asked me to represent the Company at General Vaughan's funeral. I remained in uniform all day. I went into

Folkestone in evening. As I left at 8 p.m. the sky was lit by flashes as the Dover guns fired. When I got to Hythe the Huns were answering and Folkestone was being shelled. I stopped on the top of the hill and watched it with men of the new regiment. They had come from the Isle of Wight, where all was peace. During the raid the gasworks were hit and a woman was killed.

Friday 11 December

A dark, stormy morning. Alert 9 a.m. I found Folkestone's shelling yesterday had caused greater damage than on all previous occasions. The front of one end of the Co-operative store was blown in, and a row of houses opposite, occupied by municipal dustmen, completely gutted. The rail track across the harbour and the swing bridge damaged. Tontine Street now has all but about four shops destroyed by blasts. Two gasometers were set ablaze and towards Radnor Park four houses completely destroyed. Only one person, the wife of a Jewish bookmaker named Cohen, was killed. My office had a pane broken, and the base of a shell was picked up outside. I took Gribbon and MacKie to General Vaughan's funeral service at the Parish Church (long and boring) and Shorncliffe cemetery. This was a short service, with pallbearers from the Suffolk Regiment and a bugler to sound the Last Post and Reveille. We did not get back to Gribbon's house much before 1 o'clock.

A house destroyed by a shell in Radnor Park, Folkestone (Folkestone Library/*Folkestone Herald*)

Monday 14 December
Rain at night. Alert 8.45 a.m. Hear that 'Binge' has got Rommel on the run again. I spent the day in Folkestone. Returning on the bus, I sat next to a podgy-faced American who claimed to have been in the Eagle Squadron. He gave me a cigarette impregnated with menthol.

Tuesday 15 December
Another dark morning, mild and wet. I went into Folkestone in the evening. We received a message from the Navy: 'With the steady wind blowing inshore, there was a probability of enemy drifting towards shore.' I think a word was left out! We have all our telephones in work again and during the move have been able to scrounge a number for ourselves. I hear that 'A' (Hythe) Company are to be turned into Gunners.

Wednesday 16 December
A very wet day. Alert 2 p.m. A great deal of AA fire in Lympne direction. Alert 3.15 p.m. I heard that on Sunday our ground defences fired on our own planes. The Middlesex Regiment quietly left our road this morning, their places being taken by Tank Corps personnel with a few lorries and light armoured cars.

Thursday 17 December
From 11.15 a.m. there was a succession of alerts in Folkestone. Two explosions at 4.15 p.m. News that Montgomery has cut off part of Rommel's Panzer force. BBC and papers already claim it as a great victory, but it is not that yet.

Friday 18 December
Pouring rain all day. Alert 12 noon. Alert 1 p.m. with gunfire at Hythe. Alert 2.15 p.m. There was a lot of AA and machine gun fire behind us. Rommel, after all, broke through and escaped Montgomery's round-up.

Saturday 19 December
I drove Daphne into Folkestone in the morning. She and her Guides took toys, which they had made or bought, to the children in the hospital. The bombs yesterday were on Lyminge; quite a number but no one hurt. The

Inspector brought a poor collie which was doubled up by the blast of a bomb. A Folkestone trawler, called *Britannia*, fished up part of a Dornier 217.

Thursday 24 December
Start of Home Guard holiday. I went down town and looked up Stansfield, who looks well but is weak in the legs still. Alerts 1.15 p.m. and 4 p.m. In evening, two small Saltwood girls sang carols to us.

Friday 25 December
Christmas Day. Without maids, we spent it quietly at home. I went to 8 a.m. service. It was nearly 11 a.m. by the time we finished breakfast in the kitchen, where we had all our other meals. The Tank Corps men, with mistletoe in their coats, paraded the road waiting for a girl to come and be kissed, but none appeared.

Sunday 27 December
Ethel went to a dance last night, and again failed to turn up to cook breakfast. A quiet day. Phyllis and Daphne went into Folkestone to church in the afternoon.

Tuesday 29 December
Cold wind in north. Guns firing all morning. Our planes over in afternoon. At 5.30 p.m. snow commenced falling. We have not only not advanced in North Africa, we have gone back. The hill the Guards three times captured has again been abandoned.

Thursday 31 December
Heavy rain in the night, and almost a mild morning. Alert in Folkestone at 7.30 a.m. Hythe siren was mute. At 12.30 p.m. I drove Gribbon to Shorncliffe to see the Brigade Major of the 7th Brigade to discuss orders for Home Guard. He told me he wanted me to come because they mostly concerned 'B' Company, which is true, but he has run out of petrol

coupons and would not have told me anything about it if he had someone else to drive him! I drove Phyllis in after lunch to meet a surveyor and Mrs Dix for a survey of Ingles Hall with a view to its acquisition. The Home Guard went in during August and nothing has been done. I found that my Platoon had broken into the church side [of the Drill Hall] and taken 50 chairs.

Members of 'B' Company, 8th Battalion, Kent Home Guard (Rodney Foster Archive)

1943

Friday 1 January

There was some singing by the Tank Corps at midnight. I heard nothing else. A wet day. I picked up Gribbon on my way into Folkestone in the morning and Phyllis when I came home to lunch.

Saturday 2 January

Alert 2.15 p.m. Rain in the evening. On the roads leading down to the sea, blocks of concrete have been let into the junctions. Daphne guessed, and I am told it is so, that it is to straighten the corners when tanks turning would break up the surface. This in preparation for the 'second front', as the invasion of Europe is called.

Sunday 3 January

There has been no air activity for several days, since before Christmas. This morning at 8.45 a.m. a force of our planes flew in from seawards, followed by an alert. I drove up to Shorncliffe, where I visited the Brigade Major and inspected No. 6 Platoon under Oxford and No. 1 under McHutchison. The latter had brought his men to be shown the Churchill tanks. Alert 2.45 p.m. Our planes came in, followed by four Huns who dived down from an enormous height and dropped bombs on Sandgate. Two fell in the sea, one on the beach and one in the grounds of the Star and Garter Home. There was very extensive blast damage.

Thursday 7 January

Damp and mild. I stayed in Folkestone all day, and went to a committee convened by Harward, the Town Clerk, accompanied by Vernal, the

Father and son: Hugh (right) and Hugh James McHutchison in the uniforms of the Home Guard and RAF. Hugh James was killed in action in March 1942

Battalion Head Clerk. I do not know how I got put on it; there was the usual atmosphere of intrigue, Gribbon not telling me what it was about until I received a letter this morning. Fire Service, Medical and everyone was there but it boiled down after 1½ hours' talk, mostly by Harward, a pettifogging attorney, that the Home Guard should become the town's ARP service. An RASC lorry, backing out of Oakville drive next door, went into the end of our fence and sent the small half of our garage gate flying. For three years it has escaped numerous perils, only to go down at last.

Saturday 9 January
A very cold day. Gribbon has put himself in command of all the Home Guard units in Folkestone, and reduced my command to three platoons. I wrote out my resignation. I had a restless night worrying about it.

Sunday 10 January
A thick fog stopped much of the training. I went straight to the Drill Hall and made out my letter of resignation. At 12 o'clock Gribbon made a

speech to my officers and NCOs on a talk the Army Commanders had given to the Battalion Commanders. He said it was very important, but there was nothing in it except that a Home Guard officer whatever his rank will come under the orders of the most junior regular Second Lieutenant. Afterwards, he and I got on to the orders for 'action stations' that I had written. He said first the orders were vague, then wrong and finally that they were not orders. After that he went off in a huff.

Monday 11 January
A very mild day. Sunny in afternoon. Phyllis cooked me an early breakfast. I was at Gribbon's at 9.45 a.m. and drove him up to see the Brigade Commander. Gribbon only put up small matters, but stayed nearly an hour. In Sandgate Road afterwards, sitting in the car, we had it out again. He went on to lecture 'A' Company. Street refused to give him more than half an hour on Sunday, which he refused, so had to give his lecture to half a dozen officers. It was so mild after lunch that I went for a walk round my old area, Park Lane, Garden House wood etc. and looked up Saltwood Platoon's old position at the Waterworks. The woods were full of tits.

Tuesday 12 January
At 4.30 p.m. Gribbon rang me up and said if I resigned, by Home Guard regulations I must revert to private. So I said I would withdraw my resignation and demand an interview with General Forster. He did not like that, and asked me to go over. After a fruitless argument, I agreed to carry on if he left me alone with my 'B' Company. But as soon as we had shaken hands, he suggested taking my signalling system and my quarter guard. He has a rhinoceros hide!!

Wednesday 13 January
Alert 9.15 a.m. As soon as I got in, I went and saw Gribbon. I decided I was no match for his evil cunning and told him I could not carry on. I could not now go back to the ranks, so must give up the Home Guard. The big guns round Hythe were practising most of the day, and there was a big daylight raid over France.

Thursday 14 January
Heavy rain all night. The canal overflowed, Orchard Valley estate flooded

and the bottom of Barrack Hill underwater. Going into Folkestone, I met a flooded area by the Sandgate old lifeboat house. Owing to the wet everywhere, I did not see it and drove through and the car was soaked with water, and later on the engine twice faulted.

Friday 15 January

Phyllis and I had lunch with the Gribbons at Vinson's restaurant. I had tried to get out of the engagement. Phyllis went on to her [Christian Science] reading room and I went back to the Drill Hall. Alert 4 p.m. with 'danger overhead' signal and siren hooting and screaming. Daphne said bombs were dropped on Lympne before the sirens sounded and Bofors opened up. Gribbon had a meeting in the evening of my platoon commanders to tell them whom he proposes to put in my place.

Saturday 16 January

We were woken at 4 a.m. by the tanks in our road moving off on an exercise. Vinson informed me the platoon commanders' meeting last night was heated. Stokes was rude, according to Gribbon. He proposed to bring in Major Yearsley from Hythe, a man who claims to be sick and has done nothing. In his usual method, Gribbon had fixed it up beforehand and Yearsley had enrolled in 'A' Company. He says he will only come in the morning, and not on Sundays unless he is fetched in a car! Vinson is supposed to fetch him, but tells me he will resign. He also says the platoon commanders were unanimous that they would not have him or anyone from outside Folkestone. Daphne was out all day: a Brownie officer's instructor at Folkestone gave her lunch and took her to meet all the local 'Owls'.

Sunday 17 January

News in the morning that 'Binge' had got Rommel on the run again, and that our Air Force bombed Berlin last night and only lost one plane. Gribbon rang me up suggesting I should hand over at the end of the month. I said I preferred leaving sooner, so he said 'end of the week'. I said 'whom to?', and he replied 'Vinson', and added 'temporarily'. Vinson seems quite determined he will not serve under Yearsley. Afterwards, I met some of Nos. 3, 4 and 5 Platoons, who were all very nice to me and sent me home happy. After lunch I went for a walk. There was a heavy bombardment going on across the water in the direction of Boulogne about 3 p.m. I met Molyneux and took him along into Brockhill Park. I walked round the lake and looked at the grave of old [William] Tournay on an island. What a lovely spot to be buried in, yet they called him eccentric. He died in 1903. About 8 p.m. the first Huns came over us and went straight for Canterbury. I guessed they were trying to raid London. We went up and down the road seeing what we could, and actually saw four Huns. They came over singly at intervals. We heard a bomb drop near Sellindge and saw the Hun surrounded by shell bursts. Ashford barrage opened up, and Lympne. There was heavy AA fire as each Hun arrived, and the air was full of tracer shells. Daphne saw a red flare-up in the Marsh, which might have been the destruction of a Hun. At 9.15 p.m. a Hun flew in low from the sea, taking the defences by surprise. Only one gun fired at it. We saw it plainly. At 4.30 a.m. the Huns came over again. The attack was chiefly on Canterbury.

TEN OF 60 GERMAN BOMBERS DOWN

Monday 18 January

Ten aircraft were brought down last night. Bombs were dropped in the East Cliff area, some delayed action. Bursts of AA fire at 4.15 p.m. and sporadic gunfire. A few Huns came over at long intervals and were fired at. We went out and watched, and heard one bomb explode fairly near. Speedboats were out in the Channel. Just at the end, a plane coming over Sandgate towards us was lit up by a searchlight and fired at. We saw a spot of light show and gradually grow larger and redder as it flew towards Lympne. There was no further firing. It was one of our Hurricanes which had been taking part in an exercise and had blundered into the real thing. I believe the pilot escaped. 'All clear' 8.45 p.m. Near midnight our bombers flew over to strafe Berlin again.

Tuesday 19 January

We lost 22 bombers on our raid on Berlin last night. Hard luck on the poor lads who were sent over there after the Huns had been warned. Last night, bombs were dropped on the Bayle and the Harbour in Folkestone, and a lot of windows were broken by our own AA fire. I started to hand over the Company to Vinson.

Thursday 21 January

London was caught napping yesterday. No balloons up, and many of the AA guns not manned and the alert sounded too late. The Huns dived low. The worst damage was to a school, where about 50 teachers and girls were killed. This was my first day out of harness. A few Huns came over at long intervals, and a few shots were fired at each.

Friday 22 January

A warm, sunny day. Guns of all kinds firing during morning. Good news: we must be in Tripoli by now and have stopped the German thrust in Tunisia. We have come to the aid of the French there. What are the Americans doing? Russians have also made very important gains.

Saturday 23 January

Daphne drove to her Hawkinge Guides and was given tea by their new captain, Mrs Cochrane, wife of a sailor with lots of money and a house in the Alkham Valley. Daphne gave Phyllis and me a lift. We looked at a house on the [Sandgate] Riviera owned by a Mr Kirk. It was furnished in heavy continental style, with some rooms oriental in decoration, and was full of busts, statues and china figures, mostly French.

Sunday 24 January

Alert 10 a.m. I went for a walk up Redbrooks, Pedlinge, through Sandling Park and back via Saltwood. Paths were very wet, and I had to keep to the fields. The entrance through Pedlinge to Sandling was in an extraordinary state. The tanks had churned it up into four-foot ruts and liquid mud. One tank had stuck on the right side of the chapel, so the rest crashed through the gardens and fences on the other side, obliterating everything. In the morning there was a big conference of officers at the Tank Corps Regiment Headquarters on this road, including an officer of the 2nd Canadian Corps. I thought at first it meant a change of troops, but it was probably an umpires' conference for an exercise starting tomorrow.

Tuesday 26 January

Churchill and Roosevelt have met at Casablanca in North Africa. The Germans had an idea the meeting was coming off, but thought it was to be in Washington. De Gaulle and Giraud [of the Free French] also met there. The Russians claim to have wiped out the encircled German 6th

Army. What they now give away is that the Germans had taken all Stalingrad.

Thursday 28 January
A very noisy night, with lorries and tanks passing up the road. A dark morning. Three alerts during the day. Wireless and papers give only a small paragraph with no headlines to the news of a huge Japanese [troop] concentration. The public must not be disturbed with bad news. I do hope Roosevelt and Churchill are not shutting their eyes to the danger.

Saturday 30 January
Great speculation over the Nazi anniversary celebrations on today. Goering and Goebbels spoke, the latter reading a proclamation from Hitler who said he was too busy in Russia to attend. Some of our Mosquitoes flew over in daylight and bombed Berlin, interrupting Goering's speech for an hour. The 8th Army has crossed the Tunisian border. Field Marshal Paulus and 16 Generals captured at Stalingrad.

Twenty-six year old Flight Sergeant Rawdon Hume Middleton VC, of the Royal Australian Air Force was shot down over the English Channel in November 1942, while returning from a bombing raid on the Fiat Works in Turin.

Monday 1 February
An even stronger gale at night, with many chimney pots and roof tiles down. A wild day, with rain and more wind at night. Some of our bombers came over about 9.15 p.m. The 8th Army has not after all crossed the Tunisian frontier. Body of Sergeant Rawdon Middleton VC RAAF washed ashore near Dover.

Thursday 4 February
A white frost. Our planes were over France early in the morning. Alert 9.45 a.m. I went to Folkestone in the morning and looked up 'B' Company. Gribbon still doing irregular things and generally getting away with it. Vinson has been put up for Command. He thinks Hitler has been bumped off and that the Germans are cracking.

Saturday 13 February

A warm, sunny day. Our bombers visited Wilhelmshaven last night, and caused such a huge explosion they think some arsenal must have been blown up.

Sunday 14 February

Alerts 8.15 a.m., 8.45 a.m. Our planes were active all day. In the afternoon Phyllis went to church and Daphne to her Guides, and we all met at the Central Cinema in Folkestone and saw Walt Disney's film *Bambi*; the life of a fawn, a very pretty film with none of his usual vulgarity. From 8 p.m. for half an hour our bombers flew over in a steady stream. The Russians have taken Rostov.

The station at Sandling Junction, near Hythe (Folkestone Library H/WHE/47)

Monday 15 February

I left Sandling Junction by the 11.30 a.m. train and had a comfortable journey to Guildford. As the train approached the station, we were greeted by an alert. Some time ago, a train had been bombed near Guildford, 19 people being killed. My sister Milly looked well, also Mr Blaxland [father-in-law], whom I looked up after tea.

Tuesday 16 February

We had our midday meal in the Maori Road Bridge Club; good food and interesting people. Russians have occupied Kharkov [Ukraine]. The Americans have lost Gafsa [Tunisia]. Churchill is ill with bronchitis. A large force of our bombers flew over about 8 p.m.

Wednesday 17 February

Slightly milder day. I went down town with Milly. The Americans have suffered a severe kicking in central Tunisia, losing 3,000 killed or prisoners, and most of their tanks and guns. It is the only way of waking them up. Now they will ask us to teach them how to fight.

Thursday 18 February

A warm sunny day. I went up to London; I walked up to Oxford Circus and back by back ways and had a curry at Veeraswamy. I had at my table a talkative sailor who had been to Ceylon. We got on to Gandhi and Home Rule. I took the underground to the Monument, walked to Ludgate Circus and went on the top of a bus to Charing Cross. I was surprised at the little damage to be seen in the west, but the City was truly devastated. The Huns made a supreme effort to get St Paul's. London was full of Americans and Canadians. There seemed more of the former than civilians. A regiment of airborne troops in Waterloo Station. I am of the opinion that the latter have not proved of much use. I got back [to Guildford] at 5.45 p.m.

Saturday 20 February

A man in the Bridge Club said a huge force of Canadians in full kit with tanks and guns passed through Haslemere yesterday afternoon, and the Hun plane for which we had the alert flew over them. The troops took three hours to pass through. Milly took me to an orchestral concert in the afternoon. I enjoyed it.

Sunday 21 February

I turned up at Poyle Croft after lunch to take Mr Blaxland out in the chair, and found that he had crashed at the bottom of the stairs yesterday evening, cut his forehead and hurt his arm and shoulder. The doctor did not think a bone was broken, but came to X-ray him about 6 o'clock. The Yankees have been driven from the Kasserine Pass [Tunisia]. At the end of the 9 p.m. news, a Yank, furiously angry with his people, said there was no adjustment of the line: '*We have lost the pass.*'

Monday 22 February

I went and saw Mr Blaxland. He was sleepy, and wandering slightly. His arm is broken above the elbow. The rest is unharmed. I left by the 12 noon train. They have had fog the whole time I have been away.

Wednesday 24 February

A sunny day. Alert 9.15 a.m. At midday I went to Saltwood and joined up as a Warden [ARP]. My beat includes School Road, the Saltwood half of Castle Road, Castle Close, Saltwood Castle and Home Farm. I am to sleep in the Village Hall every Monday. Alert 2.40 p.m. Work has again been started on the jetties on the seafront. There were two small cargo steamers inshore, one with its [barrage] balloon up. I saw the balloon before I saw the ship, and thought it was one from Dover broken loose. The Huns have retreated back through the Kasserine Pass, suffering heavy casualties.

Thursday 25 February

A foggy morning. Nancy phoned, saying Mr Blaxland was not so well and was being taken to a nursing home, if one could be found. Phyllis has decided to go to Guildford. At 7.30 p.m. I went to Saltwood Vicarage to meet the Lyminge regional commissioner for fire watching. Revd Peters-Jones and a Mr Allin, the two group leaders, were present. It was the same technique – threat of compulsion, no compensation and an unworkable scheme. Major Master, the Chief Warden, tried to rush me into being Chief Fire Guard, but I refused to commit myself, as I realised it would be a thankless task. Daphne has been a fire watcher from the beginning. Bombers over at night. Heard from Nancy that Mr Blaxland had been taken to a general ward in the Warren Road (County) Hospital, there being no vacancy in any nursing home. Very distressed about it.

Friday 26 February

Phyllis left for Guildford by the 11.30 a.m. train. Our planes up all day. Our bombers over at 8 p.m. About 8.30 p.m. what sounded like a Hun machine flew over us, then the alert sounded. Ten minutes later the Hun came back and flew towards Hawkinge, and was fired upon by the battery behind us. Phyllis rang up to say Mr Blaxland was comfortable and was in the best place.

Saturday 27 February

There was a bombardment across the Strait. Daphne and I went to Folkestone after tea and saw Noël Coward's film *In Which We Serve*. It was very good, but rather too much NC. AA practice again in evening. The Germans are counter-attacking the Russians, and have more than halted their advance; we have driven the Germans back to their original positions in Tunisia, but there is no sign of an advance by us. We are wasting time.

Monday 1 March

Almost a summer's day. Planes active all day. Alerts 5.30 p.m. and 6 p.m. I had my first night on duty as a Warden at Saltwood Village Hall, commencing at 9 p.m. There was a dance on in the main hall up to 10.30 p.m. Men attending the dance frequently passed through the Warden's room to the lavatories, which was very distracting. At 10 o'clock two special constables looked in and chatted for a while. I stayed awake all night, but not a plane was up, and I was relieved at 7 a.m.

Tuesday 2 March

A foggy day. Our planes went to Berlin last night and, it is said, gave it the heaviest bombing of the war. We lost 19. At 9.15 p.m. our guns commenced firing, and soon they were all at it, keeping it up for half an hour, the Huns replying vigorously.

Thursday 4 March

I was woken by an alert at 4.15 a.m. There was a continuous throb of gunfire in the distance, then a large number of planes milled around overhead. Next, single planes flew up and down and AA gunfire burst out; some of the shells burst directly overhead, rattling our windows. Australian and American airmen have done some fine work, completely destroying a fleet of 22 Japanese warships and transports.

Friday 5 March

My father-in-law Mr Arthur Blaxland died at 10 a.m. A fine character. I admired and was very fond of him. In the afternoon, Phyllis went to her church reading room and Daphne to her Guides. Alert 3 p.m.

Saturday 6 March

A foggy morning but some sun later. A notice has been put up two-thirds of the way down Stade Street saying no one must pass beyond. The small ship with a balloon was again off the seafront. These ships are stationed up and down the coast as a deterrent to sneak raiders.

Sunday 7 March

I walked into Folkestone, starting by going through the allotments and across the fields to Hythe Station then down Cliff Road into Sandgate. A cold morning with frost, but the sun came out and I was hot and thirsty by the time I reached the Drill Hall. In the orderly room I met 15 out of 19 of the officers of 'B' Company and on their behalf Vinson presented me with a handsome silver cigarette box inscribed 'From the officers of "B" Company'. It was not only a pleasant but an entirely unexpected surprise, a culmination of the loyalty they had always given me. Alerts 2 p.m. and 2.30 p.m. I heard that 'A' Company have taken over the shore guns, 20 of the RA personnel having been withdrawn.

THREE NIGHT RAIDERS DESTROYED

Three German raiders, one Heinkel 177 and two Dornier 217s, were destroyed when, shortly after midnight on Sunday, some 25 enemy aircraft crossed the coast and made scattered raids on south and south-east England and the Home Counties.

Monday 8 March

A sunny day, but a cold wind. I took my present down town and showed it to everyone I met. Met Adams and his trousered wife, and adjourned to the Castle Hotel, Saltwood, as the former said it was his birthday. He told me Gribbon when he heard of the presentation said it was against regulations. Old MacKie said Gribbon commanded the Company for two years and got nothing! Adams said Gribbon is short of cash. He owes Vinson for lunches and dinners, borrows from Salmon the barman at the Drill Hall and has even taken money from the battalion funds. Our bombers flew over in large numbers from 8.30 p.m. for more than half an hour. They came back at 2.15 a.m., some sounding quite groggy. I did my second night's duty as Warden, going on at 9 p.m. A quiet night; I read a comic story up to 4 a.m. and then slept until 7 a.m.

Wednesday 10 March

A white frost in morning, followed by a bright sunny day. No alerts. We three were driven by car to Charing Crematorium where the vicar of Lenham, with a charming manner and voice, conducted [Mr Blaxland's funeral] service. From there we returned to Ashford. I met Nancy, Herbert and Frank and brought them to the County [Hotel] restaurant, where we had lunch. We drove from there to Lympne, where the short committal service was held. Mr Burrows and two Lympne men were present. We brought Nancy and the two men home and gave them tea, and they left by the 6.30 p.m. train from Sandling. Nancy stayed with us for the night.

Thursday 11 March

An overcast day but mild. Alert 10.15 a.m. Nancy and Phyllis left for Guildford by the 11.30 a.m. train. For part of the afternoon the big guns at the back were firing. One could hear the shell as it flew over. 'Nobby' Clark, the Saltwood grocer, told me as a secret that the advance guard of the Americans had arrived in the neighbourhood. The Russians have lost much territory in the south, and the Hun has probably regained Rostov. It is obvious the Hun is defeated by the cold, not by the Russians.

Wednesday 17 March

A fine day, with not a single 'alert'. The town was full of men of a new Division. In the evening, I went to Saltwood Village Hall for instruction in Warden duties by Major Master. The Germans say the 8th Army has commenced a major

Nazi Air Scouting

The enemy have sent over single planes, flying very high, from time to time to-day. They are believed to have been on reconnaissance. Sometimes they crossed the South-East Coast and flew a little way inland.

The R.A.F. have had fighters up at a great height to deal with them.

offensive. The Swiss say that hoardings in Berlin have painted on them such slogans as 'We have had enough'. Damage from the last air raid is vast.

Saturday 20 March

Our 'Tanks' are packing up to go. We are told that it is to Scotland. The new Brigade, three Lancashire Regiments, are in Folkestone.

Sunday 21 March

A cold, foggy day. Alert 10.20 a.m. Churchill spoke at 9 p.m., chiefly telling us not to squabble over the Beveridge Report, but first win the war. He told us the 8th Army had started its attack. Alert 10.30 p.m.

Monday 22 March

I spent the day at Folkestone Library. I heard that Captain Bagshawe, the [Home Guard] Adjutant, is fed up and wants to resign his commission. A full moon. I went on duty at 9 p.m. and had to report a smouldering bonfire to the police.

Tuesday 23 March

A quiet night; no alerts since 10.30 p.m. on the 21st. As I got to my gate I saw the full silver moon in the west and the rising golden sun in the east, both an equal distance above the horizon. Much talk in Parliament and elsewhere about our shipping losses.

Wednesday 24 March

A heavy bombardment across the water from early morning. At 10 a.m., about a dozen Huns crossed our front firing, the alert sounding when they were directly overhead. They came back over the town in a quarter of an hour, with our fighters attacking them. The raid was on Ashford, where much damage was done to the town and railway, and about 35 people killed. One Hun was shot down in the heart of the town; one of ours was brought down at Pedlinge, but the pilot was safe. It seems wrong that the Hun should be able to get inland so far and dive-bomb the town, yet only lose two.

Thursday 25 March

Rain at night, the first for nearly two months. I went to Saltwood Village Hall, where I was instructed by Major Master in gas and first aid.

Friday 26 March

I had a disturbed night. More and heavier rain. Our 'Tanks' left in the early morning with much noise. I watched the new field battery arrive in Seaton Avenue. Daphne and I went into Folkestone and saw the film *Desert Victory*. Very good; heard that four photographers were killed making the film.

Saturday 27 March

Our planes were very busy early in the morning. I met a Saltwood man who is working in the BSA factory, passing out guns for the Admiralty. He says skilled workers get as much as £10 a week, girls of 17 to 19 get £5 to £7 and spend the money in the pubs drinking port, Benedictine and anything they can name. Alert 5.30 p.m. A Hun came over the Marsh, was fired at and dropped a couple of bombs. I was on the bus and heard nothing. I went in to a boxing tournament held at the Drill Hall arranged by 'B' Company Home Guard and Eastern Command. A very good show. Several champions, a pair of professionals, one Canadian, good fights, one knock-out. I had to leave at half-time owing to the bus curfew. Bombers over at 11 p.m.

Sunday 28 March

Phyllis' birthday. Sunny with a cold wind. At 11.15 a.m. there was a burst of heavy AA fire and a bouquet of shells burst at a Hun high up above Hythe. Daphne heard a whistle as of a dud shell falling, and there was a clatter of tiles as a piece of shrapnel hit our roof. We picked up one piece. A lot of damage was done to roofs in Hythe.

Monday 29 March

Our planes were very busy from dawn throughout the morning. Phyllis went to meet Mr Burrows to make a valuation of the contents of 18 Kingsnorth Gardens. I spent the day at Folkestone Library. Alert 1.10 p.m., and sirens continued to yell until 1.30 p.m. I went to my Warden duty at Saltwood at 9 p.m., and at 9.25 p.m. had a warning. Good news of Montgomery flank thrust forcing Rommel to retreat from the Mareth Line [Tunisia]. Rain at night.

Tuesday 30 March

I slept from 2.15 a.m. to 6 a.m. A mild day. The 8th Army has captured Gabès [Tunisia] and 10,000 prisoners and all forces are pushing on slowly. Our bombers went to Berlin and Ruhr last night and 33 are missing! A terrible price to pay. Alert 10 p.m.

Wednesday 31 March

I kept Phyllis and myself awake all night coughing, and have a sore throat. There were alerts during the night and, Phyllis said, a bomb

explosion. All through the day planes were droning overhead. Alert at
2 p.m. The house was shaken as though by an earthquake. Alert 4.15 p.m.
I heard an intriguing account of a base in Norway we have established,
which we reinforce from the air and from which parties go out to
sabotage.

Monday 5 April

Alert 9.45 a.m. Guns firing at regular intervals Dungeness way all day.
Alert 2.45 p.m. At 3 p.m. I saw 16 large bombers (American, I guessed) pass
slowly high up overhead, moving northwards. I went on Warden duty at
9 p.m. Bones, Saltwood's head special constable told me that German shells
came over at 11 a.m. and killed two people at the bottom of the Road of
Remembrance in Folkestone.

Sunday 11 April

I had a coughing fit in the night. I was next woken up by the roar of our
bombers sailing over. They seemed to be only treetop high. They returned,
flying higher, at 5 a.m. A mild day. Alert 8 p.m. HM the Queen made a
very moving speech thanking British women for their war effort. Rommel
is in full retreat in Tunisia, and has abandoned Sousse and an airfield
further north. A thrust by the 1st Army seems likely to have pierced their
inner defences round Bizerta.

Monday 12 April

In afternoon Phyllis and I went into Folkestone and saw Somerset
Maugham's *Moon and Sixpence*. I did not think much of it. The other
film was of the BBC's 'Brains Trust', with that bounder Joad and Miss
Jennie Lee, the miner's daughter, with fingers and arms covered in
jewellery, Elliot, Huxley and Campbell. On our return we found my
niece Joan had rung up to say that on her return from the office in the
evening she had found her mother lying unconscious at the bottom of
the stairs – she must have been there since midday. Warden duty at
9 p.m. with an alert at 12.45 a.m. Rommel has gone back to a position
around Tunis. The 1st Army took Kairouan [Tunisia] and the 8th Army
following later entered Sousse after the last German had left, but
Montgomery claims all the credit. The Budget out, only indirect
taxation.

Tuesday 13 April

I slept for two hours from 4.30 a.m. Alert 8.50 a.m. Whilst I was shopping in the town Phyllis rang up several places to catch me. Joan had rung up to say Eva had died that evening. Phyllis and I left about 12.30 p.m., had lunch in Folkestone and caught the 1.30 p.m. bus to Canterbury. We found Joan had been taken in by a friend of Eva, a Mrs Quested.

Wednesday 14 April

I decided to return to Canterbury to help Joan, so left Hythe at 3.30 p.m. and arrived there about 4.15 p.m. We looked up her landlord and an undertaker and tried the Registrar's Office, which was shut, then looked up a Miss Kingston, a JP, to have Joan's signature attested. She was a frowzy old thing like a landlady in a novel, a fat shapeless body, a chin and neck in one and a moustache. From the books and pictures in the room she seemed to be communistic in outlook. Picking up my suitcase at Mrs Quested's, we went round to Baker's Temperance Commercial Hotel in Ivy Lane and had tea and were given toast swimming in real butter! For high tea (at 6.30 p.m.), which they provide instead of supper, I had sausage and mash and coffee – three courses were provided. Two young girls of 14 waited on us. Most of, if not all, the men were commercial travellers. After tea I walked round the town; it has been badly blitzed, worse than London, and I would find it depressing to live amongst the ruins. When I went up to bed I found a Bible on my dressing table. There was an alert at 6.45 p.m. and 9.45 p.m. About 10 p.m. a very large force of our bombers passed overhead – they attacked Stuttgart. At midnight there was an alert. At 12.15 a.m., 'Tugboat Annie' hooted a dozen blasts to denote danger approaching. It hooted again at 12.30 a.m. as the AA barrage along the Thames estuary started. At 12.45 a.m., the danger siren again sounded as our AA guns opened fire. Half a dozen of the men, including myself, had by then left their rooms and were assembled on the landing of the first floor. At 1 o'clock, the siren gave one long blast, but as soon as it stopped a plane came over and there was a burst of AA fire. I heard a plane came up with lights on, but they were the wrong lights.

Thursday 15 April

Alert 8.50 a.m. I took Joan to the bank, Registrar and solicitor. Daphne came in for a Guide WVS conference and looked Joan up and we had tea in the town. Last night we lost 25 bombers and shot down four of theirs. It does not sound sense.

Friday 16 April

Another blazing hot day. Joan and I went to the Registrar and solicitor. Midday I went to an exhibition of photographs of bombed towns in Germany, Italy etc. I looked up Joan at 3 p.m., then went to a nurseryman named Smith in Franciscan Gardens to buy a wreath for Mrs Dix. Whilst there, the 'danger overhead' siren sounded. Smith, a fat, bull-necked man, and his assistant bolted down the garden, the latter calling out to me to get away from the glass. We sheltered in a stone building (a sort of summer house). Alerts all evening. At 8 o'clock I went over to Mrs Quested's, where we sat in the garden. At 9.30 p.m. a tank battalion clattered through the city. At 10 p.m. for an hour our bombers passed over the city. A very small number of our bombers returned at midnight. Alert 12.20 a.m.; a plane flew over, there was the sound of a bomb dropping through the air and an explosion.

Saturday 17 April

Another very hot day. The noise I heard last night before the bomb explosion was a Hun bomber crashing near Pelham. It is thought it dived too low and could not straighten out. I left Canterbury at 10.30 a.m. I heard the cuckoo; it was heard near Dover in March. Yesterday's raid was on Pilsen in Czechoslovakia, and we lost 55 bombers!!

Sunday 18 April

In the afternoon, our planes in large numbers were rushing about, then all was quiet at 6.15 p.m. Two minutes later the siren sounded and the sky was full of planes. At 10.35 p.m. a Hun came over and was fired at, and soon after there was the burst of a bomb. All clear 10.50 p.m., and our windows rattled from an explosion five minutes later. An alert at 12.45 a.m. woke me up, as a Hun flew past and was fired at; occasional single planes came up and a few rounds were fired at them; then a plane which might have been one of our fighters passed over unmolested. All clear 1.20 a.m.

Monday 19 April

I was woken by our planes tearing over the roof. I left for Canterbury at 10 o'clock. Between Wye and Ashford I saw two large guns on trucks in a small wood by the side of the hill. I met Joan about noon and we had lunch at the County Hotel, looked at some of the damage caused in the last raid, met Phyllis and Daphne at 2.15 p.m. and motored in a local taxi to Charing Crematorium. Mrs Dix, Miss Wheeler, Miss Desley and Molly were there. We drove back all the way to Hythe in the taxi. Joan stayed the night with us. I went on duty at 9 o'clock and had an eventless night. The shooting down of 50 transport planes off North Africa (some accounts say they were empty) is made out by everyone to be a major victory.

Monday 26 April
Heavy casualties in Tunisia, more like the last war's fighting, but I believe we are nearing developments. Russia has broken diplomatic relations with Poland. When the former overran half of Poland, they imprisoned the Polish officers separately from their men. When Russia was forced to be on our side, they released the men but nothing has been heard of the officers, some thousands of them (some say 30,000). The Germans say they have found a mass grave near Smolensk, proving that the Russians murdered them. The Poles demand a Red Cross enquiry. I went on duty at 9.45 p.m.

Friday 30 April
A wet day with a low mist. No planes up. In the town I met Captain Bagshawe, who has resigned the Adjutancy of the Home Guard and has been placed on the Reserve. He told me Gribbon nearly sent him mad, and once he just restrained himself from hitting him.

CROSS-CHANNEL GUN DUEL
LIVELY BOMBARDMENT

After a month's lull there was a lively and prolonged cross-Channel gun duel in the Straits of Dover late last night.

Monday 3 May
A strong, cold, easterly wind all day. In Tunisia we have made an important advance, the Americans taking Mateur [50 miles from Tunis]. Vichy radio repeats the passing of invasion barges through the Strait of

Gibraltar. I wonder if it is one of our blinds. I went to my Warden's post at 9.30 p.m. About midnight there was a short sham fight round the Vicarage.

Friday 7 May

Alerts 8.40 p.m. and 11.15 p.m. We heard that not only had the French and Americans entered Bizerta, but the 1st Army had taken Tunis and the enemy are finished. A very fine piece of strategy. Alexander is a genius! Tunis and Bizerta captured by British.

Saturday 8 May

My 42nd military birthday! Alert 7 a.m. A plane flew in over the allotments and the gun there fired a burst at it, but no plane was brought down. It rained all night.

Monday 10 May

Another day of strong wind and rain. I stayed in all day. Six Generals and 25,000 Germans surrendered in Tunisia. They will all give up soon. I went on Warden's duty at 9.45 p.m. It rained most of the night.

Tuesday 11 May

My relief was five minutes late. Alert 8.50 a.m. A calm sunny day after the violent gales. Guns on the seafront and at the back of Hythe fired all morning. Air activity over the Marsh in the afternoon. Alert 6.25 p.m. German prisoners now 100,000. We have cut off the southern group and are advancing up both sides of Cap Bon peninsula. I was overtired when I went to bed and could not sleep at first. I had a waking nightmare that I was lying in a pitch-dark night at the edge of a high cliff, too giddy to move, and was trying to stop Phyllis, who was coming along, as I was afraid she would trip over me.

Thursday 13 May

Summer weather returned. I spent the day in Folkestone Library. The bombardment across the Strait went on all day. As I returned in the bus, there was a ball of smoke over the French coast. At 11.15 a.m. there was another rumble in the distance; our speedboats were out, and planes which seemed to hover over the sea. Axis forces in Tunisia surrender.

Saturday 15 May

A hot night, with all the windows open. About 2 a.m. a strong northerly wind blew everything in the house about. Alerts 7 a.m., 5.45 p.m., 8.45 p.m. and 10 p.m. The bombardment broke out periodically through the day. We heard that strings of barges in tow escorted by a destroyer passed Folkestone going down the Channel in the afternoon. In the news, it was given out that rumours of German landings on our coast were not true.

GOC Inspection, Lower Sandgate Road, Folkestone, with the Victoria pier in the background

Sunday 16 May

A perfect day, atmosphere so clear. France and Fairlight Hill [Hastings] showing distinctly. Home Guard Sunday. 'A' Company had previously arranged to fire their guns at a towed target, so Street made that an excuse not to have any show. Much indignation in the town. He went over to swank as second in command of the Battalion amongst the brass hats in Folkestone, where they put up an elaborate show. Daphne went to a youth service with her Guides. In the morning, I saw 36 bombers fly over in formation. There are a number of Canadian airmen in the town.

Monday 17 May

A force of our bombers in the early morning attacked the two large dams of Möhne and Eder in the Ruhr, dispersing their waters and destroying

everything for miles and, I expect, drowning thousands of people. I went to
my Warden post at 9.45 p.m. Alert 11.10 p.m. A plane came overhead and
AA gunfire broke out at 11.40 p.m. Master turned up soon after, and Robb,
the village constable, looked in. Master and I talked on many subjects up to
12.30 a.m. when he left, as he had been up most of the night before. Alert
12.50 p.m., which brought Master back again, and he stayed till 2 a.m.

Wednesday 19 May
Last night's explosion is said to have been a Hun bomber brought down in
the sea. The other is said to have been heard in London and all over Kent.
Very little air activity. A few men of the 38th (Welsh) Division with two
lorry-loads of kit came into the Choppings'. Daphne went to a Guide
meeting, and we did not have supper until 9 p.m. Our speedboats were out
in force in the evening. Alert 11.45 p.m.

Friday 21 May
Our tranquil period finished this afternoon; a Battalion of King's Own
Lancasters occupied all the houses in the road. Our Air Force swept the
Italian airfields, destroying 113 machines and only lost one. Alerts 8.30 p.m.
and 9.50 p.m. There were further alerts and AA fire during the night. A
bomb fell behind Bluehouse Waterworks, and another at Lyminge.

Monday 24 May
Empire Day. No notice taken of it by our petty local bumbles. Steady rain
all day. We dropped 2,000 tonnes of bombs on Düsseldorf and lost 38
bombers – a bestial war. I went on duty at 9.45 p.m. Rain for part of the
night, no alerts, but I stayed up the whole night reading a third-rate crime
story.

Tuesday 25 May
Alert 10 p.m.; just before the siren sounded a flight of Spitfires rushed
treetop high out to sea. They swept round and caught the Huns which had
come in and dropped three bombs on Folkestone Harbour, one of which
fell on the beach, exploding half a dozen mines.

Thursday 27 May
My birthday (61). Big guns fired in the afternoon, and planes rushed over
the rooftops. These Canadian airmen are great on it. Alert 5.15 p.m. At

6.30 p.m. PC Mercer called. Phyllis had gone into the lower box room and turned on the light in the afternoon. It had burnt through the night and was seen by soldiers about 2 a.m. Mercer had banged on both the front and back doors, but could not wake us so he was forced to break in by ducking under the wire netting (the window was open). Our bombers were over in force in the night carrying very heavy loads.

Saturday 29 May
A blazing hot day. Hythe and Saltwood were full for Wings for Victory Week. Hythe with a stamp-covered bomb casing, and Saltwood with a bazaar. Great activity in the Strait at night.

Monday 31 May
I left Hythe at 10 a.m. for Canterbury. Alert there at noon. I looked up Kennett the auctioneers and Kingsford the solicitor. I went to Mrs Quested's at lunchtime, and had a short time with Joan. I returned by bus. At 6.30 p.m. six minesweepers going up the Channel were attacked by German planes, but gave them such a heavy burst of AA fire they sheered off. Each ship also had a balloon. I went on duty at 9.45 p.m.

Thursday 3 June
The Germans say our invasion fleets are massing in the Mediterranean. They seem to have deserted the Italians. Pantelleria [off Sicily] has been silenced. De Gaulle and Giraud have agreed; the former seems to have won all his points. The regiment here is not the King's Own but the Herefordshires, a new regiment. I met the manager of the NAAFI which used to be in our road, and asked him if he was reopening. He told me all NAAFI are now staffed entirely by women. He and his male staff are in Dymchurch waiting to go across.

Saturday 5 June
Daphne was at a Guides conference in Maidstone all day, getting back at 9 p.m. A Bren carrier ran into a car in the High Street in the morning. Everyone said 'Oh!' and looked shocked, but when they saw that the car also belonged to the Army they all grinned!!

Sunday 6 June
Churchill returned to England. A wet afternoon with thunder. No alerts,

but Eastbourne was bombed. In Margate, which was bombed on Friday, a number of soldiers were killed.

Tuesday 8 June

A cold rainy day, with mist. No air activity. The Italians say we were beaten off in an attack on Lampedusa Island [off Sicily], but we state it was a reconnaissance and lost only two men.

Monday 14 June

A heavy shower with thunder and hail in the afternoon. I was on duty at 9.45 p.m. I had a talk with Revd Peters-Jones. He has learnt that an AA Divisional Headquarters is to be stationed here. Alert 1.35 a.m. A plane came in from the north and was caught in the beam of searchlights in the Sandling direction and fired at, but was untouched and the lights switched off abruptly. Then Lympne sent up tracer shells, and a plane came zooming down over the village as if it was about to bomb us, but flew towards Hawkinge, where there was some more firing. I gave cups of tea to two policemen who turned up. All clear at 2.15 a.m.

Wednesday 16 June

The King flew over to North Africa on Saturday to be with his troops. He received a great ovation. Nancy arrived for a visit of five days. A quiet night.

Saturday 19 June

The London General Post Office was hit last night. Wavell is to be Viceroy of India in October. Planes were flying round Lympne all evening.

> **POST OFFICE WRECKED IN LONDON RAID**
>
> ————
>
> **SOLDIERS HELP TO SAVE THE MAIL**
>
> A London post office, which was hit during the short alert in the capital in the

Sunday 20 June

A perfect day. Coastal and AA guns were practising all morning (the latter need it!), and squadrons of our planes flew over to France. A short alert at 3.40 p.m. The 'danger overhead' sounded in Folkestone before the alert.

Tuesday 22 June

I went to the Town Hall and was fined 20 shillings for Phyllis' blackout offence.

Coastal gunnery crew: poster by Terence Cuneo

Wednesday 23 June

A warm day. Intensive air activity all day; flights of bombers flying over and back all afternoon. I took over the duties of Enrolling Officer in Hythe for voluntary harvest workers from Mrs Crispin. As far as I can see, there are no volunteers. News that the King has visited Malta. How grand for him and them! Alert at night.

Thursday 24 June

The 32nd anniversary of our wedding day. Air activity. Alert 11.50 a.m. Our bombers which bombed Friedrichshafen [Germany] went on to Africa. The next day they came back, dropping bombs on Italy on the way. Not one was lost.

Monday 28 June

Air activity in afternoon. A large force of American bombers flew overhead at 4 p.m. I went to my Warden duty at 9.30 p.m. At 10.50 p.m. the double alert shell warning sounded in Folkestone. At 11.15 p.m. Hythe siren sounded, and Lyminge control rang me up. Just after the 'all clear', there were two near explosions of big guns or bursting shells, and occasional gunfire. Master turned up and stayed until the 'all clear'. He told me he had slept through last Monday's bombing and was ashamed of himself. Our bombers flew overhead during the alert. I got some sleep between 4 a.m. and 6 a.m.

Thursday 1 July

I met a Colonel, Billeting Officer for south-east Kent, in our road and showed him all the houses. He wanted at least three to occupy as 'headquarters', but for whom he did not say. He said he would have to take Quarrymead, but hoped to allow us access to the gardens. Big guns fired most of afternoon.

Friday 2 July

I spent the day in Folkestone, partly in the library, and gave Phyllis lunch at Vinson's (boiled bacon) and hunted through Eva's junk at Cliff Cottage. Met Daphne at the Bayle, arranging the shifting of various chairs.

Saturday 3 July

I went into Folkestone in morning and, with the aid of four small Guides, helped Daphne to move 50 chairs to Woodward Hall. Alert 11.30 a.m. On my return Phyllis reported our onions had been stolen. I went everywhere hunting for Company Commanders, eventually meeting the Adjutant after lunch. Alert 3.50 p.m. From 10.30 p.m. and throughout the night the Herefords made an uproar going out on a night show and returning.

Monday 5 July

I spent the day at Folkestone Library. General Sikorski, Polish Commander in Chief, his daughter and two British MPs killed when their plane crashed shortly after taking off at Gibraltar. I wonder if it was sabotage. This will be a great loss to the world. Alert 8.10 p.m. We landed a raiding party in Crete. It only makes the enemy prepared, and they will round up Cretan sympathisers. I went on Warden duty at 9.45 p.m.

Tuesday 6 July

All quiet up to 2 a.m. when, finding difficulty in staying awake, I slept until 6 a.m. As far as I know, there was no alert. Coming home, I picked up half a dozen RAF French leaflets; some young pilot gone astray.

Wednesday 7 July

No alerts. Thunderstorms in afternoon and night. The Germans are making out Sikorski was murdered by us.

Saturday 10 July

At 7 a.m. the sky was full of our planes crossing over to France. A force including home county units, Canadians and Americans under Eisenhower landed on Sicily at 3 a.m. No news of its progress given to us.

Monday 12 July

I spent the day at Folkestone. I went on duty at 9.30 p.m. just as an alert sounded. About 11.30 p.m. our heavy bombers began to come over, and there was a continuous stream going over for over half an hour. About midnight, Beachborough Battle School flared up for a short time. At 2.40 a.m. a plane came roaring in from the sea flying low, and the alert sounded. After taking the call, I went out and saw a plane caught in the beams of about 10 searchlights with heavy AA bursts near it. Soon after, there was an explosion as of a bomb in that direction. I saw what I thought was a glow behind the trees, so sent a policeman to investigate. A plane flying north was next caught, but put on all its lights.

Thursday 15 July

St Swithin's Day. Phyllis and Daphne spent the day shopping in London. Twice in the afternoon the sky was full of our planes and at intervals there was the sound of heavy bombing in the Abbeville [France] direction.

Monday 19 July

I spent the day in Folkestone. More Abbeville bombing in morning. As I came home at 4.30 p.m., about 24 Spitfires in two formations skimmed the housetops. I went on duty at 9.45 p.m. Rain most of the night. Alert at 11.30 p.m. as a plane flew in from the sea.

Tuesday 20 July

I only had an hour's sleep. The Americans bombed Rome yesterday. I suppose it had to be. They claim it was daylight precision bombing.

Wednesday 21 July

An overcast day which turned to rain. Mrs Matson's furniture etc. was auctioned next door. George Matson and his wife had their lunch in our drawing room. Alerts 1.15 p.m. and 4.15 p.m. We have got half of Sicily, but all the Germans are in front of the 8th Army, who are held up. It looks as if the strategy is the same as in Tunisia.

Sunday 25 July

Sham battles all round the area in the morning. In the afternoon, the sky was full of bombers going out, and back at night. Bombers came overhead as I went to sleep. At midnight, we were told Mussolini had resigned and disappeared. King Victor Emmanuel III is Commander in Chief, and [Pietro] Badoglio is Prime Minister. They say they will fight on.

80° IN THE SHADE

Straits weather report last night:—Starlit and calm after a day of sunshine, with temperature again reaching 80deg. in the shade; light south-westerly breeze, fresh during the afternoon, dropping at dusk, temperature falling to 60deg.; moderate visibility, haze patches, some scattered cloud.

Thursday 29 July

I spent the day in Folkestone. I looked up Vinson and heard news of 'B' Company. Planes flew over the sea at 6.30 p.m., and there was the sound of heavy bombing in Boulogne direction; it was too hazy to see anything. Alert 12 midnight; a Hun flew in almost at once and others followed. Searchlights were up in dozens to the north, and AA gun barrage. After a time, I got up and looked out. There were shells bursting overhead, then,

1. The destruction of Salter's Laundry in Folkestone in 1940, which was described in a German radio broadcast as a 'powder factory' (Folkestone Library/*Folkestone Herald*)

2. Wireless aeroplane detector or 'Sound Mirror', in the Roughs, Hythe. These concrete dishes amplified the sound of approaching planes (Folkestone Library H/SER/2)

3. Platoon from the 8th Battalion Home Guard drilling on the Folkestone to Dover road (IWM HN8180)

4. A bomb disposal team with a 550lb unexploded bomb dug out from 21 Wear Bay Crescent, Folkestone, in July 1940 (Folkestone Library/*Folkestone Herald*)

5. Fighter pilots from the 32nd Squadron at RAF Hawkinge relax on the grass (Getty Images 3312673)

6. 'B' Company, 8th Battalion Home Guard, on parade at the Folkestone cricket ground (Don McHutchison)

7. Southern Railway Home Guard with their 75mm anti-tank guns during live firing practice against moving targets, Hythe range, August 1943 (Kent Messenger PD1610451)

8. Saltwood Green and Village Hall, the location of Rodney's Air Raid Precautions post (Brian Doorne)

9. The interior of the rear office of the Saltwood Village Hall where Rodney spent the night in his ARP duties, as illustrated by him (East Kent Archive)

10. A kite balloon operated by No. 961 Balloon Squadron is winched into the air amid damaged buildings at Granville Gardens, Dover, 1943 (IWM CH11026)

11. A camouflaged 2lb anti-tank gun, manufactured by Vickers Armstrong and pictured on an exercise in Kent (War and Peace Collection)

12. The tented accommodation of the US Army 125th Anti-Aircraft Artillery Gun Battalion, near Hythe, August 1944 (Hythe Library)

13. Canadian soldiers sitting upon a crashed German V-1 rocket in southern England, 1944 (Getty Images 3329347)

14 & 15. A Spitfire fighter tipping the wing of a V-1 rocket to disrupt its autopilot, 1944 (IWM CH16280/CH16281)

16. A dramatic photograph of a 'Brocks Benefit', named after the
famous fireworks manufacturer, over the skies of south Kent as
seen from one of the anti-aircraft batteries on Romney Marsh
(IWM CH13759)

in the sky over Folkestone, there was a blinding flash and an explosion, the blast hitting me in the face. I was asleep again before the 'all clear' sounded.

Wednesday 4 August
The usual air activity. No news from Sicily. I think Badoglio is waiting for us to advance and the Germans to retreat; he can do nothing until then. The heavy guns commenced firing about 11.30 p.m. I could not tell whether ours or theirs.

Friday 6 August
I spent the day in Folkestone – accountant, tailor and Eva's boxes. The former is giving me the RSPCA accounts, but cannot certify them as correct; there is £13 shown in hand but which cannot be produced.

Saturday 7 August
The Americans have captured Taormina in Sicily, a long way behind the 8th Army. In the Pacific they have at last taken Buna [New Guinea]. They are fighting well there. Notices up all over Hythe saying the coast from Dymchurch to Deal and as far inland as Barham is taken over by the Eastern Command. At present, warning of possible restrictions on the use of roads and clearing out of non-residents, to commence from 17 August. We seem in no hurry to win this war; everything will be ready for the start of the south-westerly gales. Report of all chief Nazis meeting at Hitler's HQ. Is he going like 'Musso'? Wishful thinking. Planes overhead in the night.

Monday 9 August
Weather improved during the day. Several squadrons of bombers, flying very high, went over and back during the day. I was on duty as usual. At 11.15 p.m. our heavy bombers started to go over. No alerts. I got to sleep about 3.30 a.m.

Wednesday 11 August
Storms blowing up all day. Daphne out all day at Lyminge with her Guides. At midnight, the Huns fired into Dover; reports state a packed cinema was hit. I was in Folkestone all day. The road was full with regiments moving westward. A convoy coming up the Channel looked like four warships with a lot of small craft. A force of very heavy bombers

came back high over us, and the whole sky was full of planes, convoys of Spitfires rushing over the roofs. Dover was again shelled.

Sunday 15 August
The Herefordshires left in leisurely fashion this morning. I believe they have not gone far. Before leaving, they robbed our orchard, breaking down a large bough of a pear tree. Very intensive air activity all morning; big formations of Spitfires as well as bombers. The Germans are on the run in Sicily. Rome is declared an open town, but they own they must prove it so.

Monday 16 August
All day, the sky was thick with planes. At 10 a.m. 65 Flying Fortresses came back over us. At 7.30 p.m. I went to a Wardens' meeting in Saltwood. Major Master discussed what we should do if this area was full of troops preparing for the invasion of Europe. I went on duty at 9.45 p.m.

Tuesday 17 August
Eastern Command took over the coast area today. All morning, the sky was full of bombers. I counted 36 Fortresses in one force and 32 Liberators in another. I left for Guildford by the 11.23 a.m. train via Waterloo. At the station, I heard that Messina [Sicily] had fallen; it was not a good show, the whole Hun army has got away, they say with guns and tanks. I believe Eisenhower to be the culprit. A very hot day. At Smeeth I saw two 'Boche Busters'. I did not go outside Waterloo, but amused myself looking at the comic Americans. Arrived Guildford 4.30 p.m.

"NEW LANDINGS BY ALLIES"—*Axis*

"ITALY & CRETE": NO CONFIRMATION

Friday 20 August
A stuffy day. I had a look at the Italian prisoners on Merrow Down. We have occupied the Lipari Islands [off Sicily], but are not boasting much about it.

Monday 23 August

Kharkov has been evacuated by the Germans. The Russians say they stormed it. I left Guildford at 11.30 a.m. I walked aimlessly about London and left Charing Cross by the 3.15 p.m. train. A number of Norwegian sailors on the train. Great changes in Hythe. Eastern Command had taken over the coastal area on 17 August. On every road are AV parks and latrines, with lorries parked along the road in many places. The Sappers and 'Red Caps' [Military Police] are in the newly requisitioned houses in our road; the former robbed our orchard the day they came in. Large formations overhead all afternoon. I went on duty at 9.30 p.m.

Tuesday 24 August

We lost 58 bombers in a raid on Berlin last night. In the morning, there were about a dozen ships sailing about the Strait putting down smokescreens. Dover was shelled about midday. Phyllis and Daphne went to Brabourne in the afternoon to buy plums. Alert 12.40 a.m. and air activity in the afternoon. Bombers over at night.

Wednesday 25 August

Showers in the morning. We have a new AA gun which makes a noise like an extra-vicious machine gun. Some new men came into billets in our road.

Friday 27 August

Two very large formations of Fortresses flew back at 8 a.m. to 8.30 a.m. Alert 10.55 a.m. At 4 p.m. the sky was full of planes. At 6 p.m., 60 Fortresses returned, flying high. Alert 7.30 p.m. At 10.30 p.m. our road had a line of lorries parked from one end to the other, those near us being large supply waggons. A few men walked about. They had all left again by midnight. Alert 3.15 a.m.

Monday 30 August

Eight destroyers steamed up the Strait in the morning towards Dover. In the afternoon, the town was full of Royal Tank Corps men and No. 5 Commando. I went on duty at 9.30 p.m. Our bombers did not come our way. I went to sleep at 3.30 a.m.

Tuesday 31 August

A large force of bombers flew over the Marsh at 7 a.m. and another large force came over us at 8 a.m. Phyllis and I went in afternoon out to Brabourne Lees picking blackberries and buying plums. Large formations of bombers continually came over and fighters were about in numbers. Churchill's speech told us nothing. There was no object in making it. Brendan Bracken had got into trouble for comparing Hess to a Boy Scout. The Turks say Churchill had postponed his speech in the expectation of being able to announce the surrender of the Italians.

Wednesday 1 September

Daphne's birthday. At 8 a.m. heavy gunfire broke out. The destroyers in the Strait were fired on by the Germans, one being hit. They put up a smokescreen, and our guns shelled the French coast. I went into Folkestone in the morning, and watched our motorboats go out to the scene of the action. In the afternoon, we three went into Folkestone to see the film *Forever and a Day*. Being an all-star cast, it was not very well acted but it was a pretty story. Earlier, two Claims Officers came and we showed them the damage.

Friday 3 September

Fifth anniversary of the outbreak of the war. The 8th Army and Canadians landed on the toe of Italy at dawn with very little opposition and, as yet, no Germans. Everyone wondering where the Americans are. At 8 a.m. the biggest force of planes we have seen flew over to France. It took a quarter of an hour to pass.

Sunday 5 September

Mrs Dix, Phyllis' friend, died suddenly in the morning. She had been taken to hospital the day before. It was a terrible shock to Phyllis. All morning, large formations of planes were flying over the Marsh and Dungeness. At 9.30 p.m. gunfire shook the house.

Monday 6 September

Planes were out early, a large formation returning at 8 a.m. I spent the day in Folkestone. Four destroyers, each towing four barges, were steaming down towards Dungeness, and there was a thick bank of smoke on the sea in front of Calais. I had a talk to Vinson. He agrees that the preparations around here are too apparent to be anything but bluff, and that the leisurely invasion of Italy is a farce. A raid warning came from Lyminge as I went on duty at 9.30 p.m. Major Master turned up for a short time. 'All clear' at 10.30 p.m. as the dance gramophone in the hall struck up 'God Save the King'.

Tuesday 7 September

I woke at 6 a.m. but dozed off again. A toothless hag with her hair down relieved me at 7.15 a.m., a quarter of an hour late with lame excuses. She did the same the last time she relieved me. The military authorities at midnight stopped the running of the Saltwood bus, and police traffic notices were put up on all the roads.

Wednesday 8 September

Mother's birthday. The Fire Service put up a tank under our bridge and filled it with water. Phyllis went to Mrs Dix's funeral at Charing. At 6 p.m. we heard the news of the unconditional surrender of Italy, but this is a 'phoney' war. We are told that the Armistice was signed the day we invaded Italy. Our bombers went for Boulogne. Huge orange balls went up to meet them; the

Churchill tanks and other vehicles of the 9th Armoured Division in Hythe during Exercise 'Harlequin' (IWM H32714)

bombs bursting shook our house, and streams of fire fell from the sky exactly like planes crashing in flames. Heavy bombing continued across the water, breaking out over Calais as well as below Boulogne.

Thursday 9 September

Tanks roared through Hythe town before dawn, and bombers were out again pounding Boulogne. I was told the smoke from its fires nearly reached to our shores. From 7 a.m. the sky was full of every description of plane. Alert at 7.30 a.m. At intervals, heavy bombing rattled the houses. Phyllis and Daphne left at 9 a.m. for a day in London on church matters. At about 10 o'clock, 50 barges escorted by two torpedo boats came into Hythe beach, picked up tanks and men and went out some way, then came back and disembarked their loads. There was only a slight breeze, but some of the barges pitched heavily.

Saturday 11 September

A whole train of lorries carrying bridging equipment came into our street about 6 o'clock and left at 10 a.m. Alert 7 a.m. We three went out in the afternoon to Bog Farm, Brabourne, to buy pears. It got very hot. Alert at 5.30 p.m. as we were waiting for the bus. Alert at 6.30 p.m. Practically all the Italian fleet came in and surrendered.

> ## ARMADA OF 300 SHIPS
> ———
> ### TROOPS TAKEN TO WITHIN 10 MILES OF FRANCE
> Reuter's correspondent who was on board one of the destroyers which took part in yesterday's amphibious exercise said that the ships went to within 10 miles of the French coast.
> Employing 300 craft, the Navy brought the armada on perfect schedule from a multitude of ports and embarcation beaches to within

Monday 13 September

A very sharp storm about 12.30 a.m. with vivid lightning. Troops poured along the road all night, making a deafening din. In the morning, a Brigadier and his staff passed through. Rain all morning. I spent the day in Folkestone. At 6 p.m., 37 planes came home crossed by the same number going out. In the evening, the Traffic Police took down all the road signs and dismantled the latrines. I went on duty at 9.30 p.m. An almost noiseless night!

Wednesday 15 September

The Americans are hanging on to Salerno [Italy] and the situation seems better, but they have suffered heavy casualties. It now comes out that

Badoglio wished to keep the surrender secret until we were well established in Italy, but that Eisenhower insisted on giving it out to his men before they landed. He always seems to make a hash of everything. Heavy air activity commenced in the afternoon, and went on until dusk. Paris was attacked. About 10 o'clock two Huns were lit up by searchlights and heavily fired upon by AA guns. Next, our fighters turned up and let out a green and red flare before chasing the enemy. One flew out towards France and when near the coast we saw a blazing body in the sky coming towards us. It then dropped steeply into the sea, where it burnt for a time.

Thursday 16 September
Bombs fell on Ashford last night, one man killed, and a plane was brought down at Pluckley, killing some cattle. Air activity during the afternoon. Short alert 7.10 p.m. The battery was returned to Seaton Avenue and the Herefords' advance party have come back to this road. Situation at Salerno improved, patrols of 8th Army joining up with American 5th Army.

Saturday 18 September
A distinct change to autumn. The restrictions in this area have been taken off. A poor bluff, so obvious that the Huns could hardly have been deceived. My old friend Smith, the farmer, has died at Brabourne. Our bombers out at night.

Sunday 19 September
Large formations of planes in morning and early afternoon. There have been thefts from Hayfield and Hillcrest Lodge in this road. Down, the gardener at the former, insisted from the first they were the work of an out-of-work man named Sargent and his wife in a bungalow next door. Today, from information received, a police detective visited them and found the proceeds of thefts from four houses.

Thursday 23 September
A crisp clear day, which I spent in Folkestone. Large formations of bombers were passing overhead during the afternoon. There is a yarn that one of our planes came low on Tuesday night and was brought down by an AA gun. When they examined the wreckage, they found six dead Huns in it. Short alert 8 p.m.

Saturday 25 September

The German guns sent half a dozen shells into Folkestone at 5 a.m., setting a gas cylinder alight and demolishing about four houses. A woman and her two children were killed in their Morrison Shelter. A couple in bed were unhurt, although they lost everything. A cold misty morning. Planes, mostly bombers, in the sky all day. The Russians have taken Smolensk. Our bombers came over at 9.30 p.m.

Sunday 26 September

A fine day, with a north wind. Harvest Festival, also Battle of Britain Sunday. Revd Peters-Jones preached a good sermon on sacrifice. In the late afternoon, the sky was covered with feathery white veins but, unlike three years ago, it was all our planes. It was an obvious stunt celebrating the day.

Thursday 30 September

I spent the day in Folkestone, which was full of Marine Commandos and Dutch soldiers, who looked like extra-slovenly Home Guards. At the bottom of the Road of Remembrance, the Navy have had a concrete rabbit warren built for them in the cliff under the Parish Church. September has gone, with little progress in Italy and no attempt to act elsewhere. Casualties in the American 5th Army in the fighting at Salerno are 3,500 Americans and 5,200 British! It's an astonishing war.

Saturday 2 October

The usual air activity. I counted over 60 Fortresses going out at about 5 p.m. At the same time, squadrons of Typhoons and other aircraft were going up from Lympne and Hawkinge. The Australians have captured Finschhafen in New Guinea. In the night, I had a vague idea of the sound of planes, guns and lorries, but I was too sleepy to rouse myself.

Monday 4 October

A rough day, with diminishing air activity. The town was full of Marine Commando men, a number of whom have been billeted along the Dymchurch Road. Bastia has been captured, and Corsica is in French hands.

BEER-BEER WITHOUT ACK-ACK

An east coast searchlight battery is creating a major problem for its major. Twice in 11 days it has brought down with its beams a German raider. On the first occasion the major bought the battery a barrel of beer to celebrate its " shot-less " success.' Another barrel is on order to mark the bringing down of the second aeroplane, a Junkers 88, on Saturday. The aeroplane was caught in the glare of the battery's searchlights, banked violently, and crashed into the sea.

The Germans, who have been attacking the island of Kos for two days, claim to have effected a landing. Badoglio has taken into his government two Generals who committed gross outrages in Yugoslavia. Our bombers were passing overhead from 7.45 p.m. to 8.15 p.m. I went on duty at 9.45 p.m. I forgot to take my ARP badge and armlet. A quiet night. I slept at 4 a.m.

Friday 8 October
The Germans claim that the attack on London was a heavy one, causing extensive damage and that Londoners began to squeal. Different people were put up to deny, through the BBC, the Germans' claims and to say there was no slackness or confusion in the defence. I spent the day in Folkestone. In the afternoon, all the AA batteries were practising with a towed target. Alert 8 p.m. A heavy barrage was put up from Dover, Folkestone and Hawkinge, and there were huge red flashes over the latter place as if the aerodrome was being bombed.

Saturday 9 October
A midsummer's day, hot and hazy. Daphne took her Guides out to camp in Barham. I carried her suitcase down and saw her off at 1.45 p.m. A Hurricane squadron flew down the coast from 1 p.m. and roared back, skimming our roof. At 4 p.m. a very large force of bombers and fighters returned from France.

Wednesday 13 October
A dull day. Alert 1 p.m. The Russian bridgeheads are firmly established across the Dnieper and there is a rumour the Germans are evacuating Kiev [Ukraine]. I wish we could fight as determinedly in Italy. We have occupied the Azores, though Portugal still claims to be neutral. The Italians have declared war on Germany.

Friday 15 October
A damp overcast day. Alert 7 a.m. I helped Master and two others shift Saltwood emergency rations from the cellars of Grange House to the railway van. They had got damp and were sent away to be reconditioned. In their raid on Schweinfurt, the Americans lost 60 planes! They say they shot down 120 fighters.

Tuesday 19 October

I wrote my reminiscences up to 5 a.m., then dozed for an hour. I got wet coming home. A sunny morning, and a wet and boisterous evening.

Friday 22 October

I spent the day in Folkestone. The sky was full of Hurricanes. Alert 7 p.m. Huns came roaring across the sky and an AA barrage was out up over Shorncliffe, with searchlights trying to pierce the clouds. I went outside and heard a plane dive, then the whine of a bomb coming towards me. I ducked, without realising how close I was to the porch, and hit my head against a pillar. It was probably a dud AA shell.

Saturday 23 October

No. 1, the Sargents' cottage, has a notice 'Unexploded Bomb' on its gate. It was the projectile which whistled over my head. We lost 45 bombers last night. Alert 11.15 p.m.; about 11.30 p.m. two red flares were dropped over the Marsh, and a plane flew from that direction along the coast. Over Sandgate there was the sound of a large shell coming inwards towards the Roughs. I was asleep before the 'all clear' sounded at 12.30 a.m.

Sunday 24 October

The Herefords left at dawn and by the wholesale clearance they made, they have obviously gone for good. Folkestone is also cleared of troops. A heavy rainstorm at 11.45 a.m. Ships with exchanged prisoners of war have arrived in England. Lloyd George, over 80, has married his secretary.

Monday 25 October

A huge 'V' made by clouds in the eastern sky – a sign maybe? I went on duty at 9 o'clock.

Tuesday 26 October

I woke at 6.30 a.m. and my relief was punctual. The Army in these parts has definitely gone, even the tanks in Broome Park and units in surrounding villages. I have an idea we will have Americans.

Sunday 31 October

Short alert 1.50 p.m.; our Air Force woke up and got busy. Alert 10.50 p.m. AA fire and the flash of two bombs on Dover. 'All clear' at 11.15

p.m. The Russians have cut off the Crimea, the Germans are beginning a short retreat in Italy and MacArthur has landed on Bougainville Island [New Guinea].

Wednesday 3 November
A perfect, sunny day. The last of our troops left yesterday. The 43rd (Wessex) Division are coming in. The RASC have come into billets in our road. They were a very smart Territorial Division, the first disciplined troops to come here after Dunkirk. They are probably completely altered. I had an interesting talk with a subaltern commanding the rear party of the late battery, a red-headed farmer from Ayrshire. There was the rumble of a battle in the neighbourhood of Abbeville at noon. At night, another heavy battle across the water; a naval engagement.

Thursday 4 November
The new battery came into Seaton Avenue; they seem to be digging in for the winter. They have made their lorries into a laager, covering them with tarpaulin.

Friday 5 November
Guy Fawkes Day. I spent the day in Folkestone, which was full of new troops, with a stream of lorries and marching men going east. A large force of planes went over at 1.30 p.m. and the rest of the day the sky was full of planes, and heavy bombing shook the earth. Alert 9.15 p.m. Occasional planes and short bursts of AA fire. All clear at 10.10 p.m. Vatican bombed by Americans.

Saturday 6 November
A pouring wet morning, then a sunny afternoon. Air activity in afternoon, bombers over in the evening. The Russians have taken Kiev, I believe almost the last German stronghold, and we have advanced a few miles along the whole line in Italy. It is said we could land anywhere in Albania without opposition – yet we do nothing. Alert 11 p.m., 'all clear' at 11.30 p.m. but ten minutes later the alert again and a few planes flew in from the sea. One, presumably a night fighter of ours, cruised about fairly low over the house and there was cannon fire over Lympne.

Tuesday 9 November

Hitler made a dull speech of 'no surrender' yesterday. Today Churchill made a duller one at the Lord Mayor's banquet. He had eaten and drunk too much and brushed aside the strike situation. He said next year would see the crisis, with heavy casualties.

Wednesday 10 November

A clear frosty morning, the town shrouded in thick mist. A very large force of bombers and fighters came back overhead about midday and another at 2 p.m. and again at 4 p.m. A Mr Solly and Mrs Ledger, an engaged couple from Kearsney, came for the afternoon to look over the house with a view to purchasing it after the war. She was a charming little woman; he was rather coarse. There are Turf Commissioners of the name of Solly in Dover. She, especially, seemed very pleased with the house. Bombers were overhead from 7 p.m. to 10.30 p.m.

Thursday 11 November

Armistice Day. I saw no signs of any celebrations, except the Mayor taking a wreath to the memorial. All day, squadrons flew over to France and bombers were out at night. A full moon.

Saturday 13 November

Only the Russian news is good. We are stuck in Italy and whining about the bad weather. The Germans are landing without hindrance on Leros [Greece] and claim to have taken it. We say we are 'inflicting casualties'. Yet even some of our leaders are gassing about an early end to the war.

Monday 15 November

We heard from Mrs Ledger that the house was not big enough to hold her furniture. Another cold day. I went on duty at 9 p.m. A clear night. Troops on manoeuvres in the neighbourhood burst into battle at 10.30 p.m., 1 a.m. and 4 a.m. I went to sleep at 4 a.m.

Tuesday 16 November

I slept badly, waking at 5 a.m. and again at 6.30 a.m. A fine frosty morning. The manoeuvres flowed into the town with much firing of blanks. They have to sleep in the open without coats or caps, and are nearly dead with cold. Many people in the Elham area are saving the lives of individuals

Kent Home Guard troops debriefed after an exercise escaping through a smokescreen
(Kent Messenger PD1542068)

with cups of coffee, Bovril etc. It is said we are still hanging on to Leros, and have improved our position. Our bombers went over at 9 p.m.

Wednesday 17 November

A cold day. Mrs Sargent was given nine months for her looting. Her counsel put up the plea of a blind husband, a little child and two daughters on war work and nearly got her off. We have lost Leros. The Russians have been beaten back in the south.

Friday 19 November

I spent the day in Folkestone. Vinson also has my idea that the USA and we are afraid to fight because of the possibility of heavy casualties, and that we hope that when the Russians get near the German border the Germans will beg us to come and save them. A large force of our bombers started out at 6.30 p.m. and explosions shook the house.

Saturday 20 November

A fine cold day. Much air activity. At intervals, the house was shaken by explosions. In the afternoon, Down (the 'Hayfield' gardener) asked me to telephone for the police as he had found a suitcase, packed with linen and other articles from the house, in one of the sheds.

Tuesday 23 November

I got very little sleep in the morning. Our bombers went to Berlin last night, and claim they gave it its biggest strafing of the war. We lost 26. The Germans said the 8th Army had started a major offensive in Italy, but we claim it is still stuck in the mud. The police sat up in 'Hayfield' on Saturday night without result. Down persuaded them to do so again on Sunday. Three RASC men drove up in a car at 9.30 p.m. and were caught red-handed. They had an arsenal of skeleton keys. Heavy air activity in the afternoon, including a large force of Fortresses. It is said the Air Force has been given 48 days to knock out Germany. A cold night.

Thursday 25 November

Berlin raided last night, for the third night in succession. The sky full of every description of plane during the morning. Alert 7.10 p.m. The Huns went to London up the Thames estuary and returned via Ashford and over us at 7.30 p.m. Searchlights got on to them above the clouds, and our night fighters went after them. There were several crashes of gunfire in the sky and one flash over the sea, which may have marked the destruction of one of them.

Sunday 28 November

A mild day, wet underfoot. The new troops are Pioneer Corps. I do not understand why no badges and other 'hush hush' proceedings. Alert 12.15 p.m. Bombs dropped somewhere on the coast, with no reported damage. Our bombers out at 11 p.m. and later. Alert at 2 a.m.

Monday 29 November

A clear morning. Alert 9 a.m. A big bomber force went over about 10 a.m. The sky over Hawkinge was full, with squadrons flying in every direction. The 8th Army have commenced an offensive. I went on duty at 9 p.m. A clear night, but not a plane in the sky the whole time up to 4 a.m. when I dozed off.

Wednesday 1 December

A perfect day. Slight frost and sun. Usual air activity. Alert at 8.15 p.m. Churchill, Roosevelt and Chiang Kai-shek have met in Cairo, and have given out the usual blather of terrible things going to happen to the

Japanese. The press are fed up because Lisbon gave it out on the air before they could.

Thursday 2 December
A pouring wet morning. Alert 10.15 a.m. A Hun tried a sneak dive on Dover, but despite the weather Dover and Folkestone batteries were ready and he was shot down into the sea off Capel. Churchill, Roosevelt and Stalin have met in Teheran. The 8th Army have made good progress, capturing 1,000 prisoners. Our bombers went out in force over us at 8 p.m.

Friday 3 December
We went for Berlin last night, and lost 42 bombers. They try to minimise it by adding mine laying and other activities.

Saturday 4 December
Folkestone was shelled at 3 a.m. this morning, several shells falling in the Morehall area and damaging houses. We went for Berlin, then switched over to Lübeck and claim we fooled their night fighters, yet we lost over 20 bombers. Only our Mosquitoes went over tonight.

Monday 6 December
A bitter cold east wind. In the morning I met Jack Ridley of the Bell Inn, Hythe, on 'survivors' leave for the second time. His Corvette chased a U-boat and dropped a depth charge, but the U-boat was only just below the surface and the charge blew the stern of the Corvette off, killing 28. The rudder fell on the midship deck without hurting anyone. He said the acoustic torpedo is a nasty affair, not every ship is fitted with the safety device yet. They managed to get towed to the Azores, but the skipper was wigged for taking the tug from the convoy.

Wednesday 8 December
As far as I can make out, we were driven back all along the line in Italy. We seem now to be taking places we claimed to have held a week ago.

Friday 10 December
A cold rain squall in morning and a very cold north wind in evening. I spent the day in Folkestone. A gas school has turned up here, and the

Home Guard is being saturated with gas drills. The authorities say the shore guns are useless, but have handed the whole battery over to 'B' Company. Our bombers went over about 7 p.m. for about half an hour. Poor devils. We got such a lambasting over Berlin that not a bomber got into the air for a whole week.

Saturday 11 December
Snow fell at night and lay in patches through the day. There was a primrose in bloom in the garden. Nothing has been said of where our bombers went to last night. Churchill, having quizzed American, Chinese, Russian and Turkish leaders, is now so sick Mrs Churchill has to go out to him.

Monday 13 December
Miss Phyllis Spain, our cats' meat woman, the only supplier of dogs' and cats' meat in the south-east, looked me up about her being called up. I went into Folkestone in the afternoon to the Labour Exchange. After a wait I met a very nice woman who seemed to know all the facts and thrashed the case out patiently. I went on duty at 9 p.m. The weekly dance began late, so I had to endure the gramophone up to 11 p.m. There were no planes in the night, so I went to sleep at 3 a.m.

Tuesday 14 December
I got up feeling rotten with a pouring cold. I gave in during the afternoon and went to bed with a touch of flu and bronchitis.

Wednesday 15 December
Phyllis nursed me up to 7 p.m. then gave in and joined me. Daphne was left to run everything alone.

Thursday 16 December
Daphne was out of bed by 8 a.m., cooked our breakfasts, ran her Guides, the church and the house, working without a stop up to 10 p.m.!!

Friday 17 December
A tiring and irritating day. Evidently I'm getting better.

Monday 20 December
Alerts at 2.30 a.m. and 5.30 a.m. About 5.45 a.m. there was very heavy

AA gunfire as an apparently wounded plane flew low. Daphne heard the whine of a shell (it was too 'thin' for a bomb), which seemed to fall near the house. A mild day. Our helper Beatrice Dray went home sick on Saturday, and Daphne worked the whole house on Sunday and today without us finding out. Very heavy and continuous air activity all day.

Wednesday 22 December
Another fine day. Less air activity. They say we are trying to stop the Germans putting up these rocket batteries, which they boast of as their secret weapon. The Russians say it is all bunkum.

Saturday 25 December
Christmas Day. We three spent it together with a dinner of beef and bottled plums. It is given out that Eisenhower is to be Commander in Chief of combined armies of the 'second front' and Montgomery is to command the British. It is to open in March. The Germans say the Generals are already in England.

Monday 27 December
The German battleship *Scharnhorst* attacking a convoy for Russia was intercepted by the battleship *Duke of York* and sunk with nearly all its crew drowned. I went on duty at 9 o'clock and found the post locked. There is so much 'flu' amongst the personnel that the post is closed during the day. Last Monday, when I was laid up Master risked not having anyone on duty.

Thursday 30 December
Our bombers went to Berlin last night and dropped the heaviest load of bombs dropped so far in a night. It was the anniversary of the German raid in 1941 when the city was devastated. Our Pioneers have returned to the road very much smartened up with badges etc. on them. Planes were passing over almost continuously all day. The Americans are now indulging in indiscriminate bombing.

Friday 31 December
I spent the day in Folkestone. Vinson informed me that a Wing Commander gave away in a pub the information that Montgomery was in

Folkestone a few days ago. He also pointed out that the men and vehicles with the blue cross and sword are 8th Army. 'Binge' apparently has been allowed to take his whole army with him. A huge force of Marauders flew over us about 1 p.m.

GOC inspection of the Kent Home Guard in sabotage mode

1944

Sunday 2 January

Another dull mild day. Planes about as usual. About 12 o'clock I was out for a walk on Gorsey Bank when an alert sounded. Ten minutes later, the sky over Hawkinge was black with AA shell bursts. I saw a plane in the middle of it, but it may have been one of ours getting out of the way. One dud shell whistled over my head. Canterbury searchlights were up, and then the skies over Lympne and Hawkinge were alight. At the same time AA and searchlights were ablaze on the French coast round Boulogne, and the thump of bombs shook the house.

Monday 3 January

A mild overcast day. Planes up, but not in large numbers. Our bombers lost 28 over Berlin last night. The BBC have brought on themselves the wrath of the Scotch Kirk for broadcasting a rather alcoholic Hogmanay night. I went on duty again at 9 p.m. No alerts.

Wednesday 5 January

A sharp frost at night. A fair amount of air activity. Street's son is now with the Yugoslav partisans. There is a huge dump in Seaton Avenue field; looks like petrol. Some days ago a dud AA shell fell through the roof of Manisty, North Road.

Thursday 6 January

Mild. Planes out all day and early in the evening. The Russians are 15 miles inside the Polish frontier. I wonder if we have 'sold' the Poles to Stalin?

Friday 7 January

Still mild. I spent the day in Folkestone. Usual air activity. Information about our new jet-propelled aeroplane. We claim it is faster and handier.

Tuesday 11 January

I woke at 6.30 a.m. and made myself a cup of tea and waited until 7.10 a.m. when, as no one had turned up, I locked up and went home. A wet afternoon with a cold south wind. Count Ciano and old General De Bono [Italian politicians] have been shot by the Germans. The Russians have announced that they are going to have all Poland up to the line they occupied in 1939. What are Churchill and Roosevelt doing?

Wednesday 12 January

Working for the [Volunteer] Car Pool. I went to Brockhill Road at 12.30 p.m. and picked up Mrs Learmonth, County Secretary of the Soldiers, Sailors and Airmen Family Association and drove her to Sandwich; Phyllis came too. Mrs Learmonth talked without stopping, chiefly about the immense amount of war work she does. She is the wife of the General commanding all the AA batteries in Kent, and wangles a war job in whatever place her husband is stationed. We went via Dover and Deal, as I thought the Alkham Valley would be full of army lorries. We saw very few troops. At the top of Dover Hill, there was a large field full of small AA guns (about 50) 20 yards apart in rows. Mrs Learmonth went to organise her branch and see a case. Phyllis and I had a Welsh rabbit at a café at 2 p.m. and walked twice around Sandwich and had tea at 4 p.m. I returned by the Alkham Valley. We did not meet a single lorry or car. It was dark by the time I got into Folkestone, but there was a moon behind the clouds, which gave a little light. We met some mist above Folkestone. We got back at 6 p.m.; a total of 54 miles. A large force (700) of Fortresses bombed an aeroplane factory to the south of Berlin. They met heavy opposition, the Huns sending up new planes and using new tactics. They lost 65 but claim to have shot down 150. The Huns put it the other way round. The Yankees call it a major victory, but I doubt if they will try it again.

Thursday 13 January

All day there was the sound of heavy bombing on the French coast opposite Dungeness. A thick sea mist at night. Alert 7.15 p.m., sound of enemy planes and heavy AA gunfire half an hour later. 'All clear' about 8 p.m. We are up against the Nazi Youth [Hitler Youth] in Italy, boys of 18–20; desperate fighters, and truculent when captured.

Monday 17 January

A foggy day. Big guns booming from Dungeness all morning. In afternoon, guns in every direction fired an occasional shot. I hear there are American troops in Lympne. In Folkestone, Grimston Gardens and Avenue are crammed with guns and tanks. I went on duty at 9 p.m. and found the place locked. A dark night, no planes. I settled down at 2.30 a.m.

Thursday 20 January

We were woken up by gunfire. The Huns bombarded Folkestone; the shells fell in Cheriton, where people from the shelled areas near the harbour had moved to. I heard the East Kent car depot there has been hit, and casualties were heavy. It started as usual with our guns firing at 5 a.m., and sinking a German ship off Gris Nez.

Lympne aerodrome bombed (*Rodney Foster Archive*)

Friday 21 January

I spent the day in Folkestone. I learnt that there was extensive damage in Cheriton from the shelling, but that no one was killed and less than a dozen hurt. Dover was untouched, all the shells going over into open country. Deal had about a dozen fatal casualties – there was a direct hit on a shelter. Big guns Dungeness way fired all day. At 7.30 p.m. a large force of our bombers passed overhead. Alert 8.45 p.m. Half a dozen Huns flew in from the sea and AA gunfire commenced. After a pause, an explosion shook the house and a red glow from the ground suffused the sky in the direction of

Hawkinge. AA gunfire was intense in places, one battery behind Folkestone putting up bunches of what looked like star shells. Searchlights were up, guns firing and night fighters could be heard. Owing to the gunfire, one had to go indoors and could not see what was happening. There was another explosion, which rattled the windows, and a white glare appeared Lympne way. About 9.45 p.m. searchlights in the Marsh concentrated on a raider and followed it inland when it was over Pedlinge. There were two bursts of cannon fire, and the raider burst into flames and fell in that direction. It was all over by 10 p.m., except for two flickers of gunfire later. In the middle of the raid, the electric current cut out so the 'all clear' could not be sounded.

BERLIN RAIDED
LAST NIGHT

Saturday 22 January

We lost 53 bombers last night, and brought down 16 out of 90 Huns. One from each raid was brought down near Stanford; two Huns bailed out of one bomber and were caught, one being brought into Hythe Police Station. They dropped a new type of incendiary bombs, which were scattered over large areas at Lydd and Pedlinge. In Canterbury, a large store and a garage were gutted near the station. One Hun fell into the sea off Hythe. Dover guns claimed two. We have landed a strong amphibious force at Anzio, 30 miles south of Rome, and are well established and have had practically no opposition so far. A great show! A wet day with a south-westerly gale. No air activity.

Monday 24 January

A sunny morning. Formations of bombers and fighters overhead all morning. Rain in afternoon. Daphne and I went to a WVS meeting to meet the County Chief, Lady Worsley, and the County Car Pool Organiser, a buck-stick of a woman. I went on duty at 9 p.m. Rain at midnight. No planes about.

Tuesday 25 January

A fine morning. I roused at 6 a.m., put out the fire, locked up and was starting for home when I realised I was an hour too early, so I returned and made myself a cup of tea. Planes up in the morning, a wet afternoon.

Wednesday 26 January

A wet afternoon. I fear that the Americans are going to make a mess of the Nettuno [Italy] landing; [Lieutenant General] Clarke struts up and down the beach and does not push on. Argentina, to the surprise of everyone, has broken with the Axis. The Russians have set up their own committee to investigate the mass murders of Polish officers and soldiers; about 12,000 were killed. Of course, the Russians say they have evidence the Germans did it. They have also refused American arbitration with the Polish dispute.

Thursday 27 January

At 11 a.m. in connection with the Car Pool, I picked up a Mrs Lee, an expectant mother, in Park Road and drove her to a nursing home in Broadwater Down, Tunbridge Wells. Phyllis came to look after her. On Hythe Hill we came upon three huge RAF trucks carrying the wreckage of a Hun bomber, and had to travel at 15 to 20 m.p.h. behind them all the way to Ashford. From there we got away to Sissinghurst where I stopped for oil, which I found I did not need, and the others had tea. In Tunbridge Wells I had difficulty in finding the home, eventually arriving there just before 2 p.m. We drove to the Central Station for lunch in a café opposite, but could only get coffee and cakes. We came home via Tenterden. After Sissinghurst, I missed the turning to Biddenden and drove on to Hawkhurst. Beyond that village, I again missed the turning to Rolvenden and we went on down the hill to the tiny village of Newenden with its doll's house of a church – a perfect gem. We stopped to admire it and ask the way. At the turning we had missed, we picked up a shy country girl waiting for the bus and drove her to Rolvenden. We got home at 5 p.m. A mild overcast day, the country very pretty with its brown and tan and blue-grey distances.

Friday 28 January

Our bombers went to Berlin last night: 34 missing. I spent the day in Folkestone. Last Friday, the Home Guard at Capel captured a Hun airman. We now claim to have brought down 16. Alert 10.20 p.m. At 10.45 p.m. a few Huns flew over from inland and were fired at. There was a high blanket of cloud.

Sunday 30 January

A perfect mild sunny day. I went for a walk over the golf links, which are now a tank exercise ground. A few planes over at night.

Monday 31 January

Dull and mild. A 'hoo-ha' about Japanese atrocities on our prisoners and bullying Spain to control Hun saboteurs. I went on duty at 9 p.m., and slept from 3 a.m. onwards. Not a single plane in the sky.

Tuesday 1 February

I woke about 5 a.m., then slept until 6.30 a.m. Another mild day. The Americans have landed on several of the Marshall Islands [Pacific Ocean] and captured one airfield. A bold effort, as the Japanese have been fortifying them since the end of the last war. The 5th Army in Italy are said to have cracked the German defences. The Russians have taken Kingisepp [near Leningrad].

Friday 4 February

Bombs fell one on either side of the railway tunnel east of Sandling Junction. No damage, except to a few sheep. I went to Folkestone for the day. From 11 a.m. to 3 p.m. the sky was continuously covered with planes roaring in and out. At dusk there were sounds of heavy bombers overhead. It was said on the wireless that bad weather restricted bombing by day.

Saturday 5 February

A frosty, sunny day. Am American bomber crashed into Dymchurch Police Station, killing a soldier and damaging several houses. The crew had bailed out and suffered slight injuries.

CREWLESS BOMBER'S CRASH

Sunday 6 February

I was woken at 6 a.m. by heavy AA gunfire. Planes were manoeuvring overhead, one at least a Hun, but I heard no bombs explode. In half an hour, all was quiet and I went to sleep and did not hear the 'all clear'. Another cold day. The Russians have bombed Helsinki. We have been driven back in our Anzio bridgehead and out of Cassino.

Monday 7 February

Another very mild day, with occasional drizzle of rain. I went in the afternoon to see the bomb craters. One bomb fell on the railway tunnel behind Hobbs' Farm, throwing up bricks, so it must have got very near to penetrating. I went on duty at 9 p.m. A clear sky. Expecting a possible raid about 6 a.m., I stayed awake all night.

Saturday 12 February
The bomb last night dropped near Morehall, Folkestone; no one killed. An unsettled day. It is now known that we nearly lost the bridgehead in Italy. Alert 8.40 p.m. Only one plane, probably one of our own night fighters.

Sunday 13 February
In the morning I went for a walk through Brockhill Park, up Forty Steps to Pedlinge and back by Sandling Park. Short alert at 12.15 p.m. American bombers were overhead in large numbers all afternoon, and the ground shook with the bombing across the Strait. British bombers passed over at 8 p.m. Alert 8.30 p.m. (the third night in succession); bomb explosions to the north and heavy gunfire broke out at 9 p.m. The whole northern horizon was lit up by searchlights, flares, AA shells and bomb explosions. The Huns went up the Thames estuary, only a few going back over us. They were met by searchlights, bursts of AA fire and star shells.

Tuesday 15 February
I woke at 6.30 a.m. Finland is said to be offering to stop fighting, but the Russians say the Red Army will dictate peace terms and frontiers, so the poor Finns will have to stew. Germans are giving out rumours that they are clearing out of Norway and handling over to the Quisling government. Sir Kenneth Anderson of the 1st Army has come to command the Eastern Command here. Is it promotion? I doubt it.

Wednesday 16 February
Rain all day. A rumpus about bombarding the Cassino monastery. We have got priests and bishops to say it cannot be helped, and the Americans have sent 600 planes to bomb it. The more we hear about the landing at Anzio, the more disgracefully mismanaged it appears. These Americans are hopeless. A short alert at 1.30 p.m.

Friday 18 February
Snow commenced falling at 8 a.m. and continued until 4.30 p.m., when the sun came out for a short time. I spent the day in Folkestone, but came back early because of the cold. Last Sunday, the Home Guard picked up on

the seafront in Folkestone a parachute and a haversack each with a detonator attached to it. There were printed leaflets, each with the head of a nasty-looking man on it, saying he was free or exempt from billeting and other instructions. Can't say if it is something the Hun dropped, or one of our leaflets. A Folkestone story: Mr A passing Mr B's house saw him stacking his property in a large furniture van. A said: 'Where are you off to? You surely are not afraid of a German invasion now?' B said: 'Oh no! I am clearing out before the Russians get here.'

Saturday 19 February
Sleet of varying degrees all day. The raid yesterday was on London. We publish no details, but a number of Huns seem to have got through and dropped chiefly incendiaries. Some fell on the Houses of Parliament. It is a stupid policy; the Huns claim extensive damage. Bombers over at night.

Sunday 20 February
A hard frost and bitter cold wind, but no more snow. Our bombers went to Leipzig last night and lost 79!! Americans over in afternoon.

Monday 21 February
A steady drizzle all day. I was on duty by 9 p.m. Alert 2.50 a.m., the first on my duty nights since before Christmas. A plane rushed overhead towards Lympne, and there were flashes in Ashford direction. Then the north sky was lit with a red light. All quiet for a time. At 3.20 a.m. a plane flew north-west out to sea and there were more flashes in the north-west. 'All clear' 3.30 a.m.

Thursday 24 February
A severe frost at night, and an icy cold east wind all day. At intervals all afternoon, the house shook from explosions caused by the Americans bombing the Calais area. Alert 9.45 p.m. when the Huns began to return from London, having come in another way. They sent over a large force. At 10 o'clock, the heaviest AA barrage was put up that I have ever heard in these parts. Cones of searchlights picked up planes, which were fired at. One near Ashford was shot down, and we saw the searchlights illuminate a parachute. Searchlights to the north picked up another bomber, lost it and then picked it up again and followed it out to sea over Folkestone. This was followed by Sandgate sending up tracers, star shells and flak. I saw bits

drop off the Hun and it lost height at a rapid rate; we did not see it come down (but it did). There were other cones of searchlights and A A fire everywhere.

Friday 25 February
Not such a cold day. I spent the day in Folkestone. Big forces of bombers over all day. Coming home, I saw a large force of Fortresses heading north and one of them flying very low making for Hawkinge. Fighters and fighter-bombers were also coming in.

Sunday 27 February
Some snow in morning, and again in the afternoon. In the morning I walked through Saltwood across the fields to the main road near Stone Farm and back across country further down Kick Hill. I found one of Hobbs' sheep dead in a slit trench on the tunnel.

Thursday 2 March
I was woken at 3 a.m. by a heavy barrage and cannon fire, and the sky seemed full of planes. The firing was continuous for half an hour. I was too sleepy to get up, but saw one cone of searchlights groping for a Hun over Hawkinge. At 3.20 a.m. three very brilliant white flares were dropped over Hythe town, and soon after all was quiet. Snow on the ground in the morning.

Sunday 5 March
A cold day with fog. Air activity for a short time at midday, and again in the afternoon. The Yankees went to Berlin by daylight on Saturday and lost 37 bombers and fighters, but only claimed shooting down nine of the enemy. The Huns say they drove them off, but the Yanks said they could not drop their bombs as they could not see.

Monday 6 March
A hard white frost in morning. Planes out whilst one of our convoys passed down the Strait in partial fog. The Yanks went to Berlin again in huge force today at noon. They reached its suburbs, but lost 68 bombers and 11 fighters. A shell warning at 8 p.m.; about six shells were fired by the enemy. Then a fairly large force of our heavy bombers flew over. I went on duty at 9 p.m. A quiet night. Some of our bombers returned at 3 a.m.

Tuesday 7 March

Slight snow at 6 a.m. A very cold east wind, which grew stronger by evening. A battery of American heavy howitzers passed through the town in the morning going east. Some of the men had nut-brown faces, and were Eskimo type (Red Indians?).

Wednesday 8 March

Bright sunshine with a cold east wind. A short alert at 9.30 a.m. The Americans again went to Berlin, dropping an immense load of bombs and incendiaries. Alert 9.30 p.m. to 10 p.m., but nothing happened near us.

TWO AIR STOWAWAYS FROM ITALY

The crew of an American Liberator bomber, which had flown from Italy and landed at an aerodrome in north-west England yesterday morning were surprised to see two British soldiers jump from the machine. Both men made a dash for the open country, but one of them was captured. He said that he and his companion had been on the Eighth Army front and had stowed away in the machine just before it took off in Italy.

The second soldier was captured at Bangor railway station late last night by the local police. Both men have been handed over to a military escort.

Friday 10 March

A milder day, with fog in morning. I spent the day in Folkestone. The car refused to start. Daphne was unable to go to Etchinghill, and I had to refuse a Car Pool journey tomorrow. In winding the car up, the handle slipped and I spiked my wrist on the AA badge. The Russians claim they have routed the Germans, capturing amongst other booty 100 tanks in working order. The Americans yesterday met no fighter opposition when attacking Berlin.

Saturday 11 March

A milder day. Heavy and continuous air activity from an early hour throughout the morning and again in the afternoon. Joan came to stay with us for the weekend; she had a date with a Pioneer Captain called Doug at 7 p.m. He took her for a walk then into his mess in Mrs Matson's house next door to us. We are still doing nothing in Italy, whining of bad weather and boasting of opening the 'second front'. The Americans say we have already won the war because the Luftwaffe won't attack them when they go over. Montgomery says we will make the enemy groggy this year and beat him next. He says he drove them into the sea in Tunisia and Sicily, but said nothing of Italy. He has gained a reputation on one battle – El Alamein; he never hit Rommel again. The latter retreated owing to the landing in Algiers. The 1st Army, not much more than a Brigade, with the help of the Americans and French beat the Germans. 80,000 miners on strike!!

Monday 13 March

A boisterous day. Extensive air activity throughout the day. Joan left at 11 a.m. The Americans asked southern Ireland to dismiss the German and Japanese Ambassadors. De Valera refused, so we have stopped all passenger traffic to southern Ireland. Perhaps that will learn them. I went on duty at 9 p.m. A fine night, with a short alert at 1 a.m. Not a plane was heard or any noise in our area. I went to sleep at 3.30 a.m.

Tuesday 14 March

I left duty at 7 a.m. A white frost. A deserter from the Royal West Kent has, for a week, made himself at home in the unoccupied furnished house of Spencer, Mrs Wellesley's maid, a few doors from the police station. Phyllis and Daphne in the afternoon went to meetings in Folkestone. Alert 10.20 p.m. with 'danger overhead' signals in Folkestone. About 11 p.m. Huns began to return in some numbers from London. At one time there was a roar of planes, our fighters were up, but the AA fire was sporadic. 'All clear' at midnight.

Wednesday 15 March

Frost at night, but a sunny day. Much bombing all day across the Strait. After intensive bombing and barrage, we have made a heavy attack on Cassino in Italy. Headquarters give no details, but correspondents hint we have made no progress. Alert 8.45 p.m. Planes flew in almost at once, our AA guns fired seldom and the searchlights seemed to fail to concentrate on one point. There was AA fire, and flares up over Boulougne, and some of our bombers seemed to return about 9.15 p.m. 'All clear' at 9.30 p.m. I heard that on Tuesday night two shells fell in the vicinity of Gorsey Banks; they may have been from a naval engagement in the Strait during the raid. We brought down 13 bombers that night.

Thursday 16 March

A fine day. The biggest force of Fortresses I have so far seen flew over to France about 9.30 a.m. Intense air activity again at 4 p.m., the sky full of returning planes. Alert 6.45 p.m. (an unusual hour). 'All clear' 7 p.m. A spy was executed in London yesterday. There seems to be something again wrong with our tanks; Churchill has granted a secret debate on them and said he had never said his Government never made mistakes. We lost no bombers over Stuttgart last night.

Friday 17 March

A warm spring day, which I spent in Folkestone, which is full of Americans. Daphne drove three WVS women into Canterbury to take over a semi-mobile canteen which can cater for 500 people. She was out again at Guides from 5 p.m. to 9 p.m. Alert 9.10 p.m. in a thick mist. Heavy guns commenced shelling at 9.30 p.m. 'All clear' at 9.45 p.m., after which there was another salvo.

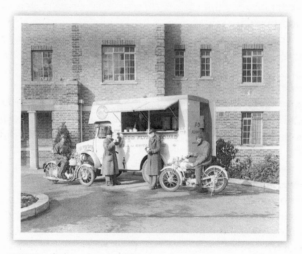

WVS Food Flying Squad mobile canteen brought American aid for Kent
(War and Peace Collection 0336)

Monday 20 March

A hundred Fortresses in two formations flew over to France at 10 a.m., followed by large forces of other bombers. As I went on duty at 9 p.m., there was practice firing with flares on the Ranges. Cross-Channel guns commenced firing at 10 o'clock; the flashes greatly emphasised by the clouded sky. It was one of the heaviest bombardments to date. Our bombers returned about 11 o'clock.

Tuesday 21 March
Slight rain at night. I left the post at 7 a.m. Air activity during the day. At 9.45 p.m. a convoy of large lorries passed down our road as the cross-Channel guns commenced firing. It was not a long affair. Alert at 12.30 a.m. which I did not hear, but I was woken by the subsequent gunfire. Being the night after my night on duty, I was too sleepy to look at the time. 'All clear' at 2 a.m.

Wednesday 22 March
Alert 9.30 p.m. There was one burst of gunfire at 10 o'clock. 'All clear' at 10.10 a.m. The Germans have occupied Hungary. The Japanese have got over the border into Manipur State [India], whilst we seem to have scattered our forces in a raid on the [River] Chindwin and an airborne expedition near Bhamo [Burma]. Mountbatten was not the man to send there. No sailor is a success with land operations.

Friday 24 March
I spent the day in Folkestone. Planes up all day and occasional bombers about 10 p.m. Alert 11.10 p.m., followed by distant AA gunfire. About midnight the cuckoo siren, which has again been installed at the school, sounded and later went off a second time. Planes came from inland, searchlights were up but could not penetrate the cloud. All round, from the north-west to the sea in the east, a pandemonium of gunfire broke out, with flashes on the ground. For a time I thought it was a sea-borne or paratroop raid by the Germans, and had visions of being taken captive to Germany. It sounded more like a Battle School practice than AA gunfire. It died down by 1 o'clock and the 'all clear' sounded at 1.10 a.m.

Saturday 25 March
A heavy raid last night, hushed up in the official announcement. We brought down eight machines. I was told that a large number of AA guns have been set up in the area; some say they are Americans. We went to Berlin last night and lost 73 bombers! A warm sunny day. Street returned

from visiting one of his battalions at Aldershot, where he watched glider-borne troops exercising.

Churchill tanks travel on a train to Kent (Kent Messenger PD1566050)

Sunday 26 March

An almost midsummer day. Air activity not that extensive. Daphne returned from her Barham Camp at 7.30 p.m. Churchill broadcast at 9 p.m. He told us nothing about the war, slobbered over Stalin, Tito and all the other villains, then talked at length on housing, education and demobilisation. He said he was giving us a land 'fit for heroes to live in' but did not use those words.

Monday 27 March

A colder misty day. Air activity restricted. The RASC in our road have been issued with khaki berets. I met 'Bone' Foster, very much under the weather. I was on duty at 9 p.m. Alert 11.40 p.m. Ten minutes later a Hun flew over from inland and was heavily fired on by guns in the Marsh. There was thick cloud high up, which the searchlights could not penetrate, and most of them switched off. The Hun retreated, but at midnight it or another returned and was again met by a noisy barrage. By this time Master and three policemen had arrived at the post. Then one of our night fighters turned up, and some of our bombers came home. It is possible the Hun was waiting for them. 'All clear' at 12.30 a.m. I settled down at 3 a.m.

Tuesday 28 March

Phyllis' birthday. I woke at 6 a.m. and left the post at 6.45 a.m. Phyllis gave me an early breakfast, and I picked up Mrs Learmonth and Mrs Daniels in the High Street. I drove them into Maidstone, where we arrived about 10.45 a.m. They went to a welfare conference at the County Hall, a huge and hideous building forming part of the wall of the county jail. I went into the town, then looked up Harriette and Jim Stanley. They are living in Boxley Road in a house called Fintonagh. It was a fairly large house with extensive grounds, the front of which had been sold for building. It was being run as a private hotel by its owner Captain Stanley-King. They only had one maid, and Mrs King had to do all the cooking. The Stanleys were out, so I went back to the town and had lunch at Lyon's Café at 12.30 p.m. I went back again about 2 p.m. and met them. They looked well and hardly a day older. The conference finished earlier then had been expected, as I had been asked to be ready at 3.45 p.m. The two ladies had lunch in the town, went out by bus to Mrs Daniels' old home, came back for tea and were late at the rendezvous. When I went to unlock the car, I found I had lost the keys. I managed to push down a window and unlock one door, and I got an ignition key from Rootes. We left about 4 p.m., getting home at 5 p.m. There was a fair amount of Army traffic on the roads, and all the woods were full of hutments. Despite the little sleep I had, I did not feel sleepy until 10 p.m. when I was dead tired and went to bed.

Wednesday 29 March

A colder day, with mist. No planes up all day; some out at night. The Government were defeated over equal pay for teachers in the Education Bill by one vote. Churchill today said he would have no criticism on even the most minor Government proposition, and if there is an adverse vote he will treat it as a vote of no confidence and resign. With [Home Secretary] Morrison's Gestapo and Churchill's dictatorship we might as well accept Hitler.

Friday 31 March

We lost 94 bombers last night in an attack on Nuremberg. No aircraft up during the day, which was fine and sunny. There was a flat calm sea but not a boat on it. A very heavy gun behind us sent the occasional shells all day into the sea. The shell made a hum like a heavy bomber as it passed over, and the column of water which rose was very high. 80,000 Yorkshire miners are on strike. General Wingate, leader of the Chindits, has been killed in a plane crash.

Sunday 2 April

Double summertime gave a change of weather. A fair amount of rain fell during the night, and in the morning the blossoms on the trees were fully out. Bullfinches have eaten all the buds on the conference pear tree.

Monday 3 April

Eight USA airmen were rescued by a trawler. I went on duty at 9 p.m.; no one to relieve, as blackout is not until then. A young Lance Corporal

U.S. AIRMEN RESCUED FROM THE CHANNEL

of the Worcestershire Regiment stopped and talked. He thought the regular Army a rough lot and believed the 'second front' was imminent, but ended by saying he thought it all a bluff. Self-educated, he had strong opinions, many erroneous. I got to sleep at 3.30 a.m.

Tuesday 4 April

I woke at 6 a.m.; a sea mist. In morning, troops were pouring up and down the town and up and down hill to Saltwood and beyond. With carrier-based aircraft, we bombed the battleship *Tirpitz* as it was leaving its Norwegian fjord. We claim 24 direct hits and that she is definitely crippled for the rest of the war. Planes passed overhead from 10 p.m. for an hour.

Wednesday 5 April

A mild overcast day with some rain. We have had a very dry spring and rain is badly needed everywhere. Some air activity in the morning. Bevin [Minister of Labour] and the TUC slating the miners; Major [Gwilym] Lloyd George [Minister of Fuel and Power] says nothing. We are told our food may be cut; that should wake people up. It is said 'Trotskyites' are causing the trouble. What are they?

Friday 7 April

Good Friday. A cold east wind. No news anywhere in Italy, Burma or the Pacific. Russians are up to the Carpathian passes. Colonel Street's son, covered in medals, is home on leave.

Sunday 9 April

Easter Sunday. Saltwood Church prettily decorated, very full including 100 men of a field battery. Phyllis was first reader at her church service in the afternoon.

Monday 10 April

Planes out early in a clear morning, then a thick sea fog came up, but did not stop the planes. Heavy bombing across the Strait from 9.15 a.m. repeatedly rattled our windows. The Russians have reoccupied Odessa and penetrated into the Crimea. I went on duty shortly after 9 p.m. (we now go on at blackout time). An almost full moon, but only a very few single planes passed over. I got to sleep by 3.30 a.m.

Tuesday 11 April

I left the post by 6.50 a.m. A convoy of ships containing large barges, each hauled by two tugs, passed down the Strait at 7 a.m. Continuous air activity up to noon. Daphne returned from camp about 3 p.m. She had had an interesting time cooking for 90 Guiders. She has been selected for the GIS Guides who are to go out to help in liberated countries. Bombers over at night.

Wednesday 12 April

Heavy bombing across the Strait all afternoon. Alert 10.50 p.m., the first for over 10 days. A few very fast raiders flew towards London. One was picked up by a cone of about 20 searchlights near Ashford, otherwise the searchlights got nowhere near them and our AA seemed to burst a long way behind. Shortly after 11 o'clock, a force of our bombers seemed to return. 'All clear' at 11.40 p.m.

Thursday 13 April

I was woken by thumping sounds, which made the house vibrate in the manner of an earthquake. A warm summer's day. All the troops in this area were charging in every direction all day, and bivouacked around Aldington and Lyminge for the night. The Huns claimed to have bombed Bristol about three weeks ago. According to Flashman, they made a mistake and dropped their loads on Weston-super-Mare, which should have been wiped out, but 50 unexploded bombs were found to be full of sand and one had a Union Jack in it!!

Friday 14 April

The great Lord Lonsdale has died, a fine gentleman. I heard the cuckoo in the morning. I spent the day in Folkestone. I saw a number of 'invasion' barges in Dymchurch bay. Rain at night.

Saturday 15 April

Overcast with some rain. No air activity. General Vatutin [Soviet military commander] has died a comparatively young man. Has he been bumped off?

Tuesday 18 April

I woke at 6 a.m. then dozed until 7 o'clock. A warm sunny afternoon. I hear that there was trouble yesterday in Hythe and Folkestone between our Commandos and Americans. I was told our lads threw the Yanks into the canal. All troops in both towns have been on manoeuvres all week. I hear that they have gone and are being replaced by Canadians. From 10.30 p.m., for half an hour our heavy bombers were passing overhead.

Wednesday 19 April

There was a raid last night from 1.05 a.m. to 1.50 a.m. and we brought down 14 Huns. I did not hear a sound. A sharp white frost in the morning. Air activity all day without a break, and speedboats and firing in the Strait. Alert 10.30 p.m. A Canadian Bofors, just set up in Castle Road, nearly blew our roof off as a plane flew over the house. 'All clear' at 11.30 p.m.

Thursday 20 April

What I thought was a gun last night was a Hun dropping bombs on a shed near a farm at Smeeth and being brought down in the Marsh by one of our fighters. Only a dog and some cats were killed. A fine day, with prolonged air activity. A nucleus of Canadian Army Service Corps arrived in our road. Big guns firing at 10.30 p.m. with a shell warning.

Friday 21 April

The Canadians are beginning to come in. The Navy have taken over the harbour [Folkestone] and the cliffs up to the Leas, and no one is allowed to enter the zone. The battalion of Oxfordshire and Buckinghamshire Lights, the only unit with an operational role in the area, has sent half its men to Italy. Their CO says that within a week the Home Guard will have no operational role except helping the ARP to put out fires. One of our Wellingtons flew back, badly hit, low over Folkestone yesterday evening and crashed near Beachborough; five of the crew were rescued.

Sunday 23 April
We lost 42 bombers last night. Another midsummer's day. I went for a walk and saw a rabbit and a stoat. Planes flew over and back all day without a stop, and in the morning a convoy sailed up the Strait covered by a smokescreen. St George's Day. Daphne paraded with her Folkestone Girl Guides at the Parish Church at 3 o'clock and at 6.30 p.m. paraded with her Hythe Guides at Hythe Parish Church. Buses were so full she had to drive a Lympne Guide home in the car. Our Pioneers have gone, including 'Cuthbert'.

Monday 24 April
All the troops are leaving Hythe and Folkestone areas, and are being replaced by Americans or Canadians. The latter appear to be attached to the USA Army, as they have the star painted on their cars. We have Army Service Corps all round us. The Americans are also taking over Lympne and Hawkinge. An AFS lorry and trailer got out of hand coming down Lucy Lane and crashed into Barnes' house, which is called Rest by the Wayside. There were six men in the truck and one had an ankle broken. The usual non-stop air activity throughout the day. I went on duty at 9.45 p.m.

US army unit in the Kent countryside in 1944 (War and Peace Collection 0318)

Saturday 29 April

Another cold day. The usual air activity. On several occasions the ground shook with explosions. One theory is that the Germans do not intend to hold the coast and are blowing up bridges etc. to obstruct our advance. A young Sapper came to tea, not quite a 'sahib' but a nice lad. A convoy of several kinds of AVs came up the road in the evening and parked in the fields at the back in the Ordnance Depot.

Tuesday 2 May

I went off duty at 6.45 a.m. Sun with a strong cold wind all day. Nancy arrived in the afternoon for a short visit. She is very nervy and strained.

Wednesday 3 May

Wind lessened but still cold. Four destroyers steamed up the Strait in the morning, followed by other vessels putting out a smokescreen. The Japanese say they have captured Imphal [Burma]. No one in England seems to take any interest in the war against Japan.

Thursday 4 May

The destroyers and invasion craft off New Romney were rehearsing a landing in the morning with smokescreens. Rain in the afternoon.

Friday 5 May

Montgomery is in the Chilham area inspecting troops. A strong cold wind with showers, and a rough sea. Alert 10.10 a.m. to 10.20 a.m. (an unusual hour) as I went into Folkestone, where I spent the day.

Monday 8 May

My 'Army birthday'. A barge over 30 feet long was towed by a tug this morning slowly across our seafront towards Romney. I went on duty at 10 p.m. Practically no planes during the night. I went to sleep at 3 a.m.

Tuesday 9 May

I slept until 6.45 a.m. White frost covered everything in the morning. A very large force of planes flew over about 8.30 a.m. At 11 a.m. a very heavy bombardment shook the ground and house; it sounded more like naval guns. The ships off Dungeness were on the move, and appeared to be practising making smokescreens. At 11 p.m. the whole town again shook from a bombardment.

Wednesday 10 May

About 3 a.m. I was woken up by what sounded like the blast of a gun alternately firing salvos and single shots, and the house rocked and windows rattled as planes flew overhead. I was too sleepy to rouse myself. A warmer day. The Russians have captured Sevastopol with two Generals. The cherry crop and early potatoes in Kent have been hit by the frosts. Bombers over at midnight.

Friday 12 May

The hottest day so far. I spent it as usual in Folkestone. All the Home Guard in East Kent, including coastal batteries, are to be called out on a surprise exercise. They are not told what form the exercise is to take, but they are warned that the balloon may go up when they are on it. Very intense and continuous air activity in the early evening. We have started a major attack in Italy.

Monday 15 May

Planes out in the early morning. A cold and windy day. Rain and sleet at 2 p.m. I went on duty at 10.15 p.m. Soldiers stole the post clock from the mantelshelf last Monday before I came on duty; they have also taken the Warden's whistles and were just prevented from stealing the wireless set. They entered by loosening the bars of the lavatory window. No planes up, heavy rain during the night.

Wednesday 17 May

In the morning I picked up a young woman and her baby and mother in the Dymchurch Road and drove them into Folkestone Hospital, getting back at 1 p.m. I do not know what was wrong with the child but 'Grannie' said he would not survive. A few bombers over at night. We had heard none for four nights. My great friend Mollie Turner passed on.

Thursday 18 May

Heavy explosions shook the house early in the morning. A flurry of planes in the afternoon. We have captured Cassino in Italy and the Chinese have taken Myitkyina in Burma. Single heavy bombers flew over at 10.30 p.m.

News emerged that Germany had shot fifty airmen who escaped from Stalag Luft III in March 1944.

Friday 19 May

The shooting of our airmen is a bad affair. Mostly British, but included in the total are Canadian, Australian, New Zealanders, South Africans, Poles, a Czech, a Norwegian, a Greek and a Frenchman. It is rumoured there have been mass escapes by French, Poles and Indian troops. I spent the day in Folkestone. Military Security Police were checking civilians' identity cards in both towns. Alert 6 p.m.; soon after, large forces of our planes passed overhead and the ground shook with explosions. I did not hear the 'all clear'. A very large force of bombers flew over sometime in the night, and explosions shook the house.

Saturday 20 May

Guides and Scouts day for collecting money for the fund to 'Help to Liberate Europe'. We employed two Guides in the morning and two Scouts in the afternoon in the garden, and an extra Guide who phoned up and said she wanted another job. A warm day. Intense air activity. Street fed up over the secret 'call out' which it was said would be sounded within 10 days and has not come off after three weeks!

Sunday 21 May

Cold wind. Very intense air activity from early morning. The warning yesterday was a shell warning. One shell fell between Dover and Canterbury roads, demolishing two houses and killing a few people. Alert 12.30 a.m. to 1 a.m.

Monday 22 May

New ration cards issued. Bombs were dropped last night on a camp near [Great] Chart, killing some men. Spurts of air activity during the day. A cloudy evening. I went on duty at 10.30 p.m. Only an occasional plane. I was asleep by 2 a.m.

Wednesday 24 May

Empire Day. I picked up Mrs Learmonth at Hill House, Sandling Road, at 9.45 a.m. and drove her to Lyminge, where she spent half an hour getting her new ration books. From there to Canterbury up the Elham Valley and on to Herne Bay. Mrs Learmonth misread the instructions of the man she had come to see, and caused us to go four miles out of our way. I had to wait two hours whilst she interviewed two local representatives. Driving down to the seafront, I had a quick lunch at a restaurant. From there we drove to the western residential part of the town, then back the way we had come to the Cottage Hospital. Herne Bay seemed empty of people and troops, and there were no boats offshore. I could find no signs of any bomb damage. We left at 4 p.m., reaching Whitstable a quarter of an hour later. Here Mrs Learmonth was closeted with the local (female) representatives for two hours. I had tea and walked over the town, which was full of narrow streets and wooden huts. A bomb had destroyed the fire station and bus office. There were fishing boats in the harbour and a naval launch outside. The town was having its 'Salute the Soldier' weekend, and had raised £90,000 in three days, which appeared absurd! Proof that the 'weeks' are put-up shows. We drove back the way we came after reaching Canterbury, arriving back at 7 p.m.; a total of 69 miles. The Home Guard were turned out on Monday night. Street did not hear the telephone and had to be roused out of bed by Hickling. Despite that, they claimed to have got 80% at the battery in an hour. 'B' Company in Folkestone took two hours, but theirs is a very complicated arrangement.

Thursday 25 May

Large formations of planes flew over in a continuous stream from 7 a.m. until early afternoon, then a strong wind got up and the sky clouded over. The main front in Italy has linked up with the Anzio bridgehead and the Hitler line has been smashed. The Manipur situation is again obscure; the Japs have started a strong attack to capture Imphal.

Friday 26 May

I drove Daphne to Sandling to catch the 9.15 a.m. train. She is to be an instructor in general duties at a Guiders' camp outside Tunbridge Wells. I then spent the day in Folkestone. Vinson has at last become infuriated with Gribbon. The new Adjutant went around 'B' Company's posts, slated the

NCOs and ordered Archie to come to him – all without Vinson's knowledge. Gribbon (as in my case) swore he had not given the Adjutant orders (a lie) and apologised, but Vinson realises he will do it again. Gribbon has also upset Axford, and his bloated headquarters staff is in such a muddle he has asked Crump to sort them out. When Street was officiating in command of the batteries sometime back, he wrote to a Folkestone man who had left but had said he might return, offering him command of the battalion. They nearly forgot to take the correspondence out of the file before Gribbon returned. The invasion exercise 'boxes' and other notices are up all over Hythe.

Saturday 27 May

My 62nd birthday. I spent it shopping and weeding in the garden. All afternoon there was an almost continuous rumble of bombing across in France.

Sunday 28 May

Whit Sunday. At 3 a.m. a powerful force of bombers flew over us and ten minutes later the house rocked and rattled from explosions on the other side. They were the heaviest we have felt so far. A hot midsummer day, with temperatures reaching 97 degrees.

Monday 29 May

Bank Holiday. An even hotter day. Air activity as intensive as ever. I went on duty at 10.45 p.m. A short 'alert' at 12.15 a.m., but nothing happened in our area. Only a very occasional plane flew overhead. I remained awake all night.

Tuesday 30 May

Dozing at 5 a.m., I was aroused by the singing of many kinds of birds. It was quite light, so I shut up at 6 a.m. Alert 6.30 a.m. to 6.50 a.m.; an unusual hour. Heavy bombing of the French coast at 9 a.m. Daphne returned from camp by the 5 p.m. train. At 3 p.m. I drove to Stanford, picked up a Miss Bull, who is deaf and dumb, drove her to the dentist in Hythe and drove her back again. Daphne had done it before. More house-shaking bombing at midnight.

Wednesday 31 May

In the morning I drove to Cannongate, picked up Coupland, a retired Indian Policeman, with two cartons of emergency rations and drove him to the Mission Hall, Seabrook, where he deposited the packages. In the afternoon, a thunderstorm travelled up the coast of France, crossed via Calais and Dover and went up north. Dover and Canterbury were flooded. We had no rain. Just before midnight, a force of fast bombers followed by a slower force flew over, and ten minutes later we were rocked with explosions. We could hear the houses the whole length of the road rattling.

Friday 2 June

A fine day. I spent it in Folkestone. Air activity recommenced midday. The town was full of Americans and Canadians and the famous 51st Highland Division. Between 6.30 p.m. and 8 p.m. the sky was black with squadrons going and coming. About midnight, a compact force of bombers roared over our heads.

Monday 5 June

We have occupied Rome and crossed the Tiber. The Hun is really on the run now. Rain early in the morning. An unsettled day. Planes out in the morning. A strong force of warships, probably destroyers, in the Strait. I went on duty at 10.45 p.m. A few planes about. After midnight, a truck pulled up in the village green from which descended three soldiers and three drunken ATSs. Each man took a girl home up Rectory Road, whilst a fourth, addressed as 'Sir', stayed in the truck. Our heavy bombers returned at 3.30 a.m. I went to sleep at 4 a.m.

> The allies have entered Rome, and the Germans have retreated beyond the Tiber after being defeated on the outskirts of the city.

The D-Day landings began on 6 June 1944.

Tuesday 6 June

We have landed on the coast of Normandy in great strength, taking the Germans by surprise. We went when the weather was unsettled and landed at low tide, having dropped airborne troops behind the lines the night before. I woke at 6 a.m. Overcast sky, cold with occasional sun. Daphne spent the whole day with her Guides on the golf links and at Scene Farm. At 2 p.m. a convoy of about 12 large ships came down the Strait escorted by destroyers and small craft. They were fired on by the French coast guns; one was hit and had to return to Dover. Everything very quiet, few troops and very few planes up. Another convoy under a smokescreen in evening.

> Nearly 11,000 first-line aircraft are available for the battle, and upwards of 4,000 ships, together with several thousand smaller craft, are engaged in the operations. On Monday night more than 5,000 tons of bombs were dropped on German coastal batteries.

Wednesday 7 June
Unsettled weather. Very little news of the invasion from our side. It's a strange mentality not letting us know what the enemy must be aware of, and leaving us to turn to the enemy's broadcasts. They are afraid of a reverse. Another big convoy passed down the Strait about 11.30 a.m. and at noon there was brisk firing by the cross-Channel guns.

Thursday 8 June
A fine day. The Germans say that they have liquidated our paratroops landing in the Channel Islands and defeated a raid in Boulogne. The Gris Nez guns seem to be out of action. A convoy passed at 11 a.m. and was not fired upon. About 12 men per regiment from the local Division went to a special service at Hythe church in the morning. I had to go to Folkestone on RSPCA work in the afternoon, so went on to Dover. There was considerable further damage from the shelling on Wednesday, when about ten shells fell in the town. A large number of small craft in the harbour. The front is still blocked off with high netting blocking out the view. I got back at 6.30 p.m. Heavy rain in the evening and during the night.

Friday 9 June
A cold day with fog, an overcast sky and some rain. No air activity. I spent

the day in Folkestone. Fishing boats on the French and Belgian coasts have been advised to stay in harbour. Another large convoy passed down the Strait. Alert 9 p.m. On Wednesday Daphne was asked to be ready to go to a castle in Sussex. The next morning, her departure was postponed to today and now they say they will give her 24 hours' notice. It is, I imagine, looking after refugees, and the postponement is due to the bad weather putting off the second landings.

Saturday 10 June

Weather still unsettled. Planes were up most of the day, flying very high. The usual convoy passed at 11.30 a.m. The Canadian RASC in our road are busy waterproofing their lorries; it is a strange process. We are officially told that the Germans on the west coast of Italy are demoralised.

Sunday 11 June

Alert 6.15 a.m., but I did not hear it. A fine morning. Planes in vast numbers were out from dawn onwards. The convoy passed down the Strait, but I did not see it. An overcast afternoon stopped all air activity, and rain fell in the evening. Both on the Normandy and Italian fronts Russians captured by the Germans are fighting against us. A French woman sniper has been shot in Normandy.

Monday 12 June

A fine day. Very large formations flew out and back from dawn onwards. The usual convoy passed down the Strait. We are now told that the Russian prisoners fighting against us are Poles and the French women snipers are German officers' wives. I went on duty at 11 p.m. About 11.30 p.m. a force of about 50 planes flew towards France with lights on. From midnight, big guns fired at intervals. At 1 a.m. another force of planes showing lights passed over. Alert 3.40 a.m., as the moon rose and a gun on Gorsey Bank fired two shots. Alert 5 a.m., then there was a furious fight over Lympne, ending with a plane zooming down out to sea as dawn broke.

The first V-1 flying bombs fell on London on 13 June 1944. Within two months, they had killed 5,000 people and destroyed 35,000 houses.

Tuesday 13 June

I made myself a cup of tea at 6 a.m., having had no sleep all night, and left at 6.30 a.m. About 30 shells and one aerial bomb, it is said, were dropped on Folkestone last night and damaged nearly every part of the town, but luckily only eight people were injured. It is said German warships approached under cover of mist and did the shelling. Rain from midday stopped all air activity.

Wednesday 14 June

A sunny day with sharp showers. Air activity intense at times. In the morning, four transports escorted by a destroyer and a lot of small craft steamed down until the leader was opposite Littlestone, then turned round and went back. In the afternoon about a dozen small ships of the minesweeper type steamed down the Strait. The news from France is not so good: our two thrusts on either side of Caen have been driven back from Troarn and Villers-Bocage; at the latter place our troops fell into an ambush.

Thursday 15 June

A windy day. A new lot of Canadians (The Royal Regiment of Canada) replaced the CASC in our road in the early hours of the morning. At 10.30 p.m. a force of our bombers went over and bombed Boulogne. I saw their golden rain flares going down, and flak and explosions, one turning the sky red. One bomber flew over at a very low altitude. They came back about 11 o'clock covered by fighters. About 11.30 p.m. the night was absolutely quiet, when there was a sound of planes flying in. As they arrived, AA guns opened up, and all the sirens screamed. The planes seemed to come in singly at intervals, one lot over the Imperial [Hotel] and our house, the other over the Marsh towards Lympne. They came in low, and the tracer shells streamed out to sea parallel to the ground. We noticed the planes were lit up, and for a time thought we were firing upon our own planes. One, alight in three places, came straight over us, the flak concentrating on it from all sides making the house rock. When our guns were not firing there was heavy gunfire in the direction of Ashford and Canterbury. The next outburst was over the Marsh; a plane was caught by six searchlights and blew up, lighting up the whole sky.

Friday 16 June

The alert of the night before was still on when I went into Folkestone, gunfire twice breaking out over us. It broke out again as I walked up under Bobby's [Restaurant] glass roof. I decided it was better to get to the other side of the road, and stood under a porch. In the sky I saw a Spitfire diving on and firing at a black object. I stepped back as the enemy plane

The first V-1 rocket was spotted by Observers Wraight and Woodland on the night of 13 June 1944 (Kent Messenger PD1563994)

blew up, and glass all over the town, including a big window of Bobby's, crashed. At 11.15 a.m. the 'all clear' sounded, practically 12 hours after last night's alert. We now know that these are wirelessly propelled pilotless planes [V-1 rockets]. The authorities suppressed the news, only saying there was a raid on the south coast, but Morrison had to get up and explain part of the situation to the House. I saw the shell damage to the houses at the top of Folkestone High Street: three of them were just a heap of rubble and matchwood. At 9.20 p.m. the first pilotless plane came over our house; there was not much firing and no alerts.

> It is now believed that the "pilotless aircraft" which the enemy has been using to attack the south of England is powered by a jet-propulsion unit. To combat the new weapon anti-aircraft guns have been sited so that the maximum fire-power can be directed against the machines before they reach populated areas.

Saturday 17 June

A strong, cold wind. Air activity early in the morning. Alert 2.10 p.m. to 2.30 p.m., and at 3 o'clock there was a burst of fire and an explosion. A

Spitfire had shot down one of the robots [V-1 rockets]. Hythe 'Salute the Soldier' week opened at 4 o'clock with a procession past the Town Hall where stood the smug Captain Few, the Mayor; our 'Yes-Man' MP [Rupert] Brabner; the local Brigadier; and a Captain RN. A good show, with Navy Marines, Ox and Bucks Gunners, Canadians, Wrens, WATS and WAAFs, Home Guard (a few under Street), Guides and Scouts. Also the tank named Hythe. At 4.30 p.m. as the procession was dismissing in Red Lion Square, a robot plane came over without warning and was fired on. A man called Beattie, a sort of inspector of pubs to the [Hythe] Brewery, fell dead in the square. Alert 11.10 p.m. and the robots came over soon after. About four came directly over our house. One, under a concentrated fire, seemed to blow up over the seafront. An explosion to the north shook the house, and a red glow covered the sky over Ashford. About midnight there was a very heavy burst of fire over the house and shrapnel showered down on the roof. The King has visited the troops in France.

Sunday 18 June
Our bombers went over at 7 a.m. Another robot flew over near us at 11.40 a.m. A convoy passed at 6 p.m. I hear that extensive damage has been created in parts of London; Charing Cross has been badly hit. American forces have cut right across the Cherbourg peninsula, bottling up a large number of Germans. A robot sailed over us without warning at 8.15 p.m. Further robots came over at 11 p.m. and the guns left them alone.

Wednesday 21 June
Twice robots came directly over our house, followed by one of our fighters. In the afternoon I saw a yellow plane sailing around, as if it was trying to land at Hawkinge. In the evening, a continuous traffic of masses of our planes flew out and back and concussions of bombs were felt. News of a big naval battle off the Philippines. About 4 a.m., I was woken by the noise of a robot passing over the house and heavy AA gunfire.

Thursday 22 June
The wind gradually died down and the sun warmed up. Last night's alert carried on up to 10 a.m. this morning. Planes, many heavy bombers, were overhead all day. 'Foddy', Miss Villiers' maid, said she saw five robots brought down into the sea early this morning. A convoy of 24 ships passed down the Strait much further out than usual at 5.30 p.m. A robot came

over us at 6.45 p.m., followed at intervals by about six others. At 2 a.m. I was woken by a robot sailing low directly over the house followed by one of our fighters, even lower, firing at it. This occurred three times. I also heard others passing further away. I heard one explode.

Friday 23 June

A convoy passed up the Strait early in the morning. I spent the day in Folkestone. Gribbon has given back all but two of the 18 signallers he took from 'B' Company. Vinson says he feels ashamed to go out with him, he is such a sight. The miscellaneous fleet anchored off Dungeness has increased lately. About 2 a.m., robots came over, but not so many as the previous night. One at least was brought down.

Saturday 24 June

Our wedding anniversary, and a perfect summer's day. We were woken about 6 a.m. by two robots sailing overhead; only a few shots were fired at them. What looked like a small aircraft carrier, heavily escorted, steamed to anchor off Dungeness. Planes flying low made a smokescreen for it. Alert at 2.30 p.m., probably a shell warning as German guns opened as a convoy of miscellaneous ships came down the Strait. When they were opposite Folkestone, they hit and set on fire the biggest ship in the convoy, which was carrying petrol. Its whole stern was alight, flames reaching to the masthead. Two tugs from Dungeness attempted to put out the fire, but the Huns continued shelling it. When I went to look at about 4.30 p.m. there was no sign of the ship. There were no robots over in daylight.

Sunday 25 June

By 7 a.m. the sky was full of our planes. Joan came over from Canterbury to church in afternoon, and came to us for tea and supper. She was full of life. The Germans say that the Americans have captured Cherbourg. The first robots came over at 8.45 p.m. Alert 11.30 p.m., and soon after a robot came straight over our house chased by a Spitfire, which shot it down beyond Saltwood. We had a good view of the machine. Other machines came over the Marsh. In that direction, there was the sound of many planes, and for a time heavy gunfire shook the house. Later a sharp shower seemed to stop all air activity.

Monday 26 June

The 'all clear' woke us at 6 a.m. A dull day. At 9 a.m. Daphne and I went down by bus, picked up the car at the Motor Cab Company and drove to Ashford railway station.

MORE FLYING BOMBS

SOME WITH A LONGER GLIDE

Here, we met another Girl Guide who came in a VCP car from Faversham, which took them both on to a camp outside Worthing, Sussex. Daphne was told that she would return in 10 days, but I believe it is the real commencement of the Guides International Service or will develop into it. I got back by 12 p.m. having driven 26 miles. A robot sailed overhead at 1 p.m. and was heavily fired at, and another at 1.30 p.m. I went on duty at 11 p.m. A robot came overhead at 12 midnight and was fired upon; others passed on either side and ten minutes later another came overhead. The alert sounded at 12.20 a.m. They came thick and fast after that, but the guns seemed to bring them down beyond us to the north-west with the greatest regularity. Later, dud shells whined across the sky. At 1.15 a.m. one from Folkestone direction was exploded in the neighbourhood of Bluehouse, the blast blowing me into the doorway of the post. At 1.45 a.m., another from Folkestone met a similar fate. It was raining by now. At 2.15 a.m. night fighters got one. By this time two policemen, Major Master and [Alex] Schwab turned up; the latter did not stay long. At 2.30 a.m. a robot passed over the centre of the hall and got away up the Ashford Road.

Tuesday 27 June

I got home at 6.30 a.m., having had no sleep all night. A gale of wind all day. Robots came over at 9.15 a.m. and at intervals all day. I slept in the afternoon. News that this time we have really captured Cherbourg. There was an alert at night and robots overhead, but I heard nothing.

Wednesday 28 June

During the morning, there was a succession of concussions across the Strait. The Military Security Police were examining identity cards in Saltwood village. I picked up Mrs Learmonth at 11.30 a.m., and drove her to Sellindge. I drove on to Chilham, where I had beer and cheese at the Woolpack. I met two local inhabitants, one of whom said the old timbered cottages would be all right to live in if they were 're-venerated'. Next, I drove Mrs Learmonth into Faversham. I wandered round; Faversham is a smallish place with no apparent reason for its existence. Mrs Neave had asked us to tea, and I met Neave, one of the brewing family but a farmer. Whilst we were there, a burst of AA gunfire started nearby. It was 6 p.m. before we left. I got back at 8 p.m. having done 68 miles. At Hythe, there had been robots, a convoy and cross-Channel shelling in the afternoon. Mrs Learmonth told me her husband had written that the new defence against the robots was brought into action on Monday night.

Thursday 29 June
I was woken at 6 a.m. by a robot flying low over the house and being heavily fired on. I slept and woke again to further robots. Later they came over in large numbers at regular intervals up to 12.30 p.m. The AA gunfire was intense and a number were brought down, one very near us by a Spitfire. Robots and AA gunfire during the night. Normandy still sticky. Italian advance should be faster. Russians claim a smashing victory.

Friday 30 June
I took the car down to fill up with petrol and to have the battery seen to. Went by bus into Folkestone for the day. A windy day. Robots came over at intervals and were invariably brought down by our fighters. A couple in Dymchurch had a wonderful escape; their house demolished and their dog, hens and goat killed. I heard the troops in this area are leaving tonight. Intense air activity by our planes in evening. I had a perfect view of a robot at 8 p.m.

Saturday 1 July
Rain at night and a thick mist up to 3 p.m. The Huns seized the opportunity to send over large numbers of robots, which the AA guns generally failed to hit. I drove Mrs Crispin [of the WVS] to Philbeach and to the Manor House to collect food and clothing for the new Rest Centre for Saltwood in Bartholomew Close. I was asked in by the Wildins whose daughter, a Wren stationed at Dover, was home after a very narrow escape from a shell. When the robots started again at 6.30 p.m. the sky was clear enough for our fighters to see and shoot them down. Robots continued coming in for an hour or more, with no apparent success for our fighters and AA guns. During a lull I got to sleep. Rain at night.

Sunday 2 July

'All clear' at 6 a.m. A thick mist all morning, but few robots came over. Our fighters and guns were powerless to bring down those that were sent. I have a theory that they cannot be fired from their platforms when it is raining. At 2 p.m., just before the mist cleared, a strong force of our bombers went over and afterwards our fighters filled the sky. There are shell warning notices put up all over Hythe. I had an interesting talk with a middle-aged Canadian whose father was MP for Alberta. His elder brother was killed in the last war and his son has just joined the Canadian Navy. He is a socialist and a great believer in the prophecies in Revelation. Heavy rain at 11 p.m. Alert at 1 a.m. as robots came over; there was heavy firing at times and an extra-shattering explosion about 3 a.m. All clear at 5.30 a.m.

Anti-aircraft batteries on Romney Marsh faced a new enemy – the V-1 rocket (Kent Messenger)

Monday 3 July

Heavy gunfire shook the house early in the morning. Tropical rain all morning stopped the robots coming over. The first came over at 2 p.m., and others followed at long intervals. One was winged by AA fire over the sea, and fell on a thickly populated street in Folkestone. I later heard that it was Bridge Street, and three were killed with 50 injured. The same area had suffered from shellfire a month ago. At 5.15 p.m. I watched a fighter chase a robot over our house and shoot it down. The explosion was very fierce. It came down in Sandling Park, injuring a number of Canadians. At 10.30 p.m. another was brought down almost in the same place. I went on duty at 11 p.m. Alert at 12 midnight, but nothing happened in the sky. From 2 a.m. for two hours there was the sound of vehicles, tanks and lorries moving along the road in the Sandling direction. I went to sleep at 4 a.m.

Wednesday 5 July
Our Canadian Army Service Corps left last night. There are now no troops in or around Hythe except AA batteries. A few robots came over at 12.15 p.m., were chased by our fighters and brought down in a clear sunny sky. They came over in greater numbers at 4.45 p.m. One robot, which passed under a large formation of returning bombers, seemed to get away unnoticed. From 8 p.m. the sky was full of bombers and fighters. A big gun to the north fired at intervals. Alert at midnight. I had a nightmare about three Hun officers covered in medals, which woke me at 2 a.m. A plane flew overhead machine gunning, the most violent explosion so far shook the house and the sirens sounded.

Thursday 6 July
From early dawn to 9 a.m. the sky was full of our planes, and the house occasionally shook with the explosions across the Strait. A robot came over at 9.30 a.m., but no more for the rest of the day. I went into Folkestone for the day and visited the area destroyed by the robot with Inspector Neville, rescuing cats. It is as bad as the damage done by the landmines. One or two planes were droning in the sky at midnight, when the house was shaken like a rat by a terrier for two minutes and the sirens sounded. There was the burr of a robot, a burst of machine gun fire followed by the cutting off of the robot's engine and the explosion. The house shook again several times.

Friday 7 July
All clear at 6 a.m. Misty rain in the morning. The first robot over at 12.15 p.m. They came over occasionally all morning. Daphne came back from her French refugee camp near Worthing at 1.30 p.m. She was driven by a VCP man from those parts, who picked up a Guide at our gates to take to the camp. It was a large camp with soldiers and ATS as well as WVS and

Guiders. There were no refugees. They cooked for about 40 of the staff, had every ration, a NAAFI and ENSA shows.

Saturday 8 July

A warm sunny day. At 3 p.m. the Huns started the cross-Channel shelling, and the shell warning sounded in Hythe for the first time. The convoy which was their object did not come opposite Hythe until 4.30 p.m., when the 'all clear' sounded. Robots came over at 9.30 p.m. when the sky clouded over. Alert 11.10 p.m. Shortly after, a robot flew directly over the house, much lower than any have come before, its whole body lit up by the long red flame from its tail. I heard a few more before I went to sleep.

> Caen has been captured by British and Canadian forces of the Second Army. The Germans fought fiercely before the city was entered, and pockets of resistance remain to be cleared up. (p. 4)

Monday 10 July

A cold overcast windy day with showers. As it cleared at 3 p.m., a number of robots came over in quick succession. Our defences did not seem quite on the spot. More came over at 8 p.m. When one flew over the house, three Spitfires were up. One seemed to signal to the other two to keep off, and chased it but did not catch it up until inland. The next flew over the town. There was a burst of machine gun fire from a plane, which caught fire and burst in the field behind Pennypot Farm. The explosion nearly pushed the side of the house in. The farm was wrecked, also roofs and windows of houses on the Dymchurch Road, including that of our maid, Mrs Dray. Eleven sheep were killed and about six people suffered from shock and glass injuries.

Tuesday 11 July

The 'all clear' at 5.30 a.m. woke me, but I was sound asleep again until 7 a.m. Robots again arrived about 9 a.m. and came over at intervals, sometimes several together. Fortresses flew out and back in the afternoon. I looked up 'Bone' Foster, who has had a breakdown through worry over his wife, who has at last been certified. I slept soundly all night.

Wednesday 12 July

The first robot of the day came over at 7.30 a.m. and was quickly disposed of by a fighter plane, and six others were shot up in quick succession. Two Spitfires racing to destroy one approached too near, and the pilot of one was killed by the blast. More flares were dropped; they came from the robots. They are, I believe, to show the Germans that the robot has successfully crossed the water. It is said that all civilian interns are to be repatriated.

Friday 14 July

A fine day. I went to Folkestone. At 3 p.m. three robots came over, two of which were destroyed. There being no other lady to take over, I have been made Local Volunteer Car Pool Controller, as Mrs Metcalf has gone away with her sick husband. I am now an honorary member of the Women's Voluntary Service.

The robots (V-1 rockets) shot down by coastal guns and Spitfires

Sunday 16 July

Robots came over at regular intervals all morning from 10 a.m. I saw one shot down over Postling, which broke windows of the church. At 10.30 a.m. there was what appeared to be a fight high up in the sky to the north-west. Tiny planes lit up by the sun flew around making white feathered rings. When they had disappeared, lines of light rippled across the sky from west to east. At noon, three planes were in the sky when a robot came over. They started for it but another cut in from a flank and shot it down with one burst. None came over in the afternoon. At 9 p.m. a thick sea fog covered the land. I slept soundly at night and heard nothing of the robots and barrage.

Tuesday 18 July

I went to sleep in my chair at 4 a.m. and was woken at 5.30 a.m. by the telephone. It was Lyminge control giving the 'all clear'. I slept again until 7 a.m. A warm summer's day. A very large convoy went up the Channel at 10 a.m. At 2 p.m. I called for Mrs Learmonth and drove her to Dover. As we went up Dover Hill, another convoy was passing up the Channel. Mrs Learmonth spent an hour with the WVS, whilst I walked about the town. There is damage everywhere, but no robots come over them. From there, I drove up to Hougham through pretty country. Mrs Learmonth visited a woman there, then we went on through Capel Street to the Main Road. As we went down the hill, a third convoy was sailing down the Strait. In Folkestone, Mrs Learmonth stopped at the WVS, found a case there, and stayed an hour. She did not think to let me know so that I could go and have tea. I did not get home until 6.30 p.m.

Wednesday 19 July

Robots came over in numbers in the morning. The AA fire was colossal, but few seemed to be brought down by the guns. Everyone exclaims at the futility and waste. Our own shells, however, set the Hythe gasometer alight, and all windows of houses on the golf links have been broken by concussions from the gunfire. Robots came over all day. At 4 p.m. Brigadier and Mrs Pease-Watkins looked over the house; at least, she did. He and I talked about the Army and India. He is a Gunner. The news from Italy is good. Alert at 11.30 p.m. as robots came over, two of which were shot down. More gunfire woke us during the night.

Claus von Stauffenberg, a German army officer, attempted to assassinate Hitler on 20 July 1944.

Thursday 20 July

Great excitement over the attempt to blow up Hitler. Most people think the war will be over in a week now. At 7 a.m. our guns seemed more successful; several robots were hit over the land and others fell into the sea. In the late afternoon and evening our planes were flying over, high up. The last of the troops in our road and the ordnance dump in Seaton Avenue left this afternoon.

Sunday 23 July
Alert 2 a.m. I was woken then and again at 5 a.m. by very heavy AA gunfire. The first robot to come over was shot down at once, but it seemed a long time between its engine cutting out and the explosion, which lit up the room. A few came over at 10 a.m. as the sky cleared. They again came over at 2.15 p.m. The guns hit the first, which Phyllis watched fly westward lurching like a dolphin. It exploded on Lympne Aerodrome, killing some airmen and wounding the Girl Guide sister of our late maid. Shell warning at 3.15 p.m. as a convoy passed down the Strait. Nothing seemed to happen; even the robots stopped coming over. 'All clear' 4.30 p.m.

Tuesday 25 July
I woke at 5.15 a.m. in time for the 'all clear' at 5.45 a.m. Fine weather again. Large formations of our planes up all day. Heavy bombing of the French coast in the evening shook the house. No robots all day, but they came at midnight. The flak was again terrific, but they seemed to bring them down with some regularity. That skunk Stalin has set up a Communist Polish Committee [Polish Committee of National Liberation], and is branching out over northern Europe without any thought of us or the Americans. Our people say nothing.

Wednesday 26 July
I was woken at 4 a.m. by terrific AA gunfire. One robot exploded over the sea opposite our windows, and the house shook like a jelly. A hot day. One of last night's robots fell and wrecked the Home Farm, Sandling, breaking windows over a wide area and made a large crater. Robots came over at 2.10 p.m. I saw two shot into the sea, and they sent up huge columns of water. Alert at midnight. The first robot heading for us was exploded over the sea, the blast blowing in our curtains. It was perhaps lucky our windows were open.

Thursday 27 July

Rain at night, and an overcast windy day. A large cargo boat, evidently hit during the shelling yesterday evening, was beached off Sandgate with two tugs in attendance. [Brigadier] Mortimer agrees with me that Montgomery is a conceited wind-bag. He is very angry at his slur on Auchinleck, whom Mortimer knows. Robots over from 3.15 p.m. to 5.15 p.m. They flew above the rain clouds, and the guns were not very successful.

Friday 28 July

I spent the day in Folkestone. A robot had been shot down in the night and fallen on Feltonfleet School [Folkestone], demolishing the building and causing extensive damage to houses as far as the Central Station. No. 18 Kingsnorth Gardens has had its front windows blown in. The boat beached off Sandgate is said to have been full of engineers; about 20 were killed, and the same number injured are in Folkestone Hospital. Robots came over at 1 a.m.; one of them was exploded in the air above Hythe and caused damage to roofs and windows. Ludlow, the baker, had his windows destroyed for the third time. A Naval man is supposed to have said our barrage is worse than anything they had on D-Day off Normandy. Hythe people are agitating about it. After midnight and at 12.30 a.m. robots came over in three waves.

> ### GERMANS ADMIT ROMMEL INJURED
>
> The German News Agency announced last night: " Field-Marshal Rommel met with a car accident as the result of an air raid in France on July 17. He suffered injuries and concussion His condition is satisfactory and his life is not in danger."—*Reuter*.

Sunday 30 July

Rain at night, fine in the afternoon. A few robots came over at 1.30 p.m. In the afternoon Daphne and I walked to the Sandling Road across fields to Garden House and down to Sandling Junction, where roofs were damaged. We went past the Newingtons' house (an awful mess) to the Home Farm, which was an absolute wreck, the fine old house and all the outhouses blown to bits. The robot fell on the edge of the front garden and made a big crater. A few robots over at 6 p.m. Alert 11.45 p.m. There was distant gunfire over the Marsh, then all was quiet. Rumours say that

Rommel was severely wounded in a bomb attack on his headquarters and is probably dead.

Monday 31 July

A muggy day. I spent the morning in Folkestone working for the RSPCA flag day. Six destroyers steamed down the Strait. Mackerel shoals off Sandgate. Mist in the morning, sun in the afternoon. No robots. I went on duty at 10.30 p.m. A quiet night. I went to sleep at 2 a.m.

The Warsaw uprising began 1 August 1944.

Wednesday 2 August

Robots over at 8.15 a.m. The first was shot down into the sea. A batch came over at 12.45 p.m. in ideal weather for them (low clouds). One flew low well below the clouds, but the guns were caught napping. Hickling told me Gribbon has at last resigned. Daphne had about 20 Cheriton Girl Guides over for tea and games during the afternoon. Turkey has broken off diplomatic relations with Germany. The Americans, at least in Normandy, are going forward. Churchill says London will next be devastated by rocket bombs. Alert 11.15 p.m. with robots coming in, in a sea fog. Then there was a lull and the 'all clear' sounded, but at midnight they came over again, half a dozen at a time and continued to do so at intervals throughout the night. Few were brought down by the guns. I do not know when I got to sleep.

Friday 4 August

A rumour says that the Germans are evacuating the Channel Islands. Perhaps that is the best way to get them back, but rather humiliating. The American advance is good but, as usual with them, it is going the wrong way. A hot day. I spent it in Folkestone on business connected to the RSPCA flag day, and repairs to 18 Kingsnorth Gardens. I also looked up Vinson, who said Gribbon got the push at General Schreiber's (GOC South-Eastern Command) inspection when he could not remember the names of his officers or see the General when he arrived. Major FW Bearne, Commander of Folkestone Company, is taking over, a retired regular officer. Vinson said he suggested me but, of course, Street would not agree. At 8.30 p.m. I went to the lookout and watched the guns shooting down robots. It was a thrilling experience.

293

Sunday 6 August

A midsummer's day. I went for a walk. The Stone Farm robot burst in the air and only blew out window frames and deroofed some tiles. Robots over at 1.30 p.m. I saw two explode over the sea. A few more came over at 5 p.m. Alert 11.15 p.m. Nothing happened here and the 'all clear' sounded at midnight.

Monday 7 August

We were woken at 6 a.m. by the AA barrage. Robots came over thick and fast up to 8 a.m., and were successfully dealt with by the guns. August Bank Holiday. The town was deserted, no visitors. I went for a walk in the morning over the golf links, and saw some 'doodles' disposed of (they came over at 10.45 a.m.) and 100 Fortresses with an equally large escort go over the Strait. We had tea and spent the afternoon in the garden. I went on duty at 10.15 p.m. Alert at 11.10 p.m. The first robots over were all destroyed, and no more came over.

Thursday 10 August

Woken at 4 a.m. by sirens, robots and gunfire. Very few robots came over, but the guns were not very successful with those that did. Mrs Pease-Watkins with her daughter and schoolboy son arrived in the morning to have another look at the house. She is almost decided to buy it. At 5.30 p.m. the guns crashed out without warning; a fairly strong west wind perhaps blew away the sound of robots. The first over was brought down beyond Lympne and sent up a column of black smoke. The next, we saw explode over Hythe Station; the greater portion of it fell on Tudor House in Cannongate, killing Mrs Galway near her shelter and demolishing half the house. All the houses around were severely damaged, and windows along Sandgate Road smashed. It is said [Major] Butler's and Hodson's houses will have to be pulled down. We saw four other robots shot into the sea. At 9 p.m. another batch came over. A quiet night.

Saturday 12 August

Robots came over at 2.15 a.m. The AA barrage was fiercer than ever, but was decidedly futile as there was no mist inland. One robot, hit in the rudder, circled twice round the town slowly. It was caught in the beams of four searchlights and, when over the sea, I saw two shells shoot up one of the beams and it exploded. As it descended, it appeared to be coming straight for us. A lull at 2.45 a.m. but they came over again at 11 o'clock. I spent the afternoon at Grimston Gardens, Folkestone, with Miss Curzon-Smith arranging for her to run the flag day. A robot had fallen on a house, two doors from my uncle's old house in Grimston Gardens, destroying it. Daphne took her Sea Rangers with the Scouts to bathe in Folkestone Swimming Pool.

Tuesday 15 August

The Times says the RAF three times bombed the Canadians near Falaise [Normandy] by mistake, the third time for an hour. 'All clear' at 6.30 a.m. and I left the post soon after. Robots at 9 a.m., the first two being quickly destroyed. They came over again at 2 p.m. Whilst I was at the Hayfield lookout,

V-1 bomb damage on Twiss Road, Hythe, where five civilians were killed

three came over together. The first got through, the second – which was travelling on the West Hythe line – seemed to swerve and come towards me. I got behind the hut expecting shrapnel might fall on me, and was shaken by the explosion. Going forward, I saw a column of smoke and dust rising from the end of Twiss Road [Hythe]. It fell on the corner house of Earlsfield Road, killing the Jacks in it and two couples in the houses on either side. A quiet night.

Wednesday 16 August

Robots came over in large numbers between 5 a.m. and 7 a.m. There was a fog, and the Gunners put up an unarmed barrage, which is not very effective. Robots over again at 8 o'clock, but the fog was clearing and all were shot down. I was told the AA firing over the town has been stopped, and a petition is being got up requesting all the guns to be removed. At 4.30 p.m. at least six robots came over in our neighbourhood, and all got through. At 5.15 p.m. the guns had better success. I saw one getting away over Bluehouse, a Spitfire fly through our flak and the 'doodle' blow up. I believe the plane got it. There was a lull at 7.15 p.m., then more came over from 7.45 p.m. to 8 p.m. A quiet night.

Saturday 19 August
The sirens sounded and the robots came over at 3.15 a.m. All were accounted for. They came over again at 6 a.m. in a dull sky, but they were brought down. 'All clear' at 7 a.m. I went into Folkestone for my RSPCA flag day at 10.30 a.m. We had very few collectors, but those we had did very well. An old lady, Mrs Ward, filled six boxes. Miss Curzon-Smith thinks only of the kudos to her in getting in a large total. She is very tactless, refusing to send a collector to the patch she asked for. She is very like Gribbon in features and character, and the ladies helping us said nobody likes her. At 2 p.m. robots came over, and a number of people came into the Town Hall to shelter. There was a loud explosion, which nearly drove in our windows and shattered the windows of Boots and other shops. A robot was brought down into the water of the harbour. A large party of 100 Wrens and Sailors bathing nearby were unhurt. Some of our collectors gave up and went home. Our last two collectors left at 6 p.m. Old Miss Ward was the last to give up collecting. The Inspector brought in the Sandgate and Cheriton boxes, and we got the money to the bank at 7 p.m. We had collected about £65, very good under the circumstances. The Inspector drove me home.

Monday 21 August
An overcast sky all day with rain at intervals. Flying bombs came over at 11 a.m. I spent from 12 noon to 4 p.m. at the Folkestone Clinic with Miss Curzon-Smith and the Inspector cleaning and counting the rest of the boxes. We got another £16. About a dozen flying bombs were sent over between 7.45 p.m. and 8.15 p.m.; all were destroyed. I went on duty at 9.45 p.m. A short alert at 10 p.m.; nothing happened. I talked to a Yankee airman who was watching the dancing. He had flown over all the beachheads from Sicily to Normandy, and had lost two brothers, with another a prisoner of war. He said the first American contingents had

given his countrymen a bad name, especially in Northern Ireland, where it was dangerous now for an American to walk through some villages alone. The driver of his 'Jeep' was keen on girls and dancing, so the airman allowed him to drive him over each evening. Last night, the driver forgot about him and the airman had to walk back to Dover.

Tuesday 22 August
I was woken by AA gunfire at 3.30 a.m. The first flying bomb to come overhead arrived at 4.15 a.m. and got through, as did several others. I got to sleep again at 4.30 a.m. All clear at 6.30 a.m. More flying bombs came over at 7.30 a.m. but were all destroyed well out to sea. Clear skies for rest of the day, with no flying bombs for the rest of day and night.

Paris was liberated on 25 August 1944.

Thursday 24 August
Rain at night. Flying bombs came over at 6 a.m. All were brought down. At noon a Major and Mrs Howell, 18th Bengal Lancers, looked over the house. We got the idea that they were not impressed. Tropical rain and thunder in the afternoon. A hole in the roof made by a bit of AA shell let water into my study. A few flying bombs were sent over at long intervals up to 7.30 p.m., the last when it was raining, which upset my theory that they cannot fire them when it is raining. More came over between 8 p.m. and 9 p.m. At 9.30 p.m., the BBC gave us a medley of noises to represent the freeing of Paris, but we learnt on the news that the Germans are fighting and refusing to quit, and the Parisian leader has asked us for help. A quiet night.

Sunday 27 August
Flying bombs came over at 6.30 a.m. when there was fog over the sea. All were destroyed. At 1.30 p.m. there was a fierce burst of gunfire, and the sky was full of rushing Spitfires. Joan came from Canterbury to church in Folkestone, and on to us for tea and supper. There was a Marine eight-gun battery of three-inch guns parked in the High Street at 8.30 p.m. The BBC's recording of the firing in Paris and attempt to kill de Gaulle was most dramatic. No flying bombs after 7 p.m., and an undisturbed night. People are already beginning to say it is the end of them.

Monday 28 August

A strong westerly wind, with some rain in the morning. At 2 p.m. the first of the flying bombs passed over Hythe and Palmarsh, and got through the barrage. The ATS, who are now in our road, were very excited over it. One of them came to us to press his uniform. They are the headquarters of an AA Brigade from Northern Ireland, where they have been living on the fat of the land, unaware there is a war on. I went on duty at 9.30 p.m.

Tuesday 29 August

A quiet night, as far as I know. The new lot of Gunners have already looted Mrs Atkinson's garden. Their Sergeant Major, who had a glass full of flowers from the garden on his table, practically owned the NCOs' mess did it. At 12 noon, a furious barrage was put up Dymchurch way. Flying bombs came our way all day. At 6.30 p.m. one was hit and on fire, coming down in flames; suddenly its engine restarted, it turned eastwards and flew towards Folkestone. I heard that it turned again and was shot down off Dover. Shell warning at 7 p.m. Flying bombs at 10.15 p.m. Shell 'all clear' at 10.45 p.m. At 11.15 p.m. there was a violent explosion, its echo rumbling on for some time.

Wednesday 30 August

The explosion was probably an ammunition dump in France, though some say it was one of our ships. A convoy was passing during the warning, and Dover and Deal were badly damaged. What a muddle they make over Army Commands! However, it gives Churchill the opportunity to promote Montgomery over Brooke and Alexander. Flying bombs came over at 6 a.m. and again at 7.30 a.m., some getting through. At 11 o'clock rain put a stop to them. At noon, the sun came out and a robot flew over Hythe and Saltwood and got away. No more came over after that, and we had a quiet night.

Thursday 31 August

At 6 a.m. a flying bomb crashed on Lyminge destroying the chapel and Rest Centre. Daphne spent the day there helping Miss Lewis to rescue WVS clothing and her own Guide stores.

Friday 1 September

Daphne's birthday. Our road is now full of Gunners without guns and

ATS. Yesterday, two Military Policemen took down all the [warning] signs in Hythe. I went into Folkestone for the day. Dover, Deal and Ramsgate were heavily shelled last night, and a few fell in Folkestone. There were casualties in Dover.

Saturday 2 September

Dover was again shelled last night and, besides other damage, Chitty's Mill was set on fire. Tropical showers during the day, sometimes with hail thrown in. I believe I heard our guns in France at noon. I got an urgent call from Barnes, the Food Officer for Hythe, asking me to drive Mr G Myer, Assistant Divisional Salvage Officer, to Dover. He had run into a lorry at Newingreen and smashed his car. He was giving a lift to a party of WAAFs. I picked him and Barnes up at the Food Office at 12.30 p.m., Phyllis having given me a scrambled lunch. I dropped Barnes off at Wood Avenue and drove through the Alkham Valley. Every house and shed in the valley has been destroyed or damaged. When we got to Chitty's Mill in the middle of the town [Dover], we found it still burning. We found Chitty's nephew Saunders, a nice fellow who had been up two nights and a day. Myer kept him up to 2.30 p.m. We met Chitty, a little man with a white goatee beard. I gathered much information about wheat and flour. After tea in the town, as there were no suitable trains, Myer asked me to drive him to Ashford. I was down to my last gallon and had no coupons, so I drove via Hythe. I found Swain's shut, but Dunkin of the Hythe Motor Works lent me a gallon. On my way back, I gave a lift from Newingreen to three soldiers. I got back at 6.30 p.m. No flying bombs all day or night. The crews are scuttling for home.

> The number of casualties in the British Empire for the first five years of the war, covering the armed forces, merchant seamen, and civilians, was 1,091,628.

Sunday 3 September

Day of Prayer on the fifth anniversary of the outbreak of war. I went for a walk and communed alone. Shell warning 1 p.m. to 2.15 p.m. Alert again at 2.30 p.m. and 'all clear' at 5.30 p.m. There was an occasional shot from guns near us, but we heard nothing of the shelling. No flying bombs. We have definitely seen the last of them.

Wednesday 6 September

A fine crisp morning. Calais was blazing in the morning as it blazed in 1940. Boulogne was hidden in the rain clouds. Shell warning at 2.30 p.m. A convoy sailed down the Strait and the sea was full of destroyers and MTBs. All clear 3.40 p.m. Phyllis and I went to the cinema. Daphne was in Lyminge and Folkestone on Girl Guide work. The film of the sniping in Paris was very thrilling, and *Captains Courageous* was very good and kept to the book. Shell warning at 8.40 p.m. I did not hear the 'all clear'.

Thursday 7 September

Pelting rain from early morning to 5 p.m. In the afternoon we went to the Central [Cinema] in Folkestone to see *Gone with the Wind*. A rather long film, but well worth seeing. Vivien Leigh, a marvellous actress, made Scarlett O'Hara very real. Leslie Howard (the late) also good. I did not like the face or the acting of Clark Gable as 'Rhett'. In the evening, a convoy passed down the Strait without a smokescreen. The Home Guard is on the eve of disbandment. Only voluntary parades once a fortnight.

The first V-2 rocket fell on London on 8 September 1944.

Friday 8 September

My Mother's birthday. A fine day with a nip in the air. I spent the day in Folkestone. Talked religion and politics with Vinson. He told me a boatload of Germans escaping from Calais gave themselves up in Dover. Sharp showers in the late afternoon.

Saturday 9 September

A cold, sunny day. Gunfire followed by a shell warning at 11.30 a.m. Phyllis and I spent the afternoon at Brabourne Lees picking blackberries. The first bus sailed past us full up, and we had to wait half an hour. Coming back we were luckier. About six rounds of gunfire, followed by a shell warning, at 11.30 p.m.

The American 1st Army crossed the German border on 11 September 1944.

Monday 11 September

Three shells fell in Folkestone yesterday, and a dozen or more in Dover. Phyllis went in the afternoon to Brabourne to get plums. Shell warning at

3.30 p.m. Guns fired a salvo just before and again after the alert, and black smoke appeared to come from Dover. 'All clear' 4.40 p.m. I went on duty at 9.30 p.m., after blackout time. All night, heavy bombers came slowly home one by one, picked up and followed by cones of searchlights. I wondered how many had failed to return. I settled down to sleep at 1.15 a.m.

Tuesday 12 September
I woke at 5 a.m., then slept until 6.50 a.m. From noon there was a continuous rumble and rattle of guns of every description from Calais to Boulogne. Nancy arrived in the afternoon for a short visit. Shell warning at 6 p.m. Bursts of shells could be heard at intervals, and some heavy guns of ours in the direction of Gorsey Bank seemed to reply. Every now and then a rumbling explosion shook the house. Three shells fell on Folkestone causing damage and a few casualties, and Dover had over a dozen. We have taken Le Havre losing only 50 killed.

Thursday 14 September
A hot day with a sea haze. More fighting across the Strait. Phyllis, Nancy and Daphne spent the afternoon at Bog Farm in Brabourne, bringing back blackberries and mushrooms. At 4 p.m. Barnes, our Food Officer, rang me up and I drove out to Lyminge, picked him and another Food Officer up and brought them back to Hythe. At 8.45 p.m. a shell burst close to Smith's house in Hillside Street, severely damaging it and the houses opposite, and breaking windows and tiles in North Road. We had a few tiles off and Oaklands next door lost some windows. This was the first shell to fall in Hythe. All quiet by 10.30 p.m., but the 'all clear' didn't sound until the early hours.

Friday 15 September
Shell warning at 11.15 a.m. One shell fell on a large house in Station Road, Hythe, killing an old woman who had lived there alone throughout the war. PC Dickinson killed in Blackbull Road, Folkestone. I met two men who had lost their wives in Stuart Road, Folkestone, on Thursday. The women had gone to the shelter; the men had stayed in the house. As the library closed when the warning sounded, I went and had a talk with Vinson. I gave Nancy a lunch at Vinson's restaurant then sat on the Leas for an hour.

Monday 18 September

Rain in the morning, and heavy clouds. A fierce battle raged all morning, mostly near Calais. Despite low visibility, some planes managed to fly over. For a short time in the afternoon the battle again burst out. I went on duty at 9.30 p.m., having told Major Master I did not see the necessity of standing to for 12 hours. The men attending the dance were mostly Americans. Guns rumbled at regular intervals during the night. I settled down at 1.45 a.m.

Tuesday 19 September

I woke at 5 a.m. and again at 6 a.m. Heavy fighting for two hours in France, and a column of black smoke rose from Boulogne. Heard from Maurice that he has got home on the repatriation ship SS *Drottningholm*. Shell warning at 11.15 a.m. In the afternoon in heavy rain the fighting increased in intensity. Despite low cloud, our fighters went over. Sound of shell bursts at regular intervals. 'All clear' 4.30 p.m. Rain all evening.

Wednesday 20 September

We were woken by the noise of armour grinding along the High Street. It was American tanks and continued for an hour. When they left, the Americans in the Marsh piled up all the furniture they couldn't take with them and made a huge bonfire of it. They also distributed hams and tinned food to the cottagers. At 9.30 a.m., I picked up Captain Croft-Cohen, Commissioner of the Board of Control, and drove him to Lydd where he visited an old lady who literally wraps herself up in *The Times*. In the paper shortage, she says she will wear nothing!

Monday 25 September

At 8.30 a.m. the sky was full of four-engined bombers. They continued passing over for half an hour, flying in a north-eastern direction. A smaller force went over at 10.30 a.m. At 11.15 a.m. three shells exploded on Folkestone, and the shell warning sounded. Explosions at intervals. 'All clear' at 3.15 p.m. One hit one of the only habited houses on the Leas, another Harvey Grammar School, which is occupied by a council office. No one badly hurt. Planes flew over at 5 p.m., and one heard the bomb explosions. All clear 6.30 p.m. As I went on duty at 9.30 p.m., the sky beyond the golf links was lit up at regular intervals by a flash like the burst

of a gigantic shell. There were few men at the dance, and no Americans.
Rain commenced at 10 p.m., and continued through the night. I settled
down at 2 a.m.

Tuesday 26 September
I woke at 6 a.m. Shell warning 9.45 a.m. Shells on Dover. Alert 12.30 p.m.
More shelling mostly Dover way, but our big guns seemed to reply.
I saw a big flash in the neighbourhood of Gris Nez. At 3.30 p.m. a
convoy of 15 ships passed down the Strait, one of which looked like a P&O
liner.

Wednesday 27 September
A very cold day, but sunny. We now know that the Arnhem airborne
landing had failed, but they claimed they have got out a third of the men.
No news about Calais, but no shell warning all day. It looks as if the shell
at 7.15 p.m. yesterday was the last of the cross-Channel guns.

Thursday 28 September
A fine, cold day. A large force of bombers flew over at 9 a.m. At
midday Daphne and I drove down to the White Hart [Inn], collected a
basket and three sacks full of jam jars and took them to Philbeach
for the WVS. In the afternoon, there were several distant and one
heavy explosion on the French coast, the latter shaking our windows.
Lyminge Control has informed us that Wardens would discontinue night
duties.

Friday 29 September
Unsettled, with some rain. I spent the day in Folkestone. Everyone there
was talking of the dangerous situations they had been in during the war. It
is said that the last German cross-Channel gun has been captured, and that
this will soon be announced officially. Armistice at Calais to evacuate the
civilian population.

Saturday 30 September
A sunny day, warm at midday. A squadron of Hurricanes in the air in the
morning. Daphne left at 9 a.m. for a weekend camp for Camp Advisers at
Sevenoaks. The AA Gunners in Castle Road left with all their belongings.
Boom of guns in the afternoon. Mrs Parry and Mrs Walsh, the wife of a

Gunner, came to tea and to look over the house. I have an idea they had meant to look at 'Bone' Foster's house. Mrs Walsh has a daughter married to an Indian Army Officer with two girls of 12 and 13 who are out in India and have never been to school. Calais surrendered to Canadian troops and the last of the German guns captured.

Sunday 1 October
Harvest Thanksgiving at Saltwood [Parish Church]. In the afternoon I looked up 'Bone' Foster, who had been in bed for a week with some form of shell shock and was still very groggy. He told me that his pension had been restored to nearly the rate before the cut. Calais has surrendered with a garrison of 7,000 troops.

Monday 2 October
Sunny but cold. What appeared to be troop carriers flew in from France. My first night off Warden duty.

Tuesday 3 October
Phyllis went for the day to Tenterden by bus. A flight of planes went over making a new sound and going fast – I wondered if they were jet-propelled. Six warships steamed up the Strait. We were rung up by Child's [estate agent] at noon suggesting they should send someone up to view the house. Daphne put them off till 3 p.m. A Mr and Mrs Langdon, GIP [Great Indian Peninsular] Railway. He wanted to be near the golf links. Warsaw has surrendered; Churchill with his tongue in his cheek praised their resistance. A filthy business. All Churchill's bad qualities are coming out in prosperity as they have done before.

Wednesday 4 October
A cold drizzle all morning. At 11.30 a.m. I saw HM the King [George VI] drive through Hythe to Lympne Aerodrome to fly to France. Heavy rain in the afternoon.

Thursday 5 October
Daphne left after lunch for London to attend a course of lectures at Guide Headquarters. At 7 p.m. a convoy of eight or ten large lorries drew up in our road for the men to have a meal at the cookhouse next door to us in Oakville. At 8 p.m. there was the rumble of heavy

explosions, obviously from Dunkirk. The Dutch say large areas of Holland have been inundated with seawater, with vast damage and loss of life. We blame the Germans, but we ourselves have bombed the dykes to let in the sea and did not give the Dutch sufficient warning to escape.

Friday 6 October
A north-easterly gale all day. I caught an early Maidstone bus which raced along and got me into Folkestone at 10 a.m. The Inspector drove me down to his house where I presented a cheque for £5 from RSPCA Headquarters to Mrs Neville. At midday I had an interesting talk to Vinson and Sergeant Mills, who was my Signalling Sergeant and is now a subaltern, about corruption in repairing bomb damage and in borough politics in general. The gale raged all night.

Saturday 7 October
A foggy November morning. A Mrs MacVittie turned up, without us being informed, to look over the house in the morning. A fine spring afternoon. Our AA Brigade Headquarters packed up and left at 4 p.m., leaving behind a small rear party.

Sunday 8 October
The AA Brigade rear party left with much noise at 5 a.m., but a plump Subaltern and a few men still remained. At 10 p.m. I drove to Sandling Junction to meet Daphne. On the way I met a young girl not more than 15 walking to the station in the pitch dark – very dangerous. The train was half an hour late and was very full, but Daphne had managed to get a seat.

Monday 9 October
An unsettled day. Noise of big guns at intervals all day. I met young 'Bone' Foster at the barbers. Recently, when in charge of a live bomb-throwing parade, one of his men dropped his grenade, Foster got the man out of the way before shifting himself and was hit in the arm and leg.

Thursday 12 October
The gale continued but with some sun. The boom of big guns (or explosions) at intervals all day. Colonel Lloyd turned up in the morning,

and insisted on seeing the house. He liked it and sent his wife over in the afternoon, but she said it was too big for an elderly couple. Torrential rain at night.

Friday 13 October
It was a Friday and a 13th that I left England in October 1901. I spent the day in Folkestone. I went without a mackintosh, but managed to dodge the showers. Phyllis also went in for the day, and we met for lunch at Vinson's. Troops of sorts arrived in our road in the evening.

Sunday 15 October
A damp day, with almost continuous drizzle. At 6 o'clock four large lorries arrived and disgorged about 100 Gunners in our road. At 9.45 a.m. more men arrived. At 10.30 p.m. we had an unexpected alert. It stopped the Gunners, who were unloading lorries with much noise and many lights up. Not a gun fired, nor a searchlight showed up. It was a robot of sorts, which is said to have passed over Ashford and Hastings and fallen into the sea. There was an explosion as if a robot had blown up, and the 'all clear' sounded at 11 p.m. Rommel is said to have now died of his accident in Normandy.

Monday 16 October
I looked up 'Bone' Foster in the afternoon. He is still not well. He has sold his house to a leading civil servant in the War Office.

Wednesday 18 October
At 11 a.m. I picked up Stainer, the Town Clerk, and the Town Sergeant at the council offices and the Mayor, Captain Few, at his house in Seabrook and drove them up the Alkham Valley to Kearsney Station, where ARP personnel were lining the road to Dover. Soon after our arrival, a special

ROYAL VISIT TO KENT

The King and Queen yesterday visited Dover and Folkestone, the first time they had been to " Hell Fire " Corner since the German cross-Channel guns had begun to shell it.

train came in and the King and Queen got out and had the Mayors of Hythe and Deal etc. presented to them. They stayed some time on the platform talking. The King and Queen came and stood at the station entrance, so I had a good view. She looked very pretty, and he was in his Naval uniform. They drove off to lunch and to be shown around Dover. They later went on to Folkestone. We came back home. Few and Stainer were terribly pleased with themselves. When I got home I found a front tyre punctured. I heard that Dover Harbour is soon to be opened for Naval and Army traffic.

King George VI and Queen Elizabeth being welcomed at the Folkestone cricket ground to inspect the troops (War and Peace Collection 0477)

Friday 20 October

The Gunners in our road smashed our fence after dark. They go out somewhere in lorries every day with picks and shovels.

Saturday 21 October

Trafalgar Day. On VCP work, I turned up at 60 Brockhill Road at 10 a.m. to convey a retired clergyman of 80, the Revd Mr Edminson, to Oxford. He was suffering from hereditary melancholia. A place had been found for him in Warneford Hospital near his niece, and they could get no car to take him there. He was accompanied by his housekeeper, a Mrs Nicholls. Daphne had a Guide Commissioners' Conference in Maidstone to attend and came too. I reached Maidstone at 11 o'clock and Daphne dropped out. Mr Edminson had one slight breakdown. At 12.45 p.m. we saw a nice-looking hotel and stopped for lunch. The hotel was run by a Frenchman. The old man ate a hearty lunch and drank a neat whisky. We got to Bagshot about 4 o'clock and stopped for tea at Queen Anne's house, where Edminson again ate well. About eight miles from Oxford, Edminson wanted his hot milk. Because of this, we got to Oxford after dark. We reached the hospital, where Mrs Rees the padre's niece had been waiting all afternoon, as 7 o'clock struck. Edminson brightened up when we neared Oxford, naming the suburbs and buildings we passed. After settling the old man, Mrs Rees got in the car and guided me to her house. The Reeses are Quakers. He was in business in Hong Kong, from which they got away just before the Jap invasion. We were given supper by Mrs Rees, who put up Mrs Nicholls, and who came with me in the car further up the Banbury Road to a little road of small houses, where she handed me over to an ugly little Italian named D'Alisandro and his young wife, a Brighton girl. They gave me a cigarette and I went to bed. The trip was 170 miles.

Tuesday 24 October
Another cold wet day. The Army Service Corps servicing the Gunners in our road smashed our fence. Nearly every unit billeted here has done it! The Gunners have started squad drill and are being issued with packs etc.

Friday 27 October
Pelting cold rain all morning, but a fine afternoon. I drove Phyllis and Daphne into Folkestone after an early lunch and saw Daphne off from Central Station by the 2.15 p.m. train. She was packed like a sardine in the corridor, off to Hitchin for strenuous weekend course training for war relief work. At 10 p.m. a large force of heavy bombers passed over.

Saturday 28 October
Sometime in the night or early morning the Gunners in our road left. Some civilian lorries loaded with bell tents and duck-board floors parked for the night in Hollowdene. Another big force of bombers over at night.

Monday 30 October
The British advance in Holland can hardly be called 'sweeping forward'. I spent the day in Folkestone. A fine day. A large convoy went up the Strait in the evening. Rain at night and heavy bombers over.

Wednesday 1 November

A still morning, with sun in afternoon. Heard that old Mr Edminson has come back by train from Oxford, and all that petrol and effort was wasted. The old chap deserves a thrashing. I saw Chapman (Percy) ex-captain of Kent [County Cricket Club] in the town.

Thursday 2 November

A fine day, except for one sharp shower. After an early lunch, Daphne drove into Canterbury for a Commissioners' Conference. In the afternoon Phyllis and I took our four hens over to Fuller for the winter. Joyce Fuller is engaged and shortly to be married to her Commanding Officer. They did not give it out, as the authorities would have parted them if they knew. Our fence has again been broken by a lorry.

Sunday 5 November

A dark overcast day, with a strong south-westerly gale. I looked up 'Bone' Foster in the afternoon, and watched him sell his car, a 1926 model Austin, for £15. Heavy rain at 6.30 p.m. Alert at 7.30 p.m. Shortly afterwards, what sounded like a flying bomb passed on a spiral course. There was a distant explosion and gunfire. Six others came over the house, one of which was fired on by a plane. Searchlights feebly traversed the sky, but could not pierce the thick clouds.

Monday 6 November

A fine, cold day. Phyllis and I had tea with Mrs Perry. Phyllis looked out her fur coat to take to London for alteration, and found it completely destroyed by moths, even the skin eaten through. Sir John Dill has died in Washington and Lord Moyne has been assassinated in Cairo. A gale and rain at night.

Tuesday 7 November

There was firing at night and in the early morning. A fine morning. The sky was full of planes, Fortresses and Super Fortresses. Phyllis spent the day in London. At 11 o'clock I conveyed clothes, food etc. from the Bartholomew Close [Hythe] Rest Centre, which is being given up for Philbeach. The afternoon was overcast and cold. Several times there was distant bombardment or bombing. The Germans' V-2 rocket has caused much damage in London and all over England. The Germans have forced our Government to own to it. The Queen's father [Claude Bowes-Lyon, the 14th Earl of Strathmore and Kinghorne] has died.

Thursday 9 November
A hard frost. From early morning, the sky was full of planes. A freezing cold north wind induced me to go for a walk up Blackhouse Hill across Gorsey Banks to Saltwood Castle. The Beachborough War School was again functioning. A succession of explosions and rattling of windows all evening.

Sunday 12 November
Still freezing hard. I went for a short walk at midday and met old padre Edminson, who convinced me he had some justification for leaving the Oxford hospital. Churchill in Paris having another guzzle. He has done himself well this month, with Quebec and Moscow and the Lord Mayor's banquet! *Tirpitz* sunk in Tromsö Fjord by RAF.

> The Tirpitz has been sunk by R.A.F. Lancasters which obtained several direct hits with 12,000lb. bombs as she lay in Tromsö Fjord.

Monday 13 November
The Royal Artillery Captain commanding the details in Hillcrest Road had stakes driven into the entrance to Oakville's side drive, to stop lorry-drivers using it as a short cut to Castle Road and damaging our fence.

Wednesday 15 November
There was an alert last night and at least one explosion not far away, but I heard nothing. The whole country was white with snow when we woke up. The earliest we had had for many years. The Russians, despite their claims of great victories, are further from Budapest than they were some time ago, and their drive into East Prussia has petered out.

Thursday 16 November
A very hard frost at night, which continued through the morning. About 8 a.m. the Gunners in our road pulled up the stakes blocking Oakville's

drive and drove their lorries through, damaging our fence. Another, driving out of Hollowdene opposite, mounted the pavement and scoured our front fence! All morning, bombers were going out and returning.

Friday 17 November
I spent the day in Folkestone, but came back by 4 p.m. as it was too wet to walk about. The 8th Battalion Home Guard is to have its 'stand down' parade in Dover, and have asked Churchill as Lord Warden of the Cinque Ports to take the salute. 'B' Company want to have their own parade in Folkestone another day. Phyllis and Daphne went in the afternoon to the wedding of Mrs Dix's maid Molly Rye at the Folkestone Fishermen's Church.

Monday 20 November
The whole Western Front seems to be on the move in an all-out assault. Distant heavy gun salvos in the afternoon.

Wednesday 22 November
A mild day. French in the south have broken through to the Rhine; a fine bit of work, but the river stops any swing round. Rain at night.

Friday 24 November
Still mild. I spent the day in Folkestone. I had lunch at a new restaurant on the Bayle called 'Shangri La'. Very stuffy, but they gave a huge plate of meat and vegetables. Daphne went to her Sea Rangers meeting in the afternoon, and from there by bus to Barham in the evening. A Folkestone Guider, who was to have taken the Guides out to a weekend camp, failed at the last minute and Daphne had to take her place.

Saturday 25 November
A Mr and Mrs Whiteman and their daughter looked over the house in the afternoon.

Sunday 26 November
A frosty, sunny morning. Planes in great force were passing overhead and returning between 9 a.m. and 3 p.m., when a mist came over the land. Heavy rain at 9 p.m. Alexander has been made a Field Marshal, with

seniority over Montgomery; a strange method of promotion. He has taken over command of the Middle East in place of Maitland Wilson, who is going to Washington in place of Dill.

Thursday 30 November

We received an offer of £2,500 from [a Mr and Mrs] Whiteman for our house. The Gunners in our road have gone and we now have Sappers – a mixed lot, several baldheads. They are obviously clearing up superfluous gun and other sites.

Friday 1 December

A mild day. I went over as usual to Folkestone and had lunch with Phyllis at Vinson's. In the morning, I saw a convoy come up the Strait past Folkestone, and several small ships come into the harbour and go out towards Calais. In the evening, the French coast was covered with thick black clouds.

> The King broadcast a message of thanks to the Home Guard last night, and also authorized the issue of a special Army Order, to mark the occasion of the force's official " stand down."

Sunday 3 December

Mild at first, then rather a cold rain for the rest of the day. The 8th (Cinque Ports) Battalion Home Guard had their 'stand down' parade at Dover in the morning. They had a rather miserable time, and Churchill did not take the parade. The American 3rd Army have crossed the Saar; this might produce good results. In Burma we have reached the [River] Chindwin at Kalewa.

Monday 4 December

A short fall of snow in the early morning. My car is again in dock. The battery, which has carried on for four years, is said to have petered out. Planes up at 3 p.m.

Tuesday 5 December

Frost early, then a perfect autumn day. Accompanied by Phyllis I picked up in Cinque Ports Avenue a Mrs Honey (née Boorman), and drove her via Ashford to Tenterden to an emergency hospital in the Milnes' house, Kench Hill. I did the 28 miles in 1¼ hours. Phyllis and I drove back into Tenterden. We had tea at the Spinning Wheel, and drove back via Hamstreet and Lympne. The country was lovely. At one place we saw seven magpies in a clutch. At another, a house with nothing but fields all round had had a direct hit and was a pile of rubble. Bombers came in from the east, flying over us to land at an aerodrome somewhere near St Mary-in-the-Marsh. We got back at 5.15 p.m. A total of 49 miles.

Thursday 7 December
A fine day and fairly mild. Rumbling in the direction of Boulogne. The Germans claim that their frogmen have blown up the lock gates of Antwerp Harbour. Our attacks on the Western Front have all come to a standstill.

Monday 11 December
A fine day; no frost. Several hundred heavy bombers flew overhead at 10 a.m., some going east and others south, with and without fighter escort. Air activity continued into the

> **BLACK-OUT RELAXED IN COAST TOWNS**
> For the first time since the war black-out restrictions were relaxed a little on Monday night in Dover, Folkestone, Hythe, New Romney, and Lydd, with rural areas adjoining.

afternoon. Alert 11.30 p.m. A heavy explosion to the north, and the 'all clear' at 11.45 p.m. Hythe etc. are to be advanced from blackout to 'dim out'.

Tuesday 12 December
A mild, overcast day. At 1.40 p.m. I picked up Mrs Crispin on Blackhouse Hill and drove to Sandling Junction, where Few (the Mayor), Stainer (the Town Clerk) and the Vicar were present to welcome the Hythe children returning from Wales in a special train due shortly after 2 p.m. At 3 o'clock the Station Master suggested we should adjourn to his office, where there was a fire, and instructions were phoned to the mothers waiting at Hythe School to disperse for tea. We sat and gossiped, Few talking in his self-satisfied way. He and Stainer are unutterable asses. The train arrived at 4 o'clock, with the children looking very fit and cheerful. I drove the nurse and conducting officer, Mr Chin, to their billets in

Douglas Avenue. At 8 p.m. the sky was full of heavy planes with searchlights trying to pierce the cloud. The Germans seem to be beginning a retreat behind the Rhine.

Wednesday 13 December

I was up by 6.30 a.m. and at Douglas Avenue by 7.15 a.m. and drove the nurse and Chin to Sandling Junction in the dark. They had 20 minutes to wait for their train. In the afternoon I went down to Child's office, where Marks senior informed me that Whiteman agreed to buy our house for £2,700 with vacant possession at the end of June 1945.

Thursday 14 December

I drove to Sandling Junction at 2 p.m. to meet a train bringing children from Cornwall; Mrs Crispin went in Miss Steven's car. We again had to wait in the Station Master's office. About 4 o'clock the Vicar and Stainer arrived from a council meeting, and the train arrived at 4.15 p.m. We were told there would be five to seven attendants. There were actually four, who had arranged to go back as far as Ashford for the night, so we had had our wait for nothing. I drove Mrs Crispin round cancelling their billets. Full blackout restrictions relaxed.

Friday 15 December

A large advance party of the Royal Warwickshire Regiment came into our road in the morning. It is said 8,000 are coming into the area to finish their training, and will eventually leave from Dover and Folkestone. I spent the day in Folkestone. Brigadier Gribbon is dangerously ill with a heart attack and not likely to recover. I saw his RNVR son in the town.

The Battle of the Bulge began when the German army counterattacked in the Ardennes on 16 December.

Sunday 17 December

Rain and a fierce gale. Bombers over at 8.45 p.m. The German offensive is so serious we have shut down on the news. Not a word has come from Montgomery for a month. I wonder if he has been knocked out as Rommel was.

Monday 18 December

A very mild day. All day, flights of light bombers were flying low out and in. At 1 o'clock Mrs Crispin rang up to say a VCP car from Tunbridge Wells with an invalid in it had broken down at Newingreen. I was off in 10 minutes and found the car with a broken axle. A WVS woman was the driver. The invalid was a little woman with a broken hip from Deal, who had been four years in Pembury Hospital. I drove along the Newington Road through Folkestone and Dover to Kingsdown, short of Deal, where she was staying with a cousin. I reached Kingsdown at 2 p.m. On the way back, I gave a lift to two WAAFs to the Duke of York's Military School [Dover] and to an airman into Dover. Troops were helping to clear up the Market Square. Having had no lunch, I had fish and chips and coffee at the Dickens' restaurant in the square and got home by 4 p.m. A large force of bombers over between 7.45 p.m. and 8.45 p.m. Gribbon died last night.

Tuesday 19 December

Another mild day with fog. Some air activity. I have a pouring cold. The Germans claim they have routed the American 1st Army with 10,000 prisoners, taken Malmedy [Belgium], are halfway to Huy [Belgium] and have broken through to the south as well. They have also driven our 8th Army back in Italy and have retaken half of Faenza.

Thursday 21 December

In the afternoon I took Maurice's silver in a hatbox to Joan in Canterbury. I went both ways by the Alkham Valley, a very cold ride. I handed the box over to Mrs Quested, as Joan was at her office. I had a cup of tea at Lyon's, walked to the bus terminus and got into a bus. At Ashentree Corner I got out and walked home past Bargrove and down Blackhouse Hill, getting in at 6 p.m. There was a line of lorries in our road and troops seemed to arrive all night.

Friday 22 December

The Warwicks broke our fence last night. I spent the morning in Folkestone. Vinson, I am glad to hear, has been given an OBE in the Home Guard honours list. He thoroughly deserves it. He was at Brigadier Gribbon's funeral, so I was not able to congratulate him.

Monday 25 December

Christmas Day. A sharp frost, followed by bright sun. Intermittent air activity during the day. A heavy explosion shook the house at 4.15 p.m. We spent a quiet day, and forgot to listen to the King's broadcast.

Wednesday 27 December

An exceptionally hard frost, night and day. Foliage white with hard frost. A few planes tried to fly at noon. The troops in our road are Gunners being transformed into Infantry.

Thursday 28 December

Not such a hard frost as yesterday. A force of bombers went out between noon and 2.30 p.m. Langley the builder came to survey our house for Mr Whiteman. He was very casual over it all, perhaps because the bad parts of the house were built by him! Churchill and Eden's journey to Athens proved futile. Everything Eden does is futile.

Friday 29 December

I spent the morning in Folkestone, returning after lunch at the Shangri La. I looked up Vinson to congratulate him on his MBE (not OBE as local papers gave it). He has no intention of closing his office, although he is losing Miss Morgan and his typewriter [typist] at the end of the month.

Saturday 30 December

Thawing. Planes out throughout the day, and some very heavy bombers after dark. Colonel Macnamara MP, who was commanding the London Irish when they were in the Small Arms School early in the war, has been killed in action. He dressed them up in kilts and made a great display of them, but he was a good man.

Sunday 31 December

Frost and thaw alternately all day. A heavy explosion shook the house at 8.30 p.m. This has been labelled a 'year of achievement'. It is as much that for the Germans as ourselves. Their stubborn resistance and then their breakthrough have shown us all that we cannot yet cut up the carcase. As for affairs at home, we have gone back to grabbing and bitterness. The

Labour Party has sunk to the lowest depths of the pre-war period. The Greek situation may improve. Churchill's attitude towards Poland is indefensible and a black blot on his reputation. Our men in Burma have been magnificent.

Barrage balloon and crew in 1944 (War and Peace Collection 0289)

1945

Monday 1 January

A clear sky most of the day. Much air activity. Throughout the day our windows rattled, sometimes violently, but there was no sound of explosions. A Lance Corporal Stevenson of the Warwicks, a Yorkshireman from Leeds, spent the evening with us. First British leave steamers arrived at Folkestone.

Wednesday 3 January

A mild day. At 10 a.m. a huge force of American bombers, some Superforts, flew south. Daphne drove Mrs Daniel [SSAFA] to Canterbury then to Bekesbourne, where they had lunch on a jugged hare with General and Mrs Delano-Osborne. They got back at 4.30 p.m. Phyllis and I met Herbert Blaxland in Folkestone. Phyllis and Herbert went through the deed box and looked over the house; I came home. At 3 o'clock Mrs Crispin rang me up for a car to take an expectant mother at once to Beckenham. Daphne returned about 4.15 p.m. and I asked her to come with me. We picked up Mrs Brown with her small daughter and her mother-in-law. I drove through Ashford and Maidstone. The sky clouded over, the wind got up and the rain fell. It was dark by the time we left Maidstone. I drove on to Seal, where I handed over to Daphne. We went through Farnborough, across Hayes Common to the southern end of Beckenham, then to Elmers End, where we deposited the family. They offered us tea and to put us up for the night, but we refused. We decided to put up at a hotel, as we had not quite enough petrol to get home. We arrived at 8 p.m., just as the sirens sounded an alert and two robots flew over and exploded somewhere not far off. The 'all clear' sounded at 8.30 p.m. Daphne found a regional Civil Defence Controller, so decided to get petrol through him from a CD Headquarters. We were directed to the West Wickham control, a marvellously organised affair in a large school building. Here we got two gallons of petrol, and a cup of tea in their canteen, and started for home. Daphne drove as far as Seal, then I took the wheel. We got back by 12.30 a.m. Phyllis had stayed up to prepare boiled eggs and coffee for us. We had travelled 132 miles and Daphne had done 44 miles in the morning.

Tuesday 9 January
A heavy fall of snow at 6 a.m. and again for two hours at 2 p.m. The Warwicks crashed into our fence, wrecking it worse than it has been before.

Thursday 11 January
Slight frost all day with some snow. Hythe public services, as usual, have been paralysed.

Friday 12 January
Snow at night, rapid thaw during the day. I spent the morning in Folkestone. Vinson has sold the restaurant. He says the small man everywhere will be squeezed out by big companies. A shocking accident near here: a live mine during a demonstration exploded, killing 20 men of the Worcestershire Regiment and blinding several others.

Saturday 13 January
Thaw all day. Air activity for about two hours in the afternoon. The Russian drive through Poland is a major victory. What treachery, the way they egged on the Polish patriots to rise last year, then left them to be destroyed.

Russia captured Warsaw on 17 January 1945.

Friday 19 January
A blizzard at night, and a bitter cold wind all day. The storm yesterday broke away part of the Sandgate Parade and covered the whole area thick with shingle. Buses had to be diverted through Shorncliffe. I spent the day in Folkestone. A flurry of snow at 5.30 p.m.

Sunday 21 January
Despite a snow-filled sky, bombers passed overhead continuously between 9 a.m. and midday. Fighters active in the afternoon, and night bombers out between 7.30 p.m. and 10 p.m.

Wednesday 24 January

About three inches of snow on the ground, and the sea froze. At 11 a.m. I attended a RSPCA committee meeting at Miss Nutting's flat in Hill House. Inspector Neville gave rather a disconnected report on animal rescue and destruction during the past four years. They decided to postpone activities until the summer. I asked the treasurer if he wished to continue, and he said he would 'carry on'. I do all his work except signing cheques.

Friday 26 January

A clear indictment of Russia, over the fall of Warsaw, by the Poles. The rebels in Greece, who have committed terrible atrocities, have been proved to be in the pay of Russia, and a similar gangster group is operating in Rome. Freezing all day; no air activity. I spent most of the day in Folkestone. Had a talk with Vinson.

Tuesday 30 January

Quite two foot of snow fell during the night, but a thaw in the morning. At 1 o'clock I picked up in Theatre Street a fireman named Craig, who was suffering from cancer of the throat, and his wife and drove them to Canterbury Hospital. There was fairly thick fog. The roads were clear in places, and in others there was thick slush. In the end, my brakes were jammed with slush, and my engine was racing, something having got in behind the throttle. I could only garage the car by switching on and off the engine. The Elham Valley was impassable.

Russian forces crossed the German border on 31 January 1945.

Saturday 3 February

A mild, sunny, spring day. Intensive air activity. I slipped up in bath in the evening and bashed my nose on the sponge rack. It bled for a quarter of an hour.

Sunday 4 February

A mild sunny day, but very few planes up. I looked up 'Bone' Foster in the morning. A few planes passed overhead after dark. About midnight, four very heavy distant explosions, two like guns.

Tuesday 6 February

A wet day. Some planes about. Explosions at midday, probably in Dunkirk area. If the Russians are really over the Oder opposite Berlin, I do not see where the Huns can make a stand.

Wednesday 7 February

We had known for some time that the conference at Yalta [Crimea] was on; the Germans have also announced it, but said it was being held in Belgrade [Yugoslavia]. Stalin got his way and refused to leave Russia. Very little air activity. Bombers out at 10.30 p.m.

Thursday 8 February

A big force of bombers went out at midday. All day there was the thunder of guns or bombs in the distance, in the direction of Dunkirk. Rain in the afternoon. The Battle School at Beachborough woke up in the evening, lighting the sky with flares.

Allied forces swept through the Siegfried Line, Germany's western line of defence, on 9 February 1945.

Saturday 10 February

A sunny day, but rain fell in the evening. Intermittent air activity, bombers over at night. No further attack on Dunkirk. Roosevelt has obviously been duped, Poland is to be slaughtered, Yugoslavia is to be handed over to Tito, the Baltic States are wiped out and we are having Stalin's 'Free Germans' dumped on us. Anxiety about our prisoners 'liberated' by the Russians.

Monday 12 February

I left Sandling Junction at 11.30 a.m., got a seat with a squash to Tonbridge, where I changed and had a carriage to myself. I walked up from Guildford Station. I found Milly looking well. A large force of bombers over at night. Some day, perhaps, the Yalta Conference will be shown up as the greatest and most ghastly betrayal in the history of man. The world seems doped. It makes me sick to think of it.

Tuesday 13 February

I went down to the Angel [Hotel] at noon and met Vinson. I met Milly, and had lunch at the Tudor Café at 12.30 p.m. I went round to Nancy's and humped her six suitcases and a trunk down to the hall. Bombers again went out, passing over at 7 p.m. for half an hour. At 10.30 p.m. I went out to look at another force, which continued passing over in a clear star-covered sky for an hour; they had their navigation lights on and many had their cabins lit up. It was the most wonderful sight I have seen; the sky appeared to be a mass of moving stars.

A Lancaster bomber of 300 squadron over Bremen on a bombing raid (IWM C5101)

Wednesday 14 February

Nancy and I left by the 12 o'clock train and had a comfortable journey, reaching Folkestone at 3.30 p.m. I managed to get porters for the luggage at Guildford, Tonbridge and Folkestone. Doris was extraordinarily demonstrative, even pawing me like a dog.

Friday 16 February

Fog most of the day. I spent the morning in Folkestone and met Phyllis at lunch at Vinson's restaurant, now under new management (the woman full of nerves and snappy). The Russians are held up, and Montgomery's push is at a standstill. We have been pushed back in Italy. We and the Americans won't fight.

Monday 19 February

A few planes were up at noon, and Dunkirk was again bombarded. Churchill returned from the Crimea to Egypt, and is behaving like a clown to cover up the dirty work he has done. A large force of bombers over at 1 a.m.

Wednesday 21 February

A sunny day, with fog over the sea. Not very much air activity. At midday, we heard a distant bombardment and several single explosions. At 4 p.m. Daphne saw a flight of planes towing gliders. Bombers over from 10 p.m.

Friday 23 February

A fine day. Not much air activity. I spent the morning in Folkestone. At noon, when I was on the Leas, there was a very heavy explosion from the direction of Dunkirk. Two leave boats came in. I was told that U-boats sheltering in Dunkirk lay mines in the Thames estuary.

Saturday 24 February

Phyllis settled with Mrs Pickering-Thompson for a flat in Springfield [east Hythe].

Monday 26 February

A mild, sunny day. Light bombers flying over and sounds of distant bombardment all day. In the afternoon, I walked to Sandling, had a talk with Major Master on the way, and looked up Capt. Stuart-Lewis, who had been ill. Master has sold Slaybrook and bought Halford.

Tuesday 27 February

A mild day, but not much activity in the air. Churchill made his speech defending the Yalta betrayal, full of lies and verbal gymnastics, and to add insult to injury offered those dispossessed British nationality. A few Conservative MPs have tabled an amendment condemning the treatment of the Poles, and the consciences of some of the Socialists are pricking. We have sunk to a third-rate power without honour.

Wednesday 28 February

A mild day. The amendment deprecating the betrayal of Poland defeated. At least there are 25 honourable men in the world.

Thursday 1 March

I drove to Shorncliffe Station where I picked up a Mr Bell, Regional Dental Officer from Tunbridge Wells, and drove him through Dover to Deal, where he went into Boots and looked up a doctor (or dentist) on the front near the castle. There were a fair number of ships in the Roads [English Channel] and one beached near the castle, an American troopship which had burnt for a week. Returning to Dover, we had lunch at the Crypt then walked down to the harbour, which was full of barges with two wrecks (one a cargo boat) on the beach. After Bell had spent half an hour in the hospital, I drove him back to Folkestone. I got back, having driven 49 miles, at 3 p.m. Later, I saw about 100 heavy bombers returning from Germany. A gun or heavy mortar fired half a dozen shots at midnight.

Saturday 3 March

A very cold north wind. Planes were up continually all day. At 1.30 p.m. a force of carrier planes towing gliders flew over. Daphne said an 'alert' sounded. At 4.30 p.m. another force of carriers and gliders flew over, and a convoy of over 40 ships sailed up the Strait. A good advance in the west, but we seem to have allowed the Germans to escape over the Rhine and blow up the bridges. Occasional explosions later on.

Monday 5 March

It is said a Hun was over Lympne last night. No great air activity during the day. There was a practice air raid warning at 10 a.m. I believe a Hun was being chased over Postling at 4.30 p.m. We all three looked over the Springfield flat in the evening.

Tuesday 6 March

A very violent explosion sometime in the night woke me. Pairs of Spitfires were flying around all day. A big convoy sailed up the Strait, and bombers flew home. Alert 9.45 p.m., followed by a loud explosion and the 'all clear'.

American forces crossed the Ruhr, south of Cologne, on 7 March 1945.

Wednesday 7 March

Mostly an overclouded day. The explosion on Tuesday night is said to have been a U-boat sinking one of our ships. The petrol pipes through Hythe on to the piers are being used, it is said.

> ### GERMANS RAID NORMAN PORT
>
> PARIS, March 9.—A small number of Germans, presumably from the Channel Islands, made a raid on the port of Granville, on the Normandy coast, at 1.15 this morning.

Friday 9 March

A fine, sunny day. I spent the morning in Folkestone. All morning, two Spitfires were 'dive-bombing' the Leas. In the afternoon, a small force of carrier planes towing gliders flew eastwards. I received a communication informing me that I have had about £20 added to my pension. On first reading, I thought it would come to £200. The Hun raid on France is a blot on Churchill's policy.

Saturday 10 March

An overcast day, but a fair amount of air activity. The Americans in the USA are quite sure the war will be over in a few days. There is a rumour that Montgomery with an amphibious force is landing somewhere in the north. Italy has entirely petered out.

Sunday 11 March

The plum trees at the end of the road and our daffodils are out.

Monday 12 March

An almost summer's day. I drove Copper, the National Savings Officer for Saltwood, to a meeting at Lyminge. I looked over the church and village, then read a stupid novel *Then a Soldier* in the car. I got back at 4 p.m., a journey of 10 miles.

Tuesday 13 March

An almost summer's day, much air activity including heavy machines. Nancy came to tea. In the evening, the house was shaken by very heavy explosions and there was the rumble of a bombardment. Bombers flew over at 10 p.m.

Saturday 17 March

A large force of heavy bombers flew over at 10 a.m. One, giving out sparks, came down below the clouds and made for Lympne. Another is said to have dropped its emergency fuel tank on Folkestone. Bombers were over again at midday and 7 p.m. After tea, Mrs Whiteman brought her mother up to see the house; she expressed great pleasure at everything.

Monday 19 March

Woken early by planes flying at rooftop height and later by troops trampling in to breakfast. Phyllis left by the 12.50 p.m. train for a week in Salcombe [Devon] to see what it is like as a possible home. Mrs Whiteman was in the town, and Phyllis phoned me from Sandling that she thought Whiteman might be trying to get out of buying the house! Rain in the afternoon and rather a wild night.

Thursday 22 March

A warm, sunny day. Ships, including destroyers, in the Strait in the morning, and two seaplanes flew over together. A bombardment sounded in the Dungeness direction, heavy explosions shaking the house. Nancy came to tea. A huge fire broke out in the wood on Gorsey Banks. A bomber force came home at midnight.

Friday 23 March

A sunny day. A ten-minute alert at 7 a.m.; a V-2 flying bomb fell near Elham village, shattering many windows but no one was hurt. I spent the morning in Folkestone. Two far-off tremendous rumbling explosions about 1 o'clock. A squadron of Marauders flew towards Dunkirk. Another similar explosion at 8 p.m. Montgomery in charge of Rhine crossing: 40,000 airborne troops in two hours.

A sky full of planes: gliders are towed over Belgium en route to Germany (IWM CL2242)

Saturday 24 March

A hot summer's day. About 8 a.m., more than 1,000 planes towing gliders passed to the north going eastwards, carrying an airborne division, and the sky was full of planes all the morning. About 11 o'clock a squadron of Marauders flew low over Hythe and apparently bombed Dunkirk, as they came back singly half an hour afterwards. Daphne went to a Guiders training course in Folkestone after preparing my lunch, which I ate alone.

Tuesday 27 March

A nasty, cold morning; improved later. Everyone at the Front says the Germans are cracking. Last V-2

Field-Marshal Montgomery's bridgehead across the lower Rhine was yesterday 30 miles wide and more than seven miles deep.

rocket to come over fell near Orpington, Kent. Over 1,050 have reached England.

Wednesday 28 March

A thick sea mist followed by rain in the morning. Phyllis' birthday. She returned unexpectedly at 3.30 p.m.; we did not expect her until the evening. She left her bag containing £3, spectacles, identity card and clothing coupons in the train carriage at Sandling. Royal Navy evacuated Folkestone, and the hotels they had occupied were taken over for repatriated New Zealand prisoners of war.

American forces captured Frankfurt-am-Main on 29 March 1945.

Thursday 29 March

It seems to be presumed that Brabner [Hythe MP] is dead. He was a thorough 'yes' man. I shopped in Hythe, then went on to Folkestone for the morning. The Navy have evacuated Folkestone, and their hotels are taken over for New Zealanders from Italy.

Friday 30 March

Good Friday. A sunny day with a strong wind. Phyllis spent the day in bed with a cold. It is tantalising not knowing how far forward our armour has got. I do not believe it would help the Germans to give it out.

Saturday 31 March

A windy day. A large force of planes went out about 8 a.m. and returned at 1 p.m. Mr and Mrs Whiteman came at 3 o'clock. He cannot get relieved of his job yet, thinks there is no hope of getting away before next spring, and agrees to my suggestion that we stay on here.

Sunday 1 April

Easter. A strong wind blew in a sea fog, and it rained all day. Clocks put forward to double summer time at midnight. Rain and wind all night.

Wednesday 4 April

No fresh news, except that two men in a car and the driver were assassinated in Berlin. The huge reward offered for news of the murderers seems to point to a very big person being involved. Stockholm says Hermann Goering was killed, the *Daily Mail* says it was Goebbels.

Friday 6 April
I was in Folkestone up to 3 p.m. I had a talk with Adam, 7th Rajputs. Enemy mines laid off Folkestone last night. Minesweepers were busy all day. Air activity midday. A large four-engined plane escorted by two fighters came back from France about 2 o'clock.

Saturday 7 April
Warm sun, cold wind. Polish government in London announce that a delegation of about eight, including a deputy prime minister, who had received a safe conduct to confer with a Russian General in Poland have not since been heard of.

Tuesday 10 April
A warm day. At night and during the morning, shattering explosions occurred at intervals. Planes were up in large numbers all day, and well into the night. I drove Daphne to Sandling Junction to catch the 12.53 p.m. train. She left for a week's camping at Braithwaite in the Lake District, and expects to be put through her final test for foreign service.

Wednesday 11 April
A shattering explosion woke us at 2.45 a.m. In the morning, there was a large vessel off Dungeness attended by smaller ones and a lot of smoke. Gossip says the explosion was a depth charge, but it was more likely a ship being torpedoed. German midget submarines are in the Strait and it is known that two ships were torpedoed on Monday night. Varied air activity all day, and depth charge explosions. Many of the leading residents, who had left Hythe at the beginning of the war, have returned.

Thursday 12 April
A hot day. In the morning, eight minesweepers off the town were steaming round in a circle, having evidently located a submarine. I met Street, Admiral Hall-Thompson and others queuing up for fish.

The war must be coming to an end! The Americans are across the Elbe.

The bane of Rodney's shopping trips – queuing for fish (IWM D24983)

Friday 13 April

Roosevelt is dead. How will that affect the war? The last barrier against the dictator Stalin gone. There was a thick sea fog all

> **OBITUARY**
> President Roosevelt died suddenly at Warm Springs, Georgia.

morning. Folkestone was full of soldiers and airmen from the Western Front, many of them drunk by 11 o'clock. There were also a lot of greasy-haired youths and girls, evidently members of ENSA. At midnight, a large force of very heavy bombers took half an hour to pass overhead. About 2 a.m. there were two heavy explosions.

Sunday 15 April

A hot day. Spasmodic air activity. All afternoon, Dunkirk appeared to be under bombardment. At 3 p.m. two Spitfires tore over the house at rooftop height apparently firing their guns. At every point on the Western Front we and the Americans have been checked, and the latter have lost one of their bridgeheads over the Elbe. So much for their talks of victory parades and holidays! We have, however, captured von Mackensen, von Papen and Prince Albert.

Allied forces liberated Bergen-Belsen concentration camp on 17 April 1945.

Tuesday 17 April

A slight breeze. Explosions at intervals all day. About 100 Fortresses came home about 6 p.m. We heard the 'cuckoo' [siren] at 7 p.m. Daphne got home at 8.30 p.m. She had a strenuous week in very grand surroundings. She was not tested.

Wednesday 18 April

Another hot day. In the morning, I met and talked with 'Bone' Foster, Thom, Tidmarsh, Butterworth, Kerr and finally Street. Generally I only meet women. The German pocket near Bordeaux has been cleared, and Dunkirk has an armistice to evacuate French civilians. Let's hope it will be wiped out now.

Friday 20 April

I spent the morning in Folkestone. About noon, I saw two columns of men from overseas march down the Road of Remembrance, the first mostly Royal Air Force. In the afternoon, six rather drunk Canadians carrying their kit came down the Leas accosting every girl they met. At the other end of the seat I was sitting on, there was a well-dressed spinster with grey hair and an attractive rather young face. After they passed us, one came back, bent over her and kissed her! She drew back and presented her cheek, but appeared not to dislike it. I should have stopped the man; instead, I was amused and thought it was a harmless amusement. She did remark, when I said they were off to the Front, that they ought to be controlled. A small convoy went up the Strait, with three minesweepers dropping depth charges in front of them.

Saturday 21 April

An overcast day with a strong cold north wind. The papers are full of the horrors of the German concentration camps.

Sunday 22 April

Sun in the morning; overcast in the afternoon. I have had to start cutting my hedges a fortnight earlier than normal. Bombers over at night.

Monday 23 April

St George's day. As usual, no one took any notice. Much air activity. The Germans say Hitler is in Berlin.

Tuesday 24 April

A fine day. Not much air activity. An exciting bit of news: two Household Brigade armoured cars shooting up a huge black limousine guarded by SS troops, leaving it and its occupants a charred wreck.

Wednesday 25 April

A fine day, much air activity. Explosions at intervals during the afternoon. Stalin insists on the Lublin government representing Poland at the San Francisco conference. Either we lied when we said an agreement had been reached at Yalta, or Stalin has broken his word. Eden owns now that the Polish delegates from London who went to Russia have disappeared.

> Göring has asked to be relieved of his command of the *Luftwaffe* because of his serious heart trouble, and Hitler has agreed.

Friday 27 April

Shopping kept me in Folkestone until 3.30 p.m. Mussolini has been taken by Italian partisans. The Russians say Goering has fled with family and jewellery. The meeting of Americans and Russians was a flop. Everyone knew it had come off several days ago, but it had to be staged with photographers etc. and Stalin and Churchill spouting about 'Liberty'.

Sunday 29 April

A cold wind, with some sun in the afternoon. Himmler of all men offering to surrender!! Mussolini shot. Hitler said to be dying.

Russian forces captured Berlin, after a nine-day battle, on 30 April 1945.

Tuesday 1 May

Cold north wind, and several sleet showers. Nancy came to tea. Hitler and

Goebbels are said to have
committed suicide as Berlin fell.
Everyone aching for the end of the
war now. Admiral Dönitz
appointed himself as successor.

German radio announced late last night that Hitler died in the afternoon. His successor is Admiral Dönitz.

Wednesday 2 May
A cold morning, but warmer in the evening. I am glad that the first large-scale surrender of Germans was to Alexander [in Italy].

Thursday 3 May
A cold wet day; heavy rain at night. In afternoon I looked up old Captain de Berry RM and had a great talk. Germans everywhere in front of us have collapsed, but they still fight the Russians. We hear no more of co-operation with our gallant allies. Montgomery dashed across the base of Denmark to keep the Russians out, and Patton is poaching into Czechoslovakia. The capture of Rangoon is a fine piece of work; the Burma campaign was a very brilliant affair.

German forces in western Europe surrendered on 4 May 1945.

Friday 4 May
A cold morning, which I spent in Folkestone. All Germans in north Holland, Denmark and north-west Germany have surrendered to Montgomery.

Saturday 5 May
A wet day. Some Germans in south Germany have now surrendered to the Americans; up to now we have had all the glory. After two months' secrecy, the Russians allow that they have imprisoned the Polish delegates to whom they gave a safe conduct.

Sunday 6 May
A milder day. The whole country making an ass of itself dithering about VE Day. Apparently even the new Führer [Karl Dönitz] has decided that the game is up.

Monday 7 May

A warm, sunny day. I met Mrs Daniel in Red Lion Square at 10.30 a.m. and drove her to Sittingbourne. The country was green and lovely, bluebells in the woods and hops in the fields. At Mrs Daniel's direction, I drove on and turned north at Key Street on to Sheppey Island, past Bobbing and Iwade. At King's Ferry we were held up crossing the Swale to allow two barges through. From there, the road twists about between dykes, like a [Romney] Marsh road, to Sheerness. I drove to Dockyard House, where Mrs Daniel had a meeting and lunch with Mrs Sinclair-Thompson, wife of the Admiral. I got a badly cooked meal in the small town, which is full of pubs and sailors' eating houses. I strolled along the seafront, watched several gunboats sail out and saw what looked like a wreck being raised in the mid-channel. I called for Mrs Daniel at 2.30 p.m. and was given a cup of coffee and played with Mrs Sinclair-Thompson's two red dachshunds (sisters). Returning, we came through Hernhill, where Mrs Daniel's daughter is married to the vicar, once a curate in Hythe. She gave us tea and I played with her black and tan dachshund. I got back at 6 p.m., having travelled 94 miles. Most of the towns and villages were putting up bunting.

> In a broadcast address to his peoples last night the King paid tribute to all whose service had helped to win the war in Europe, and to the faith and unity that "have carried us to victory through dangers which at times seemed over-whelming."

Tuesday 8 May

VE DAY. This day, I obtained my commission 44 years ago. I shopped in the morning. There was an assembly of civic officials at the Town Hall, followed by a service at the Parish Church, but we did not go to either. Daphne decorated the balcony and gate with flags. A violent thunderstorm at 12.30 p.m. Folkestone sounded the 'all clear' on their sirens at 4 p.m. after the Prime Minister's speech, which we did not listen to. We heard the King's speech at 9 p.m. Daphne switched on to Prague at 11.45 p.m. and heard them calling for help. Germany's complete surrender was announced at midnight. I got to bed at 12.30 a.m.

Wednesday 9 May

No morning papers published. In the afternoon, large four-engined bombers in fours and fives flew over, going north.

Thursday 10 May

Motorboats in the Strait and heavy smoke coming from the French coast, presumably from Dunkirk. Large planes flew north all day. It is said they are carrying repatriated prisoners of war. The Germans in Dunkirk and the Channel Islands have surrendered at last. Blackout ended; I was again not in bed until midnight.

Friday 11 May

I went into Folkestone and had to stay there up to 3 o'clock and then did not get the provisions I wanted. A blazing hot day, almost unbearable. I saw two drunken officers careering about the town with a blonde woman. We had our lights unscreened for the first time since the war was declared. It gave me a feeling of being unprotected.

Victory in Europe Day – street celebrations in Kent (War and Peace Collection 0239)

Saturday 12 May

I picked up Mrs Crispin at 10.30 a.m. and drove to Palmarsh, collecting clothes from the WVS depot there, and left some at a cottage in West Hythe. We then drove to Scene Farm, where I dumped some of Daphne's camp kit and Mrs MacGregor gave us lemon squash. Dropping Mrs Crispin at her house, I drove down to the town to finish my shopping and did not get home until after 1 o'clock. Daphne left to join her Sea Rangers in a truck to Scene Farm, where she had a weekend camp.

Sunday 13 May
Thanksgiving Sunday. I went to Saltwood Church in morning. Phyllis went to hers in afternoon. Daphne with her Sea Rangers trekked into Folkestone and attended service at the Parish Church and marched in procession. She got home at about 9 p.m. having trekked back to Scene Farm, cooked a meal, struck camp and taken her Rangers back to Cheriton. Hythe also had a service, Street and 'A' Company Home Guard turning out. A much cooler evening.

Monday 14 May
A windy day, much cooler. I picked up Coupland at 10.30 a.m. and we collected bowls, cups and other utensils from the Emergency Food Depot in Seabrook and the Food Office in Hythe, and took them to the corporation yard, handing them over to the overseer.

Thursday 17 May
Another hot day. A great convoy of more than 30 ships sailed down the Strait in the morning. In the afternoon, I went over to 18 Kingsnorth Gardens and helped a little furniture man to move Nancy's furniture and carpets up and down stairs and from room to room . I was very done in by it. Daphne and her Sea Rangers were taken over Folkestone Harbour by the Royal Navy.

Friday 18 May
Explosions as of depth charges in the morning. I went into Folkestone as usual. I had a talk with a New Zealander, who had been captured in Italy. He told me of champagne, cigarettes and prisoners' parcels being found hidden in a farm occupied by German officers. He was rescued by the Americans in Austria. Daphne left for a county camp at Lorenden Hall near Faversham.

Saturday 19 May

Rations are to be cut all round still further, and food we are supposed to live on is not obtainable. Churchill has now got a headache over his 'gallant ally' Tito, who won't leave Trieste and is infiltrating into south Austria, with Stalin grinning in the background.

Tuesday 22 May

A fine day. At 5 p.m. I picked up Mrs Crispin, loaded up with clothes and a big trunk and took them to the Manor House. From there, we took a barrel of milk to Victoria Hospital in Folkestone and dropped off clothing at several houses on the way. I drove Mrs Crispin home and met her younger daughter, a modern girl, caterer to the RAF Pathfinder and Bomber Command. I got home at 7.30 p.m. Cuts in rationing not so severe but irritating. Rain at night.

Wednesday 23 May

Phyllis gave me a return ticket to London as a birthday present. I left by the 9.15 a.m. train. The train was full. I passed through a carriage into the corridor and fell up against Inspector Neville and his wife. I stood in the corridor all the way, talking to two very nice New Zealand NCOs, ex-prisoners of war. It rained all morning. I went to an exhibition of paintings by a Captain Scanlon of the 8th Gurkhas. His types were excellent, but his action pieces were cubist and unfinished. I talked to a Rajput officer, two Sikhs and a Dogra; the Sikhs had been prisoners. I had lunch at Veeraswamy, then wasted some time making up my mind to go to the Royal Academy. I decided to go to the National Gallery, where I saw some of its pictures and some recent purchases by the Liverpool Art Gallery – a portrait of Henry VIII being outstanding. A very heavy rainstorm came down just as I got to a Lyon's teashop. I bought collars and a hat, then walked to Cannon Street Station. I left at 6.15 p.m., arriving home at 8.15 p.m.

Friday 25 May

I spent the morning in Folkestone. A lot of planes overhead. The troops in our road have become very noisy, a sure sign that they are leaving shortly.

Saturday 26 May
I met Mrs Crispin at the old Manor House, filled the car with clothing and placed a large trunk in the boot and drove to Church House, where Mrs Mackeson and her gang of women were getting ready for a jumble sale. I did three such journeys.

Sunday 27 May
My 63rd birthday. I stayed in practically all day by myself. Phyllis and Daphne went to church in the afternoon.

Tuesday 29 May
The afternoon sky was full of planes coming home. Everyone is more excited over the capture of 'Lord Haw-Haw' [William Joyce] than over Hitler's death.

Thursday 31 May
Bean, the painter, has been repairing our war damage all week. We feed in the drawing room, Daphne sleeps in my dressing room, and I dress in the box room.

Friday 1 June
I went into Folkestone in the morning. After lunch, I called in Cheriton on a paper salvage man named Whitling, who asked me into his kitchen where I met his family: a buxom wife, hoydenish daughter and a son, a Bevin Boy absent without leave. The wife offered me a cup of tea, and the son drove me back home in his lorry and took away my portfolios of pictures. After tea, I drove Phyllis to Kingsnorth Gardens on our first basic petrol, which we have got back after three years. We took Joan's silver in and shifted furniture; no extra cars were on the roads.

Sunday 3 June
We had an early breakfast and Daphne went off in a special bus to Canterbury for a Rangers day. In the afternoon, I drove Phyllis in to church and went to the service. We picked up Nancy and her Hoover at Kingsnorth Gardens and brought her back to a late tea. Rain in the evening; I got soaked going down to Earlsfield Road for a letter.

Monday 4 June

A fine day. Troop-carrying planes coming home in fair numbers, planes also over at night. Eden is sick and Churchill has taken over. Was he given a six-week rest because he was too 'pro' or 'anti' French?

Tuesday 5 June

I drove in the morning to Mrs Rose-Price in Sandgate Road to pick up some miscellaneous books and some 30 volumes of an old edition of the *Encyclopaedia Britannica*, which latter I handed over the counter of the Post Office as a gift to the forces' libraries. The two girl clerks were highly amused.

Wednesday 6 June

We have handed half of Germany over to the Russians, and the Americans have had to retreat. The King and Queen visited the Channel Islands. Plumbers in the house.

Saturday 9 June

The Russians now say Hitler married an Austrian blonde named Eva Braun two days before Berlin fell, and that he probably got away by aeroplane. The Japs say we have landed in the south of Borneo.

Tuesday 12 June

I rang up Mrs Crispin and the Honourable Mrs Cosgrove in Maidstone about an old woman, Mrs Myers of West Hythe, who wants to see her dying husband in the infirmary. For some silly reason it cannot be called a VCP journey, and I had to send my car registration book for special coupons.

Wednesday 13 June

We had an early breakfast of eggs, and I drove Phyllis to 18 Kingsnorth Gardens by 9 o'clock. Mr Stevens of Burrows' firm came shortly after to make an inventory of the furniture etc. for the sale. I returned after shopping in Folkestone and Hythe. Daphne and I had a punctual lunch and I reached West Hythe before 2 o'clock and drove Mrs Myers and her son (on leave) up to the infirmary in Etchinghill. They stayed with Myers for an hour and a half.

Friday 15 June

I spent the morning in Folkestone. Although I got to the Tatler by

12.30 p.m. I only got fish for lunch, the rest all eaten, and it shut at 1 o'clock. The troops in our road have been stealing our blackberries.

Saturday 16 June
Although it was only given out last night, apparently we had captured Ribbentrop some days ago. The Russians are trying the Poles they treacherously seized and the poor devils have pleaded guilty. Is it torture or mesmerism the Russians employ?

Monday 18 June
Another warm day. William Joyce brought up before a Bow Street magistrate and accused of treason.

Tuesday 19 June
A blazing hot day. Daphne in a rush all day preparing for her camp for Hawkhurst Guides. After tea, she drove with camp kit to Coote's field, Redbrooks, where the Hythe Guides erected the tents.

The massive guns at Cap Gris Nez which rained shells on Dover and Folkestone (Folkestone Library/*Folkestone Herald*)

Wednesday 20 June
Slight rain flurries and muggy. I went down town and shopped.

Daphne drove down in the car at 11.15 a.m., and I drove her up to Captain Coote's field and helped her to get the camp ready for the Hawkhurst Guides, who arrived at noon as I left. After a quick lunch, I drove to West Hythe and took Mrs Myers and a neighbour to the infirmary. On my way home, I drove again up Lympne Hill and deposited some tins at the Guide Camp. I picked up a fat woman waiting in the rain at the top of Hythe hill.

Thursday 21 June
Some rain. Daphne came in from her camp at 5 p.m. and left for a Sea Rangers meeting in Cheriton at 6 p.m. I drove her back to her camp after supper in the evening, Phyllis coming too.

END OF NAZI BIG GUNS

People sunbathing on the Dover beach yesterday saw the end of the concrete emplacements from which German cross-Channel guns used to shell the area. Explosions shook Dover, and great columns of smoke rose from the clearly visible French coast as the emplacements were blown up.

Friday 22 June
A blazing summer day. I drove Phyllis to a sale in Cheriton, where she met Nancy and bought a kitchen cabinet for £21. I spent the day in Folkestone, and we met again at the Tatler for lunch. Explosions on the French coast are said to be the blowing up of big gun emplacements. In the evening, we went to the cinema and saw Ronald Colman and Marlene Dietrich in *Kismet*. Coleman was good and the colouring of the film was excellent.

Sunday 24 June
Our Wedding Day. I did not go out. Daphne brought her Hawkhurst Guides to a picnic lunch on our front lawn. Phyllis went to church in Folkestone in the afternoon, and had one of our wedding day hymns sung.

Wednesday 27 June

I shopped in the morning, standing in a fish queue for a quarter of an hour. After lunch, I drove to West Hythe and took Mrs Myers to Etchinghill Infirmary. She was accompanied by Miss Harrold, a retired Army nurse who, like so many nurses, was very brusque and unkind to the old lady. After tea, I drove to Redbrooks, packed the car with Daphne's camp kit and brought her home.

Thursday 28 June

All morning, planes were flying over to France. A wet day. Miss Desley came to tea, and I drove Phyllis and her over to a Christian Science lecture in Blackfriars Hall in Canterbury. I did not go in, but walked about Canterbury in the rain. We got home at 7.30 p.m. On the way to Canterbury, we let a rabbit that Doris caught loose in a wood. Daphne went to a Sea Rangers meeting and did not get back until 10 p.m.

Friday 29 June

I went into Folkestone in the morning. After lunch, I had a long talk on the Leas with a nice young New Zealander. He was captured in North Africa. A Bavarian NCO in his camp, seeing he was keen to escape, offered to help him. He expected the Hun would shoot him and claim a reward, but chanced it and was let out by the Bavarian who, he learnt later, did not report his absence

Newly repatriated New Zealand prisoners of war share a joke as they enjoy a pint of beer in Margate, Kent
(IWM D24533)

for 24 hours. He made his way towards his own people in Italy and reached a mountain valley in Austria. The weather had got cold and he had been begging a bed for several nights. He was shown the pass and told to climb high above the road to avoid patrols. He decided to spend one more night in the valley, and was given food and a bed by a woman living below the pass. At dawn, he was woken by the police and taken to a nearby prison. There, he met others who had been betrayed by the same woman. He was eventually sent back to the camp he escaped from. He said the Czechs had a marvellous system sending on escaped prisoners from one place to another. They gave you the forward address on a paper which you had to memorise and hand back. The Poles stoned our prisoners; a pal of his lost an eye by one.

Sunday 1 July
A day of heavy showers. The Russians refuse to allow us into Berlin until we give up Schleswig-Holstein and give them an entry to bolshevise Denmark. They have also taken territory from Czechoslovakia and are threatening Turkey. Heavy rain about 10 p.m. Folkestone had a tornado and water spout.

Monday 2 July
Six people were injured, and much damage was done by the tornado last night. Phyllis and I went to Hospital Hill, Seabrook, and picked up a Mrs Black, a tall girl with a bush of peroxide hair, and her husband, a dark Scot in the Marine Commandos, and drove them to Pembury, short of Tunbridge Wells. The maternity hospital was out of the way down a narrow hilly lane. Dropping the girl, we had a good lunch at a roadhouse whilst Black had a glass of beer and a stroll. On our return, the hills to the north were black with rain, and when we got to Lympne it was pitch black, but only a short shower fell in Hythe. The trip was 90 miles. Daphne spent the day hunting for campsites for her Guides round Hatch Park. For two days, Canadians have been rioting in Aldershot.

Tuesday 3 July
I timed my standing in the fish queue: it was exactly half an hour. I had a busy morning. After supper, we all went to see Deanna Durbin in the film *Can't Help Singing*; quite amusing in parts.

Wednesday 4 July
An overcast day. At 2 p.m. I drove Mrs Myers to the infirmary. My last trip, as I am being relieved by Captain Graham Brown. I got back at 4 p.m. Daphne went to a youth sport meeting, not getting back until 10.30 p.m. She met General AL Forster.

Thursday 5 July
Polling Day. I voted in the morning. It took me half an hour to walk down the High Street being button-holed by all and sundry, and about five minutes to vote. Colonel HR Mackeson [Conservative] is said not to be popular because people are angry with George Mackeson for staying away during the war, and Mrs George was never liked. Widdecombe, the Labour candidate, had a strong organisation and, as most of the old gang had no vote in Hythe, the bet is that Labour has a good chance of getting in. Daphne voted in the afternoon and Phyllis after tea.

Friday 6 July
I picked up a milk churn for Mrs Crispin at the Manor House and drove into Folkestone in the morning. After seeing the Inspector, shopping and lunch I dropped some papers at the church for Phyllis and the churn at the hospital and drove back via Kick Hill, where I stopped for an hour and read the papers. Stalin is already making his demands for participation in the war against Japan. He will probably take Manchuria and perhaps Korea. In the meantime, we are treated in Berlin as underdogs.

Monday 9 July
Gunfire all morning made the windows rattle. I met Mrs Crispin at Oakville at 10.30 a.m. and drove her to South Road, Redbrooks, Palmarsh, Philbeach and Manor House carrying clothes and other WVS stuff. A hot, muggy day. Clouds obscured the eclipse of the sun in the afternoon. It was strange how the wireless increased in volume whilst it was on. Heavy rain with thunder at night.

Tuesday 10 July
An overcast, rather cold day. At 5.30 p.m. I picked up a Miss Compton and drove her to the Folkestone Hospital and back, getting home at 7 p.m.

I saw a number of large amphibious tanks on trailers come up from the harbour and go out through Cheriton; two lost their way and got on to the Sandgate Road.

Wednesday 11 July
An overcast morning but fine later. The Warwicks were stacking stretchers, collecting cardboard and showing signs of leaving all day. A violent explosion at 8.45 p.m. The Japanese have got a force back across the Sittaung River [Burma] and there are still several thousands west of Mandalay. Although there is nothing to be alarmed at, neither *The Times* nor *The Telegraph* say a word about it.

Thursday 12 July
A hot day. Explosions of many kinds, including Lydd guns, all day. Coming up from the town I saw black smoke issuing from the gasworks like an oil tank on fire. Rumour got about in the town that a strange plane had bombed it. It was the Army doing a stunt. The Warwickshires in our road have considerably increased in numbers.

Sunday 15 July
I drove Phyllis into 18 Kingsnorth Gardens, where she and Nancy spent the day, whilst four of Burrows' men ticketed the lots for the sale. A blazing hot day, but after 5 p.m. we had several heavy showers. We heard that the Warwickshires were leaving in a week, and no other unit was coming in. A wild stormy night.

Monday 16 July
I drove Phyllis into Kingsnorth Gardens in the morning. The porters were already there, having arrived at 9.30 a.m. Nancy arrived late; I met Burrows near the station and walked back with him. He is over 80 but looked well, only moving slowly. The auction commenced at 11.30 a.m. There were very few people, owing to Stevens the clerk having forgotten to advertise the sale locally. Prices in all but a few cases shockingly low – a bath chair in perfect order for 17/-. We watched from the bathroom on the first floor. The total was about £500. Burrows did not seem to push the bidding. It was over by 3.45 p.m.

Tuesday 17 July

All the Warwickshires left our road by midday. They walked all over our blackberries before leaving, but did not steal anything.

Wednesday 18 July

Explosions at intervals all the morning. The Whitemans came at 6 p.m. to look over the house and eat raspberries from the garden.

Thursday 19 July

A warm day. The NAAFI from our road left in the morning.

Sunday 22 July

A French Guide Commissioner staying with Miss Lewis in Lyminge came to tea. Whilst Daphne got tea ready, Miss Wheeler, headmistress of Hythe School, who had been asked to meet her, and I had to entertain her. Miss Wheeler said she could not speak French and jabbered at a rapid rate at the poor woman.

Tuesday 24 July

I learn that the troops have definitely left our road, and the houses will be de-requisitioned.

Wednesday 25 July

A hot day. Mines exploding all day.

Thursday 26 July

I drove Mrs Crispin with blankets etc. to the Folkestone Hospital, my last VCP journey. In the town afterwards, I saw something of the effect of the shock at the Socialists' overwhelming victory. Poor old Barnes nearly died of fright. In my opinion, the Tories with no policy and sheltering behind Churchill's skirts, deserved to be beaten. Results – Labour 393 MPs, Tory 213 and Liberals 10. Colonel Mackeson in for Hythe, Churchill in, but his son and son-in-law and his trumpeter Brendan Bracken and more than half his Cabinet are out. In the afternoon, I brought Mr and Mrs Briggs from Folkestone to tea. He is a bank manager who recently had a stroke. The Overalls, sister and brother, came by bus. Thunder and lightning and rain at night.

Friday 27 July

A cold day. Heavy rain early. In Folkestone in the morning, the town was full of men on leave from Germany. I met Stokes and had a long talk about the election, Gribbon and the Home Guard. He said everyone was fed up and wanted a change, so said let's try Labour. He told me Gribbon offered the MBE to him and Axford, but Vinson went crying to the Brigadier commanding the area and got it. All the same, it was absurd

Soldiers arrive back in Dover for demobilisation
(IWM BU8051)

for Axford or Stokes to have got it. I had a most inadequate lunch at the Tatler, although I went at 12.15 p.m. the hour it was supposed to open.

Sunday 29 July

An American comment: 'Now Churchill has gone, there are no gentlemen among the "Big Three".' There were never more than two.

Tuesday 31 July

The end of the Women's Voluntary Service and the Volunteer Car Pool. I handed in my last return and all the books. Railwaymen threaten to strike on the bank holiday. People, like Mrs Wood, who voted Labour are very indignant.

Friday 3 August

I went into Folkestone in the morning. It was crowded with visitors and 2nd Army leave men, and I had a miserable lunch of fish and chips and a cup of coffee for 2s 11d at Stricklands. The family at my table had to wait half an hour before being served.

Saturday 4 August

A blazing hot day. I drove down town and shopped. Daphne joined me at 11 a.m. and drove me out to Smeeth crossroads then to Joe Farm, where we met four Guides from Ashford. I stayed till noon helping her to shift their camp kit to a site on the edge of Hatch Park woods. I brought the car back. Miss Desley came after supper and stayed till 10.30 p.m. Phyllis slept in the front porch.

Sunday 5 August

A warm, sunny day. In the afternoon I drove Phyllis and Miss Desley to church. I picked up the groundsheets for Daphne from the police station under the Town Hall, and returned in time for the service. Strikes on the railways in several places.

> *The Allies dropped two atomic bombs on Japan to bring the war in the Pacific to a close. Hiroshima was bombed on 6 August 1945, and Nagasaki on 9 August 1945. Japan surrendered on 15 August 1945.*

Monday 6 August

Bank Holiday. Heavy rain at 3.30 p.m. and 6.30 p.m. Most people shocked at the atomic bomb. Stalin will be given the formula – and then what?

Tuesday 7 August

A cold day. Daphne came in from camp at lunchtime. Harry and Cynthia Collins and their small daughter Ann came to tea. The latter a sweet child. At 9 p.m. I drove out with Daphne to her camp, taking groundsheets, apples etc. and stayed until dusk. She spent the night alone in the camp, her Ashford Guides having gone that morning, and her Hythe girls were not due till next day.

Wednesday 8 August

The atomic bomb the chief subject of discussion. Scientists make feeble suggestions that the discovery can be turned to use for the good of mankind. Everyone else, except the ignorant, condemns its use. The skunk Stalin has come in just in time to rob China of Manchuria. Heavy rain at 7 p.m.

Friday 10 August

I went into Folkestone in the morning, and hung about until 3 p.m. trying to get fishcakes and went without lunch. About 2 p.m. when on the Leas I heard that the Japanese Emperor had agreed to surrender unconditionally. The holiday crowd showed no excitement, and even the leave men were not as drunk as usual.

Monday 13 August

An overcast day. I spent the afternoon picking a whole tree of apples. The Japs seem to be foxing, or perhaps it has to take time. They obviously know they are beaten.

Tuesday 14 August

Rumours everywhere, chiefly from America. Premature orders, speeches and rejoicings. Australian troops rioting in Australia. They are making their own country suffer from their hooliganism this time. At midnight, I woke to a fusillade in the town and thought it strange that the troops, with all the country to play in, should hold their night operations in the town. The last discharge sounded in our road.

> In a broadcast talk to his peoples last night the King spoke with pride of their unconquerable spirit during six years of war and of the difficult part to be played by the Commonwealth and Empire in restoring the shattered fabric of civilization.

Wednesday 15 August

The WAR is ended. Attlee announced the Japanese surrender at midnight. What I mistook for a battle practice was the firing of crackers. A bonfire was lit in the centre of Red Lion Square, and the snowplough was burnt. Rain midday, which soaked Daphne and her Guides just as they were striking camp. She returned in Newman's lorry with half the kit about 4 p.m. The King broadcast at 9 p.m. in a strong voice with no hesitation. After dark there were a few bonfires on the front, rockets over Shorncliffe and the youths milling in the High Street.

Thursday 16 August

A fine, sunny day. We spent most of it gardening and did not go near the celebrations.

Observation post, Folkestone Leas, 1945 (Kent Messenger L120180)

Friday 17 August

I went into Folkestone in the morning. Soldiers burnt all the seats on the Leas and did other damage. They were stopped from burning the bandstand piano.

Sunday 19 August

Thanksgiving services everywhere. In the morning, Daphne went to Folkestone Parish Church with some of her Guides, and I went to Saltwood, where the parson of the local AA Brigade preached a rather rambling sermon. In the afternoon, Phyllis and Daphne went to their church in Folkestone.

Monday 20 August

Practically no food in the town. I had to go down again in the evening to get some fish.

Tuesday 21 August

A wet morning. In the afternoon, Phyllis and Daphne drove out to Joe Farm, Smeeth and Hatch Park to pick blackberries.

Wednesday 29 August

A thick mist, followed by heavy rain in the morning. At 3 p.m. I went to the Church House for the meeting to wind up Hythe Women's Voluntary Service. Stainer, the Town Clerk, was in the chair as Captain Few, the Mayor, is still sick. Mrs Crispin read a very good and comprehensive report on the six years' work. She received a very deserved ovation from the members.

Thursday 30 August

I filled up with petrol in the morning, and shopped from the car. Daphne left for a GIS camp near Amersham, Buckinghamshire.

Friday 31 August

Overcast but fine. I was in Folkestone up to 3 p.m. For a short time, the sky was full of planes. Neville informed me that his younger son is coming out of the Navy and he is setting him up in Hythe with an animal clinic. He who, in the course of his profession, is supposed to prosecute unqualified veterinary practitioners.

Saturday 1 September

Daphne's birthday. We spent the day as usual.

Sunday 2 September

Anniversary of Pearl Harbor. In the morning, I walked past Saltwood Church and Waterworks, along the top of Sandling tunnel to the junction and back through Saltwood village. A heavy rainstorm midday.

Thursday 6 September

In the afternoon, Phyllis looked up several people in Folkestone. Daphne looked up Miss Villiers and Miss Wheeler, and I had a chat with Captain de Berry. In each case we took them pears from our orchard.

Saturday 15 September

An RAF pageant to celebrate the turning point in the Battle of Britain. For some reason, nothing was arranged to happen over us. Perhaps they thought we had seen too much of the real thing.

Tuesday 18 September
Mrs Stuart, her daughter Stephanie, a rather sweet child with fawn's eyes, and her parents Mr and Mrs Grigsby came to tea. He is a retired rubber planter of Malaya and Ceylon, a chatty little man.

Thursday 20 September
Daphne drove Phyllis and me to Sandling for the 12.50 p.m. train to London. We stopped the night there.

Friday 21 September
We left by the 10.40 a.m. train from Paddington, changed at Newton Abbot [Devon] and Brent and arrived Kingsbridge, where we went by bus seven miles to Salcombe, arriving 6 p.m.

Saturday 22 September
We walked round Salcombe morning and afternoon, and looked up Mr H Triscott to negotiate for his bungalow.

Tuesday 25 September
Triscott met us in the morning and informed us that Mrs Winder, his housekeeper, would not agree to the sale of the house. Phyllis spoke to her, and she asked for time to consider it. In the afternoon, we went into Kingsbridge to look at a house.

Wednesday 26 September
Triscott again came and said the sale was definitely off. I walked to Batson in the afternoon, hunting for houses.

Thursday 27 September
We left, after an early lunch, by bus for Thurlestone, changing at Kingsbridge. Spent the day looking at houses. Triscott and Mrs Winder followed us in his car to tell us they would sell the bungalow after all. They did not find us, but we went up after supper and came to an agreement.

Friday 28 September

We went up in the evening and took measurements of the bungalow.

Saturday 29 September

We left by the 10.40 a.m. bus, got a through carriage to Paddington at Kingsbridge, crossed to Charing Cross and arrived at Sandling Junction at 8.30 p.m., half an hour late.

Epilogue

Daphne, rear centre, with her cousin Joan and her children Peter and Anne on holiday in Dartmoor in the 1960s

When peace prevailed, Rodney, Phyllis and Daphne sold Upper Fold and moved to Torrington House in Kingsbridge, Devon. The family enjoyed the relative quiet of the countryside, and made many car journeys around the county. Rodney continued sketching, and researching and writing his memoirs. He thought his detailed diaries would be an antidote to nostalgia: 'One good at least will come from my writings. I shall not be the bore most old men become to their relations and friends, with their accounts of the good old days.'

Daphne, who spoke German and who had trained with the Girl Guides for humanitarian work, served in the Guide International Service during 1945 and 1946 – one of only 100 Girl Guides to do so. Her unit's work included caring for and rehabilitating people who had been imprisoned in Bergen-Belsen Concentration Camp, in north-western Germany, which was liberated in April 1945. When she returned to Devon, she continued to be active in the Girl Guides as a District Commissioner.

Rodney died in Kingsbridge in 1962, at the age of eighty. Phyllis had predeceased him. Daphne continued to live in Torrington House. When she died, unmarried, on 31 July 2000, the house was cleared out by the local council and – in the absence of any known family – her possessions, including her father's diaries and archive, were sold. Nothing is known of their immediate fate, but the material now known as the Rodney Foster Archive was sold at auction by Maggs Brothers of London in 2004 to Sailesh Jaswa, and the Second World War diaries that form the basis of this book were sold at a car boot sale in Exeter before being bought on eBay by Shaun Sewell in January 2009. The archive consists of twenty-two volumes: eighteen of autobiography, written and illustrated after Rodney retired in 1932, two of drawings and watercolours, one of newspaper cuttings related to Rodney's life and times, and one relating to the relief of Chitral in 1904.

Rodney also wrote and illustrated a 400-page volume called *Hythe 1939–1945*, based on his daily diaries, which he donated to the town and which is now in the East Kent Archive in Dover.

The Rodney Foster Archive

Rodney has left us numerous accounts of his life, of which the Rodney Foster Archive is by far the most comprehensive.

The Archive contains twenty-two bound volumes consisting of some 5,600 pages of which eighteen volumes comprise the chronological account of his life and times. This was to be Rodney's main project, which started during his retirement in 1933, and he was probably still tinkering with it up to his death in 1962.

The Archive is blessed with countless drawings, watercolours and photographs mostly by Rodney's hand which add to his textual entries and help the reader more accurately imagine the times and places he writes about. The majority of the watercolours contained in this book were taken from the Archive and form only a fraction of the depth of material available. The Archive is also rich with added ephemera such as the train ticket he kept of his journey to Sandhurst to begin training in 1900.

The first volumes concentrate on his family history, childhood and cadet training, which leads on to his early days in the Indian Army during the early part of the twentieth century. Rodney's time in the Survey of India is covered comprehensively, only interrupted by the outbreak of the First World War when he reverts back to a military life, commands a double company and is promoted to Major. During his time with the Survey he has an active life with a busy social diary of quintessential English pastimes of cricket, tennis, cards and then bagging the odd tiger or bear. Rodney's skills as a cartographer are clear to see with some wonderfully executed maps, pinpointing the places that are mentioned in the entry for that day.

The later volumes cover his retirement in Hythe and Kingsbridge; two of the volumes are dedicated to his life during the Second World War.

The Archives are currently in the ownership of Sailesh Jaswa who has been their guardian since purchasing them from the rare booksellers Maggs Bros in London in 2004.

Sailesh Jaswa can be contacted at ab1209@live.com.

Acknowledgements

I would like to take this opportunity to express my grateful thanks to a host of individuals and organisations who have made it possible to bring Rodney's wartime adventures to fruition and allow his work to be read.

I'd like to thank Anne Kingston for trusting and allowing me to bring Rodney's wartime exploits to life; Eleo Gordon and Viking for their belief and enthusiasm in producing this wonderful book; Sailesh Jaswa for allowing Rodney's artwork to adorn this book; Ulrike Paradine for opening the doors of Upper Fold to let me see where Rodney wrote his diary; all those who have kindly lent their time and efforts to help in the research and hunt for photographs which has made this book come alive: Rex Cadman at War and Peace, Barry Hollis and Linda Evans at the *Kent Messenger*, Rosanna Wilkinson at IWM, the staff at Folkestone Library, Cerys Russell at East Kent Archive, Tony Hill at Hythe Civic Society, Brian Doorne at Saltwood Village Society, Judith McCormick, James Craufurd-Stuart, Don McHutchison and Alan Taylor at Folkestone and District Local History Society.

My boyhood hero, Brian Clough, always surrounded himself with the best players and assistants and they loyally followed him from club to club; perhaps this was the key to his success. Although I'm no Brian Clough, I have benefited greatly from the loyal service of both Gordon Wise and Ronnie Scott and they are, and have been, major cogs in the production of this and previous books. I would like to take this opportunity to especially thank the both of them. Ronnie has again weaved his magic pen, adding warmth to the book through his careful editing and insertion of historical notes, embellishing the read and allowing the reader to understand and place in context the themes of Rodney's entries. Without doubt in my unbiased view, Gordon Wise would win *The X Factor* if it was just for literary agents!

Lastly, I would like thank my partner, Joan Bower, who has now lived through two World Wars with me, for her unending support, encouragement and most importantly her life-saving tea-making skills.

Shaun Sewell
Northumberland 2011

Illustrations Acknowledgements

The author and publishers are grateful to the following for permission to use illustrations appearing on the following pages and in the inset sections:

Material by Rodney Foster

The Rodney Foster Archive by permission of Sailesh Jaswa on pages iii, xvii, 1, 5, 16, 29, 34, 47, 83, 86, 89, 101, 107–108, 125, 149, 162, 187, 205–207, 237, 253, 255, 353 and nos. 2–10, 12–14 in the colour section

Ulrike Paradine on pages vii, viii-ix, xiv, xv, xix, 1, 3 and 15

East Kent Archive/Hythe Council on pages 35, 157, 289, no. 9 in the black-and-white section and nos. 1, 11 in the colour section

Additional material

Kent County Council, Libraries and Archives (Folkestone Library) and Aisha Affejee on pages 20, 24, 50, 96, 113, 131, 134, 149, 214 and no. 2 in the black-and-white section. We have not always been able to establish the copyright on some of the Folkestone Library photographs

War and Peace Collection, Kent Photo Archive, on pages 9, 111, 122, 165, 264, 271, 307, 317, 335 and no. 11 in the black-and-white section

Imperial War Museum on pages 38, 85, 97, 148, 176, 180, 239, 322, 327, 330, 342, 347 and nos. 3, 10, 14–16 in the black-and-white section

Kent Messenger and Barry Hollis on pages 41, 49, 153, 156, 247, 266, 281, 286, 350 and no. 7 in the black-and-white section

Folkestone Herald and Folkestone Library on pages 57, 167, 183, 203, 340 and nos. 1 and 4 in the black-and-white section, all from *Front-Line Folkestone*

Hythe Library on pages 65, 295 and no. 12 in the black-and-white section

Folkestone and District History Society on pages 77 and 170

Andrew Instance on page 36

Don McHutchison on pages 208, 227, 252 and no. 6 in the black-and-white section

Getty Images on page 231 and nos. 5 and 13 in the black-and-white section

Brian Doorne on page 129 and no. 8 in the black-and-white section

James Craufurd-Stuart on page 182

Anne Kingston on page 355